# Twice [obscured]

## *Supporting and Educa[obscured]g Bright and Creative Students with Learning Difficulties*

**EDITED BY**

**SCOTT BARRY KAUFMAN**

OXFORD
UNIVERSITY PRESS

OXFORD
UNIVERSITY PRESS

Oxford University Press is a department of the University of Oxford. It furthers the University's objective of excellence in research, scholarship, and education by publishing worldwide. Oxford is a registered trade mark of Oxford University Press in the UK and certain other countries.

Published in the United States of America by Oxford University Press
198 Madison Avenue, New York, NY 10016, United States of America.



CIP data is on file at the Library of Congress
ISBN 978–0–19–064547–2

9 8 7 6 5 4 3

Printed by Webcom, Inc., Canada

# Twice Exceptional

# CONTENTS

## PART IV Models

# ACKNOWLEDGMENTS

Sincere thanks to Kim Busi for her early encouragement of this project, and to Andrea Zekus at Oxford University Press for helping to make this book a reality.

## ABOUT THE EDITOR

**Scott Barry Kaufman, PhD,** is an author, researcher, speaker, and public science communicator who is interested in using psychological science to help all kinds of minds live a creative, fulfilling, and meaningful life. He is author and/or editor of 7 other books, including *Ungifted: Intelligence Redefined* and *Wired to Create: Unraveling the Mysteries of the Creative Mind* (with Carolyn Gregoire). His writing has appeared in *The Atlantic, Scientific American, Psychology Today*, and *Harvard Business Review*, and he writes a blog at *Scientific American* called Beautiful Minds. Kaufman is also host of *The Psychology Podcast*.

# CONTRIBUTORS

**Edward R. Amend, PsyD**
Amend Psychological Services, PSC

**Lois Baldwin, EdD**
Independent Educational Consultant

**Susan Baum, PhD**
Director, 2e Center for Research and Professional Development
Bridges Academy, Studio City, CA
Professor Emeritus
College of New Rochelle

**Kristin Berman, PhD**
The Quad Preparatory School

**Kevin Besnoy, PhD**
Director, ACCESS Virtual Learning
Associate Director K-12 Programs
College of Continuing Studies
University of Alabama

**Kimberly Busi, MD**
The Quad Preparatory School

**Mary Ruth Coleman, PhD**
Senior Scientist, Emerita
FPG Child Development Institute
University of North Carolina, Chapel Hill

**Maryam Trebeau Crogman, MA**
University of California Merced, Psychological Sciences

**Susan Daniels, PhD**
Professor
California State University San Bernardino
Cofounder and Educational Director
Summit Center—Walnut Creek, CA

**Joy Lawson Davis, EdD**
Virginia Union University

**Megan Foley-Nicpon, PhD**
Associate Professor
University of Iowa

**Jeffrey Freed, MEd**
Author and Special Education Counselor

**Michelle Freeman, PsyD**
Assessment Director
Summit Center—Walnut Creek, CA

**C. Matthew Fugate, PhD**
Assistant Professor
University of Houston–Downtown

**Judy Galbraith, MA**
President and Founder, Free Spirit Publishing

**Jeffrey W. Gilger, PhD**
Professor of Psychology
University of California Merced
Carlston Cunningham Chair in Cognitive Development
Director, UC Merced Alliance for Child and Family Health and Development

**Barbara (Bobbie) Jackson Gilman, MS**
Associate Director, Gifted Development Center, Westminster, CO
Cochair, Assessments of Giftedness Special Interest Group, National Association for Gifted Children

**Rebecca M. Girard, LICSW**
Stony Brook University

**Erik M. Hines, PhD, NCC**
University of Connecticut

**Fumiko Hoeft, MD, PhD**
University of California San Francisco
Psychiatry and Weill Institute for Neurosciences

**Scott Barry Kaufman, PhD**
University of Pennsylvania

**Matthew D. Lerner, PhD**
Stony Brook University

**Deirdre V. Lovecky, PhD**
Gifted Resource Center of New England

**Renae D. Mayes, PhD, NCC**
Ball State University

**James L. Moore III, PhD**
The Ohio State University

**Daphne Pereles, MS**
Independent Educational Consultant
Austin, TX

**Dan Peters, PhD**
Licensed Psychologist
Cofounder/Executive Director, Summit Center
Cochair, Assessments of Giftedness Special Interest Group, National Association for Gifted Children

**Steven I. Pfeiffer, PhD, ABPP**
Professor
Florida State University

**Shawn Anthony Robinson, PhD**
Independent Scholar and Dyslexia Consultant

**Carl A. Sabatino, MA**
Head of School
Bridges Academy

**Robin Schader, PhD**
Trustee, Bridges Academy
Executive Board Member, 2e Center for Research and Professional Development

**Rich Weinfeld**
Executive Director
Weinfeld Education Group, LLC

**Christopher R. Wiebe, EdD**
High School Director
Bridges Academy

**Richard O. Williams, PhD**
Chairman Emeritus, Board of Trustees
Beacon College, FL
Professor of Genetics, Retired

**Susan Winebrenner, MS**
Education Consulting Service

# Twice Exceptional

# Introduction

SCOTT BARRY KAUFMAN ■

> One school fixed its attention upon the importance of the subject-matter of the curriculum as compared with the contents of the child's own experience. Not so, says the other school. The child is the starting point, the center, and the end. His development, his growth, is the ideal. Not knowledge, but self-realization is the goal.
>
> —John Dewey (1902)

*Mark is an inquisitive 13-year-old African American boy with a sarcastic wit, keen observation skills, and an extraordinary ability to draw life-like renditions of birds, including albatross, petrels, and penguins. He is able to recreate, in exquisite detail, the large wingspan of the albatross as it cuts through the air and the flippers of the penguin as it wades its way through ice. The highlight of his young life so far was a trip to SeaWorld Orlando when he was 11, where he was able to see the South Pole through the eyes of a penguin. As if that weren't exciting enough for Mark, he was able to go on the Penguins Up-Close tour afterward, and even touch a penguin! It was all he was able to speak about for months, and even today he still dreams of returning someday.*

*Mark also has high-functioning autism. Diagnosed around the age of seven, you can clearly see some common characteristics of autism if you are actively looking for them. For instance, his language development was delayed, he does not naturally maintain eye contact when someone else is speaking to him, he likes order and repetition, and he often has tantrums if there is too much stimulation happening in the environment that he cannot control. To the great pain of Mark and his family, he is bullied quite frequently. While he doesn't get nearly as much time as he would desire to work on his paintings, in a few instances where he was able to work on them during recess, a few bullies teamed up and ripped them up, teasing him and calling him a "retard." During school, Mark's self-esteem is low, and his anxiety levels are high. At home, however, when he is working on his paintings in the quiet of his studio (which his parents set up for him), he feels confident, in control, and even normal.*

*Susan is a 10th-grade Caucasian girl with curly blonde hair, bright blue eyes, and a love for entrepreneurship and humanitarian issues. She is especially proud of the lemonade stand she created when she was seven years old, in which she advertised that 25% of the proceeds would go toward making a free candy stand for everyone. This idea, which the kids absolutely loved (because what kid doesn't like free candy?), earned her more revenue than any other lemonade stand in the area! Now in her second semester in high school, she runs a nonprofit organization dedicated to ending domestic abuse. Her mentor is a professor at a local community college who responded to Susan's cold-call email to give her advice on how to start a nonprofit. Her nonprofit brings in celebrities who have some association with domestic abuse to speak about the issue at her school. The proceeds from the tickets go toward providing resources and shelter for women who have been abused and need a safe space to live. She is passionate about this topic because she watched her own mother get physically abused through much of her childhood, before her mother left her father when she was eight.*

*Susan is also dyslexic. Even to this day, she has difficulty sounding out unfamiliar words, frequently misspells common words, and struggles to remember concepts she has learned in school. She also struggles with organization and attention and spends most of her classroom time daydreaming about new business models. She is often inspired, but when she starts to work on projects or homework assignments, she loses motivation quickly and finds it difficult to stay on task and complete them. Her older brother John, whom she adores and looks up to tremendously, gives her constant encouragement. When he notices she is having trouble focusing, he will gently nudge her to get back on track. Despite her learning difficulties, Susan's nonprofit is thriving, and she has already raised half a million dollars to support victims of domestic abuse.*

*Juan is a seventh-grade Latino with a big heart, a big, beaming smile, and a big mind. Not only is he a voracious learner, but he likes to think deeply about the philosophical implications of what he is learning. Juan is particularly fond of the existentialists, including Kierkegaard, Nietzsche, and Alan Watts. He asks so many questions in class, but unfortunately the teachers find it frustrating, not enlightening. Juan lives in a very low-income neighborhood, and his public school can barely afford the chalkboard the teachers use to present their lesson plan. His parents work hard to provide resources for Juan, but it's difficult. His father is a salesman at AT&T, and his mother is a server at TGI Fridays. Even so, they still don't make enough to support Juan's intense interest in philosophy books, and his school does not have a gifted and talented program. As a result, Juan is bored out of his mind, and this once spirited boy has recently started to show some signs of depression and listlessness.*

*To compound the issue, Juan also has an auditory processing disorder. As a young child, he had a lot of fluid in his ears, which made it very difficult for him to hear the teachers. After an ear operation that ate up most of his family's savings, it still took him an extra moment to process incoming auditory information. Yet with his extremely high general intellectual ability, he was able to compensate so much that not only was his disability not noticeable, but he still seemed brighter than the other students. This did not make him eligible for special education (which did exist in his school), and it made him a prime target for bullies in school. All Juan wants to do is learn much more, much faster, and with greater depth. He can feel it in his bones, but he feels held back. Also, he knows that if he could just have a few accommodations in the classroom (e.g., sit in the front row, have permission to record the lectures to listen to after class, etc.), he could learn at a much faster rate. He dreams of one day getting a scholarship to college and becoming one of the most famous Latino philosophy professors of all time. It is this dream that fills him up with hope and helps him get through the day.*

These three vignettes, which can only give the slightest portrait of these children, illustrate the joy, frustrations, and promises of children who simultaneously have extraordinary potentialities coupled with extraordinary disability. To many, this may seem like a contradiction in terms. *How can someone be both exceptionally abled and exceptionally disabled at the same time?* But therein lies the problem: society's inability to even imagine such a paradox has contributed to many children not receiving the support required for them to truly flourish. In recent years, this complex profile has been labeled "twice exceptional," but it is still a relatively unknown concept in education (compared to either gifted and talented education or special education). This is due in large part to the history of the field—in which both gifted and talented education and special education developed essentially in isolation of each other, further reinforcing the artificial mutual exclusiveness of these two forms of support.

I can only give the briefest of reviews of the history of the field here, but I direct the reader who wants a more detailed history to consult Baldwin, Baum, Perles, and Hughes (2015), Baum, Schader, and Owen (2017), Kaufman (2013), Kay (2003), or Reis, Baum, and Burke (2014).

## HISTORY OF 2E

As early as the 1920s, Leta Hollingworth, a pioneering psychologist and educator, noticed instances of normal intelligence among many of the so-called defective children she administered IQ tests to at the Clearing House for Mental Defectives (Kaufman, 2013). Hollingworth really took the time to get to know the children she worked with, including a sample of extremely high-IQ children. She noted that many of the difficulties she witnessed were a result of social isolation, adolescent adjustment, and educational neglect and that, once these issues were corrected, many of their earlier vulnerabilities disappeared. Hollingworth believed in opportunities for all children to flourish, especially those who lie outside the norm.

In *Special Talents and Defects: Their Significance for Education*, Hollingworth (1923) describes students who display special talents and general mental ability coupled with learning difficulties in subjects such as reading, basic arithmetic, spelling, and handwriting. She noticed that such learning difficulties occur across a range of the IQ spectrum, and she remarked on the need for schools to take into account individual differences and to differentiate curriculum in the classroom: "The most important single cause of truancy is that the curriculum does not provide for individual differences. . . . Not only is the curriculum not adapted to individual differences in general intelligence, but it is far less adapted to individual differences in special defects and aptitudes" (p. 200).

In the mid-20th century, more such cases of twice exceptionality became evident. In the early 1940s, Leo Kanner (1943) referred to a particular profile of high-IQ children with repetitive behaviors and reduced social skills as having "autism." The Austrian pediatrician Hans Asperger (1944/1991) noticed that many of his young patients with the same characteristics also displayed exemplary logical thinking and intense interest in a specific area. He referred to them as his "little professors," and in later years he came to believe that the characteristics that Kanner called autism may be more likely to appear in children with high intelligence than children in the general population (Asperger, 1979).

Similarly, Strauss and Lehtinen (1947) observed "disturbances" among children with at least normal levels of general intellectual aptitude, and Kirk (1962) and Cruickshank, Bentzen, Ratzeburg, and Tannhauser (1961) helped lay the groundwork for the emergence of the field of "learning disabilities." Even so, the focus was on "minimal brain dysfunction" and "perceptual disorder" (Kaufman, 2013; Shepherd, 2001). Notably absent was a search for the *strengths* of this population of children, with the rare exception of Gallagher (1966), who discussed the patterns of strengths and weaknesses for children with learning disabilities, and Elkind (1973), who was the first to explicitly introduce the idea of "gifted children with learning disabilities."

Traveling on a parallel path was the emergence of the field of gifted education, with Terman's classic studies of his high-IQ sample (e.g., Terman, 1924, 1925, 1947). Terman not only equated high IQ with giftedness, but he also believed that from high-IQ children "and no where else, our geniuses in every line are recruited" (Terman, 1924). It is notable that Terman did not report any learning difficulties among his population. This is not surprising considering that his original intent was to showcase his high-IQ children as the pinnacle of mental and physical health. Nevertheless, other high-ability researchers did note the co-occurrence of high ability with disability. For instance, in their pioneering study, Goertzel and Goertzel (1962/2004) scoured the biographies of 300 highly accomplished adults and found that most of them felt "different" from the other kids growing up and disliked school (a more recent analysis of eminent adults by Ludwig [1995] found similar conclusions). Virtually all of them displayed characteristics as children who are included in prominent definitions of giftedness today.

Curiously, however, the fields of special education and gifted and talented education continued to travel mostly on separate pathways throughout the 1970s, with students identified as gifted receiving enrichment *or* students identified with a learning disability receiving remediation, and with very little overlap among the classifications. While two major pieces of legislation in the mid-1970s—the Education for All Handicapped Children Act (1975) and the Gifted and Talented

Children's Education Act (1978)—helped provide guidelines for meeting the educational needs of each of these populations, neither one acknowledged that a student could be both high-ability *and* have a disability.

Nevertheless, it is notable that there was a shift during the 1970s and 1980s for gifted and talented education to become more expansive in supporting a wider range of abilities than just high IQ, to also include specific aptitudes, visual and performing arts, creativity, leadership, psychomotor abilities, and even nonintellective traits such as task commitment (Gardner, 1983; Marland Report, 1972; Renzulli, 1978; Sternberg, 1984; Torrance, 1984). There was also a shift away from viewing giftedness as something a child either has or does not have, to a talent development model, in which all abilities are always in a state of development in a specific context over the lifespan (e.g., Bloom, 1985; Gagné, 1985; Horowitz, Subotnik, & Matthews, 2009).

Perhaps due in part to these expanded notions of giftedness, researchers and educators increasingly began to recognize the need to provide services to students with both exceptional ability and disability. In 1977, June Maker published her influential book, *Providing Programs for the Gifted Handicapped*, in which she described the dual diagnosis of children with exceptional abilities and talents but who also experienced physical and cognitive disabilities. Additionally, in 1978, Meisgeier, Meisgeier, and Werblo (1978) argued in an article in *Gifted Child Quarterly* that students identified as gifted who also had a learning disability have a need for both learning supports *and* advanced programming. They also pointed to the unique emotional needs of these students, who faced such a striking discrepancy between their strengths and their disability (Baum et al., 2017).

In the 1980s, school programs and associations also started to crop up specifically to support gifted students with a learning disability (e.g., the Board of Cooperative Educational Services, the Association for the Education of Gifted Underachieving Students), and the National Association for Gifted Children (NAGC) created a division that supported research on special populations of gifted students, including gifted students with disabilities. As a result, there was a substantial increase in the number of articles and books pinpointing more precisely the characteristics, needs, and best practices of these students, including the influential 1991 book *To Be Gifted and Learning Disabled* (Baum, Owen, & Dixon, 1991), which is now in its third edition.

In the 1990s, more state and federal funds (e.g., the National Research Center for the Gifted and Talented) as well as school programs (e.g., Talented Learning Disabilities Programs in Montgomery County, Maryland) became available. In 1996, Ellen Winner's timely book, *Gifted Children: Myths and Realities*, included a chapter titled, "Unevenly Gifted, Even Learning Disabled." In 1997, Brody and Mills provided recommendations to help ensure that gifted students with learning disabilities receive the interventions needed to help them flourish. In their review, they noted:

> Many people have difficulty comprehending that a child can be gifted and also have learning disabilities. . . . (p. 282) Individualized instruction is optimal for

all students so that pace, level, and content can be geared to ability, interests, and learning style, but it is essential for students whose abilities are clearly discrepant. Ideally, a continuum of alternative placement options should be available, so that teachers can develop a plan that builds heavily on students' strengths but also provides remediation and support for social and emotional needs (Brody and Mills, 1997, p. 292).

The start of the 21st century brought with it even more substantial changes for twice exceptional students. In 2004 the reauthorization of the Individuals with Disabilities Education Improvement Act finally recognized the disabled student that has "not failed or been retained in a course, and is advancing from grade to grade." This was the first time that the federal government explicitly acknowledged the profile of the child with a disability that may also have an exceptional learning potentiality. Today, newsletters such as the *Twice Exceptional (2e) Newsletter* and the *Smart Kids with Learning Differences Newsletter* offer valuable information for parents, teachers, and other professionals, and some states have explicit policies and guidelines for the identification of 2e (e.g., Colorado, Maryland).

While there is not complete agreement on best practices for identification (e.g., Lovett & Lewandowski, 2006), recent reviews do conclude "that gifted students can have a coexisting disability" (Foley-Nicpon, Allmon, Sieck, & Stinson, 2011, p. 13) and that these students "are among the most frequently under-identified population in our schools" (National Education Association, 2006, p. 1). Indeed, it is estimated that there are between 360,000 and 385,000 twice exceptional students in America's schools (National Education Association, 2006; National Center for Education Statistics, Department of Education, 2013, see Pfeiffer & Foley-Nicpon, this volume). However, if we view giftedness as much broader than merely a high IQ—the approach we take in this volume—the numbers are most certainly much higher. As Baum (2017) notes, "it is . . . reasonable to assume that every school has twice exceptional students whose unique learning needs must be met." Even if a student with a disability does not display an obvious exceptional potentiality at any given moment in time, it is still fair to assume that he or she has at least *some* strengths that are lying dormant due to frustration, low self-esteem, and low expectations and that can be built upon for personal growth. As the Oak Foundation notes,

Approximately 20 per cent of children (10 million students) in United States public schools have learning profiles that are not aligned with the expectations and teaching methodologies prevalent in mainstream school systems. Referred to as learning differences, this includes but is not limited to: dyslexia; attention issues; and learning disabilities.

As a result, these students are often perceived as not being capable of performing well in school, unmotivated or just not trying hard enough. These students often disengage with school, perform poorly, and may not graduate from high school. Those who do graduate often choose not to pursue post-secondary educational opportunities. As adults, many are unemployed or can even end up in prison.

However, this is a loss of a critical resource in our society. Paradoxically, these learners bring the strengths of persistence, alternative problem-solving approaches and creativity along with their capable mind—to school, and later to the workplace and society.

## DEFINITION OF 2E FOR THIS BOOK

This book is an attempt to present the most up-to-date review of the science of supporting 2e children, written by the leaders of the field. But which children fall within the purview of 2e? I wanted to give autonomy to the experts in this volume to define 2e as they wished (as long as they explicitly defined it somewhere) and to present their own perspectives on the identification and/or support of 2e. Nevertheless, for the sake of a coherent structure to the book, I present a modified version of a definition that reached consensus among 26 organizations that support the research and educational needs of 2e students (Baldwin et al., 2015):

> Twice exceptional individuals demonstrate exceptional levels of capacity, competence, commitment, or creativity in one or more domains coupled with one or more learning difficulties. This combination of exceptionalities results in a unique set of circumstances. Their exceptional potentialities may dominate, hiding their disability; their disability may dominate, hiding their exceptional potentialities; each may mask the other so that neither is recognized or addressed.
>
> 2e students, who may perform below, at, or above grade level, require the following:
>
> - Specialized methods of identification that consider the possible interaction of the exceptionalities.
> - Enriched/advanced educational opportunities that focus on developing the child's interests and highest strengths while also meeting the child's learning needs.
> - Simultaneous supports that ensure the child's academic success and social-emotional well-being, such as accommodations, therapeutic interventions, and specialized instruction.
>
> Working successfully with this unique population requires specialized academic training and ongoing professional development. Critically, these behaviors occur in certain people, at certain times, and under certain circumstances, especially when the environment is supportive (e.g. high expectations) and in environments that challenge them appropriately in the area(s) of their highest potentiality.

The following changes were made to the original definition:

- Capacity, competence, commitment, and creativity were added as indicators of exceptional ability, based on recent expanded definitions of giftedness (e.g., NAGC, n.d.; Renzulli, 1978; Sternberg, 1997; Kaufman, 2013). *Capacity* is defined as an exceptional ability to reason and learn in a particular domain; *competence* is defined as documented performance or achievement in the top 10% or rarer; *commitment* is defined as exceptional levels of energy brought to bear on a specific task or performance area, including fascination, perseverance, dedicated practice, self-belief, and action applied to one's area(s) of interest; and *creativity* is defined as exceptional levels of originality, insight, and motivation to create something meaningful in a domain.
- The wording "develop the child's interests, gifts, and talents" was changed to "develop the child's interest and highest strengths."
- It was made explicit that these characteristics of 2e are dynamic and occur at particular times and in particular environments (Renzulli, 1978). Indeed, consideration of the environment is crucial to this definition. The capacities, competencies, commitments, and creativity seen in 2e children are only expressed under *optimal circumstances*. Most 2e children hide their strengths or their strengths are not developed to the level of giftedness due to low self-esteem and an unstable identity; low expectations from peers, parents, and teachers; and a lack of resources that would allow them reach their highest expression.

Each of these four potential manifestations of ability—capacity, competence, commitment, and creativity—can be mixed and matched in nuanced, unique ways. For instance, it is possible that the 2e student does not demonstrate his highest potentiality through formal standardized tests or school grades but demonstrates an exceptional aptitude for reasoning and soaking up knowledge in the classroom (something that can be observed by teachers). Or perhaps the 2e student is a poor test taker but is extraordinarily committed, passionate, and curious about learning more about a domain. Or perhaps the 2e child shows an intense interest in creating something, or doing a project relating to a domain. Or perhaps the 2e child is high achieving on tests but does not appear to be a fast learner in the classroom. There are, of course, many more possible combinations of these four strengths among 2e students.

*Domains* are defined by the NAGC as any structured area of activity with its own symbol system (e.g., mathematics, music, language) and/or set of sensorimotor skills (e.g., painting, dance, sports). *Learning difficulties* can include (but are not limited to) specific learning disabilities, speech and language disorders, emotional/behavioral disorders, physical disabilities, autism spectrum disorders (ASD), attention deficit hyperactive disorder (ADHD), or other health impairments (Reis, Baum, & Burke, 2014).

I believe this definition of 2e is broad enough to capture most of the 2e population while being narrow enough to distinguish among (a) 2e children, (b) children who are in gifted and talented education but who do not demonstrate a disability, and (c) children with a disability who do not require gifted and talented programming at a given time.

With that said, I dream of a day in which *every single student* receives his or her own individualized educational plan and is challenged appropriately and supported at every step of the way. Indeed, my Theory of Personal Intelligence (Kaufman, 2013) argues for a shift from an educational model that compares children to each other on a single dimension (e.g., IQ, academic performance) to an appreciation of the *whole child*, which includes a unique pattern of strengths and weaknesses, but also recognizes the importance of ability, engagement, and personal goals working together and changing over time. Only by supporting the whole child, and supporting their own unique personal goals, hopes, and dreams, will they become fully engaged in their future. I'm pretty sure that Hollingworth would have been on board with such an approach and that all of the contributors to this volume also dream of such a world.

Unfortunately, we currently live in a world in which labels are often necessary to help students receive the resources they require to thrive. Living with that reality, I hope this book is a good start toward increasing awareness and support of a long-neglected population of students: the *twice exceptional*.

## OUTLINE OF THIS BOOK

This volume is divided into three sections. Part I focuses more generally on the identification of twice exceptionality. Bobbie Gilman and Dan Peters lead this section with an examination of the implications of changing federal law policies for the identification and assessment of 2e students. Through a combination of a case study, review of educational policy changes and testing procedures, and personal experience with 2e students, the authors show how easily a 2e child with unidentified disabilities can fall between the cracks. Furthermore, they advocate for a comprehensive assessment and provide guidelines to properly identify and support 2e students.

In chapter 2, Susan Baum and Robin Schader take a strengths-based approach to the identification of 2e. Using the metaphor of "green" (a mixture of blue and yellow), they argue that the 2e child is neither high ability nor learning disabled but the dynamic interaction of both. They then describe their approach to collecting information about a student's strengths, interests, and talents, called the Suite of Tools™, with the goal of developing a personalized list of options for talent development opportunities as well as a strength-based option to access the curriculum and enhance school performance.

In chapter 3, Edward Amend discusses the unique challenges of identifying 2e students and emphasizes how the talents of 2e students are often hidden behind many years of frustration and pain. Echoing the other contributors, Amend discusses the importance of using a diverse array of tools but also discusses the importance of educators having knowledge and experience working both with students labeled gifted and talented as well as students in special education. Amend also offers some best practices and tools for finding the "hidden potential" of 2e students to avoid misdiagnosis or missed diagnosis.

In chapter 4, Deirdre Lovecky dives deeply into the issue of misdiagnosis and presents evidence suggesting that ADHD-related characteristics, such as inattention, hyperactivity, and impulsivity, are not more common among high-ability children (focusing particularly on high-IQ children). Instead, Lovecky argues that certain "overexcitabilities" (e.g., intellectual, imaginational, etc.) are really the source of the issue and should not be conflated with traits and behaviors that look like ADHD. She also reviews the evidence on the link between high ability and the risk for developing a mental disorder and argues some best practices in the identification of high-ability students to determine both strengths and weaknesses for academic, social, and emotional planning.

Steven Pfeiffer and Megan Foley-Nicpon wrap up this section nicely in chapter 5 with a discussion of the current state of the field and what issues remain to be investigated. They draw on their expertise as academic clinicians, as well as their first-hand experience working with 2e children. In addition to discussing the major challenges with identifying and supporting 2e children, they also review the methodological weaknesses in existing empirically validated intervention options. They urge caution when reading clinical reports or studies, considering the samples are usually small and biased (the children brought to the clinician are brought in for a reason), and they offer best clinical practices.

Part II of this volume moves away from issues primarily surrounding identification to the various ways twice exceptional study can be supported. In chapter 6, Susan Winebrenner tackles the challenge of how to devote equal time and attention to both of the 2e child's exceptional learning needs. Winebrenner also gives helpful strategies, such as "curriculum compacting," to teach 2e students to build on their learning strengths to help improvement with their areas of challenge.

In chapter 7, Judy Galbraith addresses the social-emotional challenges and needs of 2e students, including positive character strengths, resilience, and a growth mindset. Through the research she has conducted for over 30 years, Galbraith shows why these social-emotional needs matter and how, when they are addressed, 2e students are more likely to feel supported and succeed in school and in life. Her survey looks at a wide range of factors, including experiences with peers and at home, and how they felt about themselves as they were growing up. Galbraith also includes strategies for helping 2e students deal with their social-emotional challenges.

In chapter 8, Rich Weinfeld discusses ways that educators, professionals, and parents can advocate that every child receive a meaningful individualized educational program. Weinfeld argues that effective advocating for 2e students requires an understanding of the law and the challenges of identification, as well as best practices for supporting these students. Based on his experience in over four decades of advocating for special needs students, Weinfeld offers a guide for how to think through each of these areas in a collaborative way with the school team in order to develop appropriate educational programs. Critically, Weinfeld argues that the ultimate goal is for 2e students to eventually become their own *self-advocates*, understanding their own unique strengths and challenges, learning the tools to help remove barriers to learning, and learning how to access these tools.

In chapter 9, Mary Ruth Coleman, Lois Baldwin, and Daphne Pereles combine research and case studies to explore how the needs of 2e students change over time and how it takes a coordinated team of family members, teachers, friends, coaches, special service providers, counselors, psychologists, and sometimes medical professionals to help these students grow and flourish. In particular, the authors present problem-solving guidelines to help foster collaboration, instructional strategies for learning and differentiated instruction, and family partnership approaches to support the students' success. The emphasis in this chapter is on flexibility, innovation, and teamwork to address the academic, social, and emotional success of 2e students.

In chapter 10, Kevin Besnoy also addresses the team approach, helping parents of 2e children navigate the often confusing school policy concerning services for their children and offering strategies that school officials can implement to create stronger school-to-home partnerships to empower parents to be part of the problem-solving process. Besnoy argues for a culture in which school officials connect with parents through a variety of mediums, including inviting parents to special events and establishing social network groups focused on parents' needs. Besnoy argues that by recognizing that parents are concerned about their child's future, and providing a culture that is inviting for parents to address their concerns, educators will be more likely to produce individualized programming that meets the need of 2e students.

In Part III, we take a look at special populations, including ADHD, Asperger's, dyslexia, and culturally diverse learners. Following many of the other contributors to this volume in taking a strengths-based approach, Charles Fugate discusses ADHD in chapter 11. Fugate argues that educators should view ADHD through a new lens—as ADHG (attention divergent hyperactive gifted)—and he discusses the implications of this approach for educators as they create classrooms environments to foster creativity. Fugate believes that such a paradigm shift in our conceptualization of ADHD would shift the focus from remediation to the motivation, strengths, perseverance, and resilience that make students with ADHD so special.

In chapter 12, Matthew Lerner and Rebecca Girard focus on students with ASD, noting that many of these children have exceptional intellectual capacity and deep knowledge of specific topics but often have difficulty flexibly applying this knowledge, particularly in social situations. Adopting a strengths-based approach to ASD, Lerner and Girard reframe the often perceived social deficits of those with ASD as "social creativity" (defined as the ability to come up with novel, creative responses to social situations) and argue that not only can these abilities act as a source of social connection for many children and adolescents but they can be fostered, nurtured, and supported among children with ASD. Lerner and Girard highlight the power of improvisational comedy and engaging creatively in an area of special interest as ways of bringing out the social creativity of students with ASD.

Richard Williams and Jeffrey Freed also address ASD in chapter 13, noting some of the exceptional similarities between ASD students and 2e students in general. They review genetic and neuroscience evidence to support their claim that many of the learning difficulties seen in each group result from exceptional sensory processing issues. They argue that this hypersensitivity of the senses can cause learning difficulties in the classroom but that both groups of learners (2e and ASD) share cognitive styles that can make them excellent visual-spatial thinkers and learners. Critically, they emphasize the wide spectrum of these skills and offer some teaching suggestions to accommodate the sensory and learning difficulties of these two groups.

In chapter 14, Maryam Trebeau Crogman, Jeffrey Gilger, and Fumiko Hoeft do an extensive, nuanced review of the current state of visuospatial skills in "atypical learners"—those with developmental dyslexia or reading disorder (RD). Their review suggests that even though individuals with RDs do not generally display gifted-level visual-spatial abilities (VS), they do tend to display specific types of VS skills that RD individuals may show strengths in. Their comprehensive review suggests that this may be particularly true for a subset of those with RD who the authors refer to as "2e-RD." The authors argue for the need for a diverse array of methodologies to assess these skills, and they offer some recommendations for future research to more finely delineate the unique VS processing mechanisms in both RD and 2e-RD populations.

In chapter 15, Susan Daniels and Michelle Freeman frame dyslexia as a different pattern of brain organization and information processing and focus on the intersection of dyslexia, creativity, and "MIND-strengths," such as material reasoning, interconnected reasoning, narrative reasoning, and dynamic reasoning. Drawing on individual cases of "gifted dyslexics" (which the authors have experienced in their own clinical practice), the authors recommend teaching and learning strategies to build upon the strengths of these individuals.

In chapter 16, Joy Lawson Davis and Shawn Robinson go beyond 2e and focus on students who are "3e": those who are culturally diverse (e.g., Black, Latino), high ability, and have exceptional conditions requiring special education services. The authors argue that being 3e presents a unique set of conditions that require educators to view these students through a different set of lenses and employ a more creative tool box of strategies to bring out the best in these learners. Toward this aim, Davis and Robinson explore the specific challenges of this population, include real-life cases, and offer strategies for educators and families to help 3e learners have high expectations, capitalize on their strengths, and help them thrive in life.

In chapter 17, Renae Mayes, Erik Hines, and James Moore also go beyond 2e by taking into account the intersection of giftedness, disability, and cultural identities that can significantly shape the experience of students in school. The authors illustrate the importance of this intersection through a case study of a high-ability

African American student with a learning disability, and they discuss the academic, personal/social, and career implications for bringing out the best in culturally diverse 2e students. The authors also offer practical solutions and strategies for teachers and school counselors to collaborate with families to promote the student success of 2e students with multiple identities.

The last section of this volume, Part IV, includes two examples of schools that are intentionally designed to support 2e learners and apply evidence-based practices. In chapter 18, Carl Sabatino and Christopher Wiebe discuss the strengths-based approach to 2e that they take at Bridges Academy in Los Angeles, California. Bridges Academy serves Grades 4 to 12 and is grounded in the Multiple Perspectives Model, which emphasizes a diverse range of students' gifts and talents, learning differences, and family contexts. The authors also emphasize the importance of making decisions in a dynamic educational environment and the importance of a "culture of appreciation" in which students' strengths are celebrated alongside differentiation of curriculum to move students forward to appropriate levels of depth and complexity in their learning. The authors also argue for more flexible school policies that embrace creative problem-solving and that place the needs of the student above external rules and regulations.

In the final chapter of this volume, chapter 19, Kimberly Busi and Kristin Berman discuss the model that lies behind the Quad Preparatory School (TQPS) in New York City. Their model integrates best practices from the fields of psychology, speech pathology, occupational therapy, special education, and gifted pedagogy. Their model also incorporates a strengths-based teaching approach in which social skills are not developed in isolation but in which social and emotional development is completely interwoven with academic and executive functioning. TQPS also uses a curriculum framework that allows students the opportunity to conduct projects initiated by their own unique strengths and interests. The authors encourage parents and community partnerships, and the importance of developing a sense of autonomy in students, echoing common themes that are seen throughout this volume.

**My Own Personal Journey**

I would be remiss if I did not admit that this book project has a deeply personal component to it for me (Kaufman, 2013; Kaufman, 2018). As a kid growing up with my own auditory learning difficulty (central auditory processing disorder), I remember vividly (and painfully) what it was like to grow up with a dual identity. On the one hand, I felt as though something was very wrong with me, as though I was broken. On the other hand, I was yearning deep inside for more intellectual and creative challenges and felt capable of something more. But who was I to challenge the authorities? These conflicting identities led to a lot of confusion and an unstable sense of self as a child. Thankfully, I had a special education teacher who saw beyond my label to some hidden strengths that were bursting to come out from deep within me. She inspired me to sign up for more challenging classes and after-school activities (e.g., school orchestra, choir, musicals, etc.), which allowed me to finally put my ravenous curiosity and desire to take on creative projects to good use. Eventually, through a lot of hard work as well as a love of learning, I worked my way up to a Yale PhD in cognitive psychology, where I was able to propose a new definition of intelligence. But I will never forget where I came from, and what it was like to grow up 2e. It may only be a sample size of one, but I personally know what is possible with even a little encouragement and support, and I truly hope this book can help many more children become what they are capable of becoming.

## ACKNOWLEDGMENTS

The "History of 2e" section was written in consultation with Susan Baum.

## REFERENCES

Asperger, H. (1991). "Autistic psychopathy" in childhood. In U. Frith (Ed.), *Autism and Asperger syndrome* (pp. 37–92). New York, NY: Cambridge University Press. (Original work published 1944)

Asperger, H. (1979). Problems of infantile autism. *Communication, 13*, 45–52.

Baldwin, L., Baum, S., Perles, D., & Hughes, C. (2015). Twice-exceptional learners: The journey toward a shared vision. *Gifted Child Today, 38*(4), 206–214.

Baum, S., Owen, S., & Dixon, J. (1991). *To be gifted and learning disabled: From identification to practical learning strategies*. Mansfield Center, CT: Creative Learning Press.

Baum, S., Schader, R., & Owen, S. (2017). *To be gifted and learning disabled: Strength-based strategies for helping twice-exceptional students with LD, AHDD, and other disorders* (3rd ed.). Austin, TX: Prufrock Press.

Bloom, B. (1985). *Developing talent in young people*. New York, NY: Ballantine Books.

Brody, L. E., & Mills, C. J. (1997). Gifted children with learning disabilities: A review of the issues. *Journal of Learning Disabilities, 30*, 282–296.

Cruickshank, W. M., Bentzen, F. A., Ratzeburg, F. H., & Tannhauser, M. T. (1961). A teaching method for brain-injured children and hyperactive children. Syracuse, NY: Syracuse University Press.

*Education for All Handicapped Children Act of 1975*, U.S. P.L. 94–142. U.S. Code. Vol. 20, secs. 1401 et seq. (1975).

Elkind, J. (1973). The gifted child with learning disabilities. *Gifted Child Quarterly, 17*, 45–47.

Foley-Nicpon, M. F., Allmon, A., Sieck, B., & Stinson, R. D. (2011). Empirical investigation of twice-exceptionality: Where have we been and where are we going? *Gifted Child Quarterly, 55*, 3–17.

Gagné, F. (1985). Giftedness and talent: Reexamining a reexamination of the definitions. *Gifted Child Quarterly, 29*, 103–112.

Gallagher, J. J. (1966). Children with developmental imbalances: A psychoeducational definition. In W. Cruickshank (Ed.), *The teacher of brain-injured children* (pp. 23–43) (Syracuse University Special Education and Rehabilitation Monograph Series 7). Syracuse, NY: Syracuse University Press.

Gardner, H. (1983). *Frames of mind: The theory of multiple intelligences*. New York, NY: Basic Books.

Goertzel, V., & Goertzel, M. G. (2004). *Cradles of eminence*. Scottsdale, AZ: Great Potential Press. (Original work published 1962)

Hollingworth, L. (1923). *Special talents and defects: Their significance for education*. Ithaca, NY: Cornell University Library.

Individuals with Disabilities Education Act of 2004, P.L. 108–446, § 118 Stat. 2647 (2004).

Horowitz, F.D., Subotnik, R.F., & Matthews, D.J. (2009). *The development of giftedness and talent across the life span*. Washington, DC: American Psychological Association.

Kanner L. (1943). Autistic disturbances of affective contact. *Nervous Child*, *2*, 217–250.

Kaufman, S. B. (2013). *Ungifted: Intelligence redefined*. New York, NY: Basic Books.

Kaufman, S.B. (2018). My quest to understand human intelligence. In R.J. Sternberg (Ed.), *The Nature of Intelligence*. New York, NY: Cambridge University Press.

Kay, K. (2003). *Uniquely gifted: Identifying and meetings the needs of the twice-exceptional student*. New Hampshire: Avocus Publishing.

Kirk, S. (1962). *Educating exceptional children*. Boston, MA: Houghton Mifflin.

Lovett, B. J., & Lewandowski, L. J. (2006). Gifted students with learning disabilities: Who are they? *Journal of Learning Disabilities*, *39*, 515–527.

Ludwig, A. M. (1995). *The price of greatness: Resolving the creativity and madness controversy*. New York, NY: Guilford Press.

Maker, C. J. (1977). *Providing programs for the gifted handicapped individuals*. Reston, VA: Council for Exceptional Children.

Marland, S. P. (1972). *Education of the gifted and talented* (Report to the Subcommittee on Education, Committee on Labor and Public Welfare, US Senate). Washington, DC: US Government Printing Office.

Meisgeier, C., Meisgeier, C., & Werblo, D. (1978). Factors compounding the handicapping of some gifted children. *Gifted Child Quarterly*, *22*, 325–331.

National Association for Gifted Children. (n.d.). Definitions of giftedness. Retrieved from http://www.nagc.org/resources-publications/resources/definitions-giftedness

National Education Association. (2006). *The twice-exceptional dilemma*. Washington, DC: Author.

Reis, S. M., Baum, S. M., & Burke, E. (2014). An operational definition of twice-exceptional learners: Implications and applications. *Gifted Child Quarterly*, *58*, 217–230.

Renzulli, J. S. (1978). What makes giftedness? Re-examining a definition. *Phi Delta Kappan*, *60*, 180–184, 261.

Shepherd, M. J. (2001). History lessons. In A. S. Kaufman & N. L. Kaufman (Eds.), *Specific learning disabilities and difficulties in children and adolescents: psychological assessment and evaluation* (pp. 3–28). New York, NY: Cambridge University Press.

Sternberg, R. J. (1984). *Beyond IQ: A triarchic theory of human intelligence*. New York, NY: Cambridge University Press.

Sternberg, R. J. (1997). *Successful intelligence: How practical and creative intelligence determine success in life*. New York, NY: Plume.

Strauss, A., & Lehtinen, L. (1947). *Psychopathology and education for the brain-injured child*. New York, NY: Grune and Stratton.

Terman, L. (1924). The physical and mental traits of gifted children. In G. M. Whipple (Ed.), *Report of the society's committee on the education of gifted children* (pp.

157–167) (Twenty Third Yearbook of the National Society for the Study of Education). Bloomington, IL: Public School Publishing.

Terman, L. (1925). *Genetic studies of genius,* Vol. 1: *Mental and physical traits of a thousand gifted children.* Stanford, CA: Stanford University Press.

Terman, L. M., & Oden, M. (1947). *Genetic studies of genius,* Vol. 4: *The gifted child grows up: Twenty-five years' follow up of a superior group.* Stanford, CA: Stanford University Press.

Torrance, E. P. (1984). The role of creativity in identification of the gifted and talented. *Gifted Child Quarterly, 28*(4), 153–156.

US Department of Education. (1978). Gifted and Talented Education Act (H.R. 11533). Retrieved from http://www.govtrack.us/congress/bills/95/hr11533

US Department of Education, National Center for Education Statistics. (2013). *Digest of education statistics, 2012* (NCES 2014-2015). Washington, DC: US Government Printing Office.

Winner, E. (1996). *Gifted children: Myths and realities.* New York, NY: Basic Books.

# PART I

# Identification

1

# Finding and Serving Twice Exceptional Students

## *Using Triaged Comprehensive Assessment and Protections of the Law*

BARBARA (BOBBIE) JACKSON GILMAN AND DAN PETERS ■

Imagine yourself as a gifted child. You have advanced conceptual ability and awareness. You learn quickly, with little repetition, and you reason abstractly before your age peers. In many ways, you think like an older child—which can be both wonderful and frustrating. Your chronological age imposes physical developmental limits on your high expectations. Your hands may not meet your high standards in creative endeavors. Your understanding and awareness of troubling topics may overpower your emotional maturity, especially if you are highly sensitive and intense. You may appear to be one age in one situation and another age when circumstances change. In school, you need accommodations to be taught at your level and depth and true peers who share your interests. These needs may or may not be recognized due to the varied tapestry of characteristics you present.

Giftedness has been defined by this developmental asynchrony, or uneven development.

> Giftedness is asynchronous development in which advanced cognitive abilities and heightened intensity combine to create inner experiences and awareness that are qualitatively different from the norm. This asynchrony increases with higher intellectual capacity. The uniqueness of the gifted renders them particularly vulnerable and requires modifications in parenting, teaching and counseling in order for them to develop optimally.
>
> —The Columbus Group (1991)

Now imagine that you are both gifted and have a coexisting disability; you are "twice exceptional" or "2e." Your asynchrony just skyrocketed! You have all of the characteristics of giftedness described earlier but are dually challenged with any of a variety of weaknesses that is significant enough to be diagnosed as a learning, developmental, emotional, or behavioral "disorder" or "disability." Reis, Baum, and Burke (2014) write that you have the "potential for high achievement or creative productivity in one or more domains such as math, science, technology, the social arts, the visual, spatial, or performing arts or other areas of human productivity" to qualify for gifted programs at school but may not be able to demonstrate it. In addition, you have "one or more disabilities as defined by federal or state eligibility criteria . . . specific learning disabilities; speech and language disorders; emotional/behavioral disorders; physical disabilities; Autism Spectrum Disorders (ASD); or other health impairments, such as Attention Deficit/Hyperactivity Disorder (ADHD)," but your high intelligence allows you to compensate for your weaknesses, moderating their appearance or even hiding them.

The 2014 Twice Exceptional Community of Practice, a diverse group of educators, psychologists, and advocates, concurred on a definition of twice exceptionality and its ramifications:

> Twice exceptional individuals evidence exceptional ability and disability, which results in a unique set of circumstances. Their exceptional ability may dominate, hiding their disability; their disability may dominate, hiding their exceptional ability; each may mask the other so that neither is recognized or addressed.
>
> 2e students, who may perform below, at, or above grade level, require the following:
>
> - Specialized methods of identification that consider the possible interaction of the exceptionalities.
> - Enriched/advanced educational opportunities that develop the child's interests, gifts, and talents while also meeting the child's learning needs.
> - Simultaneous supports that ensure the child's academic success and social-emotional well-being, such as accommodations, therapeutic interventions, and specialized instruction
>
> Working successfully with this unique population requires specialized academic training and ongoing professional development. (Baldwin et al. 2015, pp. 212–213)

Is it any surprise that your 2e tapestry of strengths and significant weaknesses is confusing and frustrating and causes you to doubt yourself? Some think you are very bright, but you know you struggle with things your classmates do readily. You question your strengths and become anxious about your areas of challenge. The adults in your life may misinterpret your struggle. You work hard, but when you come up short, your parents may think you're not trying. Your teachers may see you as bright but lazy, disabled and not gifted, or fail to notice your struggle because you manage to meet grade-level expectations. While giftedness has been defined by developmental asynchrony (see previous definition), significant discrepancies that result in clinical, developmental, and learning diagnoses is what characterizes the 2e student. Despite the confusing tapestry that is apparent to others, 2e children have legitimate and significant areas of deficit that impact their ability to learn, show what they know, and manage the multiple daily challenges of school and life.

Public education generally acknowledges the existence of twice exceptionality, accepting the premise that a child can be both intellectually gifted and have disabilities. However, identification of twice exceptional students, and the provision of appropriate services and accommodations to meet their needs, has never been assured in American public schools—especially now.

In 2010, the authors and other psychologists, educators, and gifted advocates—all members of the Assessments of Giftedness Special Interest Group (SIG) of the National Association for Gifted Children (NAGC)—shared a growing concern. All wondered why we were observing a surprising increase in gifted students with learning and developmental disabilities (2e), brought to us for assistance, and overlooked for identification by schools. Our resulting 2013 article, "Critical Issues in the Identification of Gifted Students with Co-Existing Disabilities: The Twice Exceptional" (Gilman et al., 2013), explores this question. As we soon discovered, the 2e children we saw had minimal access to comprehensive assessment (a new and disturbing trend), and their performance was at grade level or above. We were able to diagnose them using individual assessments that school psychologists were no longer providing. However, parents reported resistance at their schools to the notion that gifted children can actually have significant disabilities if they are performing at grade level.

To illustrate what we were seeing, the article presented five case studies. All were of gifted young people, performing largely at average or higher levels. The students' disabilities varied, but all were significant enough to undermine success in school without accommodations or services.

Three of the students profiled were diagnosed with specific learning disabilities (SLDs)—a common cause of referral to private psychologists. What qualifies a student as having SLDs? The Individuals with Disabilities Education Act (IDEA; 2004) defines an SLD as

> a disorder in one or more of the basic psychological processes involved in understanding or in using language, spoken or written, which disorder may manifest itself in the imperfect ability to listen, think, speak, read, write, spell, or do mathematical calculations. (Title I/A/602/30/A)

If such disorders are missed, what challenges does the unidentified, gifted student with SLDs face? How do such students fare as they mature without support? Next we look at a high school student with SLDs who was missed.

Max (pseudonym) exemplifies the student for whom the lines are blurred between *bright* and *intellectually gifted,* lazy and struggling—due to hidden SLDs.

Max was the younger of two children, both with high ability. The elder sibling was identified at school as having a SLD in reading (dyslexia). At that time, states routinely provided comprehensive assessment by school psychologists and other specialists for children with suspected disabilities. Through such testing, Max's sibling was able to document a SLD in reading by earning a high IQ score, coupled with significantly depressed reading scores, evidence of dyslexia, and a history of struggle in reading. The elder child qualified for a special education Individualized Education Program (IEP) that included resource room assistance, help from a reading therapist, and classroom accommodations. Max's sibling needed and benefitted from these services, successfully graduating from high school and college.

Max was a few years younger and attended a small K-8 school. He also had symptoms of dyslexia, but teachers were supportive and provided informal accommodations. Max was a delightful child, full of personality, and teachers liked him. He was able to perform fairly well in this environment until the demands of his education increased. When his mother finally requested evaluation, teachers told her that Max didn't need it. She concluded her younger child's dyslexia must be less severe than her older child's. Two years later, when Max's struggle became pronounced, she requested an evaluation at his high school. "We don't do that anymore," his mother was told.

Max and his sibling's disabilities were handled differently due to a change in federal special education law. The elder child was identified under the previous law; Max's issues presented after passage of its most recent reauthorization, the Individuals with Disabilities Education Improvement Act of 2004 (IDEIA, 2004). Max had only casual accommodations and no formal evaluation at school prior to the new law's full implementation around 2008. He and his parents had no idea that this change had occurred and no warning of its implications for Max. His state was one of many that interpreted IDEIA 2004 to mean that access to comprehensive assessment could now be significantly limited. Without comprehensive individual evaluation to clarify his strengths and weaknesses, Max *appeared* far too capable to qualify for services. Highly verbal and undeniably gifted, he performed lower than expected but still mostly at grade level on school assessments. Previously identified as *gifted* in art and leadership, his teachers assumed he was just lazy in his academic subjects.

Max received no comprehensive assessment until age 16 when his parents requested a private evaluation. His mother wrote, "We know he is smart. Why does he struggle in a traditional school environment?" For four semesters, Max had earned *F*s—three *F*s in the semester just prior to assessment. Only two classes could be made up in summer school, and he was again failing. By that time, his mother described his competitive high school as "a nightmare."

Max's developmental history, degree of struggle, individual assessment on intelligence and achievement tests, and further evaluations with specialists provided the answers. All are critical elements of his evaluation. We have documented his history and increasing struggle over several years. What complex scoring patterns within and between his comprehensive intelligence test and individual achievement test might we expect? For a gifted child with SLDs, we would expect to see intellectual strengths in the IQ subtests most heavily loaded for abstract reasoning ability. Gifted children have advanced reasoning ability. Areas of the IQ test that assess processing skills (e.g., working memory and processing speed) often show lower scores related to the child's weaknesses. We would expect scores in at least one area of academic achievement (reading, math, or writing) on the individual achievement test to be significantly lower than scores reflecting intellectual strengths on the IQ test. We might see significant differences between areas of achievement, or we might not. All academic areas might be depressed by the learning disability. One academic achievement score might reflect a strength that approaches the child's intellectual strengths. When taken together, the weaknesses should coincide and explain the challenges the child experiences. This is one variation of a "third-method" approach to diagnosing learning disabilities, such as that described by Flanagan, Fiorello, and Ortiz (2010), in which patterns of strengths and weaknesses are interpreted, no single element is *required* for diagnosis, nor is one single method considered *sufficient* for diagnosis.

The Wechsler Adult Intelligence Scale–Fourth Edition (WAIS-IV) administered to Max yielded the Composite scores indicated in Table 1.1 (the mean score is 100).

Max earned a Verbal Comprehension Composite of 141, Perceptual Reasoning of 105, Working Memory of 95, and Processing Speed of 86. Composite scores varied by 55 points (between 3 and 4 standard deviations); a discrepancy of 40 or more points occurs in just 1.0% of individuals taking the test. Individual subtest scores varied by 13 points, ranging from the 99.9th percentile to the 9th percentile (over 4 standard deviations [SD]). According to Silverman (2013), a 30-point discrepancy (2 SD) in composite scores or a 9-point discrepancy (3 SD) in subtest scaled scores suggests the need for further evaluation of a 2e child for a possible learning disability (p. 179). Max meets both requirements. The 30-point composite discrepancy exceeds a common rule of thumb that variance of 1.5 standard deviations (23 points) usually signals a learning disability. This is because gifted children show more natural variance in composite scores than average children, and the larger discrepancy is needed to account for their typical asynchrony. A NAGC Task Force study of 334 gifted children on the Wechsler Intelligence Scale for Children–Fourth Edition (WISC-IV) found a discrepancy of 21 points between the highest composite (Verbal Comprehension 133.17) and the lowest (Processing Speed 112.02) (Gilman, Robinson, Kearney, Wasserman, & Silverman, 2010). In contrast, the WISC-IV control group's scores varied by less than 4 points, from 106.7 to 102.8 (Wechsler, 2003, p. 77).

Max's WAIS-IV test composites provided critical information. Verbal Comprehension documented Max's "very superior" or *gifted* abstract verbal reasoning, language ability, and store of knowledge, at the 99.7th percentile when compared with age peers. At the same time, there was unusual variation between the subtest scores within Verbal Comprehension. Max scored approximately 2 SD higher in the subtests requiring him to reason abstractly in novel situations (Similarities, 99.9th percentile and Comprehension, 99.6th percentile) than in the subtests requiring long-term memory for information taken in auditorily

*Table 1.1.* MAX'S PERFORMANCE ON THE WAIS-IV

| Composite/Index Scores | Scaled Scores | Percentile | Range |
|---|---|---|---|
| Verbal Comprehension | 141 | 99.7 | Gifted |
| Perceptual Organization | 105 | 63 | Average |
| Working Memory | 95 | 37 | Average |
| Processing Speed | 86 | 18 | Low Average |
| Full Scale IQ | NA | | |
| **Verbal Comprehension Subtests** | **Scaled Scores** | **Percentile** | **Range** |
| Similarities | 19 | 99.9 | Highly Gifted |
| *Vocabulary | (12) | (75) | High Average |
| Information | 13 | 84 | High Average |
| Comprehension | 18 | 99.6 | Highly Gifted |
| **Perceptual Reasoning Subtests** | | | |
| Block Design | 12 | 75 | High Average |
| Matrix Reasoning | 11 | 63 | Average |
| Visual Puzzles | 10 | 50 | Average |
| **Working Memory** | | | |
| Digit Span | 10 | 50 | Average |
| Arithmetic | 8 | 25 | Low Average |
| **Processing Speed** | | | |
| Symbol Search | 6 | 9 | Low |
| Coding | 9 | 37 | Average |

NOTE: WAIS–IV = Wechsler Adult Intelligence Scale–Fourth Edition.

or through reading (Vocabulary, 75th percentile, Information, 84th percentile). Central auditory processing disorder (CAPD) was subsequently diagnosed, likely affecting both the information Max had been able to take in auditorily and contributing to his lower (auditory) Working Memory score (95, 37th percentile). CAPD can affect phonemic awareness and sequencing ability important to hearing speech correctly, learning sound-symbol relationships, and sequencing letters and words.

These challenges are also seen in dyslexia. Most conspicuous was Max's low average Processing Speed (86), at the 18th percentile. Visual processing weaknesses were subsequently confirmed by a specialist, contributing both to his slow speed on paper-and-pencil tests and *average* Perceptual (visual) Reasoning (105, 63rd percentile). Verbal Comprehension and Perceptual Reasoning tend to score similarly unless a visual or auditory weakness lowers scores; both weaknesses together require careful interpretation. We have found that sensory modality issues are common in children with learning disabilities. The WAIS-IV provided a powerful diagnostic tool to probe issues hidden in the classroom. The achievement test and resulting conversation with Max during the test added significantly to this picture (see Table 1.2).

Max's scores on the Woodcock Johnson III Tests of Achievement (WJ-III ACH) ranged from the 75th to the 1st percentile. We would expect his standard scores to

*Table 1.2.* Max's Performance on the Woodcock-Johnson III Tests of Achievement

| Area Assessed | Standard Score | Percentile | Grade Equivalent | Range |
|---|---|---|---|---|
| Letter-Word Ident. | 96 | 40 | 9.5 | Average |
| Passage Comprehension | 110 | 75 | >18.0 | Average |
| Reading Fluency | 101 | 54 | 11.2 | Average |
| Word Attack | 88 | 21 | 4.5 | Low Average |
| BROAD READING | 102 | 56 | 11.4 | Average |
| Calculation | 101 | 51 | 11.0 | Average |
| Applied Problems | 101 | 54 | 11.4 | Average |
| Math Fluency | 67 | 1 | 3.9 | Low |
| BROAD MATH | 94 | 33 | 8.6 | Average |
| Spelling | 85 | 15 | 5.9 | Low Average |
| Writing Samples | 103 | 59 | 13.0 | Average |
| Writing Fluency | 92 | 29 | 7.6 | Average |
| BROAD WRITTEN LANGUAGE | 90 | 26 | 7.5 | Low Average |

**Max scored as follows (using age-based norms):**

| Area Assessed | Standard Score | Percentile | Grade Equivalent | Range |
|---|---|---|---|---|
| Letter-Word Identification | 96 | 40 | 9.5 | Average |
| Passage Comprehension | 110 | 75 | >18.0 | Average |
| Reading Fluency | 101 | 54 | 11.2 | Average |
| Word Attack | 88 | 21 | 4.5 | Low Average |
| BROAD READING | 102 | 56 | 11.4 | Average |
| Calculation | 101 | 51 | 11.0 | Average |
| Applied Problems | 101 | 54 | 11.4 | Average |
| Math Fluency | 67 | 1 | 3.9 | Borderline |
| BROAD MATH | 94 | 33 | 8.6 | Average |
| Spelling | 85 | 15 | 5.9 | Low Average |
| Writing Samples | 103 | 59 | 13.0 | Average |
| Writing Fluency | 92 | 29 | 7.6 | Average |
| BROAD WRITTEN LANGUAGE | 90 | 26 | 7.5 | Average |
| ACADEMIC SKILLS | 92 | 31 | 8.4 | Average |
| ACADEMIC FLUENCY | 88 | 21 | 7.8 | Low Average |
| ACADEMIC APPLICATIONS | 105 | 63 | 13.0 | Average |

*approach* the best indication of intellectual potential from his IQ test: his WAIS-IV Verbal Comprehension Composite of 141, which predicts success in advanced classes. However, instead of earning scores in the 130s or 120s, Max's achievement scores ranged from 67 to 110—well below his Verbal Comprehension score of 141. There was also a discrepancy of 43 points (almost 3 standard deviations) between his achievement scores.

The patterns of discrepancies within Max's WAIS-IV intelligence test, within his WJ-III ACH, and between the tests are consistent with a gifted student with learning disabilities. His diagnosed CAPD further correlates with his lower scores in Vocabulary and Information (general knowledge). CAPD can limit the information individuals take in from their environment, especially when they cannot compensate by avid reading. CAPD is often a factor in lower auditory Working Memory scores. Many students with CAPD struggle learning arithmetic operations from teachers who explain them sequentially in complex sentences. Max's diagnosed visual processing weaknesses correlate with his relatively poor Perceptual (visual) Reasoning performance, when compared with Verbal Comprehension on the IQ test, and his slower Processing Speed (visual-motor and visual discrimination speed). His strengths and weaknesses evident through these evaluations are consistent with his observed strengths and academic struggle.

It is important to note that the ability-achievement discrepancy (AAD) still plays an important role in the diagnosis of twice exceptional children. Just because IDEA 2004 stated that schools "Must not require the use of a severe discrepancy between intellectual ability and achievement for determining whether a child has a specific learning disability" does not mean that the AAD cannot be used as part of the evaluation. The key issue is that recent literature and research indicates that AAD *alone* does not reliably and validly identify all students with SLDs (Flanagan et al., 2010). Brock and Fernette Eide, authors of *The Mislabeled Child* and *The Dyslexic Advantage*, further address the use of AAD for the twice exceptional:

> The use of ability-achievement discrepancy is essential and irreplaceable in the diagnosis of learning and cognitive challenges, particularly for children of high conceptual ability who may struggle greatly despite exceeding percentile thresholds that identify disability in children with average IQ. Ability-achievement discrepancy is not the only tool needed for identifying significant learning challenges, nor is discrepancy always needed to validate learning disorders, but it is a critical tool that must not be discarded. (personal communication, October 13, 2012)

We concur and find that the AAD is most informative when the IQ score compared represents the best estimate of the child's intellectual potential on subtests that emphasize reasoning without processing skills (Working Memory and Processing Speed). For the reasons discussed previously, processing skills scores fall for 2e children; thus, the Full Scale IQ score is rarely the most valid indicator of intellectual potential because it averages the child's strengths and weaknesses. This lowers the Full Scale IQ, diminishing the ability-achievement discrepancy. The WISC-V Technical Report #1, Expanded Index Scores (2015), recommends two new methods to calculate AADs for determination of learning disabilities that emphasize reasoning without processing skills. Both utilize broad index scores that include both core and supplementary subtests for AAD comparisons: the

Verbal (Expanded Crystallized) Index and Expanded Fluid Reasoning Index. (An Expanded General Ability Index, now under development, may soon be helpful for this purpose.) It is also important to avoid confounding the AAD by imposing limits on how high the IQ score can be or how low the achievement score must be to constitute a true disability. Some states have imposed such limits (e.g., the child has a major IQ score of 132, but only scores up to 120 may be used in the AAD calculation), effectively requiring a gifted child to demonstrate a much larger discrepancy to qualify for services than an average or high average child.

Despite Max's multiple, strong indications of learning disabilities, only one score, Math Fluency, fell at or below the 12th percentile—the *cut score* required by his state to qualify for special education services for a SLD. Looking at both his IQ and achievement tests, most of Max's scores are average or above. While his scores show the requisite complex pattern of strengths and weaknesses, does he actually have a learning disability significant enough to require an IEP or 504 Plan? Let's look more closely.

Max's scores on timed tests of simple sentence reading, math facts, and basic sentence writing (i.e., Academic Fluency) document processing weaknesses that are typical with learning disabilities. Timed tests of very basic skills (not challenging work) account for most of his lowest scores. He could use his advanced reasoning to compensate best for his weaknesses in untimed situations; timed tests limited his compensation. Math Fluency, which assesses whether math facts are recalled automatically, yielded a score of 67 (1st percentile, third-grade level). Max revealed that he could never learn multiplication facts. Although Broad Math was average, knowledge of arithmetic operations showed holes significant enough to cause frequent confusion. Broad Reading was average, but nonsense word reading (Word Attack) was low average (fourth-grade level). Max admitted that he never learned to sound out words. Spelling was low average, at the fifth-grade level. Writing Samples showed writing weaknesses combined with the interesting content of a gifted mind. Such weaknesses are classic dyslexia symptoms in a gifted student, despite his grade-level appearance.

Taken together, Max's comprehensive testing demonstrated gifted verbal intelligence, a reading disorder, a mathematics disorder, and visual and central auditory processing weaknesses. At the time of testing, he was expressing suicidal ideation. How could a student with so many overlooked deficiencies navigate the heavy reading, writing, and listening demands of a competitive high school? How could he possibly succeed in math or science classes with his math weaknesses? His history demonstrated clearly that Max could not function successfully without identification and services. Inattention to his increasing struggle and the lack of competent school assessment to diagnose him undermined his ability to succeed and his self-confidence. Max managed to compensate reasonably well in his K-8 school due to strong reasoning ability and the kindness of teachers, but untreated deficits eventually sabotaged his success as the demands of education increased. Only with significant accommodations could Max continue to be successful, and he would particularly need a way to limit the number of courses per semester that carry heavy reading demands to avoid overload.

Max attended the posttest conference and was relieved to find real reasons for his failures and interventions likely to help. For so long, he had felt the burden of disappointing adults in his life and being called "lazy." Now there was a glimmer of hope. When the recommendations were discussed, he said, "I want to fix this." His mother reported that he said upon leaving, "Drive carefully. We finally have a reason to live."

With documented evidence of learning disabilities, Max should have received the support he needed, but he was deemed ineligible for an IEP because he performed too well (generally above that 12th percentile cut score). He should have qualified based on emotional need, if for no other reason. The 504 Plan he was offered provided some accommodations suggested by specialists but no way to make up all failing classes or to take fewer classes per semester to avoid overload. Without sufficient accommodations to allow him to succeed, he left school. Max's parents were never advised of their right to formally request a special education evaluation or a 504 Plan evaluation, so they never thought to do so in writing. His mother was told he didn't need testing. His parents were unaware of their right to due process if such assessment is refused, nor the time limits for reporting such issues.

Max's school failed to guarantee him a free appropriate public education (FAPE), and Max is not alone. He is one of many twice exceptional students with unidentified disabilities, no services, minimal or no accommodations, and a future in peril. As clinicians who work daily with these children, we see how 2e children become invisible when service eligibility hinges upon absolute low performance and proper assessment is unavailable. We see parents who struggle to provide private assessments and interventions so that their children can be successful. We do not see the families who must rely solely upon school assessment and services. Students are being denied services who cannot successfully complete school without them. How did we reach this point?

## EDUCATIONAL POLICY CHANGES THE SPECIAL EDUCATION LANDSCAPE

### Determining Specific Learning Disabilities

IDEIA 2004 resulted in systemic changes in the ways most states evaluate children for disabilities. Most notable was the new way in which SLDs would be identified and addressed. Instead of referring students with potential SLDs for comprehensive assessment with the school psychologist and determining service eligibility based on a significant discrepancy between (higher) IQ and (lower) achievement scores in the area of disability, IDEIA 2004 initiated a new process. The law stated that the criteria adopted by each state ("Assistance to States," 2006, p. 46647):

- Must not require the use of a severe discrepancy between intellectual ability and achievement for determining whether a child has a SLD;

- Must permit the use of a process based on the child's response to scientific, research-based intervention; and
- May permit the use of other alternative research-based procedures for determining whether a child has a SLD.

First, states could no longer *require* a significant IQ/achievement discrepancy to qualify a child for services. According to the *Federal Register*, they could still use it diagnostically within the body of evidence of a disability analysis ("Assistance to States," 2006), but the words "must not require" caused considerable confusion as to whether or not schools could use it. The IQ/achievement discrepancy remains an important red flag for SLDs in gifted children who may not show obvious low performance; however, as noted earlier, learning disorders can be identified in students who do not have a significant discrepancy. According to *The Diagnostic and Statistical Manual of Mental Disorders* (5th ed. [DSM-5]), "The phrase 'unexpected academic underachievement' is often cited as the defining characteristic of SLDs in that the SLDs are not part of a more general learning difficulty as manifested in intellectual disability or global developmental delay" (American Psychiatric Association, 2013, p. 69). The IQ test provides the measure of *ability* essential to determine an appropriate expectation for the child's performance, while the achievement test yields information about the child's actual learning to date. A significant discrepancy between the two (additional discrepancies are considered as well) warrants careful examination of a possible learning disability.

Second, instead of a special education evaluation, a *regular education* process became the new first step toward special education. Classroom teachers were directed to first locate students performing *below grade level* and offer scientifically based interventions of increasing intensity to mitigate the observed problem (often called Response to Intervention [RTI]). Those students responding with improvement to grade level required no additional services. Those deemed "nonresponsive" because they failed to improve sufficiently would be referred for a special education evaluation but not until Tier 2 or Tier 3 of leveled RTI interventions. Considerable time may pass as the RTI process continues, during which the exact nature and degree of the child's disability remain unclear—and opportunities for targeted early intervention slip away.

Even more troubling, gifted students with learning disabilities often elude RTI identification altogether because they perform too well. Having teachers seek out children performing *below* grade level is not the safe approach it might appear to be to locate virtually all children with learning disabilities. By using their advanced reasoning and hard work, many gifted children with SLDs compensate for their weaknesses well enough to meet "minimum grade criteria." Gifted students with disabilities are not the only children with this problem but the tip of the iceberg of bright children with significant weaknesses, performing at grade level, who may miss needed opportunities for classroom interventions and fail to be referred by teachers to special education.

Parents can still request evaluations under IDEIA 2004. According to the US Department of Education (DOE; 2007), they have the option to formally request a special education evaluation to determine if a child qualifies for an IEP, with interventions and accommodations. Or they may request a 504 Plan evaluation to assess the need for classroom and testing accommodations. Such evaluations may be requested even if the child has been located for RTI and RTI interventions are ongoing. Parents can act independently, but only if they suspect a problem and are aware of their options. Parents are often the first to notice when a child is developing differently from other family members and needs unusual support. However, parents who are unaware of a problem, or cease to be concerned because teachers assure them their child is "right where he should be" (at grade level), will not know to act or be provided with the necessary information about the process to act.

## Determining Service Eligibility for ADHD, ASD, and Other Disabilities

Some schools have also required below-grade-level performance of students seeking services for a variety of other disabilities, less directly related to learning. Regardless of a child's absolute level of performance, any child can have significant executive functioning issues, problems navigating the social landscape of school, mental health issues, or other problems that require services. As federal legal clarifications have shown, gifted students with such disabilities, such as ADHD and ASD, may still qualify for services and accommodations, regardless of higher academic performance.

## Special Education Protections Still Exist

Federal law provides more protection for "children with disabilities with high cognition" than most realize (Musgrove, 2013, 2015; Posny, 2010). The general protections of special education law, and spirit of the law, should not have allowed Max's situation to occur. In the first special education case heard by the Supreme Court, *Board of Educ. v. Rowley* (1982), fundamental issues were addressed. According to *Rowley*, special education law was largely enacted to provide access to public education for students who had been previously excluded or, not unlike Max, were "sitting idly in regular classrooms awaiting the time when they were old enough to 'drop out'" (p. 179).

The Rowley case provided no guarantee of the level of education to be provided, except that it should provide "benefit." *Rowley* further states: "In addition, the IEP, and therefore the personalized instruction . . . should be reasonably calculated to enable the child to achieve passing marks and advance from grade to grade" (*Board of Educ. v. Rowley*, 1982, p. 204). Educators in Max's school should not have felt their hands were tied, nor assumed that they could do nothing that would allow Max to continue in high school. Legal scholar Michael Eig believes there is considerable support for twice exceptional students to receive services and accommodations for disabilities through both IEPs and 504 Plans and that there is even support for gifted students to develop their strengths. In "Legal Issues in Identifying and Serving Twice Exceptional Gifted Learners," Eig, Weinfeld, and Rosenstock (2014) write:

> If the protections of 504. . . are to have any meaning for a qualified handicapped person of superior intelligence, then the student must be entitled to implementation of a Section 504 Accommodation Plan which allows him to achieve educational success reasonably commensurate with his ability.

It is reasonable to assume that a twice exceptional student should be able to complete high school and pursue higher education, with support. As students like Max mature without services, the extreme cost of current policy becomes clear. Twice exceptional students missed for services may find high school graduation at risk and college out of reach. Is it any wonder that unidentified 2e children are frustrated, anxious, depressed, underachieving, and feeling helpless about their future?

## WHAT CAN BE DONE?

> Evolving clarifications of federal law offer additional support for children of high potential, pinpointing specific areas in which state, school district and individual school policy changes are needed. The full texts of DOE clarifications of federal law are available online (US DOE, Special Education Services, Office of Special Education Programs [OSEP] Policy Letters, n.d.). All resulted from concerns individuals shared with the DOE and offer an interpretation of law.

Letter to James Delisle was the response to a December 12, 2012, meeting in Washington, D.C., between the authors and colleagues James Delisle and Michael Postma, representing the NAGC Assessment SIG, and Melody Musgrove, US DOE, director, Office of Special Education Programs, and Michael Yudin, US DOE, acting assistant secretary, Office of Special Education and Rehabilitative Services. Musgrove expressed concern about the gifted. She explained that DOE administrators anticipated that fewer gifted children with disabilities would qualify for IEPs since IDEA 2004. She hoped they were at least getting 504 Plans. We all shook our heads "no" and explained that many schools (in 2012) set the same requirement of below-grade-level performance for a 504 Plan as an IEP, and some states set low absolute performance limits to qualify (e.g., at or below the 5th or 12th percentile). Musgrove referred us to a DOE employee who shared federal legal clarifications that address students of high potential. Later, Musgrove, in response to our correspondence and that of others, firmly established each state's responsibility to assess children of high potential. Key issues include the following:

1. Letter to James Delisle (December 20, 2013) states: "it would be inconsistent with the IDEA for a child, regardless of whether the child is gifted, to be found ineligible for special education and related services under the SLD category solely because the child scored above a particular cut score established by State policy" (Musgrove, 2013).
2. OSEP policy letter 15-08 (April 17, 2015) from Melody Musgrove, director, Office of Special Education Programs, to state special education directors reminding them of Letter to Delisle and the following: "In spite of the guidance provided in Letter to Delisle, we continue to receive letters from those who work with children with disabilities with high cognition, particularly those with emotional disturbance or mental illness, expressing concern that some local education agencies (LEA) are hesitant to conduct initial evaluations to determine eligibility for special education and related services for children with high cognition. In transmitting OSEP Memo 15-08, I am requesting that you widely distribute Letter to Delisle to the LEAs in your state, and remind each LEA of its obligation to evaluate all children, regardless of cognitive skills, suspected of having one of the 13 disabilities outlined in 34 CFR §300" (Musgrove, 2015).
3. OSEP policy letter (February 29, 2012) clarifies that "Each state must ensure that FAPE is available to any child with a disability who needs special education and related services, even though the child has not failed or been retained in a course, and is advancing from grade to grade." 34 CFR §300.101(c). A State has an obligation to make FAPE available to an eligible child with a disability even if that child meets the State's academic achievement standards" (Musgrove, 2012).
4. Letter to Anonymous (January 13, 2010) states: "the IDEA and its regulations do provide protections for students with high cognition and disabilities who require special education and related services to address their individual needs." Therefore, students with high cognition and disabilities such as Asperger's syndrome or ASD "could be considered under the disability category of autism and the individualized evaluation would address the special education and related services needs in the affective areas, social skills and classroom behavior, as appropriate" (Posny, 2010).
5. Dear Colleague Letter: Access by Students with Disabilities to Accelerated Programs (December 26, 2007): "The practice of denying, on the basis of disability, a qualified student with a disability the opportunity to participate in an accelerated program violates both Section 504 and Title II. Conditioning enrollment in an advanced class or program on the forfeiture of needed special education or related aids

and services is also inconsistent with the principle of individualized determinations, which is a key procedural aspect of the IDEA, Section 504 and Title II" (Monroe, 2007).

6. OSEP Policy Letter (Redacted February 29, 2012) addresses "children with disabilities who have high cognition" and states: "It has been the Department's longstanding position that the education needs of a child with a disability include non-academic as well as academic areas." The term "educational performance" as used in the IDEA "means more than academic standards as determined by standardized measures" (Musgrove, 2012).

In our practices, and in those of our colleagues in the NAGC Assessment SIG, we have repeatedly seen these rules violated by schools. Federal clarifications appear to have been slow to trickle down to local schools.

## THE CRITICAL ROLE OF COMPREHENSIVE ASSESSMENT

If schools are responsible to assess children of high potential who may have disabilities, how can it be done accurately? Gifted children with coexisting disabilities are complex. Educators experienced with twice exceptional students may spot them immediately; others may not. Some 2e children have observable strengths but lack academic success due to hidden weaknesses. Others have observable weaknesses that leave parents and educators questioning any advanced capability. A third group seems "average" because their strengths and weaknesses cancel each other out. The combination of advanced cognition and weaknesses can lower scores on brief intelligence measures used to screen for giftedness and moderate the appearance of disabilities, making weaknesses seem less severe or nonexistent. Common measures available to teachers to find 2e students may miss them.

The DSM-5 is quite specific in its discussion of diagnosing a SLD. It states, "Comprehensive assessment is required" (American Psychiatric Association, 2013, p. 70). The NAGC concurs in its position statement, "Ensuring Gifted Students with Disabilities Receive Appropriate Services: A Call for Comprehensive Assessment" (NAGC, 2013). The NAGC recommends that schools "Provide comprehensive assessment (including norm-based, psychometrically sound, comprehensive individual intelligence and achievement tests and measures in all areas of suspected strengths and disabilities) whenever a disability or second exceptionality is suspected in a gifted child or when students identified with a disability show signs of advanced reasoning, creativity or problem solving."

What kinds of information do comprehensive assessment provide? A detailed assessment of intelligence includes an individual, comprehensive intelligence test with multiple core subtests assessing abilities in different ways and supplementary subtests to explore anomalies or provide additional evidence of a strength or weakness. Comprehensive assessments also go beyond the standardized testing data. Other important factors include a child's motivation, perseverance, and focus. Additional situational factors such as family circumstances and emotional and behavioral issues are also considered. The trained examiner is able to observe and interact with the child, one on one, as he or she completes the activities, and the tester can compute scores comparing each measurement to that of age peers.

While a typical child who earns a high average Full Scale IQ score (110–119 IQ) on a comprehensive IQ test would be expected to earn 7 to 16 subtest scores clustering around the high average level, the gifted child with a learning disability might earn a high average Full Scale IQ with highly variable scores. It would not be unusual to see subtest and composite scores ranging from the 99.9th percentile on reasoning subtests to the 5th percentile on measures of processing skills. Another 2e child might earn high scores in reasoning but a low score in social judgment and processing speed—typical of some children with ASD. Yet another 2e child might score high in all untimed reasoning tasks but score dramatically lower on anything visual or visual-motor that is timed. Such profiles of individual scores are invaluable, but the resulting Full Scale IQ scores lack meaning because they hide a dramatic pattern of strengths and weaknesses. The same occurs on brief intelligence tests, which offer limited assessment and scores that tend to average strengths and weaknesses.

Like comprehensive IQ tests, individual achievement tests provide considerable detail, assess over many grade levels (important where the 2e child is very advanced), and have multiple additional options. Such tests explore aspects of reading, math, and writing through core subtests that all children take and supplementary subtests to explore particular weaknesses. The psychologist might choose to add assessments of nonsense word reading (phonemic awareness), oral reading, math concepts and numeracy, and ability to combine sentences. Such information is essential to diagnose a learning disability in a gifted child who may show gifted reading and a math disability.

It is important to explore all possible areas of suspected ability and disability. Children may need tests of executive function, empathy, or behavior assessments to evaluate a variety of strengths and weaknesses. We find that many 2e children have several related weaknesses, so targeted assessment of one area of potential disability cannot be recommended. Children with reading disabilities often have related writing and math problems, as well as weaknesses in sensory, auditory, and visual processing. Children with ASD typically have sensory processing weaknesses and symptoms of ADHD.

Because 2e children do not easily meet the separate requirements for identification as gifted *and* as having disabilities, it is critical that schools adapt the requirements to identify a student as "gifted with co-existing disabilities" or twice exceptional. Ideally, the identification can be made based on the child's comprehensive assessment. Some states, districts, or individual schools have a gifted identification matrix in which a child must meet three of four criteria: IQ score, achievement, Renzulli identifier, and so on. It is wise to have a Plan B for twice exceptional students, even allowing one good identifier of giftedness to be sufficient to include them in gifted programming on a provisional basis. Allowing many choices but requiring just a few for the required *body of evidence* would be ideal. These might include teacher recommendations, evidence of high ability from a portfolio, outside testing by a qualified psychologist (this should always be allowed as there is similar acceptance of outside testing for special education disabilities), Characteristics of Giftedness, interview, grades (if high), and so on. Twice exceptional children often fail to meet criteria for gifted identification on a brief intelligence screener (e.g., Cognitive Abilities Test, SAGES, or Naglieri) but can usually demonstrate high ability on the portions of a comprehensive individual intelligence test less affected by the child's weaknesses. Common problems with brief tests include the averaging of strengths and weaknesses (final summary scores are not high enough), visual weaknesses undermining scores on tests of visual reasoning (e.g., Naglieri, Ravens), and visual-motor weaknesses lowering scores on timed written tests. The body of evidence most schools require to document either giftedness or disability must be adapted to the complexity of the twice exceptional child's situation.

How can test results be used to guide interventions and accommodations? The examiner should meet not only with parents but also with teachers, gifted coordinators, and special education personnel to explain areas of strength and weakness, help create a learning plan, and determine accommodations. This role is critical to clarify a disability (several issues may be present) and to help educators address both exceptionalities, emphasizing the giftedness. Twice exceptional students respond optimally when taught to their advanced conceptual level, with accommodations added secondarily for their weaknesses.

## TRIAGING COMPREHENSIVE ASSESSMENT

How can increased comprehensive assessment peacefully coexist with lean budgets and limited staffing? We suggest *triaging* requests to limit comprehensive testing to the children most likely to need it. The "Parent/Teacher/Counselor Checklist for Recognizing Twice Exceptional Children" by Silverman, Gilman, and Maxwell (2016) can be used to decide if assessment with the school psychologist or other specialists is needed—and may also alert the examiner to possible problems. The checklist is not designed to diagnose disabilities but is helpful in recognizing symptoms of a variety of issues commonly encountered. Have the parent complete the form as well. If it generates concerns, *The Mislabeled Child*, by Brock and Fernette Eide (2007), offers further explanation and helps parents determine which private evaluations may be helpful (e.g., sensory, auditory or visual processing evaluations; an ADHD evaluation with a psychiatrist). It can be surprising how many issues one child with disabilities may have. (See the "Parent/Teacher/Counselor Checklist for Recognizing Twice Exceptional Children" later in this chapter.)

## NAVIGATING REGULAR/SPECIAL EDUCATION SYSTEMS TO OBTAIN IEPS OR 504 PLANS

Mild learning disabilities should respond well to thoughtfully created 504 Plans and include accommodations for the classroom and testing. The most common are preferential seating, extra time, reduced writing, use of a keyboard with spell check, use of a calculator, and testing in a quiet room. Include any classroom or testing accommodations recommended by specialists. Virtually all of the 2e children we see should qualify, at the very least, for 504 Plans. Casual accommodations should not be substituted for a 504 Plan because they have no clout when a history of formal accommodations is needed for future accommodation requests (e.g., for College Board exams). Keep in mind that learning disabilities are lifelong, so we would expect a student to continue to need some 504 accommodations even after a special education IEP is discontinued.

Moderate and more severe disabilities would require an IEP. Many 2e children we assess require interventions—not just accommodations—to learn basic skills and strategies for the learning problems they experience. They require unusual help from parents and may require three times the usual time to complete homework. They should have IEPs based on their degree of current struggle and history of the problem(s). Access to resource teachers, counselors, and therapists may be needed, as well as accommodations for the classroom and testing. For 2e children located by RTI and receiving interventions, avoid prolonged RTI before assessing the child. Without evidence of the child's high ability as a guide, it is easy to underestimate the degree to which the child is falling behind.

## CONCLUSION

Federal law ensures all students with disabilities the right to a FAPE. For gifted students with disabilities—the twice exceptional—this assumes an education that both reasonably supports the gifted student's strengths and provides services/accommodations for disabilities that the student needs to be successful. Current policies that emphasize below-grade-level performance as a criterion for service eligibility contribute to the underidentification of twice exceptional students—and are not supported by federal clarifications of special education law. Instead, these clarifications guarantee the student of high potential the right to assessment and the right to services for learning problems, ADHD, ASD, emotional issues, and other disabilities. Educators have the responsibility to identify and serve even the average-performing student whose advanced reasoning may hide the presence of a disability.

Twice exceptional students are complex to diagnose and require individual, comprehensive assessment by trained personnel to identify them. Training in the characteristics of twice exceptionality (e.g., the use of a twice exceptional checklist) can help educators locate students and "triage" comprehensive assessment requests. The use of such practices will not only identify twice exceptional learners, maintain their civil rights, and ensure FAPE, but it can save a student from being undereducated and underemployed and never fulfilling his or her potential.

## GUIDELINES FOR EDUCATORS, SCHOOL PSYCHOLOGISTS, COUNSELORS, SOCIAL WORKERS, AND ADMINISTRATORS

1. Consider any child who exhibits indications of unusual strengths and coexisting relative weaknesses a potential twice exceptional child warranting additional review. *Performance need not be below grade level.* Monitor capable children who display unexpected struggle in certain areas, have low self-esteem, or need unusual help from adults. Consider children who excel in some areas but seem unmotivated or lazy in others. Especially scrutinize bright children whose parents have expressed concern about their academic, social, or emotional development. Parents are quick to spot unusual development not seen in other family members or issues similar to those of a family member with a disability.
2. Ensure that parents who report concerns are informed of their right to request comprehensive assessment of their child for special education or a 504 Plan evaluation. Inform them of the appropriate process to request such evaluations. The parent's right to request a formal evaluation exists whether or not the child's needs have been or are being addressed by RTI.
3. "Provide comprehensive assessment (including norm-based, psychometrically sound, comprehensive individual intelligence and achievement tests and measures in all areas of suspected strength and disability) whenever a disability or second exceptionality is suspected in a gifted child or when students identified with a disability show signs of advanced reasoning, creativity, or problem solving. Include students with suspected learning disabilities, Attention Deficit Hyperactivity Disorder (ADHD), Autism Spectrum Disorder (ASD), and mental health concerns. Utilize comprehensive assessment by qualified school psychologists and other specialists for diagnosis, eligibility determinations, and to guide interventions and accommodations" (NAGC, 2013).
4. Identify the child as *gifted with coexisting disabilities* or *twice exceptional* based on evidence from comprehensive assessment. Comprehensive assessment clarifies the interaction of strengths and weaknesses in the 2e child. States, districts, and schools that require a *body of evidence* to identify a child as gifted and a separate body of evidence to identify a child's disability must adapt these requirements to reflect the interaction of both exceptionalities (e.g., weaknesses lower scores on brief intelligence tests and strengths mitigate the appearance of disabilities

on performance assessments). If multiple measures of giftedness and of disability are required, allow more possible types of evidence, more discretion, and fewer mandated specific measures. Accept outside assessment by qualified professionals.

5. Proceed with an IEP application for children who need school-based interventions, as well as classroom and testing accommodations. Create a 504 Plan for children who primarily need accommodations. Avoid arranging casual accommodations. Evidence of a formal 504 Plan or IEP is necessary to provide an acceptable history of accommodations for the disability if the child later applies for accommodations on the SAT or ACT.
6. Create a classroom learning plan that emphasizes the child's strengths while secondarily accommodating/addressing weaknesses. Consider an expanded view of strengths that goes beyond cognitive ability and may include leadership, communication, creativity, and visual and performing arts.
7. School special education and 504 Plan coordinators need to be aware of federal legal clarifications that relate to students of high potential; for example, special education does not depend on absolute low performance.
8. "Adapt Response to Intervention to ensure that screening identifies all potential twice exceptional children. In addition to using below-grade-level performance, look for students whose performance is discrepant across major academic areas, highly variable across academic tasks, or whose school performance, as reported by parents, differs greatly from outside of school learning and achievement. Refer these children for further assessment" (NAGC, 2013).
9. Include gifted education specialists in planning RTI interventions that may involve gifted or 2e students. Scientifically based interventions should meet the higher conceptual needs of the gifted: the most effective interventions take both exceptionalities into account (Yssel, 2012) and continue as long as the child continues to progress (NAGC, 2013).
10. Provide in-service training in twice-exceptionality to improve recognition of 2e student characteristics, ensure identification, and optimize educational approaches that emphasize the student's strengths while gently providing services/accommodations for weaknesses. Explore the use of the "Parent/Teacher/Counselor Checklist for Recognizing Twice Exceptional Children" by Silverman et al. (2016) as an aid to identifying potential 2e children in the classroom who may need comprehensive assessment.
11. Contact the DOE Office for Civil Rights for information about 504 Plans. Office for Civil Rights (OCR) attorneys are available for staff training and parent questions. See https://wdcrobcolp01.ed.gov/cfapps/OCR/contactus.cfm to find an office near you.

*Gifted Development Center a service of*
*The Institute for the Study of Advanced Development*

**Parent/Teacher/Counselor Checklist for Recognizing Twice Exceptional Children**

Child's Name: ____________________Gender: M___F___

Birth Date: _________

Your Name:____________________________Date: _________

(check one) Parent: ________Teacher: ________Counselor:________

INSTRUCTIONS

The purpose of this checklist is to assist you in recognizing some common characteristics of gifted children with learning disabilities. This is **not** a diagnostic tool. This checklist has **not** been validated and there are no norms. If a child fits many of the characteristics, it would be wise to refer the child for assessment.

Please answer each item as well as you can. Mark "Sometimes" if you have **ever** observed this behavior.

| Item | General Characteristics of the Twice Exceptional Learner | Sometimes/ Often | Not Observed |
|---|---|---|---|
| 1 | Appears smarter than grades or test scores suggest | | |
| 2 | Has a sophisticated speaking vocabulary but poorer written expression | | |
| 3 | Participates well in class discussions but does not follow through with implementation | | |
| 4 | Has uneven academic skills, inconsistent grades and test scores | | |
| 5 | Does well when given sufficient time but performs poorly on timed tests and takes much longer to complete assignments and homework than other students | | |
| 6 | Experiences loss of confidence and self-esteem in area(s) of weakness | | |
| 7 | Excels in one area or subject but may appear average in others | | |

| Item | General Characteristics of the Twice Exceptional Learner | Sometimes/ Often | Not Observed |
|---|---|---|---|
| 8 | Performs well with challenging work but struggles with easy material | | |
| 9 | Needs unusual parent support in academic learning, social interaction, organization, etc. | | |
| 10 | Has wonderful ideas but has difficulty organizing tasks and activities | | |
| 11 | Has facility with computers but illegible or slow handwriting | | |
| 12 | Resists demonstrating weaknesses; may deflect attention with humor, etc. | | |
| 13 | Thrives on complexity but has difficulty with rote memorization | | |
| 14 | Understands concepts easily and gets frustrated with the performance requirements | | |
| 15 | Fatigues easily due to the energy required to compensate | | |
| | **Comments:** | | |

| Item | Visual Processing Weaknesses | Sometimes/ Often | Not Observed |
|---|---|---|---|
| 16 | Struggles with reading | | |
| 17 | Mixes up plus and minus signs | | |
| 18 | Has difficulty lining up numbers in calculations | | |
| 19 | Has difficulty copying from the board | | |
| 20 | Puts face close to the paper when writing or reading | | |
| 21 | Skips lines and loses place in reading | | |
| 22 | Poor spacing when writing | | |
| 23 | Tires easily when reading or writing | | |
| 24 | Makes "careless errors" in written work | | |
| | **Comments:** | | |

| Item | Auditory Processing Weaknesses | Sometimes/ Often | Not Observed |
|---|---|---|---|
| 25 | Does not seem to hear you; may need several repetitions before responding | | |
| 26 | Mispronounces words or letter sounds | | |
| 27 | Confuses similar sounding words (e.g., "agent" and "ancient") | | |
| 28 | Makes grammatical errors in speech | | |
| 29 | Misunderstands information | | |
| 30 | Watches other students to find out what to do | | |
| 31 | Does not pay attention when being read to or during lectures | | |
| 32 | Weak grasp of phonics affects spelling and pronouncing unfamiliar words | | |
| 33 | Has a loud voice, especially when there is background noise | | |
| 34 | Responds better to directions when shown examples of what is expected | | |
| 35 | Is exhausted after prolonged listening, particularly in the afternoon | | |
| | **Comments:** | | |

| Item | Sensory Processing Issues | Sometimes/ Often | Not Observed |
|---|---|---|---|
| 36 | Is clumsy and awkward | | |
| 37 | Has an odd pencil grip | | |
| 38 | Does not hold paper in place when writing | | |
| 39 | Has illegible handwriting and tends to avoid writing | | |
| 40 | Is poor at athletics | | |
| 41 | Wears very similar soft clothes every day | | |
| 42 | Gets upset when brushed against accidentally, as in standing in line | | |
| 43 | Props self in chair rather than sitting up straight | | |

| Item | Sensory Processing Issues | Sometimes/ Often | Not Observed |
|---|---|---|---|
| 44 | Becomes easily overstimulated and may throw tantrums | | |
| 45 | Has low energy and tires easily | | |
| 46 | Uncomfortable with crowds | | |
| 47 | Has difficulty with transitions | | |
| 48 | When younger, had difficulty deciding handedness | | |
| | **Comments:** | | |

| Item | Attention Deficit Hyperactivity Disorder Symptoms | Sometimes/ Often | Not Observed |
|---|---|---|---|
| 49 | Has difficulty awaiting turn | | |
| 50 | Acts impulsively without awareness of consequences | | |
| 51 | Intrudes on others | | |
| 52 | Is in motion as if "driven by a motor" | | |
| 53 | Has difficulty remaining seated | | |
| 54 | Fidgets with hands or feet or squirms in seat | | |
| 55 | Easily distracted | | |
| 56 | Classroom and test performance are variable | | |
| 57 | Spaces out during assignments and homework, often not completing tasks | | |
| 58 | Forgetful; may only remember part of an instruction | | |
| 59 | Concentrates deeply when interested and not at all when not interested | | |
| 60 | Responds to partial information, thinking understands fully | | |
| 61 | Complains of boredom, unless work is novel, stimulating, or self-selected | | |
| | **Comments:** | | |

| Item | Dyslexia or Stealth Dyslexia | Sometimes/ Often | Not Observed |
|---|---|---|---|
| 62 | Reads at a lower level than expected for ability; reading may be average but reasoning is superior | | |
| 63 | Struggles to learn sound-symbol relationships | | |
| 64 | Reading comprehension is stronger than phonetic decoding of words | | |
| 65 | Shows reversals; may confuse right and left | | |
| 66 | Has difficulty learning to read analog clocks | | |
| 67 | Sequential and rote memory lack permanence | | |
| 68 | Spelling and math facts may be forgotten after practice | | |
| 69 | Spells the same word in several different ways | | |
| 70 | Written output is more difficult than verbal discussion | | |
| 71 | Struggles to sequence ideas on paper | | |
| 72 | Anxious about reading aloud | | |
| 73 | May leave out words or substitute words with similar meanings or appearance | | |
| | **Comments:** | | |

| Item | Autistic Spectrum Disorder (includes Asperger Syndrome) | Sometimes/ Often | Not Observed |
|---|---|---|---|
| 74 | Struggles to read social cues: thoughts/ feelings of others, nonverbal responses, body language, motivation of others, and others' response to own behavior | | |

| Item | Autistic Spectrum Disorder (includes Asperger Syndrome) | Sometimes/ Often | Not Observed |
|---|---|---|---|
| 75 | Does not respond appropriately to others' feelings | | |
| 76 | Shows rigidity: once a decision has been made, it is very difficult to change it | | |
| 77 | Shows sensory issues (e.g., poor fine/ gross motor coordination, difficulty with loud sounds, tactile sensitivity, and transitions) | | |
| 78 | Experiences anxiety, particularly regarding social expectations and conventions | | |
| 79 | May have flat affect | | |
| 80 | May have difficulty with unfamiliar inferential language, idioms, etc., tending to be more literal, black and white | | |
| 81 | Has limited eye contact | | |
| 82 | Unexpected changes often elicit strong emotional distress | | |
| 83 | Limited initiation of social interaction; difficulty responding to overtures by others | | |
| | **Comments:** | | |



## REFERENCES

American Psychiatric Association. (2013). *Diagnostic and statistical manual of mental disorders* (5th ed.). Washington, DC: Author.

Assistance to states for the education of children with disabilities and preschool grants for children with disabilities; Final rule. (2006, August 14). *Federal Register 71*(156), 46540–46845. Retrieved from idea.ed.gov/download/finalregulations.pdf

Baldwin, L., Baum, S., Pereles, D., Hughes, C. (2015). Twice-exceptional learners: The journey towards a shared vision. *Gifted Child Today*, *38*(4), 206–214.

*Board of Educ. v. Rowley*, 458 U.S. 176 (1982).

Columbus Group. (1991, July). Unpublished transcript of the meeting of the Columbus Group. Columbus, OH.

Eig, M. J., Weinfeld, R., & Rosenstock, P. (2014). Legal issues in identifying and serving twice-exceptional gifted learners. *Excellence and Diversity in Gifted Education (EDGE), 1*(1), 21. Retrieved from http://cectag.com/wp-content/uploads/2014/07/Weinfeldjj0625I-PDF-revised.pdf

Flanagan, D. P., Fiorello, C. A., & Ortiz, S. O. (2010). Enhancing practice through application of Cattell-Horn-Carroll theory and research: A "third-method" approach to specific learning disability identification. *Psychology in the Schools, 47*(7), 739–760.

Gilman, B. J., Lovecky, D. V., Kearney, K., Peters, D. B., Wasserman, J. D., Silverman, L. K., . . . Rimm, S. B. (2013). Critical issues in the identification of gifted students with co-existing disabilities: The twice-exceptional. *SAGE Open, 3*. doi:10.1177/2158244013505855

Gilman, B. J., Robinson, N., Kearney, K., Wasserman, J. D., & Silverman, L. K. (2010, November). *Exploring ideal elements of tests of ability for gifted students.* Paper presented at the 57th annual convention of the National Association for Gifted Children, Atlanta, GA. [Available from Gifted Development Center, 8120 Sheridan Boulevard, Suite C-111, Westminster, CO 80003]

Individuals with Disabilities Education Improvement Act of 2004, P.L. 108-446, 20 U.S.C. § 1401, 118 Stat. 2657 (2004).

Monroe, S. (2007, December 26). [Dear colleague letter]. Washington, DC: US Department of Education, Office of Special Education Programs, Office for Civil Rights. Retrieved from http://www2.ed.gov/about/offices/list/ocr/letters/colleague-20071226.pdf

Musgrove, M. (2012, February 29). [OSEP policy letter (redacted)]. Washington, DC: US Department of Education, Special Education & Rehabilitative Services, Office of Special Education Programs. Retrieved from https://www2.ed.gov/policy/speced/guid/idea/letters/2012-1/redacted022912fape1q2012.doc

Musgrove, M. (2013, December 20). [Letter to James Delisle]. Washington, DC: US Department of Education, Special Education & Rehabilitative Services, Office of Special Education Programs. Retrieved from https://www2.ed.gov/policy/speced/guid/idea/memosdcltrs/13-008520r-sc-delisle-twiceexceptional.doc

Musgrove, M. (2015, April 17). [Letter to James Delisle]. Washington, DC: US Department of Education, Special Education & Rehabilitative Services, Office of Special Education Programs. Retrieved from https://www2.ed.gov/policy/speced/guid/idea/memosdcltrs/041715gilmantwiceevceptional2q2015.pdf

National Association for Gifted Children. (2013, October). Position statement. [Index listing: Comprehensive assessment to ensure gifted students with disabilities receive appropriate services]. Washington, DC. Retrieved from https://www.nagc.org/about-nagc/nagc-position-statements-white-papers

Posny, A. (2010, January 13). [Letter to Anonymous]. Washington, DC: US. Department of Education, Office of Special Education and Rehabilitative Services, Office of Special Education Programs. Retrieved from http://www.flspedlaw.com/letter_to_anonymous.pdf

Raiford, S. E., Drozdick, L., Zhang, O., & Zhou, X. (2015, August). *Expanded index scores*. Technical Report #1, 1-21, NCS Pearson. Retrieved from http://images.pearsonclinical.com/images/assets/WISC-V/WISC-VTechReport1_FNL_v3.pdf

Reis, S. M., Baum, S. M., & Burke, E. (2014). An operational definition of twice-exceptional learners: Implications and applications. *Gifted Child Quarterly, 58*, 217–230.

Silverman, L. K. (2013). *Giftedness 101*. New York, NY: Springer.

US Department of Education. (2007, January). Building the legacy: IDEA 2004. Q and A: Questions and answers on response to intervention (RTI) and early intervening services (EIS) [Formal Answer to Question C-1]. Retrieved from http://idea.ed.gov/explore/view/p/%2Croot%2Cdynamic%2CQaCorner%2C8%2C

US Department of Education, Special Education Services, Office of Special Education Programs. (n.d.). Policy letters. Retrieved from http://www2.ed.gov/policy/speced/guid/idea/memosdcltrs/index.html?exp=0

Yssel, N. (2012). Twice-exceptional students. In T. L. Cross & J. R. Cross (Eds.), *Handbook for counselors serving students with gifts and talents: Development, relationships, school issues, and counseling needs/interventions* (pp. 245–257). Waco, TX: Prufrock Press.

Wechsler, D. (2003). *The WISC-IV technical and interpretive manual*. San Antonio, TX: Psychological Corporation.

## SUPPLEMENTAL READING

Amend, E. R., & Beljan, P. (2009). The antecedents of misdiagnosis: When normal behaviors of gifted children are misinterpreted as pathological. *Gifted Education International, 25*, 131–143.

Assouline, S. G., Foley-Nicpon, M., & Huber, D. H. (2006). The impact of vulnerabilities and strengths on the academic experiences of twice-exceptional students: A message to counselors. *Professional School Counseling, 10*(1), 14–24.

Baum, S. M. (2009). Learning disabilities. In B. Kerr (Ed.), *Encyclopedia of giftedness, creativity and talent* (Vol. 2, pp. 527–529). Thousand Oaks, CA: SAGE.

Baum, S. M., & Owen, S. V. (2004). *To be gifted and learning disabled: Strategies for helping bright students with LD, ADHD, and more*. Mansfield Center, CT: Creative Learning Press.

Davis, R. D. (with E. M. Braun). (2010). *The gift of dyslexia: Why some of the smartest people can't read . . . and how they can learn* (Rev. ed.). New York: Perigee.

Eide, B., & Eide, F. F. (2006) *The mislabeled child*. New York, NY: Hyperion.

Eide, B., & Eide, F. F. (2011). *The dyslexic advantage*. New York, NY: Hudson Street Press.

Foley-Nicpon, M., Allman, A., Siek, B., & Stinson, R. D. (2011). Empirical investigation of twice-exceptionality: Where have we been and where are we going? *Gifted Child Quarterly, 55*, 3–17.

Gilger, J. W., & Hynd, G. W. (2008). Neurodevelopmental variation as a framework for thinking about the twice exceptional. *Roeper Review, 30*, 214–228.

Gilman, B. J. (2008a). *Academic advocacy for gifted children: A parent's complete guide*. Scottsdale, AZ: Great Potential Press.

Gilman, B. J. (2008b). *Challenging highly gifted learners*. Waco, TX: Prufrock Press.

Hoagies Gifted Education. (n.d.) Home page. http://www.hoagiesgifted.org/

Hoagies Gifted Education. (n.d.). Twice-exceptional page. http://www.hoagiesgifted.org/twice_exceptional.htm

Kennedy, D. M., & Banks, R. S., with Grandin, T. (2011). *Bright not broken: Gifted kids, ADHD, and autism.* San Francisco, CA: Jossey-Bass.

Lovecky, D. V. (2004). *Different minds: Gifted children with ADHD, Asperger Syndrome, and other learning deficits.* London: Jessica Kingsley.

Postma, M., Peters, D., Gilman, B., & Kearney, K. (2011, June). RTI and the gifted child: What every parent should know. *Parenting for High Potential,* 16–23.

Silverman, L. K. (2000). The two-edged sword of compensation: How the gifted cope with learning disabilities. In K. Kay (Ed.), *Uniquely gifted: Identifying and meeting the needs of twice exceptional children* (pp. 153–165). Gilsum, NH: Avocus. [Updated and revised in 2009 for *Gifted Education International, 25*(2), 115–130.]

Silverman, L. K. (2009). Searching for asynchrony: A new perspective on twice-exceptional children. In B. MacFarlane, & T. Stambaugh (Eds.), *Leading change in gifted education: The festschrift of Dr. Joyce Van Tassel-Baska* (pp. 169–181). Waco, TX: Prufrock Press.

2e Twice-Exceptional Newsletter. (n.d.) www.2eNewsletter.com

Webb, J. T., Amend, E. R., Beljan, P., Webb, N. E., Kuzujanakis, M., Olenchak, F. R., & Goerss, J. (2016). *Misdiagnosis and dual diagnoses of gifted children and adults: ADHD, bipolar, OCD, Asperger's, depression, and other disorders* (2nd ed.). Tucson, AZ: Great Potential Press.

Wrightslaw Special Education Law and Advocacy. (n.d.) www.wrightslaw.com/

2

# Using a Positive Lens

## *Engaging Twice Exceptional Learners*

**SUSAN BAUM AND ROBIN SCHADER**

It is all too common for twice exceptional (2e) students—defined as those whose high abilities are coupled with learning and/or behavioral challenges—to be seen and treated primarily through the lens of their disabilities. We believe this emphasis is misguided. Our research and experience have shown that if good learning is to take place for these learners, we must understand and respond to the individual combination of abilities and challenges each child brings to his or her education. Indeed, recent trends in psychology, motivation, social services, business, and education reinforce a growing consensus that there is more to be gained by focusing on strengths, interests, and talents than on deficits (Baum, Schader, & Hebert, 2014; Hallowell, 2006; Hiemstra & Van Yperen, 2015; Kaufman, 2013; Rath & Conchie, 2008; Seligman & Csikszentmihalyi, 2000). Students learn optimally when they feel valued and respected as learners. This chapter explores how getting to know students through their positive attributes along with any obstacles to their success can result in academic, social, and behavioral growth.

### MEET DIANA

Diana was failing third grade. Recognized as an avid reader, she was colorfully verbal, dramatic, and bright but with an extremely short attention span. Easily frustrated, Diana disrupted the class with noises and could not complete her written work reliably. She had experienced difficulty with social interactions since preschool. Her teacher noted that when Diana did find success, it was because she had put in an incredible effort that took additional toll on her self-esteem. She also reported that Diana appeared to be much less happy than her peers.

Her parents were continually called into conferences, and finally a 504 Plan was put in place to address her nonattentive and increasingly antisocial behaviors.

The plan included putting her into a gifted program for reading, a remedial social skills program, and occupational therapy for handwriting. In addition, her parents took her to both a psychologist and an educational therapist weekly.

Unfortunately, the 504 Plan did not have the desired effect on Diana's academic progress—her grades actually declined and her behaviors worsened. By fifth grade, she had completely shut down when asked to write. With more required written assignments, she became frustrated to the point of temper tantrums in the classroom and refused to complete work. At this point she was referred to an outside psychiatrist. His diagnosis included oppositional defiant disorder (ODD), attention deficit hyperactivity disorder (ADHD), and generalized anxiety disorder (GAD). Diana's lack of social awareness and emotional volatility coupled with high cognitive abilities led to an additional diagnosis of Asperger syndrome (AS). With so many acronyms describing her, Diana appeared to be an "alphabet child" (Baum & Olenchak, 2002; Baum & Owen, 2004). Today we would likely recognize her as 2e.

Why weren't the solutions proposed in Diana's 504 Plan working? The school did seem to recognize that she had both high abilities and challenges and tried to address each. However, the advanced reading class for gifted readers required considerable writing (reports and journaling). Diana's inability to explain her ideas in writing made it impossible for her to express her complex insights articulately. She felt ashamed and doubted her own abilities because her classmates seemed to have little trouble turning in their papers. The gifted program teacher complained that she did not belong in this setting because of her noncompliant behaviors.

In the social skills class, there were no other youngsters at her intellectual level, nor any peers with superior verbal skills. How does one teach generalizable social skills in a group if the students have little in common with each other? Occupational therapy to refine her motor skills was not successful either because the issue was not actually a deficit in handwriting. Instead it was one of organizing and structuring her flood of complex ideas into coherent statements.

By the end of fifth grade, the education team saw an anxious, unhappy, defiant youngster. They added more remediation and, possibly because of time and energy constraints, the adults in Diana's life began to ignore her areas of interest and advanced abilities—even though those were the times she was motivated and successful. Simultaneously Diana's peers only saw her in situations where she struggled and frequently failed. What they did not see, and more importantly what Diana did not feel, was a joy in sharing and a sense of accomplishment about what she could do well.

## THE METAPHOR OF GREEN

To better represent what being twice exceptional means, as well as to explain why conventional educational plans may not be as effective as intended, our research and experience has led us to the metaphor of green. The color green is a mix of blue and yellow. Even though green always has elements of both blue and yellow, it is a truly distinct color. Twice exceptionality might be explained as what happens when gifts and disabilities present together. A 2e individual is neither gifted (think yellow) nor disabled (think blue)—rather he or she is the dynamic interaction of both (think green) (Baum, Schader, & Owen, 2017). Recognition and understanding that even though 2e learners have both the challenges of giftedness (exceptionality #1) *and* the challenges of learning differences (exceptionality #2), they are distinctly different from either of the discrete groups. This point is critical to understand in order to address their needs (Baum et al., 2017).

It is the mix of abilities and disabilities that makes living and working with 2e students perplexing in several ways. Educationally one must address at least two distinct needs: the need for advanced-level, intellectually stimulating work and the simultaneous need for accommodating and addressing deficits. We cannot view gifts and challenges as entities to be treated entirely separately. What we know about a student's "yellow" and "blue" qualities should lead to dually differentiated solutions that recognize the "green" and capitalize on the opportunities it offers. In short, developing plans that address and isolate one exceptionality without consideration of the other will not allow students to learn optimally and make academic progress.

For educators, working with 2e students demands a particular kind of awareness and attention, as well as creativity. For example, a student who is poor in decoding but advanced in comprehension might be given a picture book of Emily Dickinson's poetry. Her simple and elegant language reveals profound truths:

A WORD is dead
When it is said,
Some say.
I say it just
Begins to live
That day.

(From the *Complete Poems of Emily Dickinson*, 1924, Part One: Life LXXXIX)

Likewise, beginning a unit with a hands-on activity to introduce advanced mathematical concepts to bright students with ADHD allows those students to engage fully in the topic with sustained attention. For example, making origami models can introduce a geometry unit about the relationships between shapes and angles. Students are guided through a series of folds that result in a three-dimensional figure. By unfolding the model, geometric patterns then appear, revealing a variety of shapes and angles. They can then ponder how the folds created the shapes. This kinesthetic and spatial experience can be used later in the unit to help students explore geometric proofs such as why sum of a triangle's interior angles equals 180°.

In Diana's case, she could neither do the work required nor feel success in programs that depended on written work. But she was able to show the richness of her perceptions and understandings as a reader when there were other opportunities to articulate her thoughts using her oral skills, her art skills, or some combination.

## WHY FOCUS ON STRENGTHS, INTERESTS, AND TALENTS?

Research over the past 25 years has contributed to the body of evidence for focusing on strengths, interests, and talents with twice exceptional students. In 1988, Baum researched the impact of using enrichment with seven identified gifted learning-disabled students. Prior to the study, the students were in general education classrooms and received resource room support for their deficits. After the students participated in a year-long, 2½-hour weekly enrichment program designed for gifted students, both qualitative and quantitative data supported findings that included improved attitudes about school and self, improved self-regulation and independence in learning, and the ability to produce creative products judged to be comparable to those of gifted students without any learning issues. In addition, there were unanticipated academic gains (Baum et al., 2017).

Baum, Renzulli, and Hébert (1995) used individual and small group investigations of "real world problems" based on the Enrichment Triad Model (Renzulli, 1976) as an intervention with gifted underachieving students. Many of these gifted underachievers had ADHD, social and behavioral challenges, or undiagnosed learning disabilities. The most compelling finding was that 82% of the students reversed their pattern of underachievement during the course of the year or within the following year, and they improved in achievement, attitude, or behavior (Baum et al., 2017).

In 2000, Oreck, Baum, and McCartney conducted longitudinal research on 23 children and young adults who had been identified by professionals as having talent in the arts. The study followed the students over three different stages of development in music and dance—elementary school; intermediate school; and secondary school, including professional or semiprofessional careers. Over 85% of the students came from economically disadvantaged circumstances. More than half of the students had been labeled as at risk for school failure due to poor grades, absences, behavioral, attention, or family issues. The results indicated that the process of artistic talent development bolstered their talents, skills, and confidence to pursue both artistic and academic goals. After the intervention, the students showed a sense of purpose, poise, independence, and determination that was striking in contrast to many of their peers.

Finally, Baum et al. (2014) studied the experiences of a cohort of students who entered a strength-based private school for twice exceptional students during middle school and successfully completed graduation requirements. They found that students demonstrated growth in cognitive, emotional/behavioral, and social domains and identified five underlying factors: psychological safety, tolerance for asynchrony, time, positive relationships, and the consistent use of a strength-based, talent-focused philosophy. Data also revealed four benefits from the talent development opportunities offered by the school. Participating in talent development activities enabled students to become part of a social group; to overcome social, emotional, and cognitive challenges within a meaningful context; to develop ongoing mentor and professional relationships with people in talent areas; and to increase knowledge and skills in an area of talent.

A commonality among these studies is that talent development complemented the more traditional approach of providing only compensation strategies, remediation, and social skills classes. While elements of the conventional approach may be necessary, findings from these studies suggest the need for a paradigm shift, away from accommodation and remediation as the primary emphases, to a broader model that includes "talent focus" as an integral, essential component.

Emerging from these studies are three guidelines for creating programs where 2e students feel safe, valued, accepted, and successful. The first is the purposeful collection of data to gain knowledge of students' strengths, interests, and talents—information not typically collected when using a deficit model. Such knowledge enables professionals to plan appropriate talent development opportunities and to develop dually differentiated strategies for use within the classroom. Second is to address student deficits (as many as possible) contextually within an enriched curriculum so students can apply and transfer skills in authentic ways. The third is to provide these students with talent development in ways that will help them be productive as adults.

## FROM THEORY TO PRACTICE: CREATING A STRENGTH-BASED, TALENT-FOCUSED ENVIRONMENT

To change things meaningfully and practically, we need to reach consensus about the terms used and what they mean. For us, "strength-based" means that we aim for alignment of curriculum and learning activities with a student's unique strengths, cognitive styles, learning preferences, profiles of intelligences, and experiences. In this strength-based approach, students will not be excused from addressing areas of weakness, nor will they be allowed to pursue activities or produce only in ways they prefer. Rather, their strengths and interests are leveraged to help them master academic and social skills, as well as to address other problematic weaknesses. "Talent focus" involves ongoing identification and recognition of a student's advanced abilities as well as budding interests, along with explicit options for exploring and expressing those abilities and interests within and outside the curriculum. Talent focus is used as an overarching term that includes talent development. "Talent development" refers to encouragement and support of identified talents and abilities that are nurtured in their own right—neither as an opening for remediation nor as a reward or motivator for achievement (Baum et al., 2014, p. 312).

The essential first step in moving from theory to practice is to personalize learning, that is, to tailor learning experiences to students' strengths, interests, and talents. We must learn about and respond to the "person" in personalized learning. To this end we have developed a comprehensive discovery process designed to build joyous, relevant, and successful learning—in stark contrast to what 2e families and children experience during more traditional diagnostic work-ups. Indeed, when we first inquire about students' strengths, interests, and talents, parents sometimes have difficulty remembering what is good about their child. Even more troubling is that once diagnostic information is collected, an examiner may still interpret the information using a deficit lens. For instance, if parents report that their youngster often spends hours building with Legos™, even forgetting about meals, an examiner might conclude that the child is demonstrating obsessive behavior or perseveration—rather than noticing that building is a passion area when the child is in flow. The challenge at hand is how to move into a "positive frame of mind" when collecting data.

Using a Suite of Tools (Schader & Baum, 2016) that highlights what is right about a child, educators and other professionals can adjust their "lens" and begin to see hope and possibilities for each individual student. We designed these tools to be used actively, not hidden away in a file.

1. *C.L.U.E.S.*™ is an acronym for **C**ollect information, **L**ook for connections, **U**ncover patterns, **E**xplore different perspectives, and **S**ynthesize findings. This tool encourages the collection and organization of information about students' strengths and challenges through a positive lens that can guide learning and counseling. The questions set the stage for open collaborative discussion between and among teachers, parents, and the student so that expectations are clear and learning can be appropriately dually differentiated.
2. *My LearningPrint*™ was developed as a nonthreatening, nonjudgmental, living document for individuals to record several dimensions of their learning: interests, curiosities, academic strengths, learning preferences, family experiences, hobbies, and collections. Responses reveal that every person has a unique "learning fingerprint" but also make it clear that there are interesting and intriguing commonalities among students, teachers, and others as well.
3. *Quick Personality Indicator*™ offers insight into basic personality styles that can help us understand how we organize our worlds, how we relate to others, as well as how we like to learn. Depending on the situation, each of us has a unique profile of preferred and less preferred ways in which we approach the world: practical manager, learned expert, creative problem-solver, or people person. When the responses are graphed, a possible 100 points is divided into the four areas, which then show the highs and lows of one's own preference. For some people, there are definite peaks and valleys. Others present a more even profile.
4. *Creating Possibilities* consists of two distinct sections. The first, *Plan for Success*™, provides a sketchpad for designing learning opportunities that leverage interests and strengths to build necessary academic and personal skills. The second section, *The Talent Development*

*Opportunities (TDO) Maker™*, is a form to organize purposefully selected opportunities that will develop a student's growth and expertise in particular areas of strengths, interests, and talent both within and outside of school.

## SEEING THE TOOLS AT WORK: A BETTER SCENARIO FOR DIANA

When we left the story of Diana, she was a defiant, argumentative, lonely sixth-grader who was not pleasant to be around at school or at home. Not only was she nonproductive, she also actively disrupted the progress of her peers. It was at this juncture that Diana's parents enrolled her in a strength-based, talent-focused school for twice exceptional learners where the Suite of Tools was created. Without relying only on past reports and scores, school personnel learned fresh information about Diana, resulting in an educational program that respected her unique set of needs. We use her story to illustrate how using the Suite of Tools can put a strength-based, talent-focused approach into practice.

The collaborative process begins with C.L.U.E.S., Section I, *Envision*. It opens with the question "What would make this a good year?" There is space to list goals, expectations, hopes, and dreams that include short- and/or long-term aspirations from student, teacher(s), and parent(s) perspectives. Oftentimes, there can be differences in expectations. Lack of awareness of these differences makes it impossible to align goals realistically and appropriately. Key persons are individually asked what they would like to see for the student. The responses for Diana, her parents, and teachers can be seen in Box 2.1.

Section II, *Taking Stock*, allows us to collect information about the student's interests, strengths, learning preferences, and experiences. Pertinent results from testing and classroom performance are also included in this section. Much of this information can be taken from screening tools such as *My LearningPrint™*, the *Quick Personality Indicator™*, multiple intelligences questionnaires, and strengths questionnaires (there are some examples in Table 2.1).

See Box 2.2 for Diana's *Taking Stock* page.

Section III of C.L.U.E.S., labeled *Potential Obstacles to Success*, is a space to list challenges and/or behaviors that stand in the way of a student's best learning in the classroom, at home, and during extracurricular activities. This information guides finding options that can smooth the road for successful learning and avoid pitfalls. We have discovered that perspective is everything. What may appear as a negative trait can in certain circumstances be refocused and used positively. See Box 2.3 for responses for Diana.

Section IV, *Times of Personal Best*, is an area for recording when, and under what circumstances, a student is thriving. The student, teachers/coaches/mentors, and parents recall moments when the student was in flow—attending, producing, and energized. Diana's section can be seen in Box 2.4.

Box 2.1

**I. Envision**

*Student:* I don't want to be trapped into anything.

*Parent 1* (mother): I want to *like* being her mother again. I want her to have friends, I want to feel as though she fits in, and I want to see her smile.

*Parent 2* (father): I don't want to argue with her every day about not wanting to go to school and hearing that she thinks the other kids are "insipid and boring."

*Teacher/Coach/Mentor 1* (middle school director): I want her to be a contributing member of her classes, without insulting or disrupting class with noises.

*Teacher/Coach/Mentor 2* (history teacher): Participate willingly. Produce and turn in assignments.

*Table 2.1.* Examples of Screening Tools

| Tool | Purpose | Publisher |
|---|---|---|
| *Starring Me* (A. Cuthbert) | Interests and learning preferences for primary-aged students | Center for Talent Development https://drive.google.com/file/d/0B6rNasUAfT1dd1Rqb05FaGhOQkE/view?usp=sharing |
| *My Learning Print*™ (R. Schader & W. Zhou) | Information about students' strengths, interests, talents, learning styles, and experiences | 2e Center for Research and Professional Development Bridges Academy, 3921 Laurel Canyon, Studio City, CA 91604 |
| *My Way* (K. E. Kettle, J. S. Renzulli, & M. G. Rizza) | Information about expression styles—preferences for products and projects | Renzulli Center for Creativity, Gifted Education, and Talent Development University of Connecticut, Storrs, CT http://gifted.uconn.edu/wp-content/uploads/sites/961/2015/10/myway.pdf |
| Quick Personality Inventory™ (S. Baum & H. Nicols) | Personality preferences (adult and student versions) | 2e Center for Research and Professional Development Bridges Academy, 3921 Laurel Canyon, Studio City, CA 91604 |
| *Multiple Intelligences Self-Assessment* (Edutopia) | An online tool to look at students' profiles of strengths and weaknesses in terms of multiple intelligences (Gardner, 2000) | Edutopia https://www.edutopia.org/multiple-intelligences-assessment |
| *Things My Child Likes to Do* (J. Renzulli & S. Reis) | Parent survey about activities children pursue at home that includes hobbies, clubs, and pastimes | Renzulli Center for Creativity, Gifted Education, and Talent Development University of Connecticut, Storrs, CT http://gifted.uconn.edu/wp-content/uploads/sites/961/2015/02/things_like_to_do.pdf |

Box 2.2

**II. Taking Stock**

*Current Interests*: Art, animé, fantasy, drama, plays chess competitively, loves entomology.

*Strengths*: Spatial intelligence, high verbal ability, abstract thinker, advanced reader, sense of humor.

*Learning Preferences*: Verbal discussion, reading, asking questions, art projects, sketching out ideas, and acting out ideas.

*Experiences*: Art school, travel, drama camp, has a personal trainer.

*Personality Indicators*: Primarily a Learned Expert. Healthy amounts of Creative Problem Solver and Practical Manager. Very little People Person.

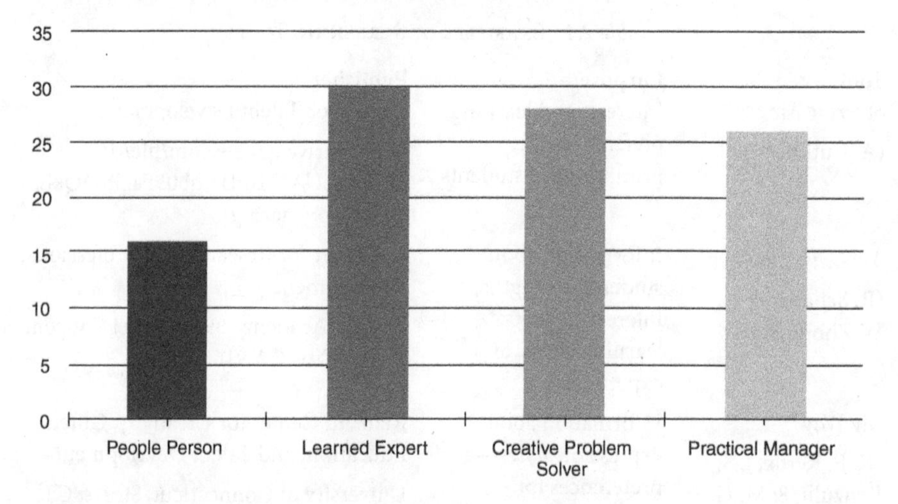


*Special Aptitudes/Talents*: Visual and performing arts.

*Educational Indicators (grades, production, etc.)*: "C" average in core subjects, "A" in art and drama, Failing PE.

*Key results from Psycho-educational Assessments*: IQ profile shows scores in the superior range in both verbal and performance areas but an extremely low score in Freedom from Distractibility (2nd percentile). High scores in linguistic, spatial, intrapersonal intelligences.

Finally, Section V, *Summary*, provides space to summarize what has been learned about this student by exploring the four main questions listed previously. Box 2.5 shows what we have discovered about Diana.

When we look at the summary of C.L.U.E.S. information, we then understand the student from various perspectives. Diana is an artist, a logical thinker, and someone who has strong opinions and a wealth of creative ideas. There are a

Box 2.3

**III. Potential Obstacles to Success**

*At School*: Inability to put ideas in writing, refusal to participate in physical education, poor attention in class, poor social skills. Shows anxiety (especially in math). Easily frustrated.

*At Home*: Argumentative and defiant with family members.

*During Extracurricular Activities*: Incites arguments. Doesn't join in group activities.

Box 2.4

**IV. Times of Personal Best**

*Student:* I feel most satisfied when I am able to finish a project that I wanted to do, no matter how long it takes me. Afterwards I feel proud and like to show what I've done. My favorite time in class is when we can talk about ideas.

*Parent 1* (mother): When she is doing her art she is so attentive and seems content. I am amazed at what she is drawing and how she can captures ideas.

*Parent 2* (father): When we are discussing/arguing moral dilemmas, politics, and current events—especially at the dinner table. I can get frustrated with her tone, but she always backs up her opinions with facts and her form of logic. I also see her focus when she's playing chess.

*Teacher/Coach/Mentor 1* (English teacher): When she is sketching, arguing a point, or discussing themes in literature. Her comments can be abstract and are often beyond the depth of those made by her classmates. She constantly doodles instead of taking notes. I used to think she wasn't paying attention but it has become clear to me that Diana is not just doodling. Her sketches are ideas from class discussion.

*Teacher/Coach/Mentor 2* (art teacher): Doing the kind of art she wants to do—currently cartooning.

*Teacher/Coach/Mentor 3* (history teacher): When she can show her creativity. She frequently takes the initiative to make something at home about what happened in class and brings it in the next day. She becomes excited when others positively respond to her work.

*Additional Input* (school psychologist): Diana spends time with me during physical education as she so often has meltdowns when asked to participate. Recently she has been asking me if she could paint a mural on my wall. Her idea is to create a series of creatures, each representing a character trait of her classmates. I am not sure if these are positive or negative at this point. In her mind, each character has its own story to tell. She has talked about this continually over the past several weeks.

Box 2.5

V. **Summary**

1. *This student is at his/her personal best when*: She is drawing or doing art projects. She becomes engaged and animated during discussions of controversial subjects.
2. *This student has strong interest and abilities in*: Drama, anime, cartooning, and politics and literature.
3. *What Potential Obstacles to Success should be noted*? Her reluctance to write is holding her back in most subjects and, because of her inappropriate social skills, she doesn't participate well in group work or team situations. She refuses to participate in physical activities.
4. *What conditions will facilitate a positive learning environment for this student? What are our hypotheses about how this student functions best?*
   *Intellectual/Academic*: advanced reading materials, issues-based content with opportunities to debate or give her opinion, opportunities for integrating art and creative expression.
   *Social/Emotional*: Opportunities to use her humor. Being able to draw or sketch to regulate when stressed. Ways to show her work so others can see her in a productive rather than destructive light. Participation in chess club for socialization. Using drama to understand and experiment with social context.
   *Physical*: A place to work on art, a place for quiet reading, may find noise-reducing headsets helpful. Sketchpads for taking notes.

number of adults in her life who will support her. This compilation of information helps as we fill out the *Creating Possibilities* tool where we begin to put the person in personalized learning.

The final tool, *Creating Possibilities*, reminds us of the importance of offering daily ways for students to experience joy in learning, especially because their anxiety and lack of confidence can be major obstacles to engagement and productivity (Baum et al., 2014; Willis, 2007). We know that magic happens when interests and abilities intersect; thus we must consciously look for possibilities that will bring engagement and light into a student's eyes. The two sections of this document (*Plan for Success*™ and the *TDO Maker*™) use the same information about a student's interests and abilities in quite different ways. First, interests and strengths are leveraged to build necessary academic and personal skills (with consideration of relevant potential obstacles) or to engage students meaningfully in a task. Second, interests and talents are nurtured in their own right so students can build toward expertise in their chosen area(s).

Leveraging strengths (in *Plan for Success*™) means using more of what one is good at to reach a goal. As Peter Drucker explains, "A person can perform only from strength. One cannot build performance on weakness, let alone on something one cannot do at all" (2008, p. 2). As a quick example, we discovered that Diana's writing improved when she could use her artistic ability to discover and shape her thinking. Her ability to use visual imagery to create metaphors provided the bridges she needed to translate her understandings into written language.

See Figure 2.1 for the Plan for Success™ form.

In contrast, talent development opportunities (*The TDO Maker*™) are purposefully selected for students so that their abilities and interests can be nurtured in authentic ways. In such instances, students are intrinsically motivated to stay in the struggle to reach their particular goal. What they produce is often of high quality, provides evidence of their potential, and allows them to dream of what they can achieve. We have seen that offering opportunities for talent development is the singular most powerful strategy to optimize growth in 2e students (Baum, 2009). Through TDOs, students are motivated to meet deadlines, work with others civilly, and build a positive sense of self and belonging. In other words, talent development is an important way to develop executive functioning, necessary social skills, and important relationships. Not only is talent development a means to support students' journeys from novice to expert, but it can also be therapeutic when the rest of their world is stressful and anxiety provoking. In a sense, it is what Robert Brooks (2001) calls, "finding an island of competence," where students can lose themselves in their strengths and talents.

It addresses ways to use information about students' strengths and interests to teach them a skill or bring them into learning about a subject. Let's return to Diana as a freshman in high school and see how using this form can help gain a fresh perspective. Box 2.6 includes a plan for a unit on the Middle Ages.

The large sketchpad section of the page is a space to brainstorm and refine ideas. Think of *Doorways* (entry points), *Bridges* (leveraging interests and strengths to achieve objectives), and *Connectors* (extending content and skills to other domains). Many problems 2e students experience in connecting with school goals (not attending, inability to access curriculum because of reading or listening skills, problems processing information, communicating what they know through written expression, etc.) diminish when curriculum and instruction respond to the four "thought-starter" prompts on the right side of the sketchpad:

1. What **ENTRY ACTIVITIES** might intrigue and engage this student?
2. What **INSTRUCTIONAL STRATEGIES** would be helpful?
3. Are there certain types of **RESOURCES** that will help this student explore core concepts and learn more deeply?
4. What **PRODUCT CHOICES or PERFORMANCE TASKS** are particularly appropriate for this student?

To reach Diana and entice her into the unit, we considered the factors listed in Box 2.7 as they aligned well to her identified strengths, interests, and talents.

When completing the sketchpad of ideas for a unit, it is helpful for the initiating teacher to brainstorm with others who know the student well. For instance, Diana's art teacher contributed several ideas during the process because she

**PLAN FOR SUCCESS™: DEVELOPING KNOWLEDGE AND SKILLS**

**Goal**
*In what particular areas (content, social skills, conceptual understandings, etc.) do you need this student to be more engaged and successful?*

**Strengths and Interests**
*Refer to Section II on C.L.U.E.S.*

**Potential Obtacles to Success**
*Refer to Section III on C.L.U.E.S.*

Doorways (entry points), Bridges (leveraging interests and strengths to achieve objectives), and Connectors (extending content and skills to other domains)

*What ENTRY ACTIVITIES might intrigue and engage this student?*

*What INSTRUCTIONAL STRATEGIES would be useful?*

*Are there certain types of RESOURCES that will help this student explore core concepts and learn more deeply?*

*What PRODUCT CHOICES or PERFORMANCE TASKS are particularly appropriate for this student?*

Figure 2.1 Plan for Success™ form.

Box 2.6

**Goals, Strengths, and Obstacles to Develop Knowledge and Skills**

***Goal***: *In what particular areas (content, social skills, conceptual understandings, etc.) do you need this student to be more engaged and successful?* She was stubbornly not involved during our previous unit on Ancient Rome. Spent most of the time arguing with her peers. I want her to contribute positively to class discussion and develop depth of knowledge in at least one aspect of life in the Middle Ages. We will be looking at the role of the feudal system in supporting the economy of a nation, along with major controversies that created social and political unrest.

***Strengths to Leverage or Interests to Engage*** (*refer to Section II in C.L.U.E.S.:* Artistic vision, interest in cultural arts, dramatic qualities, chess, love of debate and controversy, metaphorical thinking, satire, humor)

***Potential Obstacles to Success***: Lack of motivation in humanities class. Limited desire to write

Box 2.7

**Doorways, Bridges, and Connectors to Develop Knowledge and Skills**

***Entry Activities***: (ideas that are linked to her visual strengths and artistic interests but also take into account her enjoyment of sophisticated thinking and controversy) might include: Virtual tours of medieval castles and cathedrals; visits to local churches to look at stained glass windows; discussions of the origin of chess pieces and what they symbolize; viewing a film of King Henry and wives series on PBS; looking at the class system in *Downton Abbey*; watching *Monty Python and the Holy Grail*, etc.

***Instructional Strategies***: (approaches linked to her love of drama and her proclivity for arguing) could include: Role playing the situations of people in different social classes; debating the roles of church and state; holding a Socratic seminar on impact of King Henry and the advent of the Church of England, etc.

***Resources***: (a beginning list of materials that offer sophisticated information and thought-provoking information): *The Secret History of Nursery Rhymes Paperback* by Linda Alchin; *History of Cathedrals of Europe* by Elizabeth Reynolds; *The Development of Stained Glass in Gothic Cathedrals*, etc.

***Product Choices or Performance Tasks***: (options linked to her artistic ability, humor, and satirical thinking) include: Design a stained glass window illustrating the Feudal System; use humor to create caricatures of major players in the King Henry era; write and illustrate a book of nursery rhymes that represent the Feudal period; create new chess pieces depicting the roles of class systems in the 21st century, etc.

worked with Diana both in and out of the classroom and saw Diana during times of her "personal best." The art teacher was also familiar with the types of art Diana preferred and had knowledge of artistic opportunities that could be included in a unit on the Middle Ages.

In Diana's situation, the humanities teacher chose ideas that most resonated and then included them as choices for everyone in the class. Interestingly, Diana went on to work happily with two other students in developing a selection of modern-day nursery rhymes about social issues that existed during the Middle Ages and still persist today. The group project contributed to a growing friendship among the three girls that continued beyond the unit.

Moving to the *TDO Maker*™, the second section of the *Creating Possibilities* tool, we look for opportunities to develop a student's progression toward expertise in particular areas of strength, interest, and talent. The form begins with the prompt "Build a list of classes, lessons, experience, workshops, etc. that will foster this student's passion(s) in _______________. Include authentic Explorations (to broaden), Experiences (for skill development) with professionals, and Opportunities for performance and production that will support progression toward expertise." We want students to become practicing professionals as they interact with experts within specific domains and have the opportunity to explore fields related to their talent. Through these opportunities, students will be operating naturally from a position of strength.

With the guidance of Diana's advisor, we created a TDO Menu—a brainstormed list of possible classes, experiences, events, performances, workshops, mentorships, clubs, competitions, and so on that would be important building blocks to help a student develop in a specific area. For ninth-grade Diana, the options focused on her art since that was an area she talked about, and one in which she fully engaged and produced on a regular basis. From the selections listed, we were able to plan a workable, living TDO Agenda of options (shown in Figure 2.2). Notice that Diana's TDOs were selected to cover several different aspects of her growing interest and abilities. The plan continued to change and grow as each selection was completed in accordance with Diana's wishes and goals.

Diana is not unique. Every child has a complex and compelling personal story, full of clues about how they learn best. Each child deserves to build self-understanding of his or her preferences and talents. Personalizing learning for all students by using the Suite of Tools can assure that each individual in a class is positioned to engage in learning according to who they are and under what circumstances they can thrive. This quote from Diana shows how using this approach was instrumental in building self-awareness and agency for members of her graduating class:

> Now that we're seniors, all of us have found our niches. We know what we like doing. We know what we're good at. We know what we're bad at. We know what subject we're probably going to be studying and the subject we're probably not going to continue studying. (T. Ropelewski, personal communication, February 24, 2011)

**The Talent Development Opportunity Maker™ (TDO)**

**First, build a TDO Menu** by developing a list of classes, lessons, experiences, workshops, etc. that will foster this student's passion(s) in Animation & Drawing. Include authentic **Explorations** (to broaden), **Experiences** (for skill development) with professionals, and **Opportunities** for performance and production that will support progression toward expertise.

| Consider Opportunities to Explore: | Classroom and Extracurricular Options | Enriched Options Beyond School |
|---|---|---|
| | Exhibit on Anime @ Modern Art Museum | Anime Expo (May/June) |
| Take Classes or Lessons: | Watch TED Talks — Comics, Manga, Anime | Sat Art Class — manga |
| Observe or Attend events: | | upcoming lecture on becoming a visual artist |
| Create: | Paint mural on school hallway | |
| Perform: | Report on Anime Expo | |
| Find a Mentor: | | |
| Join Special Programs/Clubs: | After school "Graphic Novels" club | |
| Interview Experts: | Meet artist friend of history teacher | |
| Apprentice: | | |
| Enter Contests or Competitions: | Prepare portfolio for local gallery competition | (visit gallery) |
| Other Options: | | Summer program "Inner Sparks" |

**Then create a TDO Agenda from the possibilities above:**

| Options Selected (with dates) | Frequency and Location | Date to Revisit |
|---|---|---|
| • Watch/Select TED talks + | 1x week @school | 5/1 |
| • (develop schedule) | | |
| • | | |
| • Local Anime Expo (with parents) | 1 day event | date in May (revisit 4/1) |
| • work w/art teacher on portfolio | 3x week | 5/15 |
| • | | |
| • Sat. art classes w/expert | 1x week | 4/1 |

**Figure 2.2** TDO menu.

## A POSITIVE LENS

Throughout this chapter we have described what can happen when we view twice exceptional students through a positive lens. A key to holding this focus is keeping conversations alive about what students *can* do. Through the story of Diana we explained the unique characteristics of students who have a dual diagnosis of abilities with disabilities. We saw her blossom when attention was turned away from what she could not do to shine attention on what she *could* accomplish. Diana went on to attend a prestigious art school where she thrived. As a recent college graduate, she spoke excitedly and confidently about her future—a future we believe, that is possible because she is building on her interests and abilities.

> What I'm most looking forward to now is meeting the next level of artist . . . meeting people who are interested in things that I didn't even know

about—in the art world. The one thing I'm really interested in [now] is stop motion production and set design . . . the best thing in the world . . . which would be so crazy, but that's "in the future stuff" . . . it's something I like doing so it's something I want to do. And, . . . that's hope for the future. (T. Ropelewski, personal communication, May 31, 2015)

## REFERENCES

Baum, S. (2009). Talent centered model for twice-exceptional students. In J. Renzulli, E. J. Gubbins, K. McMillen, R. Eckert, & C. Little (Eds.), *Systems and models in gifted education*. Mansfield Center, CT: Creative Learning Press, 17–48.

Baum, S., & Olenchak, R. (2002). The alphabet children: GT, ADHD and more. *Exceptionalities, 10*(2), 77–92.

Baum, S., & Owen, S. V. (2004). *To be gifted and learning disabled: Meeting the needs of gifted students with LD, ADHD, and more*. Waco, TX: Prufrock Press.

Baum, S., Renzulli, J., & Hebert, T. (1995). *The prism metaphor: A new paradigm for reversing underachievement.* Storrs CT: National Research Center on the Gifted and Talented.

Baum, S. M., Schader, R. M., & Hébert, T. P. (2014). Through a different lens: Reflecting on a strengths-based, talent-focused approach for twice exceptional learners. *Gifted Child Quarterly, 58*(4), 311–327.

Baum, S., Schader, R., & Owen, S., (2017). *To be gifted and learning disabled: Strength-based strategies for helping twice exceptional students with LD, ADHD, ASD, and more.* Waco, TX: Prufrock Press.

Brooks, R., & Goldstein, S. (2001). *Raising resilient children: Fostering strength, hope, and optimism in your child*. Lincolnwood, IL: Contemporary Books.

Drucker, Peter. (n.d.). AZQuotes.com. Retrieved from http://www.azquotes.com/quote/372492

Drucker, Peter F. (2008). *Managing oneself.* Boston: Harvard Business School Publishing Corporations.

Hallowell, E. (2006, Fall). The problem with problems: How the pathology model destroys what could be good. *Independent Schools*, 30–38.

Hiemstra, D., & Van Yperen, N. W. (2015). The effects of strength-based versus deficit-based self-regulated learning strategies on students' effort intentions. *Motivation and Emotion, 39*(5), 656–668.

Kaufman, S. B. (2013). *Ungifted: Intelligence redefined.* New York, NY: Basic Books.

Oreck, B., Baum, S., & McCartney, H. (2000). *Artistic talent development for urban youth: The promise and the challenge.* Storrs, CT: National Research Center on the Gifted and Talented.

Rath, T., & Conchie, B. (2008). *Strengths based leadership*. New York, NY: Gallup Press.

Renzulli, J. S. (1976). *Enrichment triad model.* Mansfield Center, CT: Creative Learning Press.

Schader, R., & Baum, S, (2016). *Suite of Tools: Putting the "person" in personalized learning*. Studio City, CA: Center for 2e Research and Professional Development at Bridges Academy.

Seligman, M., & Csikszentmihalyi, M. (2000). Positive psychology: An introduction. *American Psychologist, 55*, 5–14.

Willis, J. (2007, Summer). The neuroscience of joyful education, *Engaging the Whole Child, 64*.

3

# Finding Hidden Potential

## *Toward Best Practices in Identifying Gifted Students with Disabilities*

EDWARD R. AMEND

The talents of intellectually and academically gifted students with learning disabilities or other disabilities, commonly referred to as twice exceptional (2e) students, are often hidden beneath the frustration and pain caused by years of educational misplacement. Identified as a problem child, defined by disabilities or weaknesses, or simply unnoticed for either strength or weakness, unidentified 2e individuals may create identities that mask their strengths or run counter to academic achievement. Finding and identifying intellectual or academic strengths of such students, in addition to recognizing disabilities and areas needing support, is a challenge. Someone must notice either potential gifts or weaknesses, or at least significant unevenness in performance, before a student is even referred for possible identification. These, and other factors, may result in gifted students with disabilities not even being referred for evaluation—let alone being identified as such—and ultimately not being served appropriately.

Being able to recognize the characteristics of intellectually gifted or academically talented learners in students with disabilities requires an understanding of the needs of both gifted learners and students with disabilities. Giftedness comes in many levels and varieties. Although the specific definition of a gifted student varies by state, in this chapter, "gifted" refers to students in the top 5% in a specific domain (e.g., measured intellectual ability, reading skills, math proficiency, or creativity), and, where appropriate, the type of giftedness is specified. Disabilities are likewise wide-ranging, encompassing physical challenges like vision or hearing deficits, emotional and behavioral disorders like attention deficit hyperactivity disorder (ADHD) or depression, and learning disabilities in academic domains like reading or math. Foley-Nicpon, Assouline, and Colangelo (2013) concluded that expanding professional development about the needs of 2e students both within and outside of the field of gifted education is needed for educators to understand the complex and multifaceted needs of gifted students with disabilities. They suggest that professionals working with 2e students should become familiar not only with characteristics of both gifted learners and students with disabilities but also guidelines for serving both types of students. This sentiment is echoed by clinicians and evaluators in the field.

Much of the empirical research and commentary on the identification of 2e students focuses on intellectually gifted students with specific academic or learning disabilities (G/LD). While more research is emerging related to giftedness and other disabilities such as autism spectrum disorders and ADHD (e.g., Foley-Nicpon, Assouline, & Stinson, 2012; Fugate, Zentall, & Gentry, 2013), empirical studies are limited. Drawing upon available research as well as the clinical expertise of psychologists with extensive experience in assessing 2e students, this chapter highlights methods to evaluate for potential twice exceptionalities, including special issues related to evaluating for giftedness in students already identified with a disability and evaluating for disabilities in students already identified as gifted. Examples show evaluation tools and processes that can be used as part of a comprehensive assessment battery to identify 2e learners and understand their unique profiles of strengths and weaknesses as well as strategies that provide data to help determine the services necessary for 2e students to thrive.

## UNDERLYING ISSUES

G/LD and other 2e students may not be referred for gifted services because they are defined by weaknesses that are more prominent than their strengths (e.g., Kaufman, 2013). Barnard-Brak, Johnsen, Hannig, and Wei (2015) sampled over 13,000 students with disabilities and found over 300 who showed academic achievement at or above the 90th percentile and might be identified as academically gifted. However, only 11% of the 300 (approximately 33 students) were participating in any type of gifted programming. Their data showed that students with disabilities were likely to be missed and not identified as potentially gifted, as only about 30 of the 13,000 students with disabilities were served in gifted programming even though as many as 300 may have been eligible, leaving about 270 potential 2e students unidentified and thus unserved. For other students, test results may lead to misdiagnosis, which involves having pathological explanations being applied to behavior rather than using giftedness as a frame to understand the student, his or her behavior, or his or her academic performance (Webb et al., 2016). Sometimes, only the student's giftedness is evident and served because talents are strong enough to cover any weaknesses, or the gifts and disabilities mask each other and neither is identified nor served (Brody & Mills, 1997).

An otherwise typical student who struggles in a specific academic area like reading or writing and also shows weak skills compared to age peers is easily recognized as a student who may have a disability. When eight-year-old Hunter was falling significantly behind peers in reading, an intervention phase was undertaken to determine the extent of the problem and his need for additional services.

Many schools use Response to Intervention (RTI) protocols focusing on a three-tier approach, including the general education programming, secondary interventions that are targeted and evidence-based, and finally more intensive services that can be provided on an individual basis. RTI can often recognize struggling students such as Hunter, help identify learning needs, and provide appropriate interventions. Gifted students with learning issues as severe as Hunter's challenges can be easily spotted.

*Aaron was first identified with learning disabilities in reading and written expression at the age of 10. He was struggling to keep up with his classmates and falling behind expected benchmarks in fifth grade. He was referred through his school for special needs assessment, and his parents brought him to a private psychologist for evaluation. Comprehensive assessment revealed cognitive ability above the 96th percentile—at the gifted level—with reading and written language skills well below average. The discrepancy between his ability and achievement was used to identify the learning disabilities, per state regulations. His academic scores in reading and writing were so low that he likely would have met any criteria for identification. No other explanations for his difficulties were revealed during interview, observation, or evaluation. With reading and writing skills at first-grade level, Aaron was an obvious candidate for intervention. His Individual Education Program addressed his reading and written language deficits and provided the support Aaron needed in the classroom. Additionally, he was provided opportunities to use his higher level thinking skills in gifted programming that was modified due to his learning disabilities. Despite severe disabilities, with some skills remaining at early-elementary levels, Aaron progressed through school with proper support and appropriate challenge. Subsequent reevaluations continued to show gifted-level abilities across intellectual domains as well as academic skills that, while developing, were still well below his grade placement. With accommodations, he was able to demonstrate his knowledge, and he is currently poised to attend college with continued support, carrying the G/LD, or 2e, label.*

Learning disabilities as pronounced as Aaron's have a clear educational impact and are more readily identified than subtle learning problems that interfere with a student's ability to demonstrate the full extent of his or her skills or potential. However, if Aaron's school had just used an RTI protocol for identifying the learning disability, it is not clear whether Aaron's gifted abilities would have surfaced through regular classroom performance or through RTI interventions focused solely on his weaknesses. RTI protocols are typically focused on classroom performance and grade-appropriate academic skills. Students performing above grade level are not usually the focus. As such, RTI is not designed to identify the advanced language skills, incredible memory, unique problem-solving, or creativity of a gifted student, given that interactions with a student will surround areas of difficulty, not strength. Had Aaron not been referred for *comprehensive assessment including possible gifted abilities*, his gifted abilities may have been missed because the areas of concern in school were only reading and writing.

Students with subtle learning problems are less likely to be evaluated, let alone identified. When students are intellectually gifted and yet still performing at grade level, or just slightly below, would they even be referred for assessment of either giftedness or learning disability? Or, what if they are above grade level in some areas but well below their potential or measured cognitive ability? Consider also the bright students who struggle to pay attention but who do well enough due to innate cognitive abilities, which allow them to compensate for attention problems. Will students like these be identified and served? Should they be? These are some of the very real questions that emerge and make identification difficult and the functional impairment or educational impact important to assess.

## IDENTIFICATION ISSUES

There are now specific definitions of what a 2e student is (e.g., Reis, Baum, & Burke, 2014), and most generally agree that a 2e student is a gifted or exceptional student with some of type disability (e.g., learning, physical, behavioral, or emotional). However, there is no specific educational profile or clear and researched-based approach to identifying such students. The landscape of learning disabilities is constantly changing with new information, and the field of 2e is no exception. A learning disability has traditionally been defined as a failure to learn educational information that was not due to a lack of educational opportunities or intelligence and not due to any cultural, physical, or environmental factors. While this general framework still applies, what constitutes a learning disability in a particular school or state often varies based on laws and regulations; this holds true for G/LD as well.

While the G/LD student presents a unique set of issues for identification, other disabilities present concerns as well. Attention disorders, autism spectrum disorders, and anxiety, for example, will affect performance in the classroom and can also be overlooked or misidentified in intellectually gifted students. With any disorder or diagnosis, the level of impairment and educational impact created by the symptoms must be considered in the process of identification. For a gifted student with a disability, whether that disability is a learning disorder or a mental health condition, impairment of functioning remains the key to diagnosis. The educational impact or clinical impairment refers to the extent to which the symptoms, behaviors, or problems compromise one's functioning. For gifted students with a disability—especially learning disabilities where most of the empirical research has focused—there is considerable disagreement on what constitutes impairment and ultimately what level of impairment is required for diagnosis or identification.

How impaired must one be and how much and what type of educational impact is necessary in order to be considered as having a disability? Is it enough for a student to have a discrepancy between ability and achievement? How large should that discrepancy be? What if a discrepancy is present but the relative weaknesses are still average, or even above average? What if the student is performing similarly to grade peers? While these remain empirically unanswered, some authors (Assouline et al., 2010; Gilman et al., 2013; Lovett & Sparks, 2011) provide guidelines and recommendations.

Common sense suggests that the symptoms have to get in the way of one's functioning to be identified as a disability—but does that mean the problem must interfere with one's optimal functioning, or simply average functioning for a typical student of that age or grade level? Some argue for absolute deficits, while others argue for discrepancies indicating weaknesses relative to other areas of strength. This is the crux of the difficulties faced when one attempts to determine the best way to identify a gifted student with a learning disability or other disability. Some argue that the gifted student performing at least at the average level of peers should not be identified, even if a discrepancy between ability and achievement exists, as there is no *significant* educational impact (Lovett, 2013). Others argue that the discrepancy—without evidence of another reason for the discrepancy—should be enough to lead to identification as it reveals a student's inability to demonstrate his or her full "potential." For those making this argument, *potential* is often equated with IQ, as indicated by a test that actually measures ability. They may say, after all, most schools' mission statements are not "striving for average performance from all students." In either case, any evaluation of possible disability in a gifted student will need to include assessment tools that inform the examiner of the student's strengths, weaknesses, and differences across domains, so that impairment can be assessed.

## ISSUS RELATED TO ASSESSING POSSIBLE G/LD STUDENTS

The development of gifted students across different domains (e.g., physical, emotional, and intellectual) is uneven, or asynchronous, as it is often called in gifted literature. Some skills simply outpace others, and most professionals in the field of gifted education accept that not all gifted students will be gifted in every subject or area. Not all students who are academically gifted in math will be equally gifted in reading, and not all creatively gifted students will excel in the visual arts. Likewise, not all intellectually gifted students will be equally gifted in academic areas like reading, language arts, math, science, or social studies. Common sense suggests that we do not expect giftedness in one area, like musical talent, to indicate that the same student will *automatically* have a high IQ or excel in other areas of giftedness, such as reading, creativity, or leadership, though he or she may.

That raises the question of whether we should expect intellectually gifted students to achieve at levels consistent with their ability or IQ. Given research showing a strong correlation between IQ and academic achievement (e.g., Kaufman, Reynolds, Liu, Kaufman, & McGrew, 2012), some experts argue that the intellectually gifted student's academic achievement in reading and math, for example, should generally match his intellectual ability. That thinking is consistent with the so-called *discrepancy model for identification of learning disabilities,* which flowed from the definitions in Public Law 94-142, stating that a severe discrepancy between ability and achievement is used to determine a learning disability. There are many questions and some valid concerns about the use of a discrepancy model that are too numerous to be presented here and beyond the scope of this chapter (see Feifer & DeFina [2000] for an overview).

Despite concerns, federal laws and many state policies still allow the discrepancy model to be used for identification of a student with a learning disability, though it is not the only method deemed acceptable based on current laws and policies. The discrepancy model suggests that an intellectually gifted student with an IQ of 135 (more than two standard deviations above the mean of 100) who has a reading achievement score of 100 (average overall, but more than two standard deviations below his achievement) could be identified with a learning disability. However, many times, such students are deemed to be doing *well enough* and, thus, not often identified. It seems that although their ability is higher when measured against age peers, ability is somehow judged irrelevant since the achievement is adequate and commensurate with age peers. That is, there is no *functional impairment* or *educational impact* in the academic area because they are performing adequately (Lovett & Lewandowski, 2006). This presents problems with the identification of G/LD students.

Evaluators and researchers agree that G/LD students exist (Assouline et al., 2010; Foley-Nicpon, Allmon, Sieck, & Stinson, 2011; Lovett & Sparks, 2011), and some research studies, several case studies (e.g., Wormald, Rogers, & Vialle, 2015), and many anecdotal reports (Webb et al., 2016) appear throughout the gifted literature. These reports show some students are unable to demonstrate the full extent of their knowledge and skills in traditional ways, and this leads to identification. Some are unable to read at grade level despite obvious problem-solving skills that are well above average. Some cases show intellectually gifted students achieving at average levels being identified. With these differing definitions, the challenge has, and continues to be, how to identify such students, and both clinicians and researchers agree that finding and serving 2e students is difficult (Assouline et al., 2010; Foley-Nicpon et al., 2011; Gilman et al., 2013).

While there is generally consensus from researchers and clinicians that comprehensive assessment is necessary in order to identify and serve these twice exceptional students (Assouline et al., 2010; Foley-Nicpon et al., 2011; Gilman et al., 2013; Webb et al., 2016), there is limited empirical research indicating exactly what such assessment involves. Additionally, the widely varying definitions of both giftedness and learning disabilities present additional barriers to identification (Lovett & Sparks, 2011), and Lovett (2011) expressed concern that the unclear criteria for 2e leaves a door open for parents and educators to obtain services for students who do not technically qualify for either label based on the masking of both strengths and weaknesses. Some advocate for practices such as RTI (McCallum et al., 2013) to identify and serve 2e students, but McKenzie (2010) showed that such students are less likely to be identified and served with RTI processes. McKenzie argued that RTI is more likely to produce false negatives as gifted students initially "respond" adequately to interventions, resulting in *enough* progress to prevent formal identification. Others argue for using a discrepancy model despite its problems (e.g., Assouline et al., 2010; Olenchak & Reis, 2002). Whatever process is used to identify gifted learners with a co-occurring disability must not only be able to assess gifted strengths and possible disability areas but also collect enough data to rule out other possible explanations for the school difficulties. Lack of educational opportunities, vision and hearing problems, inappropriate curriculum for a gifted learner, and cultural and socioeconomic factors, for example, must be ruled out as causes for the difficulties that are identified.

Available research as well as extensive clinical experience from several prominent clinical psychologists, school psychologists, educational psychologists, and neuropsychologists in the field of gifted education has guided the process of identification used by clinicians who work with gifted individuals and the twice exceptional. While differences are apparent, some guiding principles emerge.

## USING RESPONSE TO INTERVENTION

Fuchs and Fuchs (2006) outline how the RTI process can be effective in identifying areas falling below grade level, but Flanagan, Fiorello, and Ortiz (2010) summarize research and raise concerns about the validity of the RTI process in identifying learning disabilities. Others suggest that the probability of identifying intellectually gifted children with learning disabilities has been decreased by RTI. For example, McKenzie (2010) found that intellectually gifted students with learning disabilities are not identified as such through RTI. To avoid this, McCallum and colleagues (2013) argue for liberal criteria to be used in order to identify more false positives than false negatives so that RTI can be used to help teachers select "more relevant instructional goals" (p. 218). They argue that a false positive, while technically inaccurate, still helps guide instruction for individuals needing some level of support. In other words, they recommend educators cast a wide net and find students needing assistance whether or not they technically meet criteria for a specific learning disability.

RTI presents some problems with the G/LD identification and, while it can help spot educational impact, it is often of little help in identifying subtle learning disabilities and other disabilities (e.g., ADHD or autism spectrum disorder) in intellectually gifted students. And it is not often designed to identify giftedness at all, usually focusing on skills below expectancy and not those above. There are several places where G/LD students may be missed in the RTI process. First, a student must be deemed *at risk* to be considered for intervention, and gifted students performing *adequately* or close to grade level will likely not be selected. This concern is what McCallum and colleagues (2013) hope to avoid with more liberal criteria to determine *at-risk* students. Even when assessed *at risk*, gifted students who are significantly below average may show a temporary response to the provided interventions in a way that may improve their skills to near grade level, though still well below ability or potential, preventing identification if they are classified as a responder. If not identified in such a manner, do these gifted students still have a learning disability? Or are these students doing well enough?

This is where the level of impairment or educational impact comes into play. How impaired is enough to be identified? What responsibilities does the school system have to gifted students? Questions arise because some gifted students will show uneven skills that do not affect performance enough to be given a formal label. When a student is functioning adequately and using skills to compensate for weaker areas, should that be enough? Many clinicians argue that reaching potential, not mediocrity, should be the goal. That said, special education systems are not set up to bring intellectually gifted students to full potential but rather to remediate and bring students to adequate levels of performance. This is a fundamental difference in the thought process of clinicians who work primarily with gifted students and those who work primarily in the special education domain. It is rare to find practitioners who straddle both worlds.

## USING THE ABILITY-ACHIEVEMENT DISCREPANCY

Although much controversy and concern exist regarding the so-called discrepancy model, it can serve as a useful tool in identifying strengths, weaknesses, and relative weaknesses in gifted students. Individual intellectual and academic assessment can provide information to see discrepancies. For example, when assessment shows that a student scores in the intellectually gifted range (typically an IQ at or above 125, though the specific number is defined by each state) and scores average or even below average in a specific academic area such as reading (with a standard score of about 100 or below), a severe discrepancy exists. The discrepancy alone does not fully determine the presence of a learning disability; in such cases, finding an explanation is necessary as well as determining the educational impact or functional impairment. While a learning disability is one possible explanation, there are others that must be ruled out in such situations. Lack of educational opportunities, a curriculum that has not been meeting the student's needs, physical disabilities such as hearing and vision deficits, attention deficits, and environmental factors must be ruled out before the determination of a learning disability can be made. Some who are unaware of the reality of gifted students with learning disabilities may conclude that the discrepancies are simply the effects of extreme asynchrony in a gifted learner and not an indication of a need for service. When extreme asynchrony is viewed as inherent in a gifted individual, it becomes even more difficult to distinguish a gifted learner from a 2e learner (see Gilman & Peters, this volume).

With legitimate concerns about RTI and the ability-achievement discrepancy identifying learning disabilities in gifted students, how does a psychologist go about finding and identifying learning disabilities in gifted students? This is the dilemma clinicians face when trying to identify a twice exceptional youngster, and available research suggests that this can only be done through comprehensive assessment, including through gathering information on family and other relevant background information, assessing educational experiences, and formally evaluating intellectual, academic, and developmental abilities with standardized measures.

## COMPREHENSIVE ASSESSMENT

Comprehensive assessment is necessary to evaluate abilities and determine the presence or absence of a disability in a gifted student. However, this process can be difficult to get started for some struggling students, as there are often barriers to students being referred for evaluation. The myths that gifted students will do fine on their own or cannot have learning disabilities as well as strengths masking disabilities and average academic performance despite gifted intellect are some reasons a student may not be referred for possible services. Unless referred, one will not receive either evaluation or services. Then there are problems with the assessment process, including sloppy assessment procedures by clinicians unfamiliar with gifted students and their unique response patterns resulting from perfectionism, slow processing, or fears about being wrong or taking risks. These factors may result in poor evaluation, inaccurate results, lack of clarity in diagnosis, or even misdiagnosis. Amend and Beljan (2009) summarize some of the factors affecting accurate assessment of gifted and 2e individuals, including the effects of the stigma associated with giftedness; failing to consider giftedness or twice exceptionality as explanations; the impact of environmental, developmental, and situational factors; and even insurance influences on the assessment procedures in clinical practice.

Gilman and Peters (this volume) provide an excellent summary of the importance of comprehensive evaluation and recommendations to help parents get the assessment process started. Once an assessment is begun, it should be multifaceted and comprehensive enough to evaluate all aspects of functioning to determine the presence of a disability and its impact on functioning as well as appropriate interventions. Examples in this chapter describe what an assessment process may look like in a clinical setting and demonstrate the process of identifying intellectual and academic giftedness in student with disabilities.

When determining the appropriate tools for a comprehensive assessment, there are three types of cases that must be considered. The first is an evaluation being conducted to find a disability in an already-identified gifted student. The second type is an evaluation to find giftedness in a student already identified with a disability, and the third is to find either giftedness and/or a disability in a student not previously identified as either. Each requires an understanding of giftedness and disabilities—as well as their interaction—in order to select the proper tools to yield the most accurate data.

In the first case, when evaluating an identified gifted student for a possible learning disability, a number of factors must be considered. As noted, someone must recognize the unevenness or skill weakness so that a referral can be made. Some gifted students compensate so well that their difficulties are not noticed until middle or high school, if at all, delaying referral and intervention significantly. Once a referral is made, the evaluator must identify the area of giftedness and determine how this would impact the assessment tools in the process. It is important to select tools that allow a student's gifted abilities to be revealed, without being limited by his or her weaknesses. While this should be common sense, some evaluators fall into the trap of using a generic protocol for all assessments, sometimes without regard to the possible impact of the tools. Next, the evaluator must understand the potential areas of weakness in order to assess those areas in a way that will not be affected by the strength area. In other words, it is important to find ways for the student's weaknesses to be revealed—in a way that the student cannot use his or her strengths to compensate. Assessment will need to be completed in a way that will show the true weakness, if it exists, without the gifted child being able to mask the weakness. History and background information—including parent and teacher observations of behavior when performing challenging tasks in an area of concern—will shed light on the process of learning and educational impact of any disability.

In the second case, evaluating a student previously identified with a disability for the possibility of giftedness, the opposite concerns emerge. Barnard-Brak et al. (2015) highlighted problems with the typical disability identification process in finding giftedness, citing, among other reasons, that some disabilities may depress test scores that may otherwise indicate giftedness. With the first case, evaluators must allow weaknesses to show without impact from strengths. In the case of a disabled student being assessed for giftedness, factors such as the area of disability and the potential area of giftedness will need to be considered in determining what assessment tools must be used. Similar to assessing for disability in a gifted student, tools must be selected in a way that the giftedness can be revealed. For example, a student with a learning disability in writing will not be able to demonstrate the full extent of his or her gifted cognitive abilities on a written assessment, and the cognitive ability of a gifted student with a suspected reading disorder should not be assessed by a tool that requires reading. It is important that gifted strengths show without the impact of weakness. Background information may point the examiner toward the tools that will best allow the student to show strengths with minimal impact of weak areas.

Finally, in order to assess for a possible disability and possible giftedness in a student not previously identified in either area, the evaluation must be particularly wide-ranging. The evaluator must take care in selecting appropriate tools that will allow both abilities and disabilities to be represented. Individual assessment allows the experienced examiner to determine the accuracy of results in light of both giftedness and disability as well as assess the impact of factors associated with giftedness (e.g., perfectionism) on the test results. The issues in both of these scenarios must be considered in order to select tools properly, and multiple measures in a single domain may be needed to reveal strengths or weaknesses. For these assessments, collecting background information through history-taking is particularly important to gather anecdotal information about characteristics as well as to guide selection of assessment tools, due to possible masking of abilities. Understanding the student's preferred mode of demonstrating skills may streamline the process of instrument selection. Keep in mind that, in these types of evaluations, a student's scores may be relatively weak when compared to other areas of strength—and perhaps not below average on an absolute scale. Students with these relative weaknesses should be considered for services, as there is educational impact and functional impairment in the sense that these students are being hampered from showing their full abilities or perhaps reaching their true potential.

Identifying a behavioral or emotional disorder, such as ADHD or an autism spectrum disorder, presents additional difficulties. First, the behaviors need to be assessed, to determine their presence to a marked degree. Observations, interviews, and collection of behavioral data can provide information about whether the behaviors are present to a level that is outside the norm for the youngster's age. When the behaviors are present, further evaluation can determine the effects of giftedness and whether the behaviors of concern are better explained by giftedness rather than a disorder or disability. For example, perhaps the student is inattentive because of a curriculum well below ability level, or the student shows peer interaction difficulties because she is so advanced that she cannot relate to the other, more typically developing students. Once the behaviors are determined to be present and cannot be better explained by giftedness, the next step is assessing the level of impairment. As with learning disabilities, the extent to which behaviors are interfering with functioning is the key to making the diagnosis or identification. The presence of behaviors alone does not constitute a diagnosis—if the behaviors are not interfering with functioning or if the student has learned to compensate for the difficulties so that no noticeable negative impact is evident, a diagnosis may not be warranted.

## AVOIDING MISDIAGNOSIS OR MISSED DIAGNOSIS

*When eight-year-old Jamie was referred for assessment, his parents questioned whether he truly had ADHD. His pediatrician had collected behavioral checklists from Jamie's parents and teachers. Results showed behavioral symptoms consistent with ADHD (inattentive presentation), and the pediatrician recommended a trial of medication to address the symptoms. In Jamie's case, medication was ineffective, and parents brought Jamie for comprehensive assessment, seeking additional information and wondering if gifted intellect could be a contributing factor to Jamie's inattention in school. For the gifted student, environmental and situational factors must be considered when reaching diagnostic conclusions. Of course, it is possible that Jamie is both gifted and has ADHD. It is also possible that Jamie's giftedness explains his problems in school or that he has a learning disability that makes him appear inattentive. An educational situation that is not well matched to a student's abilities (either too high or too low of pace and level) can create difficulties that mimic ADHD. Simply completing checklists that assess behaviors consistent with ADHD will not rule out these and the many other possible explanations for Jamie's difficulties. Only comprehensive assessment, complete with diagnostic interview and individual testing of attention skills and both cognitive and academic ability, will be able to help parents understand the true nature of the problem. Evaluation revealed Jamie's measured IQ was 145 and his reading achievement was many grades higher than his current placement. These factors better explained Jamie's inattention in school and ruled out any learning problems. With this new information, interventions could then address the root cause and not simply the outward behavior. Curriculum adjustments resulted in far less inattention.*

Of course, some gifted students suffer from other exceptionalities that affect educational performance, like learning disabilities, as well as mental health concerns such as ADHD, autism spectrum disorder, depression, and anxiety. However, before jumping to a conclusion related to a possible disability or psychiatric explanation for behaviors in a gifted student, behaviors commonly seen in gifted individuals—such as perfectionism, intensity, curiosity, creativity, persistence, and willfulness—must be considered. If giftedness can explain (but not excuse) the behaviors, it can guide intervention. When these gifted behaviors are confused with pathological explanations or mistaken for a disability like ADHD due to outward behaviors, more difficulties arise. When a second-grader, like Jamie, is inattentive in reading because his abilities are much higher than the material being taught, medication will not be effective in helping him attend. And if checklists of ADHD behaviors alone are used for evaluation, his gifted intellect will not be used to explain the inattention—resulting in inappropriate interventions that will not address the root of the problem. Clinicians describe many cases like Jamie's. The comprehensive assessment allows an examiner to understand the complete picture, not just outward behavior. The interested reader is referred to Webb et al. (2016), which describes in detail the challenges associated with diagnosing gifted and talented individuals.

## TOOLS TO CONSIDER IN COMPREHENSIVE ASSESSMENTS

Comprehensive assessment is the only way to gather enough information about a student in order to determine the true nature of the difficulties and whether he or she is twice exceptional. Such assessment allows the examiner to understand multiple facets of an individual's functioning in order to determine strengths and weaknesses. Learning, nonverbal and verbal skills, thinking skills, attention, and creativity are some of the areas that can be assessed in order to determine whether a student with a disability is gifted or a gifted student has a disability. Cognitive assessment with a standardized measure such as the current versions of the Wechsler Intelligence Scale for Children–Fifth Edition (WISC-V) or the Stanford-Binet Intelligence Scales (fifth edition; the sixth edition is currently in development) will provide a wealth of data about areas of strength and weakness. While these measures should not define an individual and alone cannot determine the presence of a learning disability, such measures can serve as a point of comparison for students' learning skills. They also shed light on discrepancies across cognitive areas, like verbal and nonverbal skills, memory and reasoning skills, or timed and nontimed tasks. Viewing overall index scores like Verbal Comprehension or Working Memory as well as individual subtest scores can show functional impairment in certain domains that may not easily be seen during daily performance in a large classroom. Item analysis can prove useful in specifying inconsistency that shows impairment in a student's ability to demonstrate skills consistently and pinpoint the explanation for the educational impact observed in the classroom.

The WISC-V, for example, provides a Full Scale IQ score and a General Ability Index score, but also has a number of other index scores that provide data to inform evaluators. The standard index scores include nonverbal areas like Visual Spatial and Fluid Reasoning skills as well as Verbal Comprehension, Working Memory, and Processing Speed. Additional scores provide information on cognitive proficiency, quantitative knowledge, and expanded measures of fluid reasoning and both verbal and nonverbal development. These index scores can show the inconsistency within an individual, providing not only information to help identify challenges but also information that leads to appropriate services and interventions. Discrepancies between these areas are important. These expanded index scores can also provide alternative scores and additional data for determination of strength areas or giftedness. The Full Scale IQ or General Ability Index scores may be affected by a 2e student's disability, excluding him or her from gifted services he or she might need and ultimately receive if the disability is considered in the evaluation process. Using such supplemental index scores as markers for identification of giftedness is supported by the National Association for Gifted Children (2010).

Academic measures, such as the Woodcock-Johnson Tests of Achievement–Fourth Edition (WJTA-IV) and the Wechsler Individual Achievement Test–Third Edition, are useful tools in determining a student's academic development. Scores on these measures can be factored into determination of a learning disability based on the idea of an ability-achievement discrepancy. Additionally, as with WISC-V data, an item analysis can provide useful diagnostic data. Overall scores show *how many items* are answered correctly but not *which items* are correct. Significant inconsistency within academic subtests can indicate functional impairment in certain skill areas (e.g., long division) within a domain (e.g., math). Missing easy items, but obtaining credit for more difficult ones may indicate a learning issue, a skill gap can that can be easily remediated, anxiety, or inattention.

In assessing for possible attention deficits or a diagnosis of ADHD, one must include a variety of measures. For example, simple tasks of attention as well as behavioral checklists are a common part of most assessments for ADHD. These are necessary in the assessment of possible ADHD in the intellectually gifted student as well. Additionally, one must explore other possible explanations for any attention difficulties, as perhaps they can be better explained by a student's giftedness, curriculum or educational issues, or even anxiety and depression. Continuous performance tests, tasks of immediate attention, and tasks of sustained attention all provide additional data points to consider when ruling in or out other possible explanations for the behaviors of concern. Again, while overall performance is important, analysis of performance within tasks provides additional data. When assessing for possible giftedness in a student who has been diagnosed with ADHD and is treated with medication, optimal performance during testing is the goal, and medications should be taken during the assessment. If, however, the clinician is assessing to confirm or rule out possible ADHD in a gifted student who is already being treated with medication, sampling that student's attention without the impact of medication is preferable, unless medically contraindicated.

In addition to formal measures of ability, information gathered through interview can be particularly helpful. For example, exploring the student's strengths and whether or not he or she excels in certain areas can be gleaned from observation. Background information is necessary to determine when behaviors started, in what situations they arise, and how severe they are. Identifying the student's ability to demonstrate knowledge in certain ways is also helpful (Baldwin, Omdal, & Pereles, 2015) in determining how first to assess and then to address the identified concerns.

*Alan was a fourth-grade student when he was referred for evaluation by his parents. After reading about gifted students and their asynchronous development, parents suspected unevenness in Alan's academic profile and were determined to find the best way to educate their second child. (Their first child was a strong student who had been identified as intellectually gifted in school and excelled in all academic areas.) They wondered if Alan could also be gifted, be a more typical student than his brother, or even have a learning disability. They did not expect twice-exceptionality. In school, Alan was performing at or close to grade level in all academic areas according to teachers. He occasionally did not finish his classwork, but no teacher had raised any concerns, indicating that Alan was "doing fine" and progressing at a pace similar to his peers.*

*Evaluation with the WISC-V and WJTA-IV showed that Alan was indeed an intellectually gifted student according to state regulations with overall ability scores well above 130 but was also very uneven in both cognitive and academic domains. Strengths in verbal development and reasoning were clearly evident, but his struggles in paper-and-pencil processing speed hampered performance. Virtually every task that had a time component was lower than a nontimed counterpart. Academic assessment followed a similar pattern, with timed tasks lower than nontimed tasks, and other discrepancies were also noted.*

*Reading skills were generally consistent with what would be expected for a student of Alan's cognitive ability level. His math and writing were not. Math skills were below age and grade expectancy, though only slightly. While skills were weak overall, they were inconsistent within the domain, as Alan missed easier items and received credit for more difficult ones. Writing and spelling were more consistently weak and limited. As a fourth-grader, Alan showed math skills that were at third-grade level, while writing and spelling were at second-grade level. Both results yielded overall standard scores in the average range according to standard classification systems.*

*Both areas, math and written language, were well below Alan's measured cognitive ability—a severe discrepancy of more than 30 points (more than two standard deviations) between ability and achievement was present. In reviewing these results, context is important. While one could conclude that these discrepancies mean the presence of a learning disability in both of these areas, other factors were at play. In writing, Alan's difficulties were clear—he struggled to compose sentences and spell basic words. He misspelled words that work samples showed he had correctly spelled on recent assessments in school, indicating he was using his memory to compensate in the short term for spelling tests. The presence of a severe discrepancy between cognitive ability and written expression and the inability to demonstrate consistent writing skills showed functional impairment and educational impact. This impairment—along with the absence of other factors that could explain these difficulties—made the identification of Alan as a gifted student with a specific learning disability in written expression clear.*

*The math weaknesses presented a different profile. In mathematics, Alan showed reasoning and problem-solving skills in the gifted range, but calculations and timed calculations were in the average range and low average range, respectively. The severe discrepancy in this case, however, appeared related to two factors: mild performance anxiety (as evident during standardized testing and articulated clearly by Alan when he described his racing heart beat and sweaty palms during math testing) and lack of exposure to advanced calculation methods and symbols in his grade-level math instruction in school. He was able to correctly answer some higher level reasoning problems, but was very inconsistent in his performance. Although some functional impairment was evident, these alternative explanations were deemed more likely reasons for the discrepancy, and a learning disability was not identified in math for Alan. Instead, curriculum adjustments, including increased exposure to high level math calculations and higher level coursework overall, were recommended to decrease the discrepancy between Alan's overall ability and his math achievement. Monitoring his skills through periodic assessment indicated that, with anxiety management tools and additional exposure to advanced skills, Alan's math calculation skills developed.*

Thus, while discrepancies can be a useful tool in helping to identify gifted students with learning disabilities, solely using an ability-achievement discrepancy as the basis for identification can be problematic. Discrepancies within and across tasks and domains, differences between in-class performance and standardized test measures, performance on a variety of measures, observations, and background information are all needed to inform clinicians assessing possible 2e students. Clinical judgment and evaluation of other factors are needed. While it is clear that the discrepancy model has limitations and concerns, it is still legally allowable for the identification of learning disabilities, and clinicians specializing in working with 2e students find it useful in identifying strengths and relative weaknesses of bright or gifted students with disabilities.

## CONCLUSION

Identifying a gifted student with a disability requires comprehensive assessment with diverse tools that allow the examiner to see both strengths and weaknesses of an individual. Education and experience working with gifted students *and* special education students is invaluable in understanding the special needs of the 2e population and the unique ways they respond to assessment. While there is no single, clear profile of a gifted student with a disability, information collected through comprehensive assessment can help identify the specific strength and weakness areas. Score discrepancies provide data to guide one in the process, but the process of identification requires clinical judgment and is still an art to some extent. In straightforward cases where a student clearly shows scores and behaviors consistent with both giftedness and a disability, identification based on the functional impairment or educational impact is relatively clear. However, when there are subtle differences in performance and/or strengths mask weaknesses, or vice versa, finding hidden talents becomes more difficult. Only a skilled clinician with knowledge and experience with both populations may be able to find such students, and parents should understand the credentials of possible examiners to ensure that they will receive the best possible assessment. There are too many stories from frustrated parents about evaluations that were not comprehensive or did not identify the talents or weaknesses that were later revealed through extensive evaluations by experienced clinicians. With comprehensive assessment by qualified clinicians, more 2e kids will be accurately evaluated, identified, and served.

## REFERENCES

Amend, E. R., & Beljan, P. (2009). The antecedents of misdiagnosis: When normal behaviors of gifted children are misinterpreted as pathological. *Gifted Education International, 25*(2), 131–143.

Assouline, S. G., Foley-Nicpon, M., & Whiteman, C. (2010). Cognitive and psychosocial characteristics of gifted students with learning disability. *Gifted Child Quarterly, 54*, 102–115.

Baldwin, L., Omdal, S. N., & Pereles, D. (2015). Beyond stereotypes: Understanding, recognizing, and working with twice-exceptional learners. *TEACHING Exceptional Children, 47*, 216–225.

Barnard-Brak, L., Johnsen, S. K., Hannig, A. P., & Wei, T. (2015). The incidence of potentially gifted students within a special education population. *Roeper Review, 37*, 74–83.

Brody, L. E., & Mills, C. J. (1997). Gifted children with learning disabilities: A review of the literature. *Journal of Learning Disabilities, 30*(3), 282–286.

Feifer, S. G., & DeFina, P. A. (2000). *The neuropsychology of reading disorders: Diagnosis and intervention workbook*. Middletown, MD: School Neuropsych Press.

Flanagan, D. P., Fiorello, C. A., & Ortiz, S. O. (2010). Enhancing practice through application of Cattell-Horn-Carroll theory and research: A "third method" approach to specific learning disability identification. *Psychology in the Schools, 47*, 739–760.

Foley-Nicpon, M., Allmon, A., Sieck, B., & Stinson, R. D. (2011). Empirical investigation of twice-exceptionality: Where have we been and where are we going? *Gifted Child Quarterly, 55*, 3–17.

Foley-Nicpon, M., Assouline, S. G., & Colangelo, N. (2013). Twice-exceptional learners: Who needs to know what? *Gifted Child Quarterly, 57*(3), 169–180.

Foley-Nicpon, M., Assouline, S. G., & Stinson, R. D. (2012). Cognitive and academic distinctions between gifted students with autism and Asperger syndrome. *Gifted Child Quarterly, 56*, 77–89.

Fuchs, D., & Fuchs, L. S. (2006). Introduction to response to intervention: What, why, and how valid is it? *Reading Research Quarterly, 41*(1), 93–99.

Fugate, C. M., Zentall, S. S., & Gentry, M. (2013). Working memory and creativity in gifted students with and without characteristics of ADHD: Lifting the mask. *Gifted Child Quarterly, 57*, 234–246.

Gilman, B. J., Lovecky, D. J., Kearney, K., Peters, D. B., Wasserman, J. D., Silverman, L. K., . . . Rimm, S. B. (2013, September). Critical issues in the identification of gifted students with co-existing disabilities. *SAGE Open*, 1–16. Retrieved from http://sgo.sagepub.com/content/3/3/2158244013505855.full-text.pdf+html

Kaufman, S. B. (2013). *Ungifted: Intelligence redefined, the truth about talent, practice, creativity, and the many paths to greatness*. New York, NY: Basic Books.

Kaufman, S. B., Reynolds, M. R., Liu, X., Kaufman, A. S., & McGrew, K. S. (2012). Are cognitive *g* and academic achievement *g* one and the same *g*? An exploration on the Woodcock-Johnson and Kaufman tests. *Intelligence, 40*, 123–138.

Lovett, B. J. (2011). On the diagnosis of learning disabilities in gifted students: Reply to Assouline et al. (2010). *Gifted Child Quarterly, 55*, 149–151.

Lovett, B. J. (2013). The science and politics of gifted students with learning disabilities: A social inequality perspective. *Roeper Review, 35*, 136–143.

Lovett, B. J., & Lewandowski, L. J. (2006). Gifted students with learning disabilities: Who are they? *Journal of Learning Disabilities, 39*(6), 515–527.

Lovett, B. J., & Sparks, R. S. (2011). The identification and performance of gifted students with learning disabilities: A quantitative synthesis. *Journal of Learning Disabilities, 46*, 304–316.

McCallum, R. S., Bell, S. M., Coles, J. T., Miller, K. C., Hopkins, M. B., & Hilton-Prillhart, A. (2013). A model for screening twice-exceptional students (gifted with learning disabilities) within a response to intervention paradigm. *Gifted Child Quarterly, 57*, 209–222.

McKenzie R. G. (2010). The insufficiency of Response to Intervention in identifying gifted students with learning disabilities. *Learning Disabilities Research & Practice, 25*, 161–168.

National Association for Gifted Children. (2010, March). Position statement: Use of the WISC-IV for gifted identification. Retrieved from http://nagc.org/sites/default/files/Position%20Statement/Use%20of%20WISC-IV%20%28rev%203-2010%29.pdf

Olenchak, F. R., & Reis, S. M. (2002). Gifted students with learning disabilities. In M. Neihart, S. M. Reis, N. M. Robinson, & S. M. Moon (Eds.), *The social and emotional development of gifted children* (pp. 177–191). Waco, TX: Prufrock Press.

Reis, S. M., Baum, S. M., & Burke, E. (2014). An operational definition of twice-exceptional learners: Implications and applications. *Gifted Child Quarterly, 58*, 217–230.

Webb, J. T., Amend, E. R., Beljan, P., Webb, N. E., Kuzujanakis, M., Olenchak, F. R., & Goerss, J. (2016). *Misdiagnosis and dual diagnoses of gifted children and adults: ADHD, bipolar, OCD, Asperger's, depression, and other disorders* (2nd ed.). Tucson, AZ: Great Potential Press.

Wormald, C., Rogers, K. B., & Vialle, W. (2015). A case study of giftedness and specific learning disabilities: Bridging the two exceptionalities. *Roeper Review, 37*, 124–138.

# Misconceptions about Giftedness and the Diagnosis of ADHD and Other Mental Health Disorders

DEIRDRE V. LOVECKY

A large body of information about gifted children and the question of misdiagnosis has been disseminated through books, articles, websites, and conferences. This has led to misconceptions as parents, teachers, and mental health professionals have no way of knowing what information is based on research and what on opinion. Indeed, most people hearing about the question of misdiagnosis assume that information presented is based on solid research. This is not the case.

Giftedness can be defined in a number of ways. The Marland Report (1972) described gifted and talented children as showing high ability or achievement in one or more of six areas: high intellectual ability, academic aptitude in specific subject areas, creative thinking, leadership, visual and performing arts, and motor ability. For the question of misdiagnosis, the literature generally has not specified the type of giftedness or differentiated among types of giftedness. For the purposes of this chapter the terms "giftedness" and "gifted children" refer to intellectually gifted children (IQ 120+) and/or academically gifted children (scores of 90% on one or more academic subject areas of a standardized test), unless otherwise stated.

This chapter reviews research about gifted children and the diagnosis of attention deficit hyperactivity disorder (ADHD), the likelihood and frequency of mental disorders in general in gifted children, and best practices in diagnosing gifted children with ADHD and other mental disorders.

## THE ISSUE OF MISDIAGNOSIS

Some writers in the field of gifted education and psychology contend that gifted children have traits that look like those of mental disorders, particularly ADHD

(Hartnett, Nelson, & Rinn, 2004; Rinn & Reynolds, 2012; Webb, Amend, et al., 2005, 2006; Webb, Goerss, et al., 2006, among others). Webb, Amend, et al. (2006) stated that

> Many gifted and talented children (and adults) are being mis-diagnosed by psychologists, psychiatrists, pediatricians, and other health care professionals.... These common mis-diagnoses stem from an ignorance among professionals about specific social and emotional characteristics of gifted children which are then mistakenly assumed by these professionals to be signs of pathology. (p. 1)

Is this true? Do gifted children have behavioral and emotional traits that look like symptoms of mental disorders? What research supports this contention? ADHD is the misdiagnosis most often mentioned in the field of gifted education; yet, there are *no* research studies that have studied the frequency of misdiagnosis or if it occurs at all.

Webb and Latimer (1993), in a widely cited article, listed the symptoms of ADHD (inattention, hyperactivity, impulsivity), stating, "almost all of these behaviors, however, might be found in bright, talented, creative, gifted children" (p. 2). They compared two lists—symptoms of ADHD and traits of giftedness—but did not cite research evidence that any of these traits are common in any type of gifted children.

To further complicate matters, writers in gifted education equate ADHD behaviors with overexcitabilities (OEs). Overexcitabilities are an increased capacity for experiencing the world. There are five OEs: psychomotor, sensual, intellectual, imaginational, and emotional. Psychomotor OE is the capacity for intensely experiencing physical energy. Sensual OE is the intense experience of the sensual world. Intellectual OE refers to analytical abilities, curiosity, and intense desire to learn about things. Imaginational OE is the capacity for vivid fantasy and imagination. Emotional OE is sensitivity to one's own and others' feelings, empathy, and intense emotion. Gifted individuals can have any or all of these OEs in different combinations. The OEs are personality traits that are considered part of Dabrowski's Theory of Positive Disintegration (Piechowski, 1991). In other words, the OEs could be thought of as "five ways of being unusually open to experience" (Gallagher, 2013, p. 75).

There is a rough overlap between the OEs and aspects of the Five Factor Model of Personality (FFM), also known as the Big Five (McCrae, Costa, & Martin, 2005). One factor of the FFM, Openness to Experience, has six facets that show significant positive correlations with the OEs. Thus, Fantasy is related to imaginational OE, Aesthetics to sensual OE, Feelings to emotional OE, Actions to psychomotor OE, and Ideas to intellectual OE. The sixth facet, Values, does not correlate to the OEs. Most of the pairs had strong correlations. The exception was Actions and psychomotor OE with weaker correlations between them (Vuyk, Krieshok, & Kerr, 2016).

Because the focus in the field of gifted education is on gifted children and how they are being misdiagnosed due to traits and behaviors that look like ADHD, some writers in the field of gifted education have conflated together symptoms of ADHD and the OEs. In particular, symptoms of ADHD are seen to correspond to psychomotor OE (Hartnett et al., 2004; Rinn & Reynolds, 2012; Webb et al., 2005). For this reason, this chapter focuses on the research available on OEs and how they are related to ADHD, as opposed to research on openness to experience. In fact, there are no studies on the relationship of openness to experience and ADHD in gifted children and adolescents.

Thus there are two questions that need examination:

1. Does the research literature show that intellectually and academically gifted children actually have symptoms of ADHD? That is, do large numbers of these gifted children show symptoms of inattention, hyperactivity, and impulsivity?
2. What does the literature show about the presence of OEs in these gifted children? What is research evidence for a relationship between OEs and a diagnosis of ADHD in gifted individuals?

## EVIDENCE FROM RESEARCH STUDIES

### Question 1

Do gifted children show symptoms of ADHD? What is the research evidence that traits Webb and Latimer (1993) list as common in gifted children really exist in most?

If a child has ADHD, it would be expected that the child would exhibit inattention and/or impulsivity and hyperactivity depending on the type of ADHD. These are listed in the *Diagnostic and Statistical Manual of Mental Disorders* (5th ed. [DSM-5]; American Psychiatric Association, 2013) as symptoms of ADHD. Children with ADHD also exhibit deficits in executive functions, those aspects of performance that allow for learning and doing, such as focusing and shifting attention, organizing, planning and starting tasks, sustaining effort, completing tasks, and managing obstacles and frustration (Barkley, 1997; Brown, Reichel, & Quinlan, 2011).

If the behaviors found in diagnoses of ADHD were common among gifted children, we would expect tasks that measure inattention, hyperactivity, and impulsivity would show many gifted children to have symptoms of ADHD found in children of average ability with ADHD. That is, gifted children without ADHD would score higher on symptoms of impulsivity, inattention, and hyperactivity than average-ability peers without ADHD, who, of course, would not have measureable symptoms of ADHD.

#### RESEARCH STUDIES OF GIFTED CHILDREN WITHOUT ADHD

In one study, gifted children ($N = 24$) were shown to be superior in ability to self-regulate, inhibit responding, and focus (the opposite of impulsivity and inattention) compared to average-ability children without ADHD (*N* = 23). Gifted children (IQ 136–160) were also more motivated, persistent, and showed better working memories (Calero, Garcia-Martin, Jiménez, Kazén, & Araque, 2007).

In another study, gifted children (*N* = 57) scored higher on tasks of mental attention capacity, worked faster on tasks of speed, and resisted interference on tasks requiring effortful inhibition than average-ability peers (*N* = 92). Younger gifted children performed like older average-ability children, showing advanced ability to self-regulate (Johnson, Im-Bolter, & Pascual-Leone, 2003).

In a study using more complex material, such as matching figures, gifted children (*N* = 18) were more likely to use a reflective style. Of the gifted children, 66% were more reflective (slow and accurate) in their responses, with only 11% impulsive (fast and inaccurate). Another 22% were fast and accurate. Average-ability children (*N* = 20) showed a reverse pattern with only 30% reflective and 50% impulsive. Also, 15% were fast and accurate and 5% slow and inaccurate (Ramiro, Navarro, Menacho, & Aguilar, 2010).

Tasks of sustained attention, often used in the diagnosis of ADHD, show deficits in attention and ability to inhibit responding. Korean gifted children without ADHD (*N* = 106) performed better than average-ability children without ADHD (*N* = 71) on focusing attention, responding quickly and consistently, and making fewer errors. Using test cut-off scores for ADHD, gifted students were less likely to score in the ADHD range (Chae, Kim, & Noh, 2003).

On executive functions, gifted children without ADHD (*N* = 45) showed superior ability to shift focus, avoid errors, and plan and organize. Scores on tasks less related to executive functions were more average (such as underlining shapes) (Arffa, 2007).

In summarizing the literature, gifted children without ADHD scored higher than average-ability children without ADHD on tasks that measure attention, inhibition, and resistance to distraction. Gifted children scored higher on tasks of executive function, showed reflective cognitive styles, had a greater ability to shift attention rapidly, and excelled at problem-solving.

### Research studies of gifted children with and without ADHD

Gifted children with ADHD (*N* = 49) had a significantly greater number of ADHD symptoms (14.5 vs. 1.6), showed more difficulty with the Wechsler Working Memory and Block Design subtests, had lower scores on math and were more likely to be retained a grade than gifted children without ADHD (*N* = 92). Those with ADHD had more family members with ADHD, more lifetime psychiatric disorders, and more behavior problems both at school and with parents (Antshel et al., 2007).

Gifted children with ADHD (*N* = 54) had lower levels of self-concept, self-esteem, and happiness than gifted children without ADHD (*N* = 58). More than half in the ADHD group had coexisting mental disorders such as anxiety, depression, oppositional defiant disorder, or learning disabilities (Foley-Nicpon, Rickels, Assouline, & Richards, 2012).

On tasks of executive functions, gifted children with ADHD (*N* = 36) scored lower than gifted peers without ADHD (*N* = 34) on Full Scale IQ, Working

Memory, and Processing Speed on the Wechsler Intelligence Scale for Children, had more difficulty with tasks of inhibition (Radisavljevic, 2011), and scored lower on tasks of organization, planning, and problem-solving (Dillon, Hanratty, Arutyunyan, O'Callaghan, & Houskamp, 2013).

In a study of gifted children attending a summer camp for the gifted, comparisons of working memory and creativity were made between those with and without symptoms of ADHD. Gifted children with symptoms of ADHD ($N = 17$) had lower working memories but higher creativity scores than gifted children without symptoms of ADHD ($N = 20$) (Fugate, Zentall, & Gentry, 2013).

Thus, summarizing the research, when compared to gifted children without ADHD, gifted children with ADHD scored lower in working memory and processing speed, showed less ability to inhibit responding and had more difficulty with tasks of executive functioning. They displayed more symptoms of ADHD, had more relatives with ADHD, showed lower self-esteem and had greater problems with academic, social, and behavioral functioning. On the other hand, they had higher scores on creativity measures.

### Research studies of gifted and average-ability children with ADHD

In a sample of 275 Brazilian children referred for behavioral or learning difficulties, 15 children scored above IQ 120 (5%). Of these, 10 had ADHD combined type. The majority of these gifted children with ADHD showed problems in reading, mathematics, or writing. They also had a variety of coexisting disorders including mood disorders, social problems, disruptive/oppositional behaviors, and attention problems (Cordeiro et al., 2011).

On tasks of continuous performance, Korean gifted children with ADHD ($N = 10$) showed better ability to focus attention, inhibit performing on cue, and avoid distractions than average-ability children with ADHD but were similar on speed of responding and overall ADHD scores (Chae et al., 2003). In addition, using test cutoff scores resulted in a higher number of false negatives for gifted children with ADHD ($N = 64$). An ADHD diagnosis was correctly predicted for average-ability children ($N = 296$) 80% of the time, but for gifted children only 67% of the time. Thus there is a need for adjusted norms for higher IQs (Park et al., 2011).

On tasks of executive functions and memory, gifted children with ADHD ($N = 36$) scored higher than average-ability children with ADHD ($N = 33$) on tasks of planning and problem-solving but were similar on working memory, shifting attention, and inhibition (Radisavljevic et al., 2009). When compared to population norms, gifted children and adolescents with ADHD ($N = 117$) were significantly impaired on the Wechsler Working Memory and Processing Speed scales and on memory for story details. In addition, they were significantly impaired on executive functions such as activating effort, focusing attention, and sustaining attention. Some high-IQ people can have ADHD and show average scores yet experience difficulty achieving at the high level expected for their intelligence (Brown et al., 2011).

A small study of five gifted adolescent girls with ADHD found them to have problems in areas such as distractibility, maintaining attention and focus, completing work and handing it in, doing homework, and completing tasks they would rather avoid (similar to problems common to average-ability peers with ADHD). The gifted girls with ADHD were different from average-ability peers with ADHD in their awareness that ability alone was not enough to achieve success. Though they knew hard work and resiliency when frustrated were also needed, they found it hard to actually employ motivation and effort. Perfectionistic tendencies were also an issue. Use of sports and creative activities were found to be strategies for self-regulation for these girls (Fugate & Gentry, 2016).

In answering Question 1, summarizing the results described here, the research literature indicates that gifted children with ADHD, compared to gifted peers without ADHD, show significant symptoms of ADHD that their peers do not show: inattention, distractibility, impulsivity/inhibition, poorer working memory, and deficits in executive functions. Gifted children with ADHD also show problems similar to average-ability children with ADHD on some types of executive function tasks and coexisting mental health and learning disorders. Gifted children have higher scores on tasks that measure attention, inhibition, and executive functions than average-ability peers with ADHD. This can mask ADHD if cut-off scores are used that were generated for average-ability children. While gifted children with ADHD can score higher than average, they will, as a group, score lower than gifted peers without ADHD. Compared to other gifted children, their performance is impaired.

## Question 2

What does the literature show about the presence of OEs in gifted children and adolescents? What is research evidence for a relationship between OEs and a diagnosis of ADHD in gifted individuals?

### The presence of OEs in gifted individuals

The research literature indicated a relationship between giftedness and OEs when gifted individuals were compared to nongifted.

Across 11 international studies, gifted individuals scored higher on OEs than did nongifted, with intellectual OE being the most strongly related. Thus, in all 11 studies, gifted scored higher than nongifted on intellectual OE. In seven studies, imaginational OE was higher; in six studies, emotional and sensual OEs were higher; and in five studies, psychomotor OE was higher for gifted than nongifted (Silverman, Falk, & Miller, 2015).

On the older Overexcitability Questionnaire (OEQ), gifted Canadian adolescents ($N = 42$) were found to score higher in psychomotor, intellectual, and emotional OEs than average-ability students ($N = 37$), with psychomotor OE the highest (Ackerman, 1997).

On the OEQ-II (Falk, Lind, Miller, Piechowski, & Silverman, 1999), gifted students from the United States (*N* = 296) showed higher intellectual and imaginational OEs than average-ability students (*N* = 184). Elementary-age gifted children were higher in all five OEs than average-ability students. Compared to gifted middle school students, gifted elementary students were higher in intellectual and sensory OEs (Tieso, 2007).

In a similar study of Hong Kong gifted primary and secondary students, gifted students (*N* = 217) scored higher than nongifted (*N* = 229) on all five OEs. For the gifted group, intellectual OE was highest, then emotional OE. When this study was compared to Tieso's (2007), gifted students in Hong Kong scored lowest on imaginational OE, which may reflect cultural differences (Siu, 2010).

Intellectually gifted 10th-grade students in Turkey were found to score higher than nongifted on intellectual and imaginational OEs. Students who scored highest on creativity scored higher on all five OEs than did less creative students (Yakmaci-Guzel & Akarsu, 2006).

A longitudinal study of gifted students, students of average IQ, and high and average achievers found that, in adulthood, high-IQ people scored higher on intellectual OE than adults of average ability and lower on psychomotor OE. The high achievers scored higher on intellectual OE and sensual OE than the average achievers but lower on psychomotor OE. The authors stressed the point that OEs cannot be used to distinguish high intelligence or high achievement as only about 60% of each group could be correctly identified by their scores on the OEs (Wirthwein & Rost, 2011).

A meta-analysis of the five studies described here plus seven others (12 studies in all) compared OEs of gifted and average-ability children, adolescents, and adults, Researchers found that the gifted samples had higher OE scores than did those of average ability. The effect sizes (a measure of how big is the difference between the two groups) showed that intellectual and imaginational OEs had medium effect sizes. Sensual and emotional OEs had small effect sizes, and psychomotor OE showed no difference between the groups. Thus gifted people are more likely to score higher on intellectual and imaginational OEs than people of average ability, while psychomotor OE did not generally differ in most studies reviewed (Winkler & Voight, 2016).

Within the gifted population, how individuals score on the OEs varies from individual to individual. For example, at the Gifted Development Center, in Denver, Colorado, parents of 41 gifted children (ages 4–15) rated their children on their OEs. The highest score for 52% of the children was intellectual OE, for 19% emotional OE, for 14% psychomotor OE, for 8% imaginational OE, and for 8% sensual OE (Silverman et al., 2015). Thus while the majority of the children scored highest on intellectual OE, the others scored highest on one of the other four OEs.

### What is research evidence for a relationship between OEs and a diagnosis of ADHD in gifted individuals?

Rinn and Reynolds (2012) stated that impulsivity and hyperactivity found in ADHD are difficult to discriminate from psychomotor OE. In a study of 116 intellectually gifted children participating in a gifted summer program, the researchers, using the Overexcitabilities Questionnaire Two (OEQ-II) (Falk et al., 1999) and the Conners' ADHD/DSM-IV Scales-Adolescent (CADS-A) (Conners, 2001) found that psychomotor OE correlated with the CADS-A DSM-IV Hyperactive-Impulsive subscale to a weak degree ($r = .29$). They suggested that psychomotor OE essentially measures the same thing as the DSM-IV Hyperactive-Impulsive subscale, "which provides direct evidence for a possibility of misdiagnosis." (p. 43). Psychomotor OE did not correlate at all with the DSM-IV Inattentive subscale ($r = -.06$).

An examination of their data shows that the participants' mean and standard deviation scores on the 'Conners' CADS-A were well within the average range when checked against the scoring norms in the *Conners' Rating Scales–Revised Manual* (Conners, 2001). Though the authors did not give a range of scores obtained or indicate how many students scored higher than *T* 65 (the cutoff score for risk of ADHD), the mean scores and standard deviations indicate that most of the students would not have scored high enough on the Conners for an ADHD diagnosis. Also, although the authors did not indicate how many students had a prior diagnosis of ADHD, a description of the study in a later review article stated that none of them did (Mullet & Rinn, 2015). Thus the chance of misdiagnosis is not as high as the authors suggest. Also, since Rinn and Reynolds (2012) did not report the ranking of OEs in their sample, it is hard to know the significance of their findings. It may not be important that psychomotor OE correlates modestly with the DSM-IV Hyperactive-Impulsive subscale, if, for example, psychomotor OE was among the lowest of the OEs.

In actual studies of gifted children with ADHD, no relationship to psychomotor OE was found. Gifted Turkish high school students with ADHD (both medicated and not medicated) were compared to gifted students without ADHD (total gifted $N = 393$) and to average-ability students ($N = 351$). No relationship between ADHD diagnosis and psychomotor OE score was found. The entire group of gifted students scored highest on intellectual and psychomotor OEs. The authors concluded that it is unlikely that psychomotor OE is being mistaken for ADHD. In fact, ADHD and psychomotor OE are different things (Hough & Falk, 2016).

In a preliminary study, at the Gifted Resource Center of New England, in Providence, Rhode Island, parents of 26 gifted children with ADHD (ages 6–16) rated them on their OEs. The highest score for 58% of the children was intellectual OE, for 23% emotional OE, for 10% sensual OE, for 6% psychomotor OE, and for 4% imaginational OE (Lovecky, 2016). These results are similar to those found for gifted children at the Gifted Development Center (Silverman et al., 2015).

It is important to distinguish between the scores obtained on the OEQs and actual behaviors. Most of the research studies measured psychomotor OE by the scores obtained on the OE checklists. When gifted children exhibit high levels of hyperactive, impulsive, and inattentive behaviors, this set of intense negative behaviors can be greatly impairing; thus warranting a possible diagnosis of ADHD, whether or not they score high on psychomotor OE.

Overexcitabilities can be signs of positive development and have positive expressions in a person's life. For example, psychomotor OE is related to abundance of physical energy. When the abundance of energy, however, produces negative symptoms that interfere with functioning, the behaviors need investigation (Silverman et al., 2015).

In answering Question 2, summarizing the current research evidence, gifted individuals scored higher than people of average ability on some of the OEs, particularly intellectual and imaginational. Psychomotor OE was not generally elevated in gifted individuals compared to those of average ability (Winkler & Voight, 2016), which would suggest that psychomotor OE is not a defining feature of giftedness.

When scores obtained by a group of intellectually gifted children on an ADHD checklist were correlated with scores on an OE questionnaire, a weak relationship was found between psychomotor OE and the hyperactive-impulsive subscale (Rinn & Reynolds, 2012). Since none of these gifted children had a diagnosis of ADHD, even were scores to be elevated on these checklists, they were not being misdiagnosed.

Finally, research indicated that the psychomotor OE is not related to actual ADHD diagnosis in gifted adolescents (Hough & Falk, 2016).

Given that psychomotor OE is similar in gifted and average people, that only a weak correlation is found between psychomotor OE and checklist symptoms of ADHD in gifted children not diagnosed with ADHD, and that there is no relationship between psychomotor OE and ADHD in gifted adolescents, it is not likely that gifted children in general are being misdiagnosed with ADHD due to psychomotor OE.

## MENTAL DISORDERS IN GIFTED CHILDREN

Webb, Goerss, and colleagues (2006) estimated incorrect diagnoses in gifted children as: "ADHD, 34 percent; Asperger Disorder, 76 percent; Obsessive-Compulsive Disorder, 67 percent; Bipolar Disorder 96 percent" (p. 16). What is the research evidence that these and other mental disorders are being misdiagnosed in gifted children?

### ADHD

If large numbers of gifted children were being misdiagnosed as having ADHD, a greater proportion of higher IQs of children with ADHD compared to those without ADHD would be reported in the general literature (Antshel et al., 2011). In fact, this is not the case. The IQs of children with ADHD (*N* = 190) were found to be distributed along the expected bell curve for the whole continuum of IQ scores (below average to IQs in the 140s) (Kaplan, Crawford, Dewey, & Fisher, 2000).

Were large numbers of gifted children being misdiagnosed with ADHD, the mean IQ of children with ADHD would be skewed to a higher IQ level than average (Antshel et al., 2011). The mean IQ of 525 children with ADHD was found to be 100.99 (standard deviation 14.79) (MTA Collaborative Group, 1999, cited in Antshel, 2008). Antshel suggested that 10% of the ADHD population would have IQs over 120.

The actual prevalence of gifted children with ADHD is not yet known. A longitudinal study of ADHD in a cohort of children from Rochester, Minnesota ($N = 379$) found that about 7% of the entire population had ADHD. Of the group with ADHD, about 9% had IQs above 120 ($N = 34$) (Katusic et al., 2011), about what Antshel (2008) predicted. About 9.4% of Korean gifted students received diagnoses of ADHD using the Tests of Variable Attention and parent and teacher checklists (Chae et al., 2003).

What data we do have are *suggestive* that prevalence is similar to that of average-ability children (around 9%; Akinbami, Liu, Pastor, & Reuben, 2011), but until a study of prevalence is done with gifted children across geographical areas, ethnicity, and socioeconomic levels, the actual prevalence cannot be known.

Finally, if large numbers of gifted children were being misdiagnosed with ADHD, we would expect that these misidentified children would *not* have the same coexisting mental disorders found in children with ADHD. They would have an ADHD diagnosis but not accompanying anxiety, depression, learning disabilities, and so on. In fact, gifted children with ADHD diagnoses ($N = 49$) show high percentages of coexisting disorders: over half show lifetime diagnoses of depression or oppositional defiant disorder, social anxiety (21%), generalized anxiety (35%), or separation anxiety (26%) (Antshel et al., 2007).

## Autism Spectrum Disorders

Gifted children with autism spectrum disorders (ASD) show the same problems with social awareness, social interaction, and social communication as average-ability children with ASD. They also show restricted and repetitive behaviors, activities and interests as described in the DSM-5 (American Psychiatric Association, 2013), though interests can have greater depth and breadth than those of average-ability children with ASD (Lovecky, 2004).

If gifted children were being misdiagnosed with ASD in large numbers, the mean IQ of children with ASDs would be higher than average. This is not the case. In a study of children diagnosed with Asperger syndrome ($N = 37$), the mean Full Scale IQ was 98.2 with a range of scores from 66 to 144. The frequency distribution of the IQs roughly followed a normal distribution (Barnhill, Hagiwara, Myles, & Simpson, 2000). The prevalence of ASD in gifted children is unknown as there have been no research studies to date.

Gifted children with ASD can have very high IQs ($N = 40$) but suffer from deficits in cognition, academics, behavioral, social, and emotional functioning that distinguish them from gifted children without ASD ($N$ = 41) (Doobay, Foley-Nicpon, Ali, & Assouline, 2014).

Profoundly gifted children, above 160 IQ, do not fit in with age peers. It can be difficult to find peers who can comprehend the depth and breadth of the profoundly gifted child's interests. These gifted children can feel isolated and have no friends of their own age but will relate much better to older children and adults.

Profoundly gifted children without ASD, despite a lack of friends, do understand social faux pas, can hold a mutual and reciprocal conversation and are able to make eye contact. They can view things from another's perspective, regulate behavior and emotions, and show cognitive and emotional flexibility. Profoundly gifted children with ASD have trouble with the communication and perspective-taking aspect of social interaction, social reciprocity, and social interaction on a one-on-one level even with adults, unless the adult indulgently allows the child to be in total charge. Also, gifted children with ASD have difficulty with understanding and regulating emotions and with cognitive and behavioral flexibility.

A case study of two profoundly gifted girls, one of whom had ASD, found differences in attention, facial memory, affect recognition, narrative memory, social/emotional reciprocity, friendships, social skills, and adaptability (Assouline, Foley-Nicpon, & Doobay, 2009).

Gifted children with ASD ($N$ = 40) suffer from the same comorbid mental disorders as average-ability children with ASD. Unlike gifted children without ASD ($N$ = 41), they showed more risk for attention problems, hyperactivity, depression, aggression, somatization, withdrawal, social skills, and difficulty with activities of daily living. On parent rating scales of mental disorders, gifted children without ASD scored average (Doobay et al., 2014).

## Obsessive-Compulsive Disorder

Research studies on obsessive-compulsive disorder (OCD) showed no relationship to giftedness. Studies showed average to above average verbal IQs but Full Scale IQ similar to controls (Greisberg, 2005; Kohli, Rana, Gupta, & Kulhara, 2015; Yalçin et al., 2012). No relationship was found between childhood IQ and prevalence of OCD in adulthood (Koenen et al., 2009).

## Bipolar Disorders

In a meta-analysis of studies of giftedness, creativity, depression, and bipolar disorder, Missett (2013) found that high-IQ individuals may be at greater risk for bipolar disorder. Research indicated an association between high creative ability and mood disorders such as bipolar II and cyclothymia. Higher childhood IQ was associated with higher risk of adult mania (Koenen et al., 2009). In a large-scale study of Swedish children, males in particular at both the top and at the very bottom of the achievement scale in school were at higher risk for bipolar disorder in adulthood. The top 1.3% of academic achievers had a 3.34 greater risk of developing bipolar disorder in adulthood (MacCabe et al., 2010).

## Depression and Anxiety

In a review of the literature on psychopathology and giftedness, after eliminating studies of gifted children with ADHD, ASD, or learning disabilities, 16 of 18 studies found intellectually gifted children to be better socially adjusted with fewer internalizing (anxiety, depression, shyness, etc.) or externalizing problems (acting out behaviors) than nongifted peers (Francis, Hawes, & Abbott, 2016).

A meta-analysis of studies of rates of anxiety, depression, and suicidal ideation showed gifted youth significantly lower in rates of anxiety than nongifted peers and similar in rates of depression and suicidal ideation (Martin, Burns, & Schonlau, 2010).

Rates of depression and suicidal ideation in the general population of adolescents are concerning. For example, clinical symptoms of depression were found in 20% to 30% of adolescents (Evans et al., 2005), while rates for suicidal ideation were 14.5% for high school youth (Centers for Disease Control and Prevention, n.d., cited in Martin et al., 2010).

Whether adolescents develop depression depends on a number of factors. For all adolescents, good self-concepts, feelings of connectedness to parents and family, and a sense of belonging in school served as protective factors against depression. For gifted adolescents, a high IQ was also protective (Mueller, 2009).

## Eating Disorders

Studies of IQ in eating disorders indicated that patients with anorexia nervosa had average to high average mean IQ scores (Blanz, Detzner, Lay, Rose, & Schmidt, 1997; Lopez, Stahl, & Tchanturia, 2010; Rose et al., 2016; Schilder et al., 2016). Other studies have shown average mean IQ in some populations of people with anorexia nervosa (Weider, Indredavik, Lydersen, & Hestad, 2014).

Are gifted adolescents at higher risk than nongifted peers? It is hard to say. Some studies (Blanz et al., 1997, for example) eliminated subjects with IQs below 85, which could result in a higher mean IQ. The mean score depends on the range of scores in the sample as well as the distribution of scores. Thus scores might range from below average to highly gifted (IQ 68–145) (Schilder et al., 2016), or they might be clustered in the average to high average range (Rose et al., 2016). What can be concluded is that adolescents with eating disorders, especially anorexia nervosa, are more likely to have IQs in the above-average range than below average. Gifted adolescents are not more at risk for eating disorders than other adolescents with above-average IQs.

### Mental Disorders and the Gifted

In general, the risk of developing *any* mental disorder (with the exception of bipolar disorder) is not higher than average for gifted children and adolescents. In fact, a high IQ can serve as a protective factor by enhancing resiliency. Aspects of high IQ itself (problem-solving abilities) can enhance coping strategies (working hard and achieving) to produce resilient gifted adolescents (Kitano & Lewis, 2005).

Summarizing the research literature described here, there is no indication that gifted children are overrepresented in the populations of children with ADHD, ASD, or OCD. Thus it is unlikely that gifted children are being misdiagnosed in large numbers with these disorders. On the other hand, people with both higher and lower IQs are at risk for bipolar disorder. Adolescents with eating disorders showed above-average IQs in most studies. Finally, gifted children showed similar rates of depression and suicidal ideation as average-ability peers but somewhat lower rates of anxiety disorders.

## BEST PRACTICES IN DIAGNOSING GIFTED CHILDREN WITH MENTAL DISORDERS

The first caveat in diagnosing gifted children for possible mental disorders is the awareness that gifted children with mental disorders are *gifted* and do not lose the commonalities they have with gifted children who are not twice exceptional. Clinicians need to be aware of those unique needs to help gifted children and adolescents develop their full potentials. These children need both accommodations for areas of weakness and appropriate challenges built on areas of strength. To determine both accommodations and challenges, clinicians will need to conduct a full evaluation, have knowledge of the limitations of diagnostic tools, and evaluate impairment in functioning.

### Need for a Comprehensive Evaluation

Gifted children with symptoms of any mental disorder need a comprehensive evaluation, which includes assessment of IQ, achievement, executive functions, behavior, reported interests, school history, and a complete history of the child and family to aid in determining diagnosis and in creating an individual plan. Identification of twice exceptional learners needs to be done in the context of helping gifted students reach their potential, not just achieve grade-level work (Gilman et al., 2013).

Gathering an individual and family history is vital. The history points to developmental milestones, specific problems that have arisen in early years, and later issues with health, emotional/social functioning, and behavior. Family history adds information on problems that "run in the family." For example, families of gifted children with ADHD had a much higher frequency of first-degree relatives with ADHD and other mental disorders (Antshel et al., 2007).

A history of academic achievement, school behavior, and social functioning will be needed to assess both strengths and weaknesses occurring in the school environment. This is important for those gifted children whose parents report difficulties at home and in community activities but who are not identified as having school issues. Gifted children with learning disabilities and/or ADHD can mask their symptoms until their ability to compensate is too taxed by educational requirements (Foley-Nicpon, Allmon, Sieck, & Stinson, 2011). Information about academics, behavior, and social skills is also needed for children who show problems at school but not at home. Information gathered from the school can help address whether learning disabilities, attention problems, behavior problems, or social issues are impeding progress.

Assessments of gifted children should base determination of weaknesses not on age norms but on expectations based on the child's level of IQ; that is, the child's highest scores are the standard of comparison rather than age or grade expectations. Neuropsychological measures of executive function would be expected to be above average for a gifted child without a disability. Scores in the average range would indicate deficit areas. A large discrepancy between expectation and score is significant. Similarly, expressive, receptive, and pragmatic language, achievement, tests of memory, and visual-motor functioning would follow the same pattern (Lovecky, 2004).

The assessment should provide a plan for differential education, that is, accommodating for and remediating areas of weakness while also further developing areas of strength. A student may, for example, need remediation in written expression or social functioning while also needing acceleration in math and science.

Fugate (this volume) describes assessment of the twice exceptional learner from the school's perspective. Classroom strategies to enhance strengths and use of these as a means of developing or compensating for areas of weakness are described. Some of the strategies mentioned include mastery testing, use of technology, project-based learning, taking advantage of the gifted child's propensity for big-picture learning, and use of student choice. Also, accommodations such as help with breaking down big tasks and projects to smaller units are needed. Fugate emphasizes the positive aspects of gifted children with ADHD by focusing on their creative gifts and referring to them as "attention divergent hyperactive gifted."

## Knowing the Limitations of Diagnostic Tools, Checklists, and Clinical Interviews

Since there are few diagnostic instruments with norms geared toward the gifted, it is imperative that clinicians be aware of the limitations of continuous performance tests, tests of executive functions, parent and teacher checklists, and diagnostic observation protocols. Gifted children with ADHD can score average on these tests, especially those who have milder symptoms and/or have learned to compensate to some degree. Without specific norms, the problem of false negatives can arise, since cutoff scores are geared to the performance of average-ability students (Chae et al., 2003; Park et al., 2011).

A study of parent and teacher ratings on the Conners 3 (Conners, 2008) of 21 children selected as being gifted but "not thriving" indicated that about a quarter of these students had ADHD diagnoses; yet, neither teachers nor parents scored these gifted children significantly on the Conners 3 for inattention, hyperactivity, impulsivity, executive functions, and learning issues. In fact, many of the scores were lower than average. Due to discrepancies in finding gifted children with ADHD and the lack of agreement between parents and teachers in this study, the Conners 3 may not be diagnostically useful in determining whether or not gifted students have ADHD, executive function problems, or learning disabilities. In fact, the Conners 3 needs norms specifically geared to gifted students (Wood, 2012).

Diagnostic instruments such as the Conners 3 (Conners, 2008) can have false negatives; that is, they miss children who actually have ADHD. Nevertheless, when a child scores significantly on a scale such as the Conners 3, the information should be used as part of the assessment. Thus while a positive or "at risk" score indicates possible ADHD, an average score does not necessarily rule out ADHD if other indicators suggest significant symptoms and impairment.

In combination with diagnostic instruments, use of the diagnostic interview can aid in the assessment of symptoms. In addition to a comprehensive history, the clinician will need to interview the parents and child together and separately. Specific questions about possible symptoms should be asked, since not all problems are evident. For example, many teenagers hide symptoms of depression, thoughts of suicide, anxiety, OCD, and eating problems.

Parents may not mention the extent of behavior problems they deal with at home because the comparison group is so different. Some parents think all gifted children behave like their child. Parents of gifted children can also interpret questions differently than parents of children of average ability. For example, one mother described her daughter as making creative displays of her stuffed animals and dolls. Though the child had ASD, her mother did not think of her actions as "lining up toys or objects" and answered "No" to that question.

Behavior outside the home needs to be explored. How does the gifted child behave on sports teams or in art, music, dance, or gymnastics classes? Are there problems at community activities like Scouts, church, or a community center? Not only the presence but duration, frequency, and intensity of behaviors needs to be assessed.

Gifted girls with ADHD, ASD, anxiety, or depression may not show symptoms at school because they conform to rules and imitate other girls to fit in, but behavior outside of school shows their difficulties (Lovecky, 2004).

## Impairment in Functioning

The DSM-5 (American Psychiatric Association, 2013) requires that for diagnosis of ADHD and ASD, symptoms occur in two or more settings, such as home, school, with friends/relatives, or at other activities. The clinician needs to ask about each type of situation, not assuming that because the child is getting by at school or does not show problems at home the disorder is not present.

Noting the amount of structure and support available in each setting is also necessary since symptoms can be masked if there is significant support. Ryan, age eight, with a 130 IQ, was not considered a problem at school despite his hyperactivity, impulsivity, and inattention. His teacher basically provided one-on-one executive function support in his small school setting but did not see this as a problem. In fact, she marked an ADHD checklist as not significant for ADHD. On the other hand, Ryan's gymnastics coach noted increasing problems at practice. Ryan had immense talent but had made little progress for several months due to his symptoms. His coach scored Ryan significantly for ADHD symptoms. At home, Ryan had difficulty with doing homework, chores, following instructions, managing self-help skills appropriate for his age, and getting along with adults and peers. Ryan was significant for ADHD on parent checklists. Were only the school reports to be considered, Ryan would not be considered impaired, despite clear signs that he was impaired in social and home settings.

The clinician needs to assess level of impairment. "Impairment" refers to the difficulties that the symptoms cause. For ADHD, how do symptoms of inattention and/or hyperactivity/impulsivity interfere with, negatively impact, or decrease the quality of social, academic, or other functioning (American Psychiatric Association, 2013)? For children in the gifted range, the comparison group should be other gifted children. A child like Ryan who needed significant support at school was impaired compared to gifted classmates who did not need such support, because Ryan was not able to work independently. He was impaired at gymnastics because he was not developing skills at the expected rate. He was impaired at home as he was unable to follow-through on tasks, do chores, manage activities of daily living at age expectation, or get along with parents or peers.

Signs of impairment can be identified by evaluating how hard the gifted child needs to work to maintain good grades and perform in school or in other settings compared to other gifted children. If the gifted child spends all his or her spare time on schoolwork, symptoms are impairing. Similarly if the gifted child needs the parent to be an executive secretary to get homework done, symptoms are impairing, even if grades are excellent.

Impairment can also be seen in how much the symptoms of ADHD or ASD interfere with other people's academic performance. The child may not experience any problems, but others around him or her can have a very different picture.

The risk of not diagnosing and treating the gifted child with ADHD, ASD, or other mental disorder is great. If interventions are delayed, valuable time needed for development of vital skills will be lost, resulting in greater impairment.

## CONCLUSION

Based on the literature, gifted children without ADHD scored higher than average on tasks of attention, self-regulation, and reflection as well as executive function. Gifted children with ADHD showed significant symptoms of ADHD and scored lower on tasks measuring these symptoms. The literature on OEs is less clear, but, in general, gifted children and adolescents scored higher than average-ability peers on intellectual and imaginational OEs. There was no difference between the groups for psychomotor OE. While there is a weak correlation between scores for psychomotor OE and scores for hyperactivity/impulsivity on scales measuring these behaviors, none of the participants had a diagnosis of ADHD. When gifted adolescents with and without ADHD were compared, there was no correlation between psychomotor OE and a diagnosis of ADHD. Thus it is unlikely that gifted children are being misdiagnosed with ADHD in large numbers.

Gifted children with ADHD or ASD showed associated mental disorders including anxiety and depression. Gifted children without ADHD or ASD did not show elevated risk for development of anxiety, depression, OCD or other mental disorders with the exception of bipolar disorder and possibly eating disorders.

Clinicians should recognize that, for gifted children, the greater danger is not misdiagnosis but that those with ADHD and other mental disorders will not be diagnosed at all in the mistaken belief that their negative behaviors can be attributed to giftedness and boredom in school. If symptoms are attributed to giftedness, quirkiness, or OEs, the gifted child is put at risk for later failure. By the time symptoms become that severe, it can be difficult to obtain the accommodations and remediation needed.

## REFERENCES


Ackerman, C. M. (1997). Identifying gifted adolescents using personality characteristics: Dabrowski's overexcitabilities. *Roeper Review, 19*, 229–236.

Akinbami, L. A., Liu, X., Pastor, P. N., & Reuben, C. A. (2011, August). *Attention deficit hyperactivity disorder among children aged 5–17 years in the United States, 1998–2009* (NCHS Data Brief 70). Hyattsville, MD: National Center for Health Statistics.

American Psychiatric Association. (2013). *Diagnostic and statistical manual of mental disorders, fifth edition*. Arlington, VA: American Psychiatric Association.

Antshel, K. M. (2008) Attention-deficit hyperactivity disorder in the context of a high intellectual quotient/giftedness. *Developmental Disabilities Research Reviews, 14*, 293–299.

Antshel, K. M., Faraone, S. V., Stallone, K., Nave, A., Kaufmann, F. A., Doyle, A., . . . Biederman, J. (2007). Is attention deficit disorder a valid diagnosis in the presence of high IQ? Results from the MGH Longitudinal Family Studies of ADHD. *Journal of Child Psychology and Psychiatry, 48*, 687–694.

Antshel, K. M., Hendricks, K., Faraone, S. V., & Gordon, M. (2011). Disorder versus disability: The challenge of ADHD in the context of a high IQ. *The ADHD Report, 19*, 4–8.

Arffa, S. (2007). The relationship of intelligence to executive function and non-executive function measures in a sample of average, above average and gifted youth. *Archives of Clinical Neuropsychology, 22*, 969–978.

Assouline, S. G., Foley-Nicpon, M., & Doobay, A. (2009). Profoundly gifted girls and autism spectrum disorder: A psychometric case study comparison. *Gifted Child Quarterly, 53*, 89–105.

Barkley, R. A. (1997). *ADHD and the nature of self-control*. New York, NY: Guilford.

Barnhill, G., Hagiwara, T., Myles, B. S., & Simpson, R. L. (2000). Asperger syndrome: A study of the cognitive profiles of 37 children and adolescents. *Focus on Autism and Other Developmental Disabilities, 15*, 146–153.

Blanz, B. J., Detzner, U., Lay, B., Rose, F., & Schmidt, M. H. (1997). The intellectual functioning of adolescents with anorexia nervosa and bulimia nervosa. *European Child & Adolescent Psychiatry, 6*, 129–135.

Brown, T. E., Reichel, P. C., & Quinlan, D. M. (2011). Executive function impairments in high IQ children and adolescents with ADHD. *Open Journal of Psychiatry, 1*, 56–65.

Calero, M. D., Garcia-Martin, M.B., Jiménez, M. I., Kazén, M., & Araque, A. (2007). Self-regulation advantage for high IQ children: Findings from a research study. *Learning and Individual Differences, 17*, 328–343.

Chae, P.K., Kim, J. H., & Noh, K. S. (2003). Diagnosis of ADHD among gifted children in relation to KEDI-WISC and T.O.V.A. performance. *Gifted Child Quarterly, 47*, 192–201.

Conners, C. K. (2001). *Conners' rating scales-revised, technical manual*. North Tonawanda, NY: Multi-Health Systems.

Conners, C. K. (2008). *Conners' 3rd edition manual*. North Tonawanda, NY: Multi-Health Systems.

Cordeiro, M. L., Farias, A. C., Cunha, A., Benko, C. R., Farias, L. G., Costa, M. T., . . . McCraken, J. T. (2011). Co-occurrence of ADHD and high IQ: A case series empirical study. *Journal of Attention Disorders, 15*, 485–490.

Dillon, S. E., Hanratty, A. M., Arutyunyan, A.M., O'Callaghan, E. T., & Houskamp, B. M. (2013, June). *Visual planning and organizational deficits in intellectually gifted youth with ADHD*. Paper presented at the 11th annual meeting of the American Academy of Neuropsychologists, Chicago, IL.

Doobay, A.F., Foley-Nicpon, M., Ali, S. R., & Assouline, S. G. (2014). Cognitive, adaptive, and psychosocial differences between high ability youth with and without autism spectrum disorder. *Journal of Autism and Developmental Disorders, 44*, 2026–2040.

Evans, D., Beardslee, W., Biederman, J., Brent, D., Charney, D., Coyle, J., . . . Weller, E. (2005). Depression and bipolar disorder. In D. Evans, E. Foa, R. Gur, H. Hendin, C. O'Brien, M. Seligman, & B. Walsh (Eds.), *Treating and preventing adolescent mental health disorders: What we know and what we don't know* (pp. 1–27). Oxford, UK: Oxford University Press.

Falk, R. F., Lind, S. L., Miller, N. B., Piechowski, M. M., & Silverman, L. K. (1999). *The Overexcitability Questionnaire–Two (OEQII): Manual, scoring system, and questionnaire*. Denver, CO: Institute for the Study of Advanced Development.

Foley-Nicpon, M., Allmon, A., Sieck, B., & Stinson, R. D. (2011). Empirical investigation of twice-exceptionality: Where have we been and where are we going? *Gifted Child Quarterly, 55*, 3–17.

Foley-Nicpon, M., Rickels, H., Assouline, S. G., & Richards, A. (2012). Self-esteem and self-concept among gifted students with ADHD. *Journal for the Education of the Gifted, 35*, 220.

Francis, R., Hawes, D. J., & Abbott, H. M. (2016). Intellectual giftedness and psychopathology in children and adolescents: A systematic literature review. *Exceptional Children, 82*, 279–302.

Fugate, C. M., & Gentry, M. (2016). Understanding adolescent gifted girls with ADHD: Motivated and achieving. *High Ability Studies, 27*, 83–109.

Fugate, C. M., Zentall, S. S., & Gentry, M. (2013). Creativity and working memory in gifted students with and without characteristics of attention deficit hyperactive disorder: Lifting the mask. *Gifted Child Quarterly, 57*, 234–246.

Gallagher, S. A. (2013). Building bridges: Research on gifted childrens' personalities from three perspectives. In C. S. Neville, M. M. Piechowski, & S. S. Tolan (Eds.), *Off the charts: Asynchrony and the gifted child* (pp. 48–98). Unionville, NY: Royal Fireworks Press.

Gilman, B. J., Lovecky, D.V., Kearney, K., Peters, D. B., Wasserman, J. D., Silverman, L.K., Rimm, S. B. (2013, July–September). Critical issues in the identification of gifted students with co-existing disabilities: The twice exceptional. *SAGE Open*, 1–16.

Greisberg, S. (2005). Neuropsychological functioning of children with obsessive-compulsive disorder. *Dissertation Abstracts International: Section B: The Sciences and Engineering, 66* (3-B), 1719.

Hartnett, D. N., Nelson, J. M., & Rinn, A. N. (2004). Gifted or ADHD? The possibilities of misdiagnosis. *Roeper Review, 26*, 23–26.

Hough, E., & Falk, R. F. (2016, July). *Overexcitabilities and ADHD: Profile of gifted Turkish students*. Poster presented at the 12th International Dabrowski Conference, Calgary, AB, Canada.

Johnson, J., Im-Bolter, N., & Pascual-Leone, J. (2003). Development of mental attention in gifted and mainstream children: The role of mental capacity, inhibition, and speed of processing. *Child Development, 74*, 1594–1614.

Kaplan, B. J., Crawford, S. G., Dewey D. M., & Fisher, G. C. (2000). The IQs of children with ADHD are normally distributed. *Journal Learning Disabilities, 35*, 425–432.

Katusic, M. J., Voigt, R. G., Colligan, R. C., Weaver, A. L., Homan, K. J., & Barbaresi, W. J. (2011) Attention-deficit/hyperactivity disorder in children with high IQ: Results from a population-based study. *Journal of Developmental and Behavioral Pediatrics, 32*, 103–109.

Kitano, M. K., & Lewis, R. B. (2005). Resilience and coping: Implications for gifted children and youth at risk. *Roeper Review, 27*, 200–205.

Kohli, A., Rana, D. K., Gupta, N., & Kulhara, P. (2015). Neuropsychological assessment in obsessive-compulsive disorder. *Indian Journal of Psychological Medicine, 37*, 205–211.

Koenen, K. C., Moffitt, T. E., Roberts, A. L., Martin, L. T., Kubzansky, L., Harrington, H., . . . Caspi, A. (2009). Childhood IQ and adult mental disorders: A test of the cognitive reserve hypothesis. *American Journal of Psychiatry, 166*, 50–57.

Lopez, C., Stahl, D., & Tchanturia, K. (2010). Estimated intelligence quotient in anorexia nervosa: A systematic review and meta-analysis of the literature. *Annals of General Psychiatry, 9*, 40.

Lovecky, D. V. (2004). *Different minds: Gifted children with AD/HD, Asperger Syndrome and other learning deficits.* London: Jessica Kingsley.

Lovecky, D. V. (2015, October). Misperceptions about giftedness and the diagnosis of ADHD and other disorders. Retrieved from www.researchgate.net/publication/283293582. doi:10.13140/RG.2.1.1884.4886

Lovecky, D. V. (2016). [Responses of parents of gifted children with ADHD on the OIP]. Unpublished raw data.

MacCabe, J.H., Lambe, M.P., Cnattingius, S., Sham, P. C., David, A. S., Reichenberg, A., . . . Hultman, C. M. (2010). Excellent school performance at age 16 and risk of adult bipolar disorder: National cohort study. *The British Journal of Psychiatry, 196*, 109–115.

Marland, S. P. Jr. (1972). Education of the gifted and talented: Report to the Congress of the United States by the U. S. Commissioner of Education and background papers submitted to the U. S. Office of Education. 2 vols. (Government Documents, Y4.L 11/2: G36). Washington, DC: U. S. Government Printing Office.

Martin, L. T., Burns, R. M., & Schonlau, M. (2010). Mental disorders among gifted and nongifted youth: A selected review of the epidemiologic literature. *Gifted Child Quarterly, 54*, 31–41.

McCrae, R. R., Costa, P. T., & Martin, T. A. (2005). The NEO-PI-3: A more readable revised NEO personality inventory. *Journal of Personality Assessment, 84*, 261–270.

Missett, T. C. (2013). Exploring the relationship between mood disorders and gifted individuals. *Roeper Review, 35*, 47–57.

Mueller, C. E. (2009). Protective factors as barriers to depression in gifted and nongifted adolescents. *Gifted Child Quarterly, 53*, 3–14.

Mullet, D. R., & Rinn, A. N. (2015). Giftedness and ADHD: Identification, misdiagnosis, and dual diagnosis. *Roeper Review, 37*, 195–207.

Park, M. H., Kweon, Y. S., Lee, S. J., Park, E. J., Lee, C., & Lee, C. U. (2011). Differences in performance of ADHD children on a visual and auditory continuous performance test according to IQ. *Psychiatry Investigation, 8*, 227–233.

Piechowski. M. M. (1991). Emotional development and emotional giftedness. In N. Colangelo & G. A. Davis (Eds.), *Handbook of gifted education* (pp. 285–306). Boston, MA: Allyn & Bacon.

Radisavljevic, K. (2011). Diagnosing gifted children with attention-deficit/hyperactivity disorder: An exploration into the role of inhibition. *Dissertation Abstracts International: Section B: The Sciences and Engineering, 72*(5-B), 3103.

Radisavljevic, K., McDonald, L. B., Houskamp, B., Mota, E., Offinga, T., & Beljan, P. (2009, August). *Attention and executive functioning in a population of gifted children.* Poster session presented at the annual meeting of the American Psychological Association, Boston, MA.

Ramiro, P., Navarro, J. I., Menacho I., & Aguilar, M. (2010). Estilo cognitivo reflexividad-impulsividad en escolares con alto nivel intelectual. (Cognitive style: reflexivity-impulsivity among school children with high intellectual level). *Revista Latinoamericana de Psicología, 42*, 193–202.

Rinn, A. N., & Reynolds, M. J. (2012). Overexcitabilities and ADHD in the gifted: An examination. *Roeper Review, 34*, 38–45.

Rose, M., Stedal, K., Reville, M., van Noort, B. M., Kappel, V., Frampton, I., . . . Lask, B. (2016). Similarities and differences of neuropsychological profiles in children and adolescents with anorexia nervosa and healthy controls using cluster and discriminant function analyses. *Archives of Clinical Neuropsychology, 31*, 877–895.

Schilder, C. M., van Elburg, A. A., Snellen, W. M., Sternheim, L. C., Hoek, H. W., & Danner, U. N. (2016). Intellectual functioning of adolescent and adult patients with eating disorders. *International Journal of Eating Disorders Online First*, http://dx.doi.org/10.1002/eat.22594

Silverman, L. K., Falk, R. F., & Miller, N. B. (2015, November). *Overexcitabilities: Verifying the inner worlds of the gifted globally.* Paper presented at the 62nd annual convention of the National Association for Gifted Children, Phoenix, AZ.

Siu, A. F. Y. (2010). Comparing overexcitabilities of gifted and non-gifted school children in Hong Kong: Does culture make a difference? *Asia Pacific Journal of Education, 30*, 71–83.

Tieso, C. L. (2007). Overexcitabilities: A new way to think about talent? *Roeper Review, 29*, 232–239.

Vuyk, M. A., Krieshok, T. S., & Kerr, B. A. (2016). Openness to experience rather than overexcitabilities: Call it like it is. *Gifted Child Quarterly, 60*, 192–211.

Webb, J. T., Amend, E. R., Webb, N. E., Goerss, J., Beljan, P., & Olenchak, F. R. (2005). *Misdiagnosis and dual diagnosis of gifted children and adults.* Scottsdale. AZ: Great Potential Press.

Webb, J. T., Amend, E. R., Webb, N. E., Goerss, J., Beljan, P., & Olenchak, F. R. (2006). The misdiagnosis and dual diagnosis of gifted children. Retrieved from http://sengifted.org/archives/articles/misdiagnosis-and-dual-diagnosis-of-gifted-children.

Webb, J. T., Goerss, J., Amend, E. R., Webb, N. E., Beljan, P., & Olenchak, F. R. (2006). Diagnosis or misdiagnosis. *Understanding Our Gifted, 18*(2), 15–17.

Webb, J. T., & Latimer, D. (1993, July). *ADHD and children who are gifted.* (ERIC Document No. EDO-EC-93-5). Reston, VA: Council for Exceptional Children.

Weider, S., Indredavik, M. S., Lydersen, S., & Hestad, K. (2014). Intellectual function in patients with anorexia nervosa and bulimia nervosa. *European Eating Disorders Review, 22*, 15–24.

Winkler, D., & Voight, A. (2016). Giftedness and overexcitability: Investigating the relationship using meta-analysis. *Gifted Child Quarterly, 60*, 243–257.

Wirthwein, L., & Rost, D. H. (2011). Focussing on overexcitabilities: Studies with intellectually gifted and academically talented adults. *Personality and Individual Differences, 51*, 337–342.

Wood, S. C. (2012). Examining parent and teacher perceptions of behaviors exhibited by gifted students referred for ADHD diagnosis using the Conners 3 (An exploratory study). *Roeper Review, 34*, 194–204.

Yakmaci-Guzel, B., & Akarsu, F. (2006). Comparing overexcitabilities of gifted and non-gifted 10th grade students in Turkey. *High Ability Studies, 17*, 43–56.

Yalçın, Ö., Şener, Ş., Sarıpınar, E. G., Soysal, A. Ş., Güney, E., Sari, B. A., & Işeri, E. (2012). Çocuk ve ergen obsesif-kompülsif bozukluk hastalarının bilişsel işlevlerinin kontrol grubuyla karşılaştırılması: Gniş katılımlı nöropsikolojik bir çalışma. (Comparison between cognitive functions of children and adolescents with obsessive-disorder and healthy controls: A neuropsychological study of large sample). *Nöropsikiyatri Arşivi (Archives of Neuropsychiatry), 49*, 119–128. Abstract Only. Retrieved from psycnet.apa.org.

5

# Knowns and Unknowns about Students with Disabilities Who Also Happen to Be Intellectually Gifted

STEVEN I. PFEIFFER AND MEGAN FOLEY-NICPON

There is a growing interest in the gifted field—and in the world of general education as well—on the topic of the high-ability student who presents with a coexisting psychiatric or medical disorder, or special education disability—termed the "twice exceptional" or 2e student. This chapter reviews historical and contemporary perspectives on the twice exceptional student, provides an overview on some unique diagnostic challenges, and discusses two of the more high-prevalent disorders associated with gifted students, specifically attention deficit hyperactivity disorder (ADHD) and specific learning disabilities. The chapter ends with a brief synthesis of empirically supported efficacious interventions and concluding comments.

Before we begin, we felt that it was important to provide the reader with a transparent, "truth in advertising," statement about ourselves. We are both academic clinicians with primary professional affiliations working as tenured professors in major research universities—Florida State University and the University of Iowa. Our thinking and views on twice exceptional students is based on a careful reading of the scientific literature and on our own research. We both also share many years' first-hand experience in the real-world of clinical practice, working with intellectually gifted students with coexisting disabilities. What follows is a synthesis of our shared clinical and research experiences and circumspect interpretation of the major findings of published scientific papers on this unique and fascinating population.

High-ability students can have coexisting behavioral, social, and emotional difficulties. They also can have sensory, physical, or communication disabilities (Robinson, Shore, & Enersen, 2007). The coexisting difficulties can vary in terms of severity of impairment, ranging from quite mild and almost imperceptible to severe and debilitating (Pfeiffer, 2013, 2015b).

The great majority of information on the twice exceptional student is based on case study and anecdotal clinical reports. There are very few empirical studies on the topic (Foley-Nicpon, 2015; Foley-Nicpon, Allmon, Sieck, & Stinson, 2011; Robinson, et al., 2007). Most of what the field knows about high-ability students with coexisting psychiatric or medical conditions is based on reports consisting of very small and unrepresentative clinical samples (Burko & Pfeiffer, 2017; Foley-Nicpon, 2015; Pfeiffer, 2015). There is not even one prospective, epidemiological study that has examined a large community sample of nonreferred cohorts of gifted children to explore the etiology, pathogenesis, course, and prevalence for those who are twice exceptional.

We need to be cautious and conservative when reading reports based on clinical studies of the twice exceptional. There are real limitations when generalizing from small clinical samples; clinical samples are anything but representative of the general population of gifted children and youth in the community at large, a small percentage of whom we expect to have a coexisting psychiatric or medical disability. Gifted children who show up at gifted specialty treatment centers such as the Belin & Blank Center, where the second author holds an administrative appointment, or are referred to well-known therapists in the gifted field, such as the first author, tend to present with more serious symptomatology and be more impaired. And gifted children who are seen at specialty centers or by well-known therapists can be expected to come from families that feel more desperate or burdened by their gifted children's problems (Angold, Costello, & Erkanli, 1999; Pfeiffer, 2013).

As mentioned, some of the information in this chapter is based on our own clinical experiences working with gifted students with behavioral disorders, cerebral palsy, high-functioning autism spectrum disorder (formerly Asperger's disorder), orthopedic impairments, specific learning disabilities, cancer, diabetes, and a variety of psychiatric disorders. However, we have tried to emphasize what we know based on material that has appeared in peer-review journals. It is tempting to grandstand, but only very brief personal case material will be included to help illustrate a point.

It is unclear exactly when the term "twice exceptional" was first used or who, in fact, coined the term. Many contend that it was James Gallagher, and it would be nice to believe that he did, if for no other reason than because he was the first author's mentor in graduate school at the University of North Carolina. However, the earliest reference we have been able to locate appeared in a chapter titled, "Gifted Handicapped: A Desultory Duality," written by Yewchuk and Lupart (1988).

In this chapter, we operationally define twice exceptional as any student of exceptional intellectual or creative ability or promise with a coexisting disability.

We realize that there are other ways to define twice exceptional. For example, one could just as easily expand the inclusion criteria to include elite youth athletes or highly precocious young ballet dancers or musicians with coexisting disabilities as twice exceptional. In fact, we have seen in our clinic work these unique subgroups of youth, but this definition is what closely matches current perspectives in the empirical literature and from experts in the field (Baldwin, Baum, Pereles, & Hughes, 2015; Reis, Baum, & Burke, 2014):

## HISTORICAL AND CONTEMPORARY PERSPECTIVES

In their recent work, Baldwin and colleagues (2015) provide a thorough history of twice exceptionality. They demonstrate it is a relatively new concept to the educational and psychological fields, yet its origins date back to Leta Hollingworth (Hollingworth, 1923), a counseling psychologist who first noted the same person could have extraordinary talents and learning deficits. In the 1940s, Kanner and Asperger independently wrote case study analyses of children with characteristics now thought to be consistent with autism spectrum disorder, and Asperger's cases ranged in cognitive ability and included those with high intelligence (Pearce, 2005). In the 1960s and 1970s, scholars such as Gallagher (1966) and Elkind (1973) wrote about the confluence of gifts and talents with disabilities, and Maker (1977) is credited as the first to organize and identify resources and ideas for intervention in schools. This was in tandem with the 1075 authorization of PL-94-142 that mandated free and appropriate education for all students, including those with disabilities. These foundational works led the way for scholars in the 1990s to empirically investigate the phenomenon (e.g., Coleman, 1992; Minner, 1990; Reis, Neu, & McGuire, 1997; Waldron & Saphire, 1990; Vespi & Yewchuck, 1992), findings that laid the groundwork for the contemporary views held today.

Within the gifted education community, scholarly inquiry and practitioner interest in twice exceptionality has increased significantly in the past decade, yet emphasis outside the field is relatively scant (Foley-Nicpon, Assouline, & Colangelo, 2013). This could be for a number of reasons, but part of the issue may be related to identification. High ability is most often identified in schools, whereas mental health diagnoses are most often identified in medical settings; learning disabilities are the purview of both domains but how they are operationalized is somewhat distinct (Weis, 2014). This can lead to confusion about which professions should teach the concept in training programs, as well as practice setting challenges in identification and diagnosis.

## DIAGNOSTIC CHALLENGES

The term "twice exceptional" was likely borrowed from a similar concept in medicine, namely "comorbidity." In medicine, comorbidity refers to patients with an index disease (e.g., cardiovascular disease or diabetes) who also have one or more other diseases in addition to the index disease, such as asthma, migraine, rheumatoid arthritis, or cancer (Gijsen et al., 2001). Comorbidity is a frequently studied diagnostic phenomenon in psychiatry as well as general medicine (Angold et al., 1999; Pfeiffer, 2015a, 2015b). In fact, in psychiatry some have argued that comorbidity is the "premier challenge facing mental health professionals" (Kendall & Clarkin, 1992, p. 833).

There are at least three reasons for the interest in comorbidity in medicine: comorbidity is highly prevalent in the population; persons with comorbid medical conditions are associated with less favorable outcomes; and comorbidity can cloud our understanding of the etiology, course, and treatment of each medical disease and psychiatric disorder coexisting in one index patient.

In our clinical and research practices working with high-ability children and youth, it is very unusual for the referred child to present as a "pure" case of a gifted child with one very specific and clearly demarcated psychological disorder (e.g., eating disorder, bipolar disorder, ADHD). In the great majority of cases, the gifted child presents with an *admixture* of maladaptive symptoms and at times two or more distinct psychological disorders. Boundary problems are common in childhood mental disorders, just as they are in medicine (Pfeiffer, 2013, 2015b).

A number of factors can complicate the diagnostic and treatment challenges that educators and psychologists face when assessing or planning an individualized intervention program for a gifted student who is presenting with one or more coexisting psychiatric or medical disabilities. This chapter presents a brief discussion of six such issues:

## Time of Onset of the Disorder

Medicine has found it helpful to distinguish between the onsets of each disease among comorbid patients. Clinical researchers in the gifted field have not yet begun to examine the times of onset when gifted students present with two or more coexisting disorders, for example the gifted student with ADHD or the gifted student with conduct problems.

## How to Define "Gifted"

Another limitation is the vexing issue of how to operationally define "gifted." As the reader is probably well aware, there are a great many different conceptions of giftedness (Pfeiffer, 2008, 2013). There is the traditional psychometric view, talent development models, Gagné's Differentiated Model of Giftedness and Talent, Subotnik's Developmental Transitions in Giftedness and Talent, Stanley's Talent Search Model, Renzulli's Three Ring Conception of Giftedness, expert performance perspectives, Sternberg's Theory of Successful Intelligence, Gardner's Multiple Intelligences, and the first author's Tripartite Model (Pfeiffer, 2008, 2015). Published articles on the twice exceptional have, almost exclusively, adopted a traditional psychometric view. In other words, in almost all published papers on the topic, the twice exceptional student is described as a youngster with a high IQ along with a coexisting disability or disorder. Unfortunately, there are very few published articles on Sternberg's "street smart" gifted child with a coexisting disability, Gardner's interpersonally gifted youth with a coexisting disability, or Pfeiffer's high potential to excel gifted student with a coexisting disability.

## Primary versus Secondary Disorders

In medicine, a secondary condition is considered *caused* by a primary condition. For example, renal failure secondary to a myocardial infarction generally results from hypoperfusion of the kidneys, caused by a calamitous drop in the patient's blood pressure following the heart attack (Angold et al., 1999). However, very few if any of the common child psychiatric comorbidities have been shown to result from one disorder causing another. For example, ADHD and bipolar disorder can coexist in the same patient; the rates of ADHD range from 57% to 98% in bipolar patients (Borchardt & Berstein, 1995) and rates of bipolar disorder range from 11% to 22% in ADHD patients (Biederman et al., 1996). However, although ADHD and bipolar disorder show high comorbidity in multiple clinical studies, no researcher has proposed that one condition *causes* the other.

Some in the gifted field have argued that being gifted places one at heightened or increased risk for developing psychological problems and even psychiatric disorders, such as low self-concept, existential depression, or perfectionistic anxiety (Baum & Owen, 1988, 2004; Baum, Owen, & Dixon, 1991). This position is consistent with the previously mentioned medical view in which giftedness serves as the "primary condition" *causing* the psychological problem or psychiatric disorder (the "secondary disease"); purportedly the high intellectual ability and psychological disorder are based on a suspected common pathophysiology in the brain (van Weel & Schellevis, 2006). A majority of authorities in the gifted field, however, do not view being intellectually gifted as automatically increasing one's vulnerability or risk for psychiatric disorders (Neihart, Pfeiffer, & Cross, 2015; Robinson, 2002; Neihart, 2008; Pfeiffer & Stocking, 2000; Pfeiffer, 2013, 2015b). Some, in fact, argue that being gifted serves as a potential advantage, a prophylactic that serves to increase the gifted youngster's resilience and ability to effectively cope with adversity, stress, or conflict. There is some logic to this argument in that students of high intellectual ability have, by definition, more advanced cognitive skills and could be expected to better understand the day-to-day nuances of challenging social and interpersonal situations and possess a greater array of problem-solving strategies. This provocative hypothesis has yet to be empirically tested with a representative cohort of gifted youngsters.

Gifted students, as a group, are typically at least as well adjusted as their nongifted peers (Neihart, 2008; Neihart, Pfeiffer, & Cross, 2015). Some gifted students, however, do struggle with psychological problems and psychiatric disorders that can be distressful, dysfunctional, and even dangerous (Cross & Cross, 2017). Not all gifted children easily navigate the often challenging social and emotional waters of childhood and adolescence. Quite a few experience psychological problems every bit as distressful as those experienced by their same-age nongifted peers (Pfeiffer, 2003, 2013, 2015b, 2016; Pfeiffer & Stocking, 2000).

## Comorbidity Challenges Disease-Specific Guidelines

Medicine has documented that the interacting effects of two or more concurrent diseases complicates their effective management. Physicians report that effective individualized care requires more than simply the sum of separate guideline components (Kendall & Clarkin, 1992). There is little research on, and an urgent need for, testing the impact of treatment guidelines for patients with comorbid diseases. An analogous, although not parallel, case can be made for the twice exceptional student. There is no peer-reviewed research that has examined the effectiveness of evidence-based treatment protocols (e.g., behavioral parent training for ADHD, cognitive-behavioral treatment protocols for depression, or parent management training for disruptive behavior problems) when applied specifically to a clearly defined cohort of twice exceptional students. Of course, being gifted is not the same as having a medical disease such as angina, diabetes, hypertension, renal failure, or postpartum depression.

## Comorbidity versus Complexity

Comorbidity is the concurrent coexistence of two or more medically diagnosed diseases in the same patient, with the diagnoses of each disease based on clearly established and widely accepted diagnostic criteria (Nardi et al., 2007). Comorbid conditions are almost always more serious and require more comprehensive and intensive treatment (Fortin, Soubhi, Hudon, Bayliss, & van den Akker, 2007; Kerby & Hennessy, 2003). The concept of complexity is related to but not exactly the same as comorbidity. Complexity or "case mix complexity" is a term used in medicine to refer to a set of multiple patient attributes that include, in addition to comorbidity, socioeconomic factors, lifestyle factors, access to healthcare, severity and chronicity of the illness, prognosis, treatment difficulty, need for intervention, and resource intensity to manage the illness (Nardi et al., 2007; Safford, Allison, & Kiefe, 2007). The more complex the case mix, the greater the need for multiple resources and the less predictable the course and outcome. In addition, the more complex the case mix, the greater the reliance on clinical judgment and a tailored intervention plan and the more important coordination of services. In this sense, case mix complexity perhaps is a more useful concept than comorbidity when considering the twice exceptional student. In other words, it might be helpful to conceptualize the intellectually gifted student with a subclinical or even full-blown psychological or psychiatric disorder from a "complex case mix" perspective, rather than from a comorbidity model, since intellectual giftedness is not a disease but rather a relevant characteristic of the individual that can contribute to making the case more challenging to treat.

## Misdiagnoses and Missed Diagnoses

Most authorities recognize that diagnostic boundaries in medicine are not absolutely precise and that there exists a gray area and degree of overlap among disorders (Angold et al., 1999). For example, there are shared symptoms in arthritis, hypertension, ischemic heart disease, and stroke (Gijsen et al., 2001), which complicates the situation for the physician who is trying to make a correct diagnosis. The same is true in terms of diagnostic boundary issues clouding precise diagnoses with intellectually gifted students presenting with possible coexisting problems. Some experts in the gifted field contend that "misdiagnoses stem primarily from the widespread ignorance among otherwise well-meaning and well-trained professionals about the social and emotional characteristics of gifted children and adults" (Webb et al., 2005, p. xxiii). There is the potential for misdiagnosis if the practitioner incorrectly attributes characteristics of some gifted children as indicative of defining symptoms of one or more underlying disorders. For example, the high activity level, boredom, resistance to rules and regulations, or intellectual overexcitability of an intellectually gifted youngster might be misinterpreted as defining symptoms of ADHD. Some authorities estimate that as many as half of gifted children with the diagnosis of ADHD are misdiagnosed (Webb et al., 2005). We suspect that this is probably an overestimate (see Lovecky, this volume) of what is, very likely, a real problem with some gifted children being misdiagnosed. A recent survey of school psychologists in the United States found that the great majority of practitioners—all members of the National Association of School Psychologists—were provided very little graduate training on the gifted. Less than half of the national sample reported receiving any training on characteristics of gifted students, and two-thirds of the group reported receiving *no* training regarding the social-emotional needs of the gifted or any information on twice exceptionality (Robertson, Pfeiffer, & Taylor, 2011). One can understand how misdiagnosis is both a serious and a not uncommon phenomena in the gifted field. Misdiagnoses can lead to improper and even dangerous interventions. The bored, highly excitable, and intellectually impetuous gifted student incorrectly diagnosed with ADHD could very likely be improperly prescribed psychostimulant medication, for example.

In addition to misdiagnoses, there is the risk of a missed diagnosis. What this means is that the student's intellectual gift or special talent can serve to mask from the teacher or parents the presence of an actual disability. Equally probable, the adverse impact of a disability can mask or disguise the student's gift or special talent. In both instances, the student is not identified as twice exceptional. In the first instance, the student is recognized as gifted but not diagnosed as also having a coexisting disability because his or her advanced intellectual or academic abilities camouflage recognition of the disability. In the second instance, the student is not identified as gifted because his o or her disability serves to overshadow intellectual or academic gifts. In both instances, students are denied much-needed special services or programs because their twice exceptional status goes unrecognized.

A final possibility exists. It is conceivable that, in some instances, a high-ability student with a disability could go unidentified as both gifted and disabled. One could overlook both the giftedness and the disability if features of each conceal or mask one another with neither readily noticeable. We have seen this missed diagnosis phenomenon far too often in our clinical work.

The National Education Association (2006) published a white paper on the twice exceptional student, which states,

> some youngsters show a pattern of extreme strengths combined with areas of significant difficulty . . . commonly referred to as twice exceptional students; students who have outstanding gifts or talents and are capable of high performance, but who also have a disability that affects some aspect of learning. (Brody & Mills, 1997, as cited in National Education Association, 2006, p. 1)

The white paper notes that the twice exceptional "are among the most frequently under-identified population in our schools. Twice exceptional students present a unique identification and service delivery dilemma for educators" (National Education Association, 2006, p. 1). If we assume that approximately 6% of the student population is classified as gifted, then there are approximately 3 million gifted children in grades K–12 in the United States. In 2000–2001 there were nearly 6 million students in the United States served under the Individuals with Disabilities Education Act (IDEA) (US Department of Education, 2002). This equates to approximately 360,000 or 6% of the students served by IDEA as twice exceptional, academically gifted with a disability. More recent data from the Department of Education, National Center for Education Statistics (2013) indicates that 6.4 million students were served under IDEA in 2010–2011. Using the same 6% estimate for academically gifted, we now are looking at over 385,000 twice exceptional children. There are likely a considerable number of high-ability students with disabilities who have been missed and not identified in the schools.

One final point on misdiagnoses and missed diagnoses bears mentioning. Questions have been raised in the mental health field about the clinical utility of the diagnostic classification systems that we use—presently, the *Diagnostic and Statistical Manual of Mental Disorders* (fifth edition; American Psychiatric Association, 2013) and the International Classification of Diseases (10th revision [ICD]). The architects of the new ICD-11 are acutely sensitive to this issue; many authorities are advocating for a science of clinical utility that would be built into any new classification systems for mental disorders (Keeley et al., 2016). These efforts will help refine and further validate the diagnoses that are routinely applied to gifted students with coexisting difficulties, for example ADHD and learning disabilities.

## HIGH-PREVALENCE TWICE EXCEPTIONALITIES

While some have questioned the existence of high-ability students with learning disabilities (Lovett & Sparks, 2011), research findings and clinical experience demonstrate otherwise and point to the need to increase awareness within educational and clinical settings. Some have described characteristics of this population but also emphasize the heterogeneous nature of the identity itself (e.g., Reis et al., 1997; Ruban & Reis, 2005). That is, one can be outstanding at calculation but struggle with phonics and reading comprehension. Another student can demonstrate specific artistic or musical aptitude but lack organizational and problem-solving skills. In general, though, high-ability students with learning disabilities have strengths, such as advanced creativity, analytical thinking, and verbal and nonverbal reasoning, along with deficits in one or more academic domains with accompanying frustration and sensitivity to failure (Ruban & Reis, 2005).

Among the twice exceptionalities examined in the research literature, gifted students with learning disabilities have received the greatest attention (Foley-Nicpon et al., 2011), yet empirical investigation represents only 5% of the published articles, and the research rigor within this 5% varies (Lovett & Sparks, 2011). Part of the problem may be due to a low incidence rate, but the larger problem may be the unique challenges identification of both giftedness and learning disability presents (Mee Bell, Taylor, McCallum, Coles, & Hays, 2015). More recent, large-scale investigations (McCallum et al., 2013; Mee Bell et al., 2015) provide both a method of screening for twice-exceptionality using curriculum-based measures and demonstrate how the "masking effect" can manifest in schools. Identifying effective screening methods for twice exceptionality that utilize universally administered data are imperative given the cost and time associated with individualized assessment. Yet implementation of McCallum and colleagues' recommendations does not appear widespread as the practice has yet to be reported in the literature. Researchers (Mee Bell et al., 2015) next examined curriculum-based measurement data's ability to predict performance on high-stakes, end of the year assessments. Children who were gifted in reading but scored low in math did not significantly differ from their high-ability peers on end of the year assessments, but children who were gifted in math but scored lower in reading performed significantly lower on both reading and math in the end of the year assessments than their high-ability peers. The authors suggest reading deficits may therefore mask students' talents in mathematics on standardized test items that tap additional skills, such as reading, processing speed, abstract reasoning, and working memory. More studies such as these are necessary so we can best screen for twice exceptionality and refer for comprehensive assessment, understand the masking phenomenon and how to interpret school-based data, and design interventions that work to capitalize on strengths and remediate students' areas for growth.

The second most researched area of twice exceptionality is among high-ability students with ADHD. There have been case study (e.g., Moon, Zentall, Grskovic, Hall & Stormount, 2001; Zentall, Moon, Hall, & Grskovic, 2001), clinical sample (e.g., Foley-Nicpon, Rickels, Assouline, & Richard, 2012), and large-scale (Antshel et al., 2007; 2008) investigations into issues of academic performance, executive functioning, and psychosocial functioning. In general, findings suggest diagnostic determination may be later than in other children with ADHD potentially due to their higher cognitive functioning and ability to compensate for their deficits. They also tend to respond equally well as their nongifted counterparts to stimulant medication intervention (Grizenko, Zhang, Polotskaia, & Joober, 2012). It appears their high ability serves as somewhat of a protective factor as they demonstrate fewer attention and social deficits (Grizenko et al., 2012) and less underachievement (Bussing et al., 2012) than students with ADHD who are not high ability. However, in comparison to high-ability students without ADHD, they report lower overall self-esteem, behavioral self-concept, overall happiness (Foley-Nicpon et al., 2012), and greater academic concerns (Antshel et al., 2007, 2008). Finally, the complexity and symptom overlap between some symptoms of ADHD and high ability (Rinn & Reynolds, 2012) necessitate comprehensive evaluation, instead of relying only on rating-scale methods, in the diagnostic decision-making process.

## EFFICACIOUS EVIDENCE-BASED INTERVENTIONS

There are limited empirical investigations demonstrating the efficacy of interventions specifically designed for twice exceptional youth, but several exist within the wider field of child clinical psychology (e.g., Weisz & Kazdin, 2010). It is likely application of these proven strategies with twice exceptional youth would be beneficial, as long as the clinician and/or educator considers the "case mix complexity" the gifted identification presents. Among the limited studies with this specific population, and among specialists in the field, the recommendation is almost always to assume a strengths-based approach (Baum & Owen, 2004; Baum, Schader, & Hebert, 2014; Baum & Schader, this volume; Crepeau-Hobson & Bianco, 2011) and address psychosocial factors that influence academic performance (Foley-Nicpon, 2015). However, high-ability students receiving special education services in schools may be overlooked for gifted services, which is a clear and cost-effective strengths-based intervention. In the largest prevalence study to date, Barnard-Brak, Johnson, Hannig, and Wei (2015) discovered through examination of the Special Education Elementary Longitudinal Study that only 11% of those with an achievement score in the 90th percentile or above participated in gifted and talented programming, with even lower participation percentages among girls, African Americans, and Latinos (see Davis & Robinson, this volume; Mayes, Hines, & Moore, this volume). Too often the focus is on remediation of what is wrong, rather than programming for talent development (Barnard-Brak et al., 2015). These two goals should not be mutually exclusive.

When developing educationally based intervention plans for twice exceptional students, results from case study analyses suggest the value of a team approach (Coleman, Baldwin & Pereles, this volume; Wormald, Rogers, & Vialle, 2015).

This team should consider all data gathered on the child, including curriculum-based assessments, high-stakes achievement tests, observations, parent input, and outside evaluations (Pfeiffer, 2015a). The sometimes artificial, sometimes central divide between assessments completed in psychological clinics and educational settings only serves to harm the child and family. When children are continually reassessed to corroborate what has been deemed in existence through neuropsychological or psychoeducational testing only serves to waste time and money and can have a negative impact on the child (Wormald et al., 2015).

## CONCLUSION

We could have easily expanded this chapter to include a discussion on the twice exceptional gifted/student with autism spectrum disorder, physical disabilities, sensory disabilities, and a wide number of psychiatric disorders. These different types of twice exceptional students present with a unique constellation of characteristics and needs (and strengths) (Pfeiffer, 2013, 2015b).

Also, we could have expanded the chapter by broadening our definition of gifted to include a wide variety of highly talented young artists, athletes, performers, and community leaders. In other words, there exist gifted youth who are not defined exclusively by high intellectual ability but by extraordinarily precocious accomplishments in one or more culturally valued domains and fields (Pfeiffer, 2013). Finally, as we mentioned earlier, there are probably a significant number of high-ability children and youth with an admixture of two or more coexisting disorders along with their gifts—for example, the exceptionally bright fourth-grader who also has a moderate to severe bilateral high frequency hearing loss and a social anxiety disorder. We did not focus on this more complex twice exceptional student.

Identification of the twice exceptional student is often a complex and challenging undertaking. Gifted assessment must always consider *both* the type and level of giftedness and the type of disability and degree of impairment (Pfeiffer, 2015a, 2015b). Psychoeducational interventions for the twice exceptional student should take into account social/interpersonal and emotional issues; a student's background, culture, and family; and how to accommodate the student's academic strengths and interests as well as plan to address his or her weaknesses and disability (National Education Association, 2006; Pfeiffer, 2013). It is all too easy, when conducting a psychological assessment, to forget about or minimize the child's unique interests, passions, special skills, and budding gifts when the expectation is to provide reliable diagnostic and prognostic information about the child's deficits and weaknesses (Pfeiffer, 2015a, 2016). This would be a mistake.

Our own experience as academic clinicians has led us to recognize that there is high clinical utility in adopting a positive psychology viewpoint (Pfeiffer, 2016; Seligman, 2011; Seligman, Park, & Peterson, 2005). Educators, psychologists, and parents all benefit when we deliberately and thoughtfully consider *both* the twice exceptional students' specific weaknesses and deficits while at the same time paying attention to their unique assets, level of subjective well-being, engagement, positive emotions, quality of peer and adult relationships, and interests (Pfeiffer, 2016; Suldo, 2016; Suldo, Hearon, & Shaunessy-Dedrick, 2018). The overarching goal in working with the all students, including the twice exceptional—in our opinion—should be to determine how to maximize their optimal academic, social, and emotional functioning.

An interesting possibility, not yet researched, is whether twice exceptional students experience a disproportionately high level of psychological distress because of their dual "differences" from the dominant majority peer culture. Meyer (1995, 2003) developed and empirically tested a minority stress model to help explain the reasons for a higher prevalence of mental health difficulties among sexual minorities. His model describes the interaction between "minority stress processes" and protective factors that moderate positive or negative mental health outcomes for minority persons. We have often wondered, in our clinical work with twice exceptional students, if this minority stress model might operate for some gifted youngsters with coexisting disabilities. Their status as both gifted and presenting with a disability put them at double risk for being viewed by their peers (and teachers and family) as "different."

While many unknowns remain about twice exceptionality, there are enough knowns to suggest this is a diverse population with complex needs that are of growing interest to professionals. To meet this demand, we should continue to dispel myths and misconceptions and train educators and clinicians to provide best-practice interventions. For example, universities should include coursework in gifted and special education for their preservice teachers (Wormald et al., 2015), particularly since educators are often the initial referral point for many gifted programs (Barnard-Brak et al., 2015), and mental health training programs should include high ability as a contextual factor to consider in treatment. Through research, training, and professional development advances we will continue to grow the knowns about our twice exceptional youth well into the future.

## REFERENCES

American Psychiatric Association. (2013). *Diagnostic and statistical manual of mental disorders* (5th ed.). Washington, DC: American Psychiatric Association.

Angold, A., Costello, J., & Erkanli, A. (1999). Comorbidity. *Journal of Child Psychology and Psychiatry*, *40*(1), 57–87.

Antshel, K.M., Faraone, S.V., Maglione, K., Doyle, A. E., Fried, R., Seidman, L. J., & Biederman, J. (2008). Temporal stability of ADHD in the high-IQ population: Results from the MGH longitudinal family studies of ADHD. *Journal of the American Academy of Child and Adolescent Psychiatry 47*, 817–825.

Antshel, K. M., Faraone, S., Stallone, K., Nave, A., Kaufmann, F., Doyle, A., . . . Biederman, J. (2007). Is attention deficit hyper- activity disorder a valid diagnosis in the presence of high IQ? Results from the MGH Longitudinal Family Studies of ADHD. *Journal of Child Psychology and Psychiatry*, *48*, 687–694.

Baldwin, L., Baum, S., Pereles, D., & Hughes, C. (2015). Twice-exceptional learners: The journey toward a shared vision. *Gifted Child Today, 38*(4), 206–214. doi:10.1177/1076217515597277

Barnard-Brak, L., Johnsen, S. K., Hannig, A. P., & Wei, T. (2015). The incidence of potentially gifted students within a special education population. *Roeper Review, 37*(2), 74–83.

Baum, S., & Owen, S. V. (1988). High ability/learning disabled students: How are they different? *Gifted Child Quarterly, 32*(3), 321–326.

Baum, S., & Owen, S. V. (2004). *To be gifted and learning disabled.* Mansfield, CT: Creative Learning Press.

Baum, S., Owen, S. V., & Dixon, J. (1991). *To be gifted and learning disabled: From definition to practical intervention strategies.* Mansfield, CT: Creative Learning Press.

Baum, S. M., Schader, R. M., & Hebert, T. P. (2014). Through a different lens: Reflecting on a strengths-based, talent-focused approach for twice-exceptional learners. *Gifted Child Quarterly, 58*(4), 311–327. doi:10.1177/0016986214547632

Biederman, J., Faraone, S. V., Mick, E., Wozniak, J., Chen, L., Ouellete, C., . . . Lelon, E. (1996). Attention deficit hyperactivity disorder and juvenile mania: An overlooked comorbidity? *Journal of the American Academy of Child and Adolescent Psychiatry, 35*(8), 997–1009.

Borchardt, C. M., & Bernstein, G. A. (1995). Comorbid disorders in hospitalized bipolar adolescents compared with unipolar depressed adolescents. *Child Psychiatry and Human Development, 26*(1), 11–18.

Brody, L. E., & Mills, C. J. (1997). Gifted children with learning disabilities: A review of the issues. *Journal of Learning Disabilities, 30*(3), 282–286.

Burko, J., & Pfeiffer, S. I. (2017). A methodology review of empirical investigations of twice exceptionality: Strengths, weaknesses and future directions. *Roeper Review.* Manuscript submitted for publication.

Bussing, R., Porter, P., Zima, B. T., Mason, D., Garvan, C., & Reid, R. (2012). Academic outcome trajectories of student with ADHD: Does exceptional education status matter? *Journal of Emotional and Behavioral Disorders, 20*, 131–143.

Coleman, M. R. (1992). A comparison of how gifted/LD and average/LD boys cope with school frustration. *Journal for the Education of the Gifted, 15*(3), 239–265.

Crepeau-Hobson, F., & Bianco, M. (2011). Identification of gifted students with learning disabilities in a Response-to-Intervention era. *Psychology in the Schools, 48*, 102–109.

Cross, T. L., & Cross, J. R. (2017). Suicide among students with gifts and talents. In S. I. Pfeiffer, E. Shaunessy-Dedrick, & M. Foley-Nicpon (Eds.), *APA handbook of giftedness and talent* (pp. 601–614). Washington, DC: American Psychological Association.

Cross, T. L., Cassady, J. C., & Miller, K. A. (2006). Suicide ideation and personality characteristics among gifted adolescents. *Gifted Child Quarterly, 50*(4), 295–358.

Elkind, J. (1973). The gifted child with learning disabilities. *Gifted Child Quarterly, 17*(3), 45–47.

Foley-Nicpon, M., Assouline, S. G., & Colangelo, N. (2013). Twice-exceptional learners: Who needs to know what? *Gifted Child Quarterly, 57*(3), 169–180. doi:10.1177/0016986213490021

Foley-Nicpon, M. (2015). The social and emotional development of twice-exceptional children. In M. Neihart, S. I. Pfeiffer, and T. L Cross (Eds.), *Social and emotional development of gifted children: What do we know?* (pp. 103–118). Waco, TX: Prufrock.

Foley-Nicpon, M., Allmon, A., Sieck, B., & Stinson, R. D. (2011). Empirical investigation of twice-exceptionality: Where have we been and where are we going? *Gifted Child Quarterly, 55*(1), 3–17.

Foley-Nicpon, M., Rickels, H., Assouline, S. G. & Richards, A. (2012). Self-esteem and self-concept examination among gifted students with ADHD. *Journal for the Education of the Gifted, 35*, 220–240.

Fortin, M., Soubhi, H., Hudon, C., Bayliss, E. A, & van den Akker, M. (2007). Multimorbidity's many challenges. *British Medical Journal, 334*(7602), 1016–1017.

Gallagher, J. J. (1966). Children with developmental imbalances: A psychoeducational definition. In W. Cruickshank (Ed.), *The teacher of brain-injured children* (pp. 23–43) (Syracuse University Special Education and Rehabilitation Monograph Series 7). Syracuse, NY: Syracuse University Press.

Gijsen, R., Hoeymans, N., Schellevis, F. G., Ruwaard D., Sectarian W. A., & vanden Bos, G. A. (2001). Causes and consequences of comorbidity: A review. *Journal of Clinical Epidemiology, 54*(7), 661–674.

Grizenko, N., Zhang, D. D. Q., Polotskaia, A., & Joober, R. (2012). Efficacy of methylphenidate in ADHD Children across the normal and the gifted intellectual spectrum. *Journal of the Canadian Academy of Child and Adolescent Psychiatry, 21*, 282–288.

Hollingworth, L. (1923). *Special talents and defects: Their significance for education.* Ithaca, NY: Cornell University Library.

Keeley, J. W., Reed, G. M., Roberts, M. C., Evans, S. C., Medina-Mora, M. E., Robles, R. . . . Saxena, S. (2016). Developing a science of clinical utility in diagnostic classification systems field study strategies for ICD-11 mental and behavioral disorders. *American Psychologist, 71*, 3–16.

Kendall, P. C., & Clarkin, J. F. (1992). Introduction to special section: Comorbidity and treatment implications. *Journal of Clinical and Consulting Psychology, 60*(6), 833–834.

Kerby, J. R., & Hennessy, C. H. (2003). Patterns and impact of comorbidity and multimorbidity among community-resident American Indian elders. *The Gerontologist, 43*(5), 649–660.

Lovett, B. J., & Sparks, R. L. (2011). The identification and performance of gifted students with learning disability diagnosis: A quantitative synthesis. *Journal of Learning Disabilities, 46*(4), 304–316. doi:10.1177/0022219411421810

Maker, C. J. (1977). *Providing programs for the gifted handicapped individuals.* Reston, VA: Council for Exceptional Children.

McCallum, R. S., Bell, S. M., Coles, J., Miller, K., Hopkins, M., & Hilton-Prillhart, A. (2013). A model for screening twice-exceptional students (gifted with learning disabilities) within a Response to Intervention paradigm. *Gifted Child Quarterly, 57*, 209–222. doi:10.1177/0016986213500070

Mee Bell, S., Taylor, E. P., McCallum, R. S., Coles, J. T., & Hays, E. (2015). Comparing prospective twice-exceptional students with high-performing peers on high-states tests of achievement. *Journal for the Education of the Gifted, 38*(3), 294–317. doi:10.1177/0162353215592500

Meyer, I. H. (1995). Minority stress and mental health in gay men. *Journal of Health and Social Behavior, 36*(1), 38–56.

Meyer, I. H. (2003). Prejudice, social stress, and mental health in lesbian, gay, and bisexual populations: Conceptual issues and research evidence. *Psychological Bulletin, 129*, 674–697.

Minner, S. (1990). Teacher evaluations of case descriptions of LD gifted children. *Gifted Child Quarterly, 34*(1), 37–39.

Moon, S. M., Zentall, S. S., Grskovic, J. A., Hall, A., & Stormont, M. (2001). Emotional and social characteristics of boys with AD/HD and giftedness: A comparative case study. *Journal for the Education of the Gifted, 24*, 207–247.

National Center for Health Statistics. (2006). Causes of death report. Retrieved from http://www.cdc.gov/ncipc/wisqars

National Education Association. (2006). *The twice-exceptional dilemma*. Washington, DC: Author.

Nardi, R., Scanelli, G., Corrao, S., Iori, I., Mathieu, G., & Amatrian, R. C. (2007). Comorbidity does not reflect complexity in internal medicine patients. *European Journal of Internal Medicine, 18*(5), 359–368.

Neihart, M. (2008). Identifying and providing services to twice exceptional children. In S. I. Pfeiffer (Ed.), *Handbook of giftedness in children* (pp.115–137). New York, NY: Springer.

Neihart, M., Pfeiffer, S. I., & Cross, T. L. (2015). *The social and emotional development of gifted children* (2nd ed.). Waco, TX: Prufrock Press.

Pearce, J. M. S. (2005). Kanner's infantile autism and Asperger's syndrome. *Journal of Neurology, Neurosurgery, & Psychiatry, 76*, 205. doi:10.1136/jnnp.2004.042820.

Pfeiffer, S. I. (2003). Psychological considerations in raising a healthy gifted child. In P. Olszewski-Kubilius, L. Limburg-Weber, & S. I. Pfeiffer (Eds.), *Early gifts: Recognizing and nurturing children's talents* (pp. 173–185). Waco, TX: Prufrock Press.

Pfeiffer, S. I. (2013). *Serving the gifted*. New York, NY: Routledge.

Pfeiffer, S. I. (2015a). *Essentials of gifted assessment*. Hoboken, NJ: Wiley.

Pfeiffer, S. I. (2015b). Gifted students with a coexisting disability: The twice exceptional. *Estudos de Psicolegia, 32*(4), 713–723.

Pfeiffer, S. I. (2016). Success in the classroom and in life: Focusing on strengths of the head and strengths of the heart. *Gifted Education International, 33*, 95–101. doi:10.1177/0261429416640337

Pfeiffer, S. I., & Stocking, V. (2000). Vulnerabilities of academically gifted students. *Special Services in the Schools, 16*(1–2), 83–93.

Reis, S. M., Baum, S. M., & Burke, E. (2014). An operational definition of twice-exceptional learners: Implications and applications. *Gifted Child Quarterly, 58*, 217–230.

Reis, S. M., Neu, T. W., & McGuire, J. M. (1997). Case studies of high-ability students with learning disabilities who have achieved. *Exceptional Children, 63*(4), 463–479.

Rinn, A. N., & Reynolds, M. J. (2012). Overexcitabilities and ADHD in the gifted: An examination. *Roeper Review, 34*, 38–45.

Robertson, S. G., Pfeiffer, S. I., & Taylor, N. (2011). Serving the gifted: A national survey of school psychologists. *Psychology in the Schools, 48*(8), 786–799.

Robinson, A., Shore, B. M., & Enersen, D. L. (2007). *Best practices in gifted education: An evidence-based guide*. Waco, TX: Prufrock Press.

Robinson, N. M. (2002). Introduction. In M. Neihart, S. Reis, N. M. Robinson, & S. Moon. (Eds.), *The social and emotional development of gifted children* (pp. xi–xxiv). Waco, TX: Prufrock Press.

Ruban, L. M., & Reis, S. M. (2005). Identification and assessment of gifted students with learning disabilities. *Gifted Education, 44,* 115–124.

Safford, M. M., Allison, J. J., & Kiefe, C. I. (2007). Patient complexity: More than comorbidity. The Vector Model of Complexity. *Journal of General Internal Medicine, 22*(Suppl. 3), 382–390.

Seligman, M. E. P. (2011). *Flourish: A visionary new understanding of happiness and well-being.* New York, NY: Free Press.

Seligman, M. E. P., Park, N., & Peterson, C. (2005). Positive psychology progress. *American Psychologist, 60,* 410–421.

Suldo, S. M. (2016). *Promoting student happiness. Positive psychology interventions in schools.* New York, NY: Guilford Press.

Suldo, S. M., Hearon, B. V., & Shaunessy-Dedrick, E. (2018). Examining gifted students' mental health through the lens of positive psychology. In S. I. Pfeiffer, Shaunessy-Dedrick, E. & Foley-Nicpon, M. (Eds)., *APA handbook of giftedness and talent* (pp. 433–449). Washington, DC: American Psychological Association. doi: 10.1037/0000038-028.

US Department of Education, National Center for Education Statistics. (2013). *Digest of education statistics, 2012* (NCES 2014-2015). Washington, DC: US Government Printing Office.

van Weel, C., & Schellevis, F. G. (2006). Comorbidity and guidelines: Conflicting interests. *Lancet, 367*(9510), 550–551.

Waldron, K. A., & Saphire, D. G. (1990). An analysis of WISC-R factors for gifted students with learning disabilities. *Journal of Learning Disabilities, 23*(8), 491–498.

Webb, J. T., Amend, E. R., Webb, N. E., Goerss, J., Beljan, P., & Olenchak, F. R. (2005). *Misdiagnosis and dual diagnoses of gifted children and adults: ADHD, bipolar, OCD, Asperger's, depression and other disorders.* Scottsdale, AZ: Great Potential Press.

Weis, R. J. (2014). *Introduction to abnormal child and adolescent psychology* (2nd ed.). Thousand Oaks, CA: SAGE.

Weisz, J. R., & Kazdin, A. E. (2010). *Evidence-based psychotherapies for children and adolescents, second edition.* New York, NY: Guilford Press.

Wormald, C., Rogers, K. B., & Vialle, W. (2015). A case study of giftedness and specific learning disabilities: Bridging the two exceptionalities. *Roeper Review, 37*(3), 124–138. doi:10.1080/02783193.2015.1047547

Vespi, L., & Yewchuk, C. (1992). A phenomenological study of the social/emotional characteristics of gifted learning disabled children. *Journal for the Education of the Gifted, 16*(1), 55–72.

Yewchuk, C., & Lupart, J. L. (1988). Gifted handicapped: A desultory duality. In K. A. Heller, F. J. Mönks, & A. H. Passow (Eds.), *International handbook of research and development of giftedness and talent* (pp. 709–725). London: Pergamon Press.

Zentall, S. S., Moon, S. M., Hall, A. M., & Grskovic, J. A. (2001). Learning and motivational characteristics of boys with AD/HD and/or giftedness. *Exceptional Children, 64,* 499–519.

**PART II**

# Supporting Twice Exceptional Students

6

# How We Can Recognize and Teach Twice- or Multi-Exceptional Students

SUSAN WINEBRENNER

Meet Jason, a complicated sixth-grader who could tell fascinating stories for as long as he could get someone to listen to them. However, when asked to create a written product, his response was always the same. "I actually *can't* write anything down." Sadly, many of his teachers believed he was simply refusing to do his work.

One teacher finally convinced him to write by declaring that she would get into trouble if she could not get him to submit some written products. Jason liked this teacher well enough to say—"Okay, I'll give it a try." The assignment was to create interesting couplets that illustrated conflict, and he complied with:

All day my mother slaves over a hot stove,
While my father slaves over a hot secretary!

The teacher cleverly decided to find voice-to-text technology that would likely lead to less shocking outcomes. Fortunately, she recognized Jason as a student with multiple exceptionalities since there was a noticeable dichotomy between what he could express verbally and what he could not express in writing.

To hold the designation of twice exceptional (2e), one must be gifted in one or more learning areas and also be eligible for special education services. However, the strategies in this chapter may be used with any students who might benefit from them.

Dr. Sidney Parnes, the father of creative problem-solving, taught that we should begin each quest for a solution with these words: "In What Ways Might We?"(IWWMW) to create multiple solutions for perplexing problems. The benefit to this approach is if one solution does not work as expected, others are waiting in line as possible alternatives.

For 2e students, the conundrum is that often neither their areas of high ability *nor* their areas of learning challenge are actually served effectively while they are in school. This is because their "gift" makes their challenges appear less problematic, while their "challenge" makes their advanced potential appear much closer to average.

A system of teaching 2e students is described in this chapter that will help them learn that their intelligence is not being disputed. Their responsibility, working with their teachers, is to continuously search for learning methods that are most likely to lead to academic learning success.

In psychology, a belief system called phenomenology (Husserl, 1963; Kaufer & Chemero, 2015) purports that what people actually see or hear is not guaranteed to be exactly what happened. The deciding factor is the person's *perception* of the event. Therefore, it is essential to clearly communicate that the learning challenges students experience are not due to low intelligence, character weaknesses, or motivation flaws. Instead, we focus on teaching them how to continuously seek alternative learning strategies until the right match is found. Concurrently, teachers learn to use metacognitive coaching techniques in the process so the student may be empowered to become more independently successful over time.

We know strategy choices are very powerful. At many Individualized Education Program meetings, there is almost always one teacher who simply does not recognize the problematic behaviors being described. Their comments might be: "Of course I understand that we are all talking about the same student. But when he is in my class, he is generally engaged and takes an active role in what we are learning, and I have had no trouble with him at all!"

During follow-up visits to some of these teachers' classes, I made these observations:

- Based upon the students' comments to each other, their willingness to help others and even to request help when needed, they demonstrated their understanding that they are not in competition with each other for approval or grades.
- They are highly aware of necessary adjustments regarding environmental, academic, or self-talk changes and make those adjustments as needed.

One of these teachers, Mrs. Z., explained that she had been applying Carol Dweck's notion of "the Power of Yet" through which teachers avoid giving a failing grade in favor of using the comment of "Not Yet" (Dweck, 2014). This simple change communicates that students have the power to positively influence their own achievement. The video also highlights ways to motivate students to focus more on the processes they use than the grade earned by the final product.

When adults "over-help," students may perceive that the teacher actually believes they *are* helpless. The work in the area of attribution theory helps learners and adults acknowledge that welcoming hard work is the most important factor in achieving ongoing learning success, (Krakovsky, 2016).

## THE AMAZING POWER OF SHORT-TERM GOAL-SETTING

When students are not productive, power struggles ensue. Twice exceptional learners have heard all the admonitions regarding how to become more successful with school tasks. These include, "It is clear to me that you are not working hard enough. "You could do much better if you only applied yourself!" Judging from your success in other subject areas, you should be able to make better choices about how be successful in this subject." Most teachers know that those words do not move students to work harder.

Our goal with all our students should be to convince them they need your help less as we coach them into self-talk and goal setting behaviors that, over time, do make them believe they are more competent than they may have thought. Dr. Steven Landfried's work helps educator and parents avoid creating "learned helplessness." He believes that a highly significant factor in student's becoming more successfully independent is the degree to which they believe they are in charge of their own learning outcomes (Landfried, 2014).

Successful students attribute their success to having exerted enough *effort* with a task. Unsuccessful students perceive they lack the *ability* to succeed and therefore expect to fail. They do not even see the connection between their own efforts and their learning outcomes. They have learned to be helpless by observing that if they look or sound pathetic enough, some adult will come to the rescue.

The Goal-Setting Log (see later in this chapter) translates attribution theory into personal academic situations. It empowers students to believe they are actually in control of their learning experiences by being in charge of identifying their own short-term goals of what they can accomplish in a particular subject area in designated time period. When *adults* suggest that students reduce the amount of work they should do, we inadvertently set low expectations so the student can experience "contrived success." However, when we transfer the goal-setting action to the control of the students, we can observe some very interesting student behaviors.

- Goals set by students for themselves are often higher than those set by their teachers.
- Students can learn how to adjust their own goals from one learning experience to the next, based upon their levels of successful outcomes.
- When a goal is not met, students realize that the world does not end. Instead, they experience a new way to define success as the ability to set and accomplish realistic, short-term goals and repeat that process until their larger task is completed.

## Using the Goal-Setting Log

Each day, in every instructional period, nonproductive students set goals using two fractions. The denominator represents the assigned amount for the task, set by the teacher. The student sets the numerator, which represents how many sentences, problems, or ideas they predict they can successfully create in the available time. When the time is up, students record on a second fraction's numerator, their actual accomplishment in the allotted time. The sample Goal-Setting Log (Figure 6.1) illustrates one particular student's data recording in a self-contained class over two instructional periods in one day. When students change classes, they keep separate logs for each class.

Inability to reach the goal only requires the student to decide if and how to revise it. Teachers and parents need to be careful not to instantly expect higher goals as soon as a particular goal has been met one time. That may lead to a "fear of success" in which students resist higher goals because of the pain of experiencing instantly higher expectations.

| Task | Monday | Tuesday | Wednesday | Thursday | Friday |
|---|---|---|---|---|---|
| **Math Practice** | | | | | |
| Goal | 2/20 | 2/20 | 3/20 | 3/20 | 4/20 |
| Actual | 1/20 | 2/20 | 3/20 | 4/20 | 4/20 |
| **Log I Entries** | | | | | |
| Goal | 3/10 | no log | 3/10 | no log | 3/10 |
| Actual | 2/10 | no log | 2/10 | no log | 3/10 |

**Figure 6.1** Goal-Setting Log.

| | Monday | Tuesday | Wednesday | Thursday |
|---|---|---|---|---|
| Journal Writing | 3/15 | 3/15 | 3/15 | 3/15 |
| # of sentences | 2/15 | 2/15 | 3/15 | 4/15 |
| Math Practice | 2/8 | 2/8 | 3/8 | 3/8 |
| # of problems | 1/8 | 2/8 | 3/8 | 4/8 |
| Descriptive | 2/15 | 3/15 | 4/15 | 4/15 |
| Paragraph Sentences | 2/15 | 3/15 | 3/15 | 4/15 |

Adapted from Winebrenner. S., & Brulles, D. (2012). *Teaching gifted kids in today's classroom*. Minneapolis, MN: Free Spirit Publishing, pp. 19–21.

Some teachers worry that it might not be fair to other students if some students can get a grade without creating the same product or amount as their classmates. Dr. Richard Louie, a specialist in helping adults understand students with significant learning challenges, says: "Fairness does *not* mean giving all students the same work. Fairness *does* mean giving each student the work they need to consistently move forward in their learning" (LaVoie, 2004).

## THE POWER OF ADULT LANGUAGE

The words we use with our students are extremely powerful. It is essential to avoid any language that might create fear or shame for any student. Instead, we can explain how they may have been "less lucky" than successful students because they may have consistently experienced mismatches between the ways in which their brain operates most comfortably and the methods used by most of their teachers.

### Guidelines Summary: In What Ways Might We Facilitate Learning Success for 2e Students?

- Students who fail to become successful learners have rarely been taught how to use learning methods that match the way their brains could more easily understand the required standards.
- Successful students enjoy a match between the way they learn best and the ways in which most teachers teach.
- When students are not learning the way they are being taught, the teacher must try different methods that are more likely to lead that student to learning success.
- Teachers must be allowed to change strategies as evidence mounts that a specific strategy is not leading to desired outcomes.
- Most teachers would gladly "do the right thing" if they only knew what that was.
- In their areas of learning strength, 2e students who will not do "their work" must be given full credit for standards they have already mastered *rather than having to "relearn" this year's content.* (See the section on compacting)

## LEARNING ENVIRONMENT PREFERENCES

Figure 6.2 shows students' learning environment preferences.

The list on the left describes learning characteristics of students who are highly likely to enjoy success in school. Their most comfortable way taking in information is auditory—by listening and talking. Their favored thinking style is analytic

| ANALYTIC THINKERS | GLOBAL THINKERS |
|---|---|
| Bright Light | Low light |
| Silence for concentrating | Silence is distracting; needs background sound |
| Warmer room temperatures | Cooler room temperatures |
| Sitting still is comfortable | Needs more movement |
| Goes to bed early; eats good breakfast | Night owl; never eats breakfast |
| Generally enjoys reading | Reads only high-interest items |
| Consults time frequently | Unaware of current time |
| Mostly neat and well-organized | Clothes don't match; can't find his stuff |
| Can organize ideas sequentially | Requires hands-on activities to do sequence |

**Figure 6.2** Learning Environment Preferences.
Adapted from full chart, Winebrenner. S. & Kiss, L. (2014). *Teaching kids with learning difficulties in today's classroom*. Minneapolis, MN: Free Spirit Publishing, pp. 54–56.

since they enjoy figuring out the whole from the individual parts. Most teachers talk quite a bit and appreciate students who can figure things out, so students with similar learning preferences do very well in those classes. Most students with learning difficulties prefer visual, tactile, and/or kinesthetic input. When it is not readily available, frustration and school failures result.

The descriptors on the right side of the chart provide the pathways on which global learners may depend. These students *must always be able to refer to* "the whole" while making sense of how the parts fit together. They may actually encounter scary feelings of fear, inadequacy, or embarrassment when the predominant way in which their teachers communicate is by talking to them or asking them to listen to or read sources that require fluent reading skills.

When the conditions of a preferred learning environment are accommodated, formerly unsuccessful students can enjoy dramatic positive changes in their levels of success. In addition, global learners are often more comfortable with certain technologies than analytic students so we can use that information in our planning and teaching.

## WHOLISTIC ACRONYM

The teaching practices in the acronym "WHOLISTIC" describe optimum conditions that facilitate more consistent learning success for global thinkers, Each letter of the acronym describes a different element that helps us provide a much better chance for students with learning difficulties to demonstrate they can be successful with required learning tasks. Over time, most teachers can become more successful at creating learning tasks that appeal to both analytic and global learners.

*Whole* to parts means we always make available a model of the "whole" before expecting global thinkers to make sense of its specified parts. We can do this by "surveying" the entire content before actually starting instruction or by using videos and/or graphic organizers that makes the material more visual. Traditional methods of teaching usually teach content section by section. That creates a distinct disadvantage for the global learner, who often becomes confused when continuous visual access to the "whole" is not possible.

*Hands-on learning* activities provide manipulatives and technologies throughout each learning experience that are usually much easier than printed text for 2e students to understand and use successfully.

*Organize information visually* uses mind-maps and graphic organizers to allow students to keep in their mind's eye how parts of the whole are related to each other. Struggling readers are always grateful when teachers supplement any lectured information with these visual learning aids. Students might enjoy other helpful websites such as Khan Academy or YouTube. For advanced learners, check out "The Mathologer' and the work of Presh Talwalkar, as well as similar sites that cause global thinkers to respond with a comment such as, "Oh, *now* I see what you are talking about."

*Learning modality focus* shows students that their special learning needs are being accommodated when teachers proactively make available user-friendly methods and materials to all students. That attention enhances the self-respect of students who have been regularly unsuccessful in school.

*Immerse the senses* reminds us to consistently offer learning experiences that can reinforce learning by appealing to several senses simultaneously. For example, finger multiplication (Winebrenner & Kiss, 2014, pp. 162–163; Townsley, 2010) is one useful method of learning number facts for students who struggle to master that standard. Students of all ages learn how to use their fingers to show mastery of the number facts by using their visual, tactile, and kinesthetic senses without relying at all on memory. In less than a week, most students become fluent on all the multiplication number facts from 6 to 20. Other students use jump ropes or even exercise bikes as they chant rhymes they have learned to remember designated content using kinesthetic reinforcement.

Dr. Marie Carbo's methods (2007) offer significant gains in reading fluency and comprehension over a very short time as students use all their senses simultaneously to become dramatically more accurate in their efforts to comprehend not only the story's meaning, but its application to their own life experiences.

*Seek patterns and connections* applies the work on Advance Organizers by David Ausubel that describes the power of helping the brain connect new learning to something it already knows. Keep the growing graphic visually accessible to students at all times during the learning process (in Curran, J., Takata, S. et al., [September, 2003]).

*Technology assistance:* Twenty-first-century educators at all grade levels and with almost all content have learned to appreciate the assistance of various types of technology. These devices are increasingly likely to be present in almost all students' homes for added convenience and support.

*Integrate skills into content* moves students beyond learning facts to using that data in more than one learning context. Global learners are much better able to

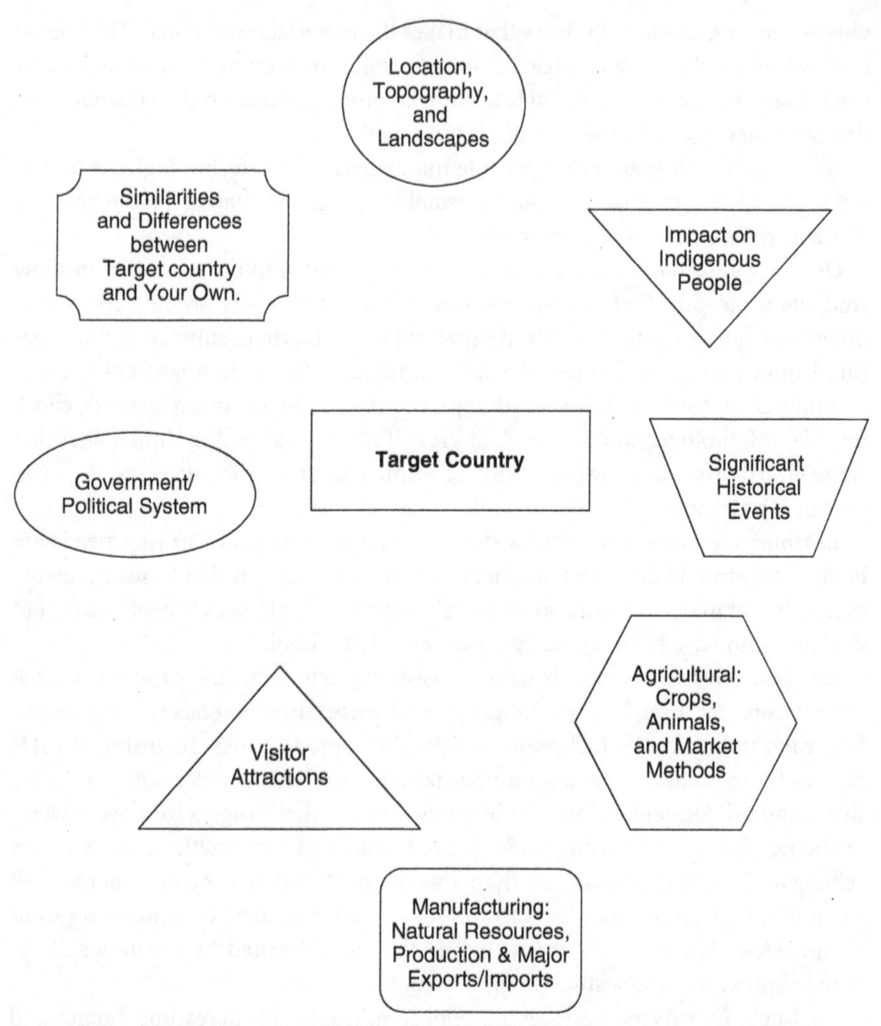


**Figure 6.3** Content Organization Chart (COC) for Study of any Countries, States, or Provinces.

remember required content once the visual and experiential connections have been made. So much of standards-based curricula emphasize problem-solving and learning through simulations. These and other active learning experiences dramatically improve students' abilities to remember content longer and understand the "glue" that holds the various elements together, especially if laughter and other emotional ties are present.

*Concrete to abstract* thinking encourages teachers to use whatever it takes ensure that required content makes good sense to students. Although "hands-on-learning" was previously relegated to elementary students, many content specialists in the secondary grades have shown their willingness to use these teaching tools that allow new concepts to be better understood. They are also helpful in showing the connections between various subject areas and between subjects and the real world. Social Studies School Service catalogs, virtual reality tours of museums and other locations, and interaction with primary documents (e.g., Jackdaw.com) also improve student understanding of abstract ideas.

The COC in Figure 6.3 includes all of the guidelines in the WHOLISTIC acronym (Winebrenner & Kiss, 2014, pp. 150–151) and illustrates how to begin an ongoing study of various world countries with some country students are already familiar with. This allows learners to concentrate on learning to use the method without having to simultaneously learn completely *new material.* Student pairs work together to complete their individual charts. The teacher demonstrates on a large version of the chart how to move clockwise from one category to another. For each category, partners use think–pair–share to find details and enter three to five phrases on "spokes" connected to the corresponding figure. The teacher hears feedback from the pairs and illustrates pertinent details on a large chart all students can see. Partners are free to add new details to their own chart as well as eliminate incorrect information.

The next country chosen (exemplar) should be one for which most students have very little information. Reinforce the idea that all the countries that will be studied will contain the same categories as were demonstrated for the first country.

As other exemplars are studied, some pairs will be able to break away from the group instruction to complete a new COC independently. Critical thinking activities may be added, such as comparing and contrasting similar categories for two or more countries.

Other examples of topics for ongoing COCs are

- Ancient civilizations
- Tall tales or folk tales
- Wars in which the us has participated
- Political candidates for a particular office
- Energy sources
- Severe weather events
- News articles about a target topic

The difference between the COC and other graphic organizers is that once the COC categories are established, they remain the same for all related exemplars. This empowers global learners to actually "see" these similarities sooner so they become able to predict them for subsequent topics.

Independent studies may be undertaken by pairs of students who appear to truly understand a particular COC. At some point, these pairs may conduct their research about a unique exemplar not being studied by the rest of the class. Sharing what they have learned with the entire class enriches the COC experience for all students.

Teachers sometimes allow students who wish to use their visual memory to first fill in a blank version of the current COC in class *before* an assessment to refresh their visual memories about the content they have learned. This may actually give them a slight advantage in content retention.

## ACCOMMODATING THE "GIFTED" LEARNING NEEDS OF TWICE EXCEPTIONAL STUDENTS

To be totally sensitive to the learning needs of all gifted students, we must be attentive to our own adult attitudes about being trapped in situations in which we feel our learning time is being wasted. Imagine that you have arrived at a professional development experience, eager to learn something new about the designated topic. With angst, you soon discover that the entire day may be a waste of your time as you are already familiar with much of the content. Many of you would do anything necessary to leave the meeting. Because you are adults, you may actually be allowed to do so.

The learning preferences of gifted students of all ages are amazingly similar to those of educated adults. They often feel "trapped" in a particular learning situation, without any hope of relief. They are simply not allowed to leave. That's when some of them may turn to mischief.

Gifted or advanced learners generally have two characteristics that educators must recognize and serve in school. First, they tend to learn new material very quickly. Sometimes, they can even understand content designed for older students, since their learning capacities in their areas of strength exceed those for typical learners their own age. Second, they have the "annoying" capacity to remember seemingly *forever* everything they have ever learned once. By those very descriptors, *grade-level standards cannot possibly provide a challenging learning opportunity for these students* when their teachers assume that all the content is new for all the students in a particular grade. Students may express their great impatience and resistance with outbursts such as "Why do we have to do this?" "This is boring" or "We had this last year!"

This usually creates power struggles in which the teacher tries to convince both the students and their parents that since what is being taught is required to be learned by all students of a certain age, all students must do the assigned work. But the irony is, some of these 2e students have already mastered those grade-level standards in their areas of learning strength.

Therefore, the first step teachers must take with gifted students of all ages and learning characteristics is to offer consistent opportunities to "compact" the curriculum by utilizing preassessment methods to allow advanced learners to spend no school time on topics they have already mastered (Winebrenner & Brulles, 2012).

This generous opportunity allows advanced learners to focus on topics related to the standards but that "extend" required content into highly interesting research topics. Twice- or multi-exceptional students must be allowed access to the same compacting opportunities as their gifted classmates who are not 2e (Winebrenner & Brulles, 2012, p. 38). For their independent research work, they receive equivalent credit for each class period during which they follow these essential working conditions:

- Don't bother anyone (that includes the teacher if he or she is doing direct instruction).
- Don't call attention to yourself or the fact that you are allowed to choose different work.
- Work on your chosen extension activity or accelerated content during all the available class time as designated by your teacher.
- Willingly and courteously participate in whole-class activities as indicated.
- Keep records of your own extension work in the manner your teacher describes.

## THE ADVANCED LEARNING NEEDS OF TWICE-/MULTI-EXCEPTIONAL STUDENTS

Gifted students are often in power struggles at school because it is perceived by educators that they will not do "their work." That is a faulty belief, as most nonproductive gifted students would be happy to be allowed to do "their work" (content that is unfamiliar to them) instead of required grade-level standards, which are often not at all challenging. What is challenging may be their inadequate executive functioning skills, for which we should offer the scaffolding they need without taking away the actual opportunity to participate in differentiated learning tasks.

**Caution:** Teachers may find themselves tempted to take learning time away from students in their areas of strength in order to provide more learning time in subject areas that appear more challenging. This is not an effective practice for several reasons:

1. When students are shown that there are learning paths more likely to lead to learning success, their areas of weakness may become less apparent.
2. When teachers use more proactive language and pedagogy and demonstrate their willingness to continue to search with the student for more successful learning methods, both groups may be surprised at the noticeable improvement demonstrated by formerly unsuccessful students. To quote Dr. Kenneth Dunn, "If students are not learning (i.e., making forward progress from their entry level) the way we are teaching them, we must teach them the way they learn" (K. Dunne, personal communication, 1994).

### Specific Compacting Strategies

The work that we plan for our students is really *our* work. It does not become *their* work until it represents true learning for them. It is a two part process—and each part is critical.

"Curriculum compacting" is the first absolutely necessary step in garnering students' support for these advanced learning options. It is very difficult to convince a really smart person of any age that doing more of anything than is absolutely necessary is an idea they should embrace.

Compacting was created first by Dr. Joseph Renzulli (Renzulli & Reis, 2014). Curriculum compacting operates like a trash compactor on a garbage truck. As the garbage is dumped from scores of containers, the truck performs a process called "compacting" by compressing the garbage into a smaller space, so new space may be created for more garbage. In the classroom, compacting allows advanced learners to document which required standards they have already mastered *before that content is actually directly taught*. However, once that mastery is documented, students need access to more challenging differentiated activities. To make these accessible for 2e learners, we must provide alternative experiences that appeal to students' visual, tactile, and/or kinesthetic learning strengths. By doing this, we can make advanced learning activities accessible to more students, including those with learning difficulties.

See the previous section on the WHOLISTIC acronym, which will help with scaffolding efforts.

## Guidelines for Fair and Effective Compacting

Compacting opportunities should be made available to all students who want to try them, and who agree to follow the required working conditions. We should not choose only students who have formerly been identified as gifted or advanced learners. Rather we explain these opportunities to all of the students. Sometimes, a 2e student whose advanced learning capacity has never been noticed or served will rise to the occasion.

In all compacting options, teachers should proactively

- Know which standards will be addressed.
- Locate or create two to three suggested extension activities that incorporate higher level thinking from any critical thinking model (Brulles, Brown, & Winebrenner, 2016).
- Make sure students are aware of the prerequisite skills or knowledge they should have to make compacting an appropriate choice for them.
- Address student suggestions for alternative extensions they would like to do instead.

## Voluntary Pretests

For pretestable content that students have probably learned earlier, offer one or more of these three options

1. *Most difficult first:* After briefly teaching upcoming skill content, have students begin their homework in class. Identify four to five problems that are the most difficult part of the entire assignment. Invite all students who want to try the most difficult to do so, knowing they have to finish those four or five, with no more than one wrong, in 15 minutes or less. Those who do that are done practicing for the day and go on to extension activities. Those who get more than one wrong are told they need more practice and that they should stay with the direct instruction group for the rest of the class period as they need more practice.
2. *Mastery of one week's work:* Students are invited to look at the week's work and those who want to take the end of the week's assessment on the first day of the week are invited to do so. Those scoring 85% or higher can work on extension activities instead of the rest of the week's work.
3. *Learning contract for one entire chapter:* Students examine the chapter content for two minutes. Those who wish to demonstrate mastery at 85% or higher of the entire chapter take a chapter assessment that day. Those who score 85% or higher receive a learning contract for the entire chapter and are expected to attend direct instruction only when concepts they missed are being taught. On other days they work on extension activities.

## Compacting When Content Is New for Students

1. Pretesting of new content invites "cramming," which is not recommended. Instead, for unfamiliar content, we "compact" the *amount of time* advanced learners need to document mastery of required standards without actually doing the related work. Students who can do this take the same required assessments, at the same time, as their classmates. However, they work on extension projects they have chosen during all time teachers make available. Since the teachers have dated evidence of these students' mastery of the required standards, students use the time they "buy back" from not having to actually do the daily work (Renzulli & Reis, 2014). Beyond documenting their content mastery, their only responsibilities are to experience the same assessments at the same time as their classmates, keep a Daily Log of their extension work, and follow the essential working conditions listed earlier. The time they save by not doing the daily work is spent working on their extension activities.
2. Many other extension options are available online or from other sources (Brulles et al., 2016).
3. Students who work on extensions must also follow all the essential working rules, so take the time to explain and clarify them carefully, including details about the content and format. Of course, extension

options may be made available to other students in ways that seem manageable.
4. Students who demonstrate mastery of required standards *before* any direct instruction are allowed to work on extension activities or ongoing research as long as they keep a Daily Log of their extension work.

### Daily Log of Project/Extension Work

All project/extension work is recorded daily on the Daily Log.

> Students who don't follow the established working conditions or who fail to document mastery of standards at assessment times leave their independent study and return to the direct instruction group for the rest of that designated unit. (Winebrenner & Brulles, 2012, pp. 89–92)

## IN WHAT WAY MIGHT WE MAKE APPROPRIATE ACCOMMODATIONS MORE AVAILABLE TO 2E STUDENTS WHO NEED THEM?

One of the practices described in *The Cluster Grouping Handbook* (Winebrenner & Brulles, 2010) shows how to include twice exceptional students in the same classroom that contains a cluster of identified gifted students. The teacher of that group is expected to have received gifted education training, including knowledge about how to recognize and accommodate the exceptional learning needs of twice-/multi-exceptional students. If your school is considering implementing a cluster grouping program, be certain the chosen program includes proper classroom placement to enfranchise the gifted qualities of 2e learners.

## CONCLUSION

The strategies in this chapter, although targeted for 2e students, should be available to all students who might benefit from them. The more accurately parents and teachers can diagnose the exact nature of any learning or behavior challenge, the more likely it is that mutually satisfying solutions will be found. Students must be treated as partners in our ongoing search for the most effective methods for creating consistent success for them in learning and productivity.

## REFERENCES

Ausubel, D. P. (2000). *The acquisition and retention of knowledge: A cognitive view.* Boston, MA: Kluwer Academic.

Brulles, D., Brown, K., & Winebrenner, S. (2016). *Differentiating content for all learners.* Waco, TX: Prufrock Press.

Carbo, M. (2007). *Becoming a great teacher of reading: Achieving highly rapid reading gains with powerful, differentiated strategies.* Thousand Oaks, CA Corwin Press.

Curran, J., Takata, S., et al. (2003, September 24). Ausubel's Advance Organizers. In *Learning Theory*, California State University.

Dweck, C. (caroldweck). (2014, September 14). The power of yet. [Video file]. Retrieved from https://youtu.be/J-swZaKN2Ic

Husserl, E. (1963). *The idea of phenomenology.* New York, NY: Free Press of Glencoe.

Kaufer, S., & Chemero., A. (2015). *Phenomenology: An Introduction.* Cambridge: Polity Press.

Krakovsky, M. (2016, November–December). When success sours. *Stanford Alumni Magazine.*

Landfried, S. (2014). [Chart on avoiding giving too much help to students]. In S. Winebrenner & L. Kiss (Eds.), *Teaching students with learning difficulties in today's classroom* (3rd ed., pp. 37–39). Minneapolis, MN: Free Spirit Publishing.

LaVoie, R. (2004). *How difficult can this be? The F.A.T. City video.* Retrieved from www.ricklavoie.com

Renzulli, J:, & Reis, S. (2014). *The schoolwide enrichment model: A how-to guide for talent development* (3rd ed.). Waco, TX: Prufrock Press.

Townsley, M. B. (2010, July 28) [YouTube demonstration for finger multiplication]. [Video file]. Retrieved from https:/www.youtube.com.

Winebrenner, S., & Brulles, D. (2010). *The cluster grouping handbook.* Minneapolis, MN: Free Spirit Publishing.

Winebrenner, S., & Brulles, D. (2012). *Teaching Gifted Kids in Today's Classroom.* Minneapolis, MN: Free Spirit Publishing.

Winebrenner, S., & Kiss, L. (2014). *Teaching students with learning difficulties in today's classroom.* Minneapolis, MN: Free Spirit Publishing.

7

# Twice Exceptionality and Social-Emotional Development

## *One Label, Many Facets*

JUDY GALBRAITH

> Having a special brain [is] like having a Great Dane and a Chihuahua. You may have all these ideas about how to raise a Great Dane, but if you get a Chihuahua, you're going to have to adjust your strategies a bit. There are so many people out there trying to raise Chihuahuas like Great Danes.
>
> —Chesner, 2012, p. 32

When I was an undergraduate in the mid-1970s studying to be a teacher, not one professor mentioned the label "gifted" or discussed what should be done on behalf of students with advanced learning abilities. These are students who, for example, learn quickly compared to same-age peers, are curious, have keen intelligence and demonstrate achievement in various domains, and are sensitive to the world around them. Although I was required to take one course related to learning disabilities (I prefer to call them learning *differences*) and one educational psychology course, these hardly prepared me for the challenges I faced once I had my own students. I was not unlike most of my colleagues, who also had very little training in terms of meeting a broad range of educational and behavioral needs. Although we all cared deeply about young people, it was a rare educator who fully grasped the value and importance of addressing children's social-emotional needs. What I learned early on in my teaching career, and current research soundly supports, is that when students' social-emotional needs are met, success in school and in life follows. This is true regardless of a student's ability levels or special needs.

A meta-analysis of 213 studies involving more than 270,000 students showed that the students who participated in evidence-based social-emotional and learning (SEL) programs had an 11 percentile point gain in academic achievement compared to students who did not participate in SEL programs. Students participating in SEL programs also showed improved classroom behavior, an increased ability to manage stress and depression, and better attitudes about themselves, others, and school (Durlak, Weissberg, Dymnicki, Taylor, & Schellinger, 2011, p. 405).

In my first year of teaching, I had six very bright sixth-graders in my classroom who completed work significantly faster and at a higher level of quality and accuracy than their peers. I felt strongly that these students were getting short-changed in school. This is partly what led me to specialize in gifted education. I also had several students with behavior challenges and learning differences, which often hindered their success in school. After several months, and as I came to know my students better, I realized that the social-emotional needs of these two groups of students were very similar and merited my attention. These needs, and the frustrations felt when these needs were not being met, were also cited in the results of surveys I have conducted with gifted children and teens over the past 30 years (Galbraith, 2009). The issues and concerns expressed by gifted students included

- Feeling frustrated with the lack of educational challenge or with the inability to keep up with peers who seem to learn more easily, even though the students sensed it was not because they were not smart
- Having low self-confidence due to social ostracism, name-calling, or a lack of self-awareness
- Feeling misunderstood by peers, educators, and parents
- Feeling that their interests, and the ways in which they learn best, are largely ignored
- Fearing people will think less of them if they make mistakes or try something new with less than stellar results

These social-emotional needs are addressed as part of the "Gifted Education Programming Standards" from the National Association for Gifted Children (see nagc.org/resources-publications/resources/national-standards-gifted-and-talented-education).

For gifted students to have their SEL needs met, they need a curriculum that accommodates their advanced abilities, alongside intentional SEL support. However, some gifted students have multiple special needs that may seem to contradict one another: they may be gifted and they may also have a learning difference such as attention deficit hyperactivity disorder or dyslexia. The giftedness of these twice exceptional (2e) students might be overlooked due to their learning challenges.

Although the recognition of 2e is relatively new, there have always been students with multiple areas of exceptionality. Publications such as *Gifted Child Today* have brought 2e issues to our attention (*Gifted Child Today*, 2015), as have newsletters such as *2e: Twice Exceptional Newsletter* (2enewsletter.com). However, given the lack of funding and mandates to support gifted education, and the fact that the opposite is true for special needs education, I believe kids' special needs exceptionalities have garnered, and will continue to garner, more attention than their gifts and talents have. We may unintentionally be focusing too much on students' disabilities and not also addressing their gifts and talents. Those of us who embrace this challenge need to continue to provide information, solutions, and professional development to educators and parents about 2e students' needs. We need to be laser focused on young people's strengths, not just their disabilities (i.e., learning differences), so that their gifts and talents are not masked or overshadowed by their challenges.

It is essential to address these SEL issues if we are going to help 2e students realize their potential. And, more importantly, addressing these needs may help these young people have more happiness in life.

According to Dr. Emma Seppälä (2016), science director of Stanford University's Center for Compassion and Altruism Research and Education,

> The great myth overarching all the other myths of success is that we have to sacrifice happiness in the short term to be successful and fulfilled in the long term. . . . Decades of research have shown that happiness is not the *outcome* of success but rather its *precursor*. (pp. 6–7)

If adding SEL to the curriculum feels overwhelming, educators should understand that social-emotional education is already happening in their schools whether they are aware of it or not. It is part of how educators address students, whether directly or indirectly; it is part of the climate that staff and educators establish for their classrooms and school; and it is part of how students are taught (or not taught) to get along with other students and staff. These daily interactions can send positive or negative messages to students about themselves and others. It is crucial, first and foremost, that a supportive school environment is created and sustained. This support comes from truly liking and respecting all students—including students who are gifted or have learning differences, or both. These students are not necessarily the easiest ones to work with. In fact, students who are the most challenging and put us out of our comfort zone are perhaps the ones who need us the most.

When working with gifted students, it is generally most effective for educators to see themselves as facilitators of learning rather than being "knowledge disseminators." In my work with gifted kids, I found that some of them were much more advanced in certain subjects than I was. It would have been demoralizing to them if I had felt threatened or inadequate because of that. In working with students identified with learning differences, it was best for me to be flexible and to learn as much as I could from specialists about how to teach and support them. This chapter presents recommendations for addressing and meeting each of the five social-emotional issues and concerns of students listed earlier. Of course, this list does not represent the *whole*-child needs of 2e students, but it does include key aspects of their experiences year to year.

## STRATEGIES FOR HELPING 2E STUDENTS DEAL WITH SEL CHALLENGES

1. When students feel frustrated with the lack of educational challenge or with the inability to keep up with peers who seem to learn more easily

> Self-advocating, taught at an early age, is a worthwhile lifelong strategy. Perhaps the core prevalent concern is educating parents/caregivers of children who are twice exceptional with the knowledge of the exceptionality, potential needs of the child, and how to advocate for the child (G. Graiewski-Moore, personal communication, September 2016).

Students benefit enormously when they learn how to be assertive and can respectfully and reasonably communicate what is going on (whether they are being underchallenged or struggling to learn), how they feel about something (if it makes them feel frustrated or demoralized), and what they would prefer to be different ("I'd like to test out of what I already know, so I can move on to more challenging projects," or "I need a study buddy to help me with math").

- Teaching 2e students how to advocate for themselves—with teachers and with others—is essential. Even though their requests may not always be granted, if students do not ask, they will never know what could have changed or improved. Even if a student hears "no," it can still be empowering because they are sticking up for themselves. They are being self-advocates and will at least know that they tried.
- Teachers can help students practice self-advocacy and assertiveness through role-playing and modeling this behavior. They can also serve as a resource by being knowledgeable about what the school and/or district can offer 2e students.

> The movement schools are making toward "personalized learning"[1] will benefit 2e students. It will encourage teachers to provide all students, including those who are twice exceptional, with classroom activities and outside assignments that are tailored to the needs and preferences of the individual student. If this is happening for all students, then 2e students will not feel like they are getting special treatment. They will be appropriately challenged just like their peers (M. Catucci, personal communication, September 2016).

1. See Hanover Research's report *Best Practices in Personalized Learning Environments (Grades 4–9)* (http://www.hanoverresearch.com/media/Best-Practices-in-Personalized-Learning-Environments.pdf) for more information on this trend.

- Talk with students about expectations—their own and those of people around them—for school and learning. Ask students which expectations they feel are realistic, unrealistic, humane, or uncaring and which expectations feel encouraging or discouraging. Talk about how students can temper expectations to keep feelings of discouragement or frustration in check. Ask students, "What can I do to help?" Then follow through, and let students know your plan of action.

2. When students have low self-confidence due to social ostracism, name-calling, or lack of self-awareness

When we talk about diversity, we are referring to many kinds of differences including race, religion, sexual orientation, gender and gender expression, mental or physical abilities, and so on. The more students learn to respect differences, and not to engage in bias-based behaviors such as bullying, name-calling, or social ostracism, the more positive the school climate will be and the less likely students will be to have chronic low self-confidence. Teachers can set the tone for the classroom environment.

- Educators need to display a positive view of diversity ("diversity makes life more interesting") and provide classroom resources from diverse sources and perspectives.
- Educators need to make it a point to learn, with students, about differences that the class does not know much about. This includes learning about 2e students and discussing varying learning differences, learning styles, and the many ways in which people are smart.

Schools with the No Place for Hate Program work hard to help celebrate talents and exceptionalities educating the school population, celebrating the students, and sharing their talents. When students learn that being different is okay, then the stigma drops, and the students who are 2e are then accepted into the general population and even looked to for assistance from others rather than being shunned. 2e is something to celebrate, not to hide or attack (B. Evans, personal communication, September 23, 2016).

- Educators can conduct class activities, such as using scenarios, to show the ways in which stereotypes are based on false assumptions.
- When teachers witness name-calling, social ostracism, or bullying, they should intervene *every* time. "It's widely known that students, rightly, feel angry and helpless when schools ignore bullying. Students are more likely to speak up for their peers when they see adults intervene as well" (Isaacs & Novick, 2011).

3. When students feel misunderstood by peers, educators, and parents
   - Educators can share this quote from 17-year-old Jennifer with students: "I can go slow if I want, fast if I'm so inclined, or skip right to the end and work backward sometimes, too. A perfect day is where I am free to think flexibly and act at my own pace. Can you even do this in school?" (Galbraith & Delisle, 2015, p. 138). Ask students to discuss or journal about how this quote relates to their thoughts about "a perfect day at school." How do students' abilities, and the rate and way in which they learn, leave them at risk for being misunderstood? What can they do and say so people are more likely to "get" them? In what situations does it not matter? Why or why not?
   - Educators need to be active listeners. Some students who feel very alone may not bring it to anyone's attention for all kinds of reasons. Ask 2e students questions in a group setting so they can hear what are likely to be similar concerns and experiences of their peers. Learning that they are not the only ones who experience feeling misunderstood can go a long way toward helping 2e students feel less different and less alone. Students can also brainstorm ways to talk about who they are and what they need from educators, peers, and parents.
4. When students feel that their interests, and the ways in which they learn best, are largely ignored
   - Educators can have students complete interest and learning style surveys, which offer a great opportunity for students to identify valuable information about themselves. While it is rare that educators can offer completely individualized education plans for 2e students, educators can use the survey results to provide assignments that use individual pacing. Educators can also use survey information to offer choices to students that include topics that interest them, different types of products to be produced, and interactions with teachers that support students' strengths, not just their weaknesses.

> Seeing the whole child and nurturing students' academic gifts while also supporting their areas of needs is one of the biggest challenges in working with students who are twice exceptional. Knowing that they need to be challenged and pushed while also given scaffolding to be successful is a hard juggle for teachers. You cannot overlook either side of the spectrum or you risk losing that balance (E. Wegener, personal communication, September 26, 2016).

   - Educators can use different student pairings or groupings for certain activities to challenge and support students. While focusing on their areas of strength, 2e students benefit from being with others who are also strong in that subject or topic. When working on subjects in which they are struggling or working below grade level, 2e students benefit by being paired with students who are naturally helpful and enjoy mentoring peers.

5. When students fear people will think less of them if they make mistakes or try something new with less than stellar results
   - To support and promote creativity, innovation, and risk-taking, educators must create an environment where trying new things and making mistakes is okay—even desirable. Students who are fearful of mistakes and new things are at risk for undue stress, anxiety, and underperforming. Educators can model healthy risk-taking by avoiding pejorative language about mistakes ("How could I be so stupid?" "What on earth was I thinking?"). Rather, students feel supported when people talk about what was learned by trying something new, even if the outcome was not as hoped or expected. Educators can offer praise for efforts that were outside of students' comfort zones ("Wow, you really showed courage and persistence when you tackled that project," "I know you'd hoped for a better score, but I also know you worked really hard and this particular part of your work showed a lot of creativity!").
   - Although some aspects of coursework in school require attention to accuracy, for example, in math and science, it is important to also offer students open-ended or ungraded learning opportunities. Some students, in particular perfectionists, may struggle with these open-ended options because there is no grade to strive for. But that is even more reason to offer these opportunities. Students can experience the freedom of being relatively unconstrained, and they can learn to be motivated by something other than a grade.

Some examples of open activities that promote risk-taking and creativity are free writing, painting or drawing whatever students want, listening to a piece of music and then writing or telling about it, picking somewhere in the world to learn about, or writing a blog post from the perspective of a cat or dog.

## CONCLUSION

Nonacademic skills are vital to success in school and in life. But social-emotional skills—which include developing positive character traits, resilience, and a growth mindset—cannot be directly measured by standardized test scores. Nonetheless, efforts must be made to create regular time in the school day for the development of students' SEL skills. It is common sense that is not common enough in education, so you may feel a bit like a maverick in these endeavors. Take encouragement from the words of Randall McCutcheon and Tommie Lindsey (2006), authors of *It Doesn't Take a Genius: Five Truths to Inspire Success in Every Student*:

> It helps if you're a bit crazy. Crazy enough to care more about your children than you do about yourself. Take heart, though, if you are among the chosen who do care. Kingman Brewster Jr., a former Yale University president, was right when he said, "There is a correlation between the creative and the screwball. So, we must suffer the screwball gladly." Respect that. Honor that. (2006, p. 280)

## REFERENCES

Chesner, J. (2012). *ADHD in HD.* Minneapolis, MN: Free Spirit Publishing.

Durlak, J. A., Weissberg, R. P., Dymnicki, A. B., Taylor, R. D., & Schellinger, K. B. (2011). The impact of enhancing students' social and emotional learning: A meta-analysis of school-based universal interventions. *Child Development, 82*(1), 405–432.

Galbraith, J. (2009). *The survival guide for gifted kids.* Minneapolis, MN: Free Spirit Publishing.

Galbraith, J., & Delisle, J. (2015). *When gifted kids don't have all the answers: How to meet their social and emotional needs.* Minneapolis, MN: Free Spirit Publishing.

Coleman, M.R., & Roberts, J. L. *Gifted Child Today* (2015), *38*(4), 204–256.

Isaacs, J., & Novick, R. (March 2011). *Factors influencing bystander behavior in bullying situations.* Poster presented at the Society for Research in Child Development Conference.

McCutcheon, R., & Lindsey, T. (2006). *It doesn't take a genius: Five truths to inspire success in every student.* New York, NY: McGraw-Hill.

Seppälä, E. (2016). *The happiness track: How to apply the science of happiness to accelerate your success.* New York, NY: HarperOne.

8

# Advocating for Twice Exceptional Students

RICH WEINFELD

According to the Individuals with Disabilities Education Act of 2004 (IDEA), every child with a disability has the right to an Individualized Educational program (iep) that develops his or her unique potential. The act clearly describes special education as preparing students for further education, employment, and independent living. Yet a study by the US Department of Education's Office for Civil Rights (2014) concluded that only 1% of students who receive IDEA services are in gifted and talented education programs, compared with 7% of their general education peers (see http://www2.ed.gov/about/officeslist/ocr/docs/crdc-college-and-career-readiness-snapshot.pdf) Fortunately, however, we have seen legal decisions and guidance from the US Department of Education increasingly provide support for the appropriate identification of twice exceptional (2e) students (Eig, Weinfeld, & Rosenstock, 2014).

The US Supreme Court, in *Endrew F. v. Douglas County Schoo District,* (2017) ruled that students are entitled to more than just minimal educational benefit and that this benefit must be judged according to each student's potential. This new standard for measuring educational benefit has already been the law in some of the judicial circuits in the United States. Now, it should be the standard for the entire country. We believe that when we consider the potential of each student, it is evident that 2e students need to be identified in relation to both their gift and their disability and that they need to be instructed and assessed according to best practices (Weinfeld, Barnes-Robinson, Jeweler, & Shevitz, 2013).

In order that 2e students are appropriately identified and receive evidence-based best practices, it is crucial that educators and parents, who understand these special learners, advocate for them. What does it mean to "advocate?" We define an advocate as "Someone who has a high degree of skill and knowledge about education and gives expert advice about this field for the purpose of supporting children" (Weinfeld & Davis, 2008). In our work as advocates for 2e students, we develop an expert opinion based on a review of records, observation of the student, conferring with all involved professionals, and conferring with parents. We then advocate for the development of an appropriate iep with appropriate goals, objectives, accommodations, supplementary aids, hours of service, and school placement.

When we speak about advocacy, it is important to remember that the ultimate goal is for 2e students to become self-advocates. As with other skill areas, this is an area that school staff and parents must help the student to develop over time. Students become effective self-advocates when they understand their own unique strengths and challenges, understand what tools work to remove obstacles to learning, and understand how to access those tools. Students must be afforded the opportunities to learn about their own profile, to experience which tools work for them, and to have practice asking for what they need in appropriate ways. In the school setting the responsibility for helping students to develop these self-advocacy skills belongs to the case manager. Comprehensive case management is described in our discussion of best practices in this chapter. While students are developing their self-advocacy skills, it is crucial for the adults in their life to continue to be responsible for advocating for appropriate identification and implementation of best practices.

For 2e students, our advocacy is first shaped by our understanding of the difficulties with identification, as the gift and disability may mask each other. Identification of 2e students may be difficult, because of 3 challenges with identification:

1. We may see the gift, but the gift may mask the disability.
2. We may identify the disability and lose sight of the gift.
3. The gift and the disability may mask one another, resulting in our identifying neither and therefore not providing the needed rigor and enrichment or the needed special education (adapted from definition of twice exceptional learners; Baldwin, Baum, Perles, & Hughes, 2015).

Our advocacy is also shaped by our understanding of the best practices for the education of 2e students. We have summarized this into four major areas of best practices:

1. Development of the gifts
2. Development of skills and strategies that are impacted by the disability
3. Accommodations and aids that remove obstacles
4. Comprehensive case management

(Weinfeld, Barnes-Robinson, Jeweler, & Shevitz, 2013)

Over the past several decades, we have advocated for 2e students on "both sides of the table," as school system administrators and as educational consultants in private practice. We have come to believe that effective advocacy only takes place in a collaborative environment, when all parties are engaged in child-centered problem solving, focusing on the one unique individual whose education is being considered at that time.

In order to effectively advocate for 2e students, the advocate must keep in mind five components of advocacy, related to any issue that is under discussion:

1. Beliefs about 2e students
2. Why it's a good thing for kids
3. Why it's a good thing for schools
4. How the law supports it
5. How this can really happen

By keeping these five components in mind, while advocating for 2e students with a collaborative, child-centered and problem-solving approach, great outcomes can be achieved. When we do advocate successfully for 2e students, we are making a difference both for them individually and for society as a whole. Without identification and supports, 2e students are at risk for emotional challenges, poor attendance, and school failure. With identification and supports, they thrive. As we think of the importance for our society as a whole, we are inspired by a quote from Mahatma Gandhi: "The difference between what we do and what we are capable of doing would suffice to solve most of the world's problems." (see http://www.dailygood.org/story/466/gandhi-s-10-rules-for-changing-the-world-henrik-edberg/) Twice exceptional students are capable of great things, making a difference for us all.

What follows is a "recipe" for thinking through advocacy for 2e students. We have taken each of the major areas that an advocate needs to attend to when advocating for these special learners/ We suggest thinking through the challenges in identification and the areas of best practices, as outlined previously, when advocating for each student.

The following is a guide to thinking about each of the identification and best-practice areas in terms of the five components of advocacy described previously. We hope this will provide a framework for thinking in depth about how to advocate for each individual 2e student.

## ADVOCATING FOR APPROPRIATE IDENTIFICATION

### Seeing the Gift But Not the Disability

1. What we believe
   When we only see the gifts in 2e kids, we cannot understand why they are not succeeding in school. Even worse, we may blame them for not being successful, thinking of them as lazy and unmotivated or as having behavior problems. When we see a gifted student who is not

being successful in school, we must explore the possibility of disability. Disabilities for this population most frequently are in the areas of specific learning disabilities, other health impairments such as attention deficit hyperactivity disorder, or autism spectrum disorders. They may also include any of the other disability areas designated by the federal and state governments, including emotional disturbance, speech and language impairment, orthopedically handicapped, visually impaired, or hearing impaired.

2. Why it's a good thing for kids
   When students are seen as gifted but their disability is not identified, their self-esteem suffers as they themselves doubt their strengths; they tend to give up out of frustration.

   When the students and the adults in life understand their disabilities, they can provide the interventions that will allow students to realize their potential.
3. Why it's a good thing for schools
   Gifted students who are not performing may be among the top performers in the school when identified appropriately and given accommodations and aids that remove the obstacles presented by their disability.
4. How the law supports it
   Special education law requires that we screen all students who are suspected of disability and consider whether or not they are eligible for an iep. Discrimination law prohibits excluding students with disabilities from the opportunities available to their nondisabled peers. Guidance from the US Department of Education has made it clear that no student can be "too smart" to qualify for an IEP. *Endrew F. v. Douglas County School District* clarifies that potential must be considered in the special education process. Many previous lower court decisions have also specified that it should.
5. How this can really happen
   Identifying the disability in students who are already identified as gifted will only happen when staff and parents are trained to suspect a possible disability in those gifted kids who are not performing up to expectations. A thorough assessment is the first step.

## Seeing the Disability But Not the Gift

1. What we believe
   When we only see the student's disability, we will not develop the gifts. The contributions that these individuals can make to society are then likely to go unnoticed and undeveloped.
2. Why it's a good thing for kids
   When we know what students are capable of, we have a benchmark by which to measure the growth in the skills affected by their disability.

When we identify gifts, students' self-esteem improves as they come to understand their own strengths and understand that the adults in their world see these strengths as well.

3. Why it's a good thing for schools
   Once the gifts are identified, 2e students may be among the top performers in school. Twice exceptional students will also be likely to be motivated to work on their areas of need when their strengths are also identified and addressed.
4. How the law supports it
   While there is not a federal requiring gifted identification, many states and local school districts have policies calling for this identification. To exclude disabled students from a fair opportunity at the same identification is a form of discrimination. In addition, the special education law calls for students to receive educational benefit from their program. Without knowing the student's capabilities, we cannot accurately measure educational benefit. *Endrew F. v. Douglas County School District* clarifies that potential should be considered when determining educational benefit.
5. How this can really happen
   Identifying the gift in students who are already identified as disabled will only happen when staff and parents are trained to look for signs of the possible gift in disabled students and, when seeing those signs, understand the importance of identifying the gifts.

## Seeing Neither the Gift nor the Disability Because of Masking

1. What we believe
   The largest group of unidentified 2e kids are those who are neither identified as gifted or as having a disability because each masks the other. For these students we are failing to educate them in accordance with either their gift or their disability and missing what they need in both areas.
2. Why it's a good thing for kids
   When we identify students as 2e students they will receive the services that they are guaranteed by law while receiving the gifted opportunities that will allow them to reach their potential and thrive.
3. Why it's a good thing for schools
   Once students are identified as 2e, students who were previously performing in a mediocre way or possibly exhibiting behavior problems have the opportunity to thrive and become some of the highest performing students.

4. How the law supports it
   Special education law requires that we screen all students who are suspected of a disability and consider whether or not they are eligible for an iep. Discrimination law prohibits excluding students with disabilities from the opportunities available to their nondisabled peers. Considering students' gifts while identifying their disabilities provides us with the opportunity to see the patterns of strengths and weaknesses indicative of a disability and to measure educational benefit in a realistic way. Again, *Endrew F. v. Douglas County School District* should provide a nationally uniform way to consider potential when looking at educational benefit.
5. How this can really happen
   Identifying students as 2e who are currently identified as neither gifted nor disabled requires staff and parents to look for evidence of both the challenge and the strength, to trust the strengths that we do see, and to investigate why they are not more consistently evident.

## BEST PRACTICES

### Development of the Gifts

1. What we believe
   If students are to lead meaningful and fulfilling lives it will be because their gifts have been identified and developed. Our ability to thrive as a society depends on developing the next generation of inventors, artists, creators, and leaders.
2. Why it's a good thing for kids
   Students will thrive when their gifts are identified, recognized, and developed.
3. Why it's a good thing for schools
   When students' gifts are identified and developed, the school as a whole achieves at a higher level and a positive climate is created for all.
4. How the law supports it
   The special education law's goal is for students to be prepared for further education, independent living, and employment. For 2e students this includes preparation for higher level learning.
5. How this can really happen
   Schools must have gifted-level options, which can include Honors and AP courses, enrichment, and other rigorous programming. Schools must have means of identifying student's gifts and must include students with disabilities in this identification. Staff needs training on how to provide appropriate adaptations and accommodations within the gifted programming so that students with disabilities can succeed.

## Development of Skills that Are Impacted by the Disability

1. What we believe
   Although we believe that focusing on the gift comes first, and that if parents are given the false choice of "Your child can be in gifted classes or in special ed but not in both" they should choose gifted education, we also believe that we have a responsibility to help students improve their own skills and learn strategies that will help them remove obstacles to learning. We believe that gifted students can learn skills and strategies through evidence-based methods provided with fidelity.
2. Why it's a good thing for kids
   Students deserve to develop all their skills as much as possible. We can teach students at any age to improve their academic, social, behavioral, and executive functioning skills. When this instruction is done with respect and in the context of gifted education, students are typically willing and motivated to work on improving these skills.
3. Why it's a good thing for schools
   Teaching students the skills that are impacted by their disability, as well as strategies that they can employ to circumvent the obstacles presented by the disability, allows students to achieve at a higher level, raising the school's overall achievement. Students who are able to access instruction as a result of improved skill levels are less likely to misbehave and more likely to have strong attendance.
4. How the law supports it
   IDEA requires specialized instruction for students who qualify for ieps. Evidence-based instruction is also part of the law. Guidance from the US Department of Education makes it clear that no student can be "too smart" to qualify for an iep.
5. How this can really happen
   The federal government's What Works Clearinghouse and other reputable websites maintain lists of evidence-based methodologies. School staff needs to be given the knowledge of these programs, training in how to use them, and access to them. They also need to be trained to provide strategy and skills instruction for 2e students.

## Accommodations and Aids that Remove Obstacles

1. What we believe
   In order for gifted students who simultaneously have disabilities to succeed in appropriately rigorous instruction, they must be provided with interventions that remove obstacles to learning. It is not enough to place 2e students in challenging classes or programs; it is crucial that the teachers in these classes and programs present information and assess understanding in ways that are not impacted by the student's disabilities.

2. Why it's a good thing for kids
   When students are placed in appropriately challenging instructional opportunities and the obstacles to their success are removed, they will flourish, preparing them for their future and helping them to realize their potential.
3. Why it's a good thing for schools
   When students' gifts are identified and developed, the school as a whole achieves at a higher level and a positive climate is created for all.
4. How the law supports it
   Antidiscrimination laws and guidance from the US Department of Education have made it clear that 2e students are to be included in appropriately challenging classes and programs and once placed in these programs continue to have the right to receive all appropriate accommodations and supplementary aids.
5. How this can really happen
   In order for this to happen, teachers and school administrators need training on how to provide instruction that is not "dumbed down" or inappropriately modified but does afford the opportunity for information to be learned in alternative ways and for understanding to be demonstrated in alternative ways. Teachers, administrators, and staff need access to a list of accommodations that have worked for 2e students and then need to carefully choose the individual accommodations that are a fit for the student in question (Weinfeld et al., 2013).

## Comprehensive Case Management

1. What we believe
   In order for 2e students to be successful in school, they need to have a case manager who thoroughly understands their educational profile, including strengths and challenges. This case manager must be able to advocate for appropriately challenging instruction, for instruction in the skills that are affected by the disability, and for accommodations and aids to be systematically provided to the student throughout the school day. The case manager must be the liaison, communicating between school staff and the parents and the providers in the community who may be part of the student's support network. Finally, the case manager should help the students to become advocates for themselves, through understanding of their own profile, knowing what works for them, and knowing how and when to ask for support.
2. Why it's a good thing for kids
   When students have an effective case manager who is supporting them throughout the school day, they will be most likely to get what they need both in terms of appropriate level of rigor and appropriate supports. When students' self-advocacy skills are gradually developed,

they become ready to independently ensure that they are getting what they need.

3. Why it's a good thing for schools
When students' gifts are identified and developed, the school as a whole achieves at a higher level and a positive climate is created for all. Twice-exceptional students, who without support may present with behavior or attendance problems and who are not succeeding academically, may become some of the top performers in the school.
4. How the law supports it
The goal of the special education law is to prepare students for further education, employment, and independent living. When a case manager advocates for the 2e student and the 2e students learn to advocate for themselves, the goal of the law can become a reality.
5. How this can really happen
Case managers must be identified by the school. Typically this will be done as part of the special education process. These case managers need training to understand 2e students in general and the individual 2e student in particular. The development of self-advocacy should be one of the iep goals and should be treated as a developmental process, similar to developing reading or writing skills.

## CONCLUSION

Twice exceptional students have the potential to achieve great things in school and beyond. It is up to us, the adults in their world, to advocate for appropriate identification and instruction so that their potential can be realized. Advocacy must take place locally and globally.

Each 2e student deserves effective advocacy to make sure they have an appropriate iep. Twice exceptional students, as a group, require our continued advocacy, making sure that we increase awareness about the strengths, challenges, and the required interventions for this special population.

## REFERENCES

Baldwin, L., Baum, S., Pereles, D., & Hughes, C. (2015). Twice-exceptional learners: The journey toward a shared vision. *Gifted Child Today*, *38*, 206–214.

Eig, M., Weinfeld, R., & Rosenstock, P. (2014). Legal issues in serving twice-exceptional gifted learners. *Excellence and Diversity in Gifted Education*, *1*, 15–23.

*Endrew F. ex rel. Joseph F. v. Douglas City School District RE-1*, No. 15-827, 2017 WL 106626, 580 U.S. ___ (Mar. 22, 2017).

US Department of Education Office for Civil Rights 1 Civil Rights Data Collection: Data Snapshot (College and Career Readiness), March 21, 2014.

Weinfeld, R., Barnes-Robinson, L., Jeweler, S., & Shevitz, B. (2013). *Smart kids with learning difficulties: Overcoming obstacles and realizing potential.* Waco, TX. Prufrock Press.

Weinfeld, R., & Davis, M. (2008). *Special needs advocacy resource book: What you can do now to advocate for your exceptional child's education.* Waco, TX. Prufrock Press.

9

# It Takes a Team

## Growing Up 2e

MARY RUTH COLEMAN, LOIS BALDWIN,
AND DAPHNE PERELES

## MEET EMMA AND JACK

*Standing on the campus green in her cap and gown with a college diploma in her hands, Emma wipes away her tears of joy. She is having difficulty believing that she is truly a college graduate. Her journey to reach this point has been filled with angst, anxiety, learning issues, and behavioral challenges. As she stands there teary-eyed and amazed, she reflects on her journey.*

*Since Jack's birth, his parents have had reason to be concerned about their son. They are aware of his wonderful cognitive strengths but are also sensitive to his cognitive and behavioral rigidity, his struggles with social skills, and his difficulties with transitions. Jack is an only child who lives with his mother, a full-time pediatric nurse, and his father, an electrical engineer. His father is currently unemployed due to a physical disability. Because the father is at home, he often transports Jack to school or takes him his lunch or homework when he forgets and leaves it at home.*

The complex patterns of extreme strengths and challenges that are part of each individual who is twice exceptional (2e) are lifelong characteristics. These patterns of "gifts" and "difficulties" help to define who they are at any moment in time and continue to influence who they are becoming as they grow and develop. In order for these individuals to experience success, they must receive the appropriate support of many people including families, teachers, special service providers, counselors, psychologists, and in some cases medical professionals. Organization and focused coordination of these support teams along the developmental journey is key to the success of 2e individuals.

A definition of twice exceptional individuals that was established by the National Twice Exceptional Community of Practice states that the characteristics of this special population of gifted individuals must be taken into consideration and specific strategies must be put into place in order for twice exceptional individuals to be successful.

The definition of "twice exceptional individuals" is

> Twice exceptional (2e) individuals evidence exceptional ability and disability, which results in a unique set of circumstances. Their exceptional ability may dominate, hiding their disability; their disability may dominate, hiding their exceptional ability; each may mask the other so that neither is recognized or addressed.
>
> 2e students, who may perform below, at or above grade level, require the following:
>
> - 2e specialized methods of identification that consider the possible interaction of the exceptionalities
> - 2e specialized enriched/advanced educational opportunities that develop the child's interests, gifts, and talents while also meeting the child's learning needs
> - 2e specialized enrichment and simultaneous supports that ensure the child's academic success and social-emotional well-being, such as accommodations, therapeutic interventions, and specialized instruction.
>
> Working successfully with this unique population requires specialized academic training and ongoing professional development. (Baldwin, Baum, Pereles, & Hughes, 2015)

In this chapter we follow the lifespan of Emma and Jack, two twice exceptional individuals, tracking their progression from birth to college. At each developmental stage we examine the trials, challenges, and strengths of each individual. Because a comprehensive plan is needed to help them meet with success, we examine the role of the problem-solving team at various developmental stages.

Parents have great hope for the children they bring into this world. When their child is born, they naturally wonder about how they will develop, what their personalities will be like, and what their interests will be. They watch them closely as they grow. When the child encounters difficulties with any aspect of development, parents worry and are often the first people to identify potential problems (Neitzel, 2011).

*Emma was born following a full-term pregnancy but the delivery was induced due to her mother's increased blood pressure. There were no complications and Emma weighed 8 pounds, 6 ounces. Emma is the middle daughter with a sister who is two years older and a brother who is four years younger. Her mother, a research scientist, works for a pharmaceutical lab and her father is a dentist with a private practice.*

*Jack was born prematurely, at 36 weeks. Following two days of labor, his birth was induced and he was delivered by caesarian section. There were no reported complications and his Apgar score was a 10. However, he presented with feeding problems almost immediately due to lactose intolerance. He demonstrated severe reflux reactions resulting in frequent vomiting. This reflux and vomiting caused him to be hospitalized at nine months of age due to dehydration.*

Reaching early milestones is critical for the young child, and pediatricians help the parents follow the child's trajectory across five developmental domains: cognition, communication, social-emotional engagement, adaptive behaviors for daily living, and physical motor skills (Kirk, Gallagher, & Coleman, 2105). This is evident with Emma's and Jack's parents.

*Emma's early developmental milestones appeared to be within normal limits. She crawled early, including moving backwards to get to objects, and once she walked at 11 months, she never stopped moving. Emma was always active. Her mother noted that "Emma would go nonstop from the time she woke up in the morning. She never, ever sat still." She preferred climbing on the furniture or playing outdoors to more sedentary games or toys. She needed very little sleep so it was very difficult to get her to bed and to keep her there. She loved to be read to especially at bedtime and quickly memorized the stories. Her parents could hear her "reading" to her stuffed animals after they put her to bed.*

*Early developmental milestones appeared to be within normal limits or even early for Jack. He was walking alone at 12 months, using words at 10 months, and forming two- to three-word sentences at 16 months. At 18 months he was able to count to 12 and could spell his own name. His parents said that he was a pleasant infant who enjoyed being held. All was well until about 15 months of age when the temper tantrums began. When things did not go as he wanted them to or he was not in control, Jack would experience a "meltdown." He would refuse to leave the house and throw or spill objects in order to get his way. Activities such as family parties, grocery shopping, or public events would often trigger these negative behaviors, and his parents began to dread taking him anywhere. Jack also developed acute sensory sensitivities. He could not stand the tags in his shirts, the texture of some foods, or anything sticky on his skin, and he hated to have his hair washed or brushed.*

While both Emma and Jack showed some early warning signs during infancy and as toddlers, in preschool (ages three to four) their difficulties intensified. As children grow up, life becomes more demanding. With each phase of growth, expectations increase across the five developmental domains (Coleman, 2011). Preschool is often the first experience of these increasing demands. In preschool the child is expected to master basic cognitive skills for emerging literacy and numeracy (e.g., interest in reading, naming letters, counting, recognizing shapes). Communication and social relationships take on more importance as a child is expected to express his or her needs and frustrations appropriately, to play cooperatively with other children, and to make friends. Preschool children are expected to remember classroom routines, delay gratification, and sit still during story time. Their fine and gross motor skills should allow the child to hold a pencil or spoon, balance on a low beam, and move with agility. All of these expectations place additional demands on the child, and, for some, these demands feel overwhelming (Gillis, West, & Coleman, 2009). Both Emma and Jack experienced challenges in preschool.

*Although she was very excited about starting preschool because she was curious and loved to learn, it was more difficult than Emma had expected. In fact, one day she came home and announced that she was quitting saying, "School gives me a hard time." She did not like sitting still, holding a pencil, writing her letters, or learning her math facts. Her favorite part of the day was free play. Emma's preschool teachers recognized her need to move so they kept her as active as they could within the constraints of the school requirements. Emma was also struggling with articulation problems, making her speech almost unintelligible. According to her mother, Emma had developed a very large and sophisticated vocabulary and was very verbal from an early age, but it was difficult to understand her speech. Her immediate family understood what she was trying to communicate and they were impressed with the sophistication of her ideas and thoughts, but others, including her teachers, could rarely understand what she was saying.*

*Preschool had its ups and downs for Jack. Although he demonstrated a great deal of curiosity, related well to the adults, and loved to learn, he continued to have temper tantrums, particularly during unstructured activities or when he needed to transition from a task he was enjoying to something new. He often "snatched" toys from other children when he wanted to play and rarely engaged in social interactions with his classmates.*

When adults recognize that a young child is experiencing difficulties that interfere with learning or with daily life skills, they must respond with appropriate support (Coleman, Buysse, & Neitzel, 2006). Early intervention and the provision of supports and services to children birth through school age and their families can be critical to establishing a foundation that will allow for later success (Kirk et al., 2015). Early intervention often begins with a problem-solving process, and preschool teachers are a critical part of the problem-solving team (West, 2011).

The problem-solving process brings together multiple sources of information in order to make decisions that will have the best outcomes for the child. The problem-solving process involves (a) defining the area(s) of strength and concern, (b) collecting and analyzing data to identify needs, (c) creating and implementing a plan to address needs, and (d) evaluating the progress of the student in relation to the plan. Effective problem-solving teams include family members and the professional personnel who can contribute their knowledge of the child's strengths and challenges as well as strategies and interventions to support the child. Besnoy (this volume) discusses the role of parents in collaborative partnership with schools. This partnership is the foundation of a solid problem-solving team. As Emma and Jack get older, we will see that the specific members of the team vary depending on the child's age and unique needs. When done appropriately, the child him- or herself will become the most important member of the team.

Jack and Emma's preschool teachers recommended early intervention and a problem-solving team was formed in each case. For Jack the concerns were around his communication and social challenges. Concerns for Emma focused on speech development and self-regulation (e.g., sitting still, reducing impulsivity). In both cases the problem-solving team also reviewed the children's strengths and included enhancement strategies that addressed their individual gifts and talents. Table 9.1 shares the members of the preschool problem-solving teams for Emma and Jack and gives the strategies for support and enhancement.

While multidisciplinary teams are important for all children with exceptionalities, these teams are essential for children who are 2e (Baldwin, Omdal, & Pereles, 2015; Coleman & Gallagher, 2015). As the team reviews data from multiple sources that address the different facets of the student, it becomes evident that a variety of strategies are often necessary to create an appropriate plan that support the unique needs of each twice exceptional student (Baldwin et al., 2015). As children transition to school age, the use of problem-solving teams becomes essential in understanding their strengths and challenges and planning to meet their needs. Much has been written about this process, the need to have representation from various perspectives, and the importance of including family members as partners in the process (Lines, Miller, & Arthur-Stanley, 2011).

*For Emma, kindergarten was challenging. Although she was more compliant about sitting for longer periods of time and participating in the classroom activities, she continued to fidget constantly. Her teachers noted that she was very bright, frequently calling out answers and asking perceptive questions. They enjoyed her enthusiasm and energy. She was very social and was often found organizing the games on the playground. While her teachers had some concerns about her ability to focus, they felt that perhaps she was just a little immature and that as she got older she would settle in.*

*Jack's preschool challenges followed him to elementary school. In kindergarten, although he said that he liked school, he often would not get on the school bus. His parents would ask him why he was upset but he could not give them a reason. The staff and parents met to see if they could come up with some solutions to make it easier for Jack to accept being in school. They discussed his strengths. He already knew his alphabet, could read books independently at the beginning of third-grade level, particularly those that focused on facts about bugs and dinosaurs, knew one-to-one correspondence, could add and subtract in his head, and was adept with the computer. They also discussed his challenges, which were his inability to socialize or work in groups with the other students, his tantrums when he was asked to change activities, and his inability to follow oral directions. His parents and teachers developed a comprehensive plan focused on strategies for developing his strength in reading and strategies to address his behavior challenges to facilitate his transition to different activities. In addition, he was placed in a social skills group, with the school's guidance counselor there to assist him with reading body language and understanding pragmatic language.*

*Table 9.1.* PRESCHOOL (AGES 3–4) PROBLEM-SOLVING TEAMS FOR EMMA AND JACK

**Jack**

| **Members of the Team** | **Areas of Strength/Interest** | **Areas of Concern** | **Strategies for Support** | **Strategies for Enhancements** |
|---|---|---|---|---|
| Parents | Large vocabulary and sophisticated language skills | Temper tantrums, refused to leave the house, throws objects to get his way | Social skills group with the psychologist | Given extra time in the science corner |
| Preschool teacher | *Playing computer games* | Sensory sensitivities | | Math puzzles and games |
| Psychologist (behaviorist) | *Memorized baseball facts* | Lack of social skills, does not play well with other students | | |
| | | Severe reflux reactions and eating problems | | |

**Emma**

| **Members of the Team** | **Areas of Strength/Interest** | **Areas of Concern** | **Strategies for Support** | **Strategies for Enhancements** |
|---|---|---|---|---|
| Parents | Physically adept | Impulsivity | A lot of movement built into her school day | *Acting out stories with classmates or stuffed animals once a week* |
| Preschool teacher | Active | Lack of self-regulation | Manipulatives for math | |
| Speech therapist | Memory | Speech difficulties | | |
| | Large sophisticated vocabulary | Holding a pencil | | |
| | Curiosity | Math facts | | |
| | Loves hearing and telling stories, memorized them and acted them out | | | |

NOTE: Areas in italics were not specifically mentioned in the case information presented.

Transition into kindergarten is a critical time for young children as they learn to manage themselves and the new environment and expectations of school. Parents are also learning how to work with school personnel as they become partners in supporting their child's success. As the child goes through the grades, academic and social demands increase. This, in combination with increased expectations for autonomy and independence, can lead to difficulties for the child. There seem to be some critical times where the demands and expectations seem to outstrip the child's capacity. First grade is often such a time, and we see that in Emma and Jack's difficult first-grade experiences.

*When Emma was in first grade, her older sister, who was in third grade, was screened and accepted into the school's gifted program. Although everyone felt that Emma was also very bright, testing and participation for the gifted program in that school did not happen until third grade. In the meantime, Emma, seemed to learn at a slower rate than her verbal precocity would suggest. She struggled when she was reading aloud, skipping words and entire lines of text, but she always seemed to understand the meaning and she could answer the comprehension questions. Writing was even more difficult. She was still having trouble holding a pencil and writing her ideas. In addition, she continued to struggle with one-to-one correspondence in math. She frequently called out because she could not wait to either ask a question or to give the answer. Recess, where she continued to organize students into teams when they were playing, was still her favorite time of day. It was clear that she was a natural leader.*

*By first grade, the school determined that a thorough evaluation was needed for Jack. At the Committee for Special Education (CSE) meeting, he was formally diagnosed with other health impairment and obsessive-compulsive disorder. As part of the evaluation, his Wechsler Intelligence Scale for Children demonstrated that Jack's cognitive ability was in the very superior range overall (Full Scale IQ 141, 99.7th percentile). His subtest scores ranged from average (Processing Speed) to very high (Fluid Reasoning) to extremely high (the rest of the subtests). It was also determined that he should continue to attend a general education class with special education teacher consultation two hours a day, speech and language twice a week for 30 minutes, as well as counseling once a week with the school psychologist.*

These difficulties that were evident in that critical first-grade year persisted into both Emma and Jack's early elementary experience. The development of an effective plan for each of them became increasingly important.

*By second grade Emma was identified with attention deficit hyperactivity disorder and a 504 Accommodation Plan was developed for her. She was allowed preferential seating (usually in the back of the room so that she did not distract anyone when she needed to get up and move), frequent breaks, chart paper for math problems rather than the workbook, and math manipulatives. Her pediatrician recommended Ritalin, which seemed to help her focus. At this time Emma's parents, who had both been actively engaged in their children's upbringing, got a divorce. This significantly decreased her father's involvement in his children's educational progress. This was a traumatic event for the entire family but particularly Emma because she was closer to her father than her mother and considered herself "Daddy's little girl." Her father remarried within the year and started a new family. While Emma's mother did not remarry, she did have several short-term relationships. In third grade, on the gifted program screener, Emma scored within the gifted range and she was identified for the gifted pullout program. The program met once a week and allowed her to worked on a special project of her choice.*

*Jack survived second grade, but by third grade the CSE Committee decided that he needed to have a one-on-one special education aide because he was continuing to demonstrate behaviors that were difficult to manage such as work avoidance, doodling, calling out, and disrespectful responses to the teacher. Jack's eating issues had improved considerably over the years but still caused him to be underweight. During second grade he was diagnosed with a food aversion restriction disorder, and his parents worked with an allergist to help with the dairy allergies and a pediatrician to deal with his diet and reflux issues. His food-related difficulties made lunch time a special trial for him and his aide. Although the teachers knew that Jack was gifted, there was no gifted program in the school, and so, other than some minor in class differentiation (e.g., he was occasionally allowed to read a book of his choice if he finished his work early), his cognitive strengths were rarely addressed in school.*

One of the important issues that is often overlooked when dealing with twice exceptional students is the need to focus on the student's strengths, gifts, and talents while also addressing their learning needs and challenges. Both Emma and Jack's problem-solving teams identified strategies to assist with the challenges but were not as consistent with addressing their strengths (see Table 9.2). Emma was evaluated and accepted into the gifted program in third grade, but this focus on her strengths did not continue the following year. Jack received some acceleration and enhancement, but it was not part of his comprehensive plan until fifth grade.

Developing a comprehensive plan is not as easy as it sounds. Guiding questions that focus on three distinct areas—strengths and interests, challenge or disability needs, and social/emotional needs—are often helpful (see Box 9.1). These questions push the team to consider aspects of a student's strengths and needs that they may otherwise overlook. It would have been great, for example, if Jack and Emma's problem-solving teams had used the guiding questions in Box 9.1 to frame a more intentional approach to integrating supports across a comprehensive plan.

Problem-solving teams play an important role during these critical times, and the collaboration between school professionals and families is essential in planning and implementing interventions and supports. An important family team member who is often left out is the child himself/herself. Studies have indicated the importance of the development of self-determination skills early for children with exceptional needs (Lee, Palmer, Turnbull, & Wehmeyer, 2006). The definition of self-determination is "acting as the primary causal agent in one's life and making choices and decisions regarding one's quality of life free from undue external influence or interference" (Lee et al., pp. 36–37). This self-determination requires goal-setting, self-regulating, and practicing independent behavior

*Table 9.2.* Elementary School (Grades K–4) Problem-Solving Teams for Emma and Jack

**Jack IEP**

| Members of the Team | Areas of Strength/ Interest | Areas of Concern | Strategies for Support | Strategies for Enhancements |
|---|---|---|---|---|
| Parents | Reading above grade level | Social skills | 1:1 aide | *No gifted program—some differentiation—read books of his choice when he finished his work early, given higher level math problems, allowed to play computer games if followed directions* |
| General education and special education teachers | Interested in facts about bugs, dinosaurs, science | Working in groups | speech and language twice a week | |
| Psychologist | Math- could add and subtract in his head | Temper tantrums | Co-teaching with special education teacher support 2 hours a day | |
| Committee for special education | Computer games and skills | Following oral directions | Social skills group with psychologist | |
| Speech teacher | *Sports statistics* | Work avoidance, doodling | Checklist for transitions | |
| Allergist | | Food Aversion Restriction Disorder | | |

**Emma 504**

| Members of the Team | Areas of Strength/ Interest | Areas of Concern | Strategies for Support | Strategies for Enhancements |
|---|---|---|---|---|
| Parents | Social skills | Lack of focus | Preferential seating | Gifted program for third grade once a week, worked on independent projects in social studies |
| Teacher | Leadership | Immaturity | Frequent breaks | No focus on cognitive and personal strengths in fourth grade |
| Gifted specialist in third grade | Organizing students into teams during recess | Self-regulation and impulsivity | Chart paper and manipulatives in math | |
| 504 team | Enthusiasm, curiosity, perceptiveness | Writing, spelling, and math skills | Word processing | |
| | | Withdrawn, keeping to herself beginning in fourth grade | Extra time for tests | |
| | | By fifth grade lethargy at home and mediocre performance at school | Medication for ADHD | |

NOTE: Areas in italics were not specifically mentioned in the case information presented.

Box 9.1

## Questions to Help with Problem-Solving Team Planning

### Questions to Help Determine Need in the Area of Strengths and Interests

- In what subjects does the student excel?
- Does the student show evidence of higher level thinking in this subject?
- What is the student's favored mode of learning information and skills?
- What is the student's favored mode of expressing him/herself?
- Does the student qualitatively extend assignments and projects beyond the requirements? (Not just writing more pages for a report but adding insights reflecting a deeper and more complex understanding.)
- In what topics does the student have interest and knowledge that is far above the level of a typical student of the same age? Does the student have an intense focus on a single topic that may be considered unusual?
- In what school-based or out-of-school activities does the student participate and/or perform at a higher level than his or her age-mates and/or has received recognition?
- To what degree does the challenge/disability impact the ability of the student to pursue this area of interest?
- How has the student utilized his or her strengths to compensate or mediate the areas of challenge?

### Questions to Help Determine Need in the Area of Challenge or Disability

- In what subject(s) does the student have difficulty?
- What is the nature of the learning difficulty?
- What is the student's favored mode of learning information and skills?
- What tasks or learning activities does the student avoid?
- Does the student demonstrate negative or unexpected behaviors during certain learning tasks or activities?
- What is the student's favored mode of expressing him/herself? Does the student prefer oral versus written responses?
- What learning/academic incongruities are present (e.g., advanced comprehension of material presented visually and/or aurally but low comprehension if read)?
- To what degree does the challenge/disability impact the ability of the student to pursue strengths and interests?

**Questions to Help Determine the Need in the Area of Social-Emotional Concerns**

- What triggers, if any, set the student off?
- What behaviors does the student exhibit that interfere with learning?
- To what degree does the student exhibit heightened empathy and sensitivity?
- Does the student make derogatory comments such as "I'm dumb" about him/herself?
- What, if any, uneven development exists physically, emotionally, and/or socially?
- What evidence exists that would indicate extreme perfectionistic tendencies that would prevent the student from taking risks?
- How does the student hide his or her strengths and/or his or her disabilities to fit in with peers?
- Does the student avoid peers, or do they avoid the student?

Reprinted with permission from Baldwin, L., Omdal, S. N., & Pereles, D. (2015). Beyond stereotypes: Understanding, recognizing, and working with twice-exceptional learners. *TEACHING Exceptional Children, 47*(4), 216–225.

---

(Korbel, McGuire, Banerjee, & Saunders, 2011). An individual's ability to problem-solve their own needs is important to his or her success in life. Developing self-advocacy requires active participation, from the beginning, using developmentally appropriate approaches that enable students to participate in the planning process. Modeling communication and problem-solving skills from team members and supported participation for the student help with the development of effective self-advocacy skills. While self-advocacy skills development is important for all students, it is imperative for students who are twice exceptional (Reis, McGuire, & Neu, 2000). Often students who are 2e to do not recognize and appreciate their own strengths and abilities. This is especially problematic if most of the emphasis in school is placed on their disabilities or their areas of challenge. We will see that this is what happened to Emma starting in the fourth grade, when her strengths were completely overlooked and the consequences were painful. If given the appropriate support and allowed to gradually increase their level of participation, assuming a more proactive role and greater say in their plan development over time (Sebag, 2010), 2e students will acquire the self-determination skills to see them through life (Hart & Brehm, 2013).

Including the child in the problem-solving process evolves over time. Encouragement will likely involve structured coaching to help the child understand how to communicate his/her needs as he or she develops the skills necessary for full participation as a partner in the problem-solving process. In order for a student to prepare for participation in plan development, it is important to consider developmentally appropriate ways to collect information to facilitate

Box 9.2

**Ways to Gather Information Across the Developmental Age Span**

**Strengths and Interests**

- Have one-on-one conversations with student regarding his or her interests at home and at school
- Discuss student interests with family and staff
- Conduct direct observations of student in area of strength/interest
- Complete student interest forms (e.g., *Interest-A-Lyzer Family of Instruments* [Renzulli, 1997])
- Review portfolios of student work
- Collect exemplars of student work samples in areas of strength and interest
- Gather information regarding gifted behaviors (e.g., *Scales for Rating the Behavioral Characteristics of Superior Students* [Renzulli et al., 2010])

**Challenge or Disability Needs**

- Review of cumulative folder to determine any discrepant scores in class-wide assessments or screeners
- Interview teachers regarding student's academic performance, including any areas of concern
- Collect samples of student work, compare when student does his or her best versus not
- Direct observations of areas of student challenges

**Social/Emotional Needs**

- Ask students if they feel safe in their learning environment
- Ask families what resources may be necessary to support their child at home
- Discuss with students when they feel like they are performing at their optimum level
- Discuss with students situations that cause them to feel overwhelmed
- Ask students if and when a time-out would be helpful
- Direct observation of peer interactions and social skills
- Collect information from family members and staff about peer interactions and social skills

their involvement and understanding of the process. Box 9.2 offers several strategies to structure the collection of informal data that can support appropriate planning by extending the information gathered through more formal assessments.

*Fourth grade brought about a lot of changes for Emma. Because of the divorce, Emma's mother and the three children moved to an apartment in a new school district. Emma no longer presented as a happy, enthusiastic child. She was still very active and energetic, but she was withdrawn and kept to herself in class. She played with her pencil, fiddled with her hair, and pulled apart her socks thread by thread. She listened to the teacher and knew the answers when called on, but she no longer volunteered to give answers or asked perceptive questions. Emma was still struggling with reading fluidly, and she scored within average range within the class. Although she had good ideas, her writing was limited to the absolute basics and she was several grade levels behind in spelling; she rarely finished writing in the time allotted. Her new school did not have a gifted program, so other than her mother reminding the teacher that Emma had scored in the gifted range, there was no focus on her cognitive and personal strengths.*

*In fifth grade, Jack transitioned to the middle school where a number of things began to change. First, he had a psychologist who was concerned that Jack's cognitive strengths had not been addressed and began to question and advocate for a focus on his exceptional abilities. Second, he was assigned a special education aide whose own rigidity and lack of training caused her to confront him and his behaviors in negative ways and Jack became very disrespectful toward her. Third, he had English and social studies teachers who recognized his incredible strengths in these two areas and were concerned about his progress and how to challenge him.*

When a child moves to a new school, whether because of a family move or as part of their natural progression across the grades, the transition is rarely seamless. The adults change, the context changes, the demands on the child change, and often the level of expectation changes as well. Parents often feel like they have to "start from scratch" to help the new teachers understand their child's strengths. Students often feel like they have been abandoned, and they worry about the "unknowns." Teachers and educational professionals also struggle with how to identify reasonable accommodations and modifications to help the student succeed. The role of the problem-solving team becomes incredibly important to the success of these transitions. It is necessary to connect with teams in the new educational setting to share critical information to contribute to a successful plan for each student.

*By fifth grade, Emma's mother had become increasingly concerned about Emma's lethargy at home and mediocre performance in school. Her teacher assured her that she was doing fine but her mother did not agree. She could see that Emma was very unhappy and struggling. Emma would isolate herself in her room after school, spending most of her time reading and listening to music. She no longer played with other students or her siblings, and her nails were bloody from her picking at them. Homework took so long that she dropped out of after-school sports because she could not finish her work and still participate. She was totally disorganized and had no sense of time management. Long-term assignments were always late. Her mother was very concerned and requested that the school do an evaluation for special education services.*

*Jack was still demonstrating challenging behaviors that were of concern to the team and his parents. He consistently slept through his first period study skills class, never got to class on time or packed up his belongings in a timely manner, and frequently called out or challenged the teacher's information. He would seek other students' attention and laughter with negative behaviors such as falling on the ground when he entered the classroom or pulling apart his pen and making a mess.*

As the child moves into their preadolescent and adolescent youth their bodies undergo changes that often affect their medications and careful monitoring of their medicines becomes critical. This can be difficult, however, because the need for close monitoring often coincides with a growing sense of autonomy as the young person fights for control over his or her identity. Preadolescence and adolescence also increases the demands for socialization and independence. Issues that often emerge during this time period include personal hygiene, setting boundaries for personal intimacy, and appropriate response to risk-taking behaviors. Emma and Jack both demonstrated increased difficulties during these stages because of the challenges they faced in addition to normal developmental issues. The problem-solving team is critical for coordinating supports and services as things become more complex for the young person.

As we see in Table 9.3, the problem-solving team for Emma continued to ignore her areas of strength and her social emotional needs. Jack's team, on the other hand, did focus in on his strengths. These decisions directly affected the experience of both students.

*Emma's middle school years were extremely difficult. She continued to be withdrawn, depressed, and frequently angry when she returned home from school. Because her math skills were so weak, she was placed in the lowest math class, which meant that her schedule would not allow her to access the higher level English and social studies classes that were more aligned with her cognitive strengths. She felt like a "dummy" and often referred to herself as such. Her parents decided that she needed counseling, but this made Emma feel even more "broken." Her participation was so minimal that her parents finally cancelled her weekly sessions. To make herself feel that she had some control of her life, she dyed her hair blue, got a tattoo, wore an earring in her nose, and refused to take her medication.*

*At the CSE meeting, it was determined that Jack should be classified with autism spectrum disorder. The math teacher agreed to pretest him and to accelerate him based on his specific needs. Because of Jack's exceptional grasp of language and great sense of humor, he enjoyed making comments in the margins or editing almost every worksheet he was given. The English teacher appreciated his skills and humor so encouraged him to start writing a book. She made time each week to discuss his progress and to help him hone his skills. The psychologist suggested that he would work with Jack on his organization and time management skills and also suggested to administration that the special education aide be reassigned to another student. His parents noted that he had established his own computer repair business in their basement. They would continue to encourage him with this but would also insist*

*Table 9.3.* Middle School (Grades 5–8) Problem-Solving Teams for Emma and Jack

**Jack IEP**

| Members of the Team | Areas of Strength/ Interest | Areas of Concern | Strategies for Support | Strategies for Enhancements |
|---|---|---|---|---|
| Parents | Advanced math | Organization and time skills (getting to class on time and completing long-term assignments) | Checklists and graphic organizers for organization and long-term assignments | Accelerated math class |
| Jack | Computer programming and repair | Challenging teachers | Co-teaching with special education teacher for science, social studies, and special courses | Independent project with English teacher to write a book |
| Special education staff | Sense of humor | Issues with 1:1 aide | Social skills with psychologist once a week | Computer repair business at home |
| Psychologist | English class (literature and writing skills) | Calling out answers | | |
| | Social studies | | | |

**Emma 504**

| Members of the Team | Areas of Strength/ Interest | Areas of Concern | Strategies for Support | Strategies for Enhancements |
|---|---|---|---|---|
| Mother | Verbal precocity | Organization and time management skills | Extra time for tests | No focus on her cognitive or personal strengths |
| Emma | Literature, reading, and listening comprehension | Avoids reading aloud | Word processor | |
| Teacher | Music | Limited writing skills | Graphic organizers for long-term assignments | |
| 504 team | History, current events | Withdrawn socially, biting nails | Meeting with psychologist once a week | |

*that he be in bed by 10 PM each night. Although Jack continued to display some very quirky and often negative behaviors, the focus on his strengths and the team planning made a difference.*

In addition to planning for the current academic and social success of the middle school student, formal planning for future transitions to college and career should begin. Formal transition planning is required by law for students who have Individualized Education Program (IEPs). The law also requires that the student be actively involved in this planning and the goal-setting for his or her future. While formal transition planning is not mandated for students with 504 Plans, it is still a good idea. Planning for a successful postsecondary transition involves identifying personal goals and looking for individual gaps in the academic and nonacademic skills needed to reach these goals (Gothberg, Peterson, Peak, & Sedaghat, 2015).

The primary focus of transition planning during middle and high school is often academic preparation, and little attention may be given to nonacademic skills (Brand, Valent, & Danielson, 2013). A growing body of research suggests that nonacademic skills (e.g., perseverance, self-discipline, self-determination, self-advocacy, positive attitude, social interactions, forming relationships, problem-solving, resourcefulness, creativity, imagination) are key factors in success both within college and beyond (Gothberg et al., 2015; Reed, Kennett, & Emond, 2015; Wessel, Jones, Blanch, & Markel, 2015; Zionts, Hoza, & Banks, 2004). Because of their importance, nonacademic skills should be explicitly taught, modeled through role-play, and practiced (Gothberg et al., 2015). These life skills can be developed in real-world settings with the support of many different adults through experiential learning opportunities like: community service projects, job shadowing, work-related internships, and extracurricular activities (Brand et al., 2013). Parents and school counselors often play a critical role in helping students with disabilities identify their strengths and gaps in both academic and nonacademic areas and supporting students as they develop the skills needed to be successful in college (Brand et al., 2013). Emma continued to struggle to find her direction because there had been no discussion about college, but Jack had a comprehensive plan that included college planning.

*It was not until her last year of high school that Emma finally felt that she was given an opportunity to prove that she had strong cognitive abilities. She took a "blind" entrance exam for a college English course and she was accepted. The course challenged her and excited her intellect. The class focused on literature with very little writing, which meant she was able to participate in high-level class discussion without worrying about her writing difficulties. She and the teacher began exchanging books and discussing the various attributes and merits of each. Her teacher became an advocate for Emma, encouraging and supporting her.*

*By ninth grade Jack was ready for the International Baccalaureate Program offered by the school. His special education resource teacher worked with him on the organization and time management skills needed for the long-term projects as well as staying on topic and not off on tangents based on his opinions rather than facts. The high school psychologist assisted him with social skills. Like always, he got A's in all of his subjects except political science where he was having a bit of an issue due to a personality conflict with the teacher.*

Planning for college takes on heightened significance during the last two years of high school as students begin to take a more serious look at their future. For students who are twice exceptional this look can be both exciting and daunting. There is a lot to think about, starting with "why do I want to go to college?" Students with disabilities, including those who are 2e, have a variety of reasons for wanting to go to college: getting a good job to support myself, fulfilling a love of learning, exploring options for life, meeting new people, pleasing parents, earning the respect of others, delaying adult responsibilities. For some students who are 2e, a big part of wanting to go to college involves proving that "I can do it" (Reed et al., 2015).

*During her senior year, Emma took a social studies elective that would change her life. There were two parts to the course—one in which she was involved with the Senior Senate and the other in which the students participated in a mock trial. The teacher was both inspirational and influential in Emma's development of a more positive self-esteem. Her greatest accomplishment was winning Law Day, an event in which teams of students from all over the county competed. Many of Emma's early leadership skills were evident again, her self-confidence grew, and her interest in law as a profession was sparked.*

*As a high school senior Jack had been identified as a gifted student as well as diagnosed with autism spectrum disorder. Although he had made significant progress academically, socially, and emotionally during his school career, this last year in high school was much more difficult because of the focus on transitioning to college. Jack was experiencing a great deal of stress and anxiety. His college of choice was Massachusetts Institute of Technology (MIT) where he wanted to major in computer science with a minor in physics. His parents and school counselors insisted that he also apply to some "safe" schools in case he did not get accepted to MIT. He, on the other hand, thought it was a waste of his time since MIT was the best program and that was where he intended to go to school. To appease his parents, he put applications in to other colleges, but his rigidity and insistence on attending only MIT escalated his parents' concerns. His parents were stressed because they were concerned about his ability to live independently and with other students in a dorm, to get to classes on his own, and to follow through with the organizational and time management skills that he has learned.*

The decision to go to college is a big one, and finding the school that is the right fit is essential. Students with disabilities are protected from discrimination by laws that address their right to nondiscriminatory access to higher education and the right to the reasonable and effective accommodations and supports needed to be successful within these settings under Section 504, Rehabilitation Act, 1973, the

Americans with Disabilities Act of 1990, and its amendments in 2008. The level and nature of supports for students with disabilities, however, vary widely across institutes of higher education, and students with disabilities may still face social and physical barriers to their success (Agarwal, Moya, Yasui, & Seymour, 2015; Hong, 2015). Because of this, finding the right college for each student's individual strengths and needs is vital. Four questions should be considered in the college selection process:

- What campus-wide programs and policies are available for all students?
- What specific supports and services are available for students with disabilities?
- What instructional and academic accommodations and/or modifications are typically provided for students with disabilities?
- What extended community resources are available?

The problem-solving team plays a critical role in helping the student find the best fit and in supporting the student's success through comprehensive transition planning (see Table 9.4). Finding this "fit" must include the student's passions, interests, and aspirations as well as their needs for support. This planning was especially important for the plans that both Emma and Jack made at this critical juncture in their lives.

*Because her grades were mediocre, Emma chose to go to the community college for her first two years. She utilized the College Help Center on a regular basis. In fact, she requested that an assessment be done to determine if she had a learning disability and was not surprised when the psychologist and educational team confirmed that to be true. After a successful two years, Emma transferred to a competitive four-year college where she majored in political science and history with the goal of becoming a lawyer. So as she stands on the campus green with her diploma in hand, Emma knows that this next part of her academic journey will also not be easy, but she is up to the challenge and has the courage and resiliency to make it happen.*

*As a 12th-grader Jack is finishing up his high school career and looking forward to his future. The rigidity, difficulty with transitions, anxiety, and social issues that he exhibited as a young child are still present but he is more aware of his strengths. He was accepted into MIT, and, while he is a little worried about all of the changes this will bring, he feels confident that with his parents' support and the services offered on campus, he can meet this new challenge.*

As we followed Emma and Jack across their lifespan we saw the multiple challenges they faced. Their success was dependent on the commitment of numerous individuals who offered support, guidance, wisdom, and love. For students who are 2e the presence of this support is essential to their accomplishments. Parents, family, teachers, counselors, coaches, doctors, therapists, and friends all contribute to their success because it takes a team.

*Table 9.4.* High School (Grades 9–12) Problem-Solving Teams for Emma and Jack

**Jack IEP**

| Members of the Team | Areas of Strength/ Interest | Areas of Concern | Strategies for Support | Strategies for Enhancements |
|---|---|---|---|---|
| Parents | Computer Science | Transition to college | Meeting with psychologist once a week | College-level math class online |
| Jack | Sense of humor | Cognitive and behavioral rigidity | | Advanced placement for all other courses |
| Committee for special education | Exceptional grasp of language including grammar and spelling | | | |
| Psychologist | | | | |
| Guidance counselor | | | | |

**Emma 504**

| Members of the Team | Areas of Strength/ Interest | Areas of Concern | Strategies for Support | Strategies for Enhancements |
|---|---|---|---|---|
| Mother | English, particularly literature | Math skills | Remedial math class | Social studies Honors elective |
| Emma | Leadership | Spelling and writing skills still weak | Extra time on tests including the SAT | Senior Senate and Mock Trial during Law Day |
| 504 team | Social studies, particularly law, politics, and current events | | Word processor | |
| Guidance counselor | | | Graphic organizers for long-term assignments | |

## REFERENCES

Agarwal, N., Moya, E. M., Yasui, N. Y., & Seymour, C. (2015). Participatory action research with college students with disabilities: Photovoice for an inclusive campus. *Journal of Postsecondary Education and Disability*, *28*(2), 243–250.

Baldwin, L., Baum, S., Pereles, D., & Hughes, C. (2015). Twice-exceptional learners: The journey toward a shared vision. *Gifted Child Today*, *38*(4), 206–214.

Baldwin, L., Omdal, S. N., & Pereles, D. (2015). Beyond stereotypes: Understanding, recognizing, and working with twice-exceptional learners. *TEACHING Exceptional Children*, *47*(4), 216–225.

Brand, B., Valent, A., & Danielson, L. (2013). *Improving college and career readiness for students with disabilities*. Washington, DC: College and Career Readiness and Success Center at American Institutes for Research. Retrieved from http://www.ccrscenter.org/sites/default/files/Improving%20College%20and%20Career%20Readiness%20for%20Students%20with%20Disabilities.pdf

Coleman, M. R. (2011). The importance of staring early. *Perspectives on Language and Literacy*, *37*(3), 9–10.

Coleman, M. R., Buysse, V., & Neitzel, J. (2006). *Recognition and response: An early intervening system for young children at risk for learning disabilities*. Chapel Hill: University of North Carolina at Chapel Hill, FPG Child Development Institute.

Coleman, M. R., & Gallagher, S. (2015). Meeting the needs of students with 2e: It takes a team. *Gifted Child Today*, *38*(4), 252–254.

Gillis, M., West, T., & Coleman, M. R. (2009). *Early Learning Observation & Rating Scale: Development manual*. New York, NY: National Center for Learning Disabilities.

Gothberg, J. E., Peterson, L. Y., Peak, M., & Sedaghat, J. M. (2015). Successful transition of students with disabilities to 21st-century college and careers. *TEACHING Exceptional Children*, *47*(6), 344–351.

Hart, J., & Brehm, J. (2013). Promoting self-determination: A model for training elementary students to self-advocate for IEP accommodations. *TEACHING Exceptional Children*, *45*(5), 40–48.

Hong, B. S. (2015). Qualitative analysis of the barriers college students with disabilities experience in higher education. *Journal of College Student Development*, *56*(3), 209–226.

Kirk, S., Gallagher, J., & Coleman, M. R. (2105). *Educating exceptional children* (14th ed.). Stamford, CT: Cengage Learning.

Korbel, D. M., McGuire, J. M., Banerjee, M., & Saunders, S. A. (2011). Transition strategies to ensure active student engagement. *New Directions for Student Services*, *134*, 35–46.

Lee, S., Palmer, S. B., Turnbull, A. P., & Wehmeyer, M. L. (2006). A model for parent-teacher collaboration to promote self-determination in young children with disabilities. *TEACHING Exceptional Children*, *38*(3), 36–41.

Lines, C., Miller, G., & Arthur-Stanley, A. (2011). *The power of family-school partnering (FSP)*. New York, NY: Routledge, Taylor & Francis.

Neitzel, J. (2011). Early indicators of developmental delays in infants and toddlers. *Perspectives on Language and Literacy*, *37*(3), 25–26.

Reed, M., Kennett, D., & Emond, M. (2015). The influence of reason for attending university on university experience: A comparison between students with and without disabilities. *Active Learning in Higher Education, 16*(3), 225–236.

Reis, S. M., McGuire, J. M., & Neu, T. W. (2000). Compensation strategies used by high ability students with learning disabilities who succeed in college. *Gifted Child Quarterly, 44*, 123–134.

Renzulli, J. S. (1997). *Interest-A-Lyzer Family of Instruments: A manual for teachers.* Waco, TX: Prufrock Press.

Renzulli, J. S., Smith, L. H., White, A. J., Callahan, C. M., Hartman, R. K., Westberg, K. L.,. . . Sytsma, R. E. (2010). *Scales for rating the behavioral characteristics of superior students: Technical and administration manual* (3rd ed.). Waco, TX: Prufrock Press.

Sebag, R. (2010). Behavior management through self-advocacy: A strategy for secondary students with learning disabilities. *TEACHING Exceptional Children, 42*(6), 22–29.

Wessel, R. D., Jones, D., Blanch, C. L., & Markle, L. (2015). Pre-enrollment considerations of undergraduate wheelchair users and their post-enrollment transitions. *Journal of Postsecondary Education and Disability, 28*(1), 57–72.

West, T. (2011). RTI approaches to early intervening supports. *Perspectives on Language and Literacy, 37*(3), 17–24.

Zionts, L. T., Hoza, T. E., & Banks, T. I. (2004). Self-advocacy, self-determination, and adolescent brain research: What are the implications for youth with EBD? *Beyond Behavior, 13*(3), 9–11.

10

# Educating the Twice Exceptional Child

## *Creating Strong School-to-Home Collaborative Partnerships*

KEVIN BESNOY

## INTRODUCTION

> We've had very flexible teachers up until now, teachers who are willing to think outside the box and not be stuck to teaching to the norm. This is how you have to do it. It will be interesting to see what happens when we get to middle school where we'll have a whole different structure and things like that, so talk to me in six months. Because, like I said, we are very new at this, so we're not sure. But up until now, teachers have been very supportive of his situation; talking to us about it, talking to him about it. My most important thing is for him to feel satisfied, not happy all the time because no one is happy all the time and that's not satisfying anyway if he were just happy-go-lucky. (Parent of gifted student with a learning disability describing the effects of strong school-to-home collaborative partnership)

Providing appropriate services for gifted students with learning disabilities requires school officials to communicate with parents about federal education legislation, educational terminology, and pedagogy while simultaneously utilizing parent language that is not intimidating, overwhelming, or confusing. Furthermore, educators must assume the responsibility of connecting with parents of gifted children with disabilities and help them craft an effective educational experience for their children. While there are several interventions and strategies that educators can implement, one of the most effective is building strong school-to-home partnerships.

Given the difficulty with identifying precociousness among students with disabilities, this chapter discusses giftedness from the framework of Robert Sternberg's *Tiarchic Theory of Intelligence* (1985). Thinking about the manifestation of giftedness through this lens allows stakeholders to be open to the notion that students with disabilities may not necessarily exhibit stereotypic gifted behaviors. As a result, teachers and parents might begin to recognize that a child with a disability can display amazing talents through analytical, creative, and/or contextual ways.

Despite the existing body of research documenting the positive outcomes associated with strong school-to-home collaborative relationships, teachers and parents alike know that establishing and maintaining a trusting relationship is difficult. Establishing collaborative partnerships requires that parental confidence that school officials are willing and equal partners. Similarly, school officials must trust that parents are making good-faith efforts to formulate pedagogically sound interventions without questioning their professional judgment.

In addition to receiving training at the preservice teacher level, school officials receive in-service training and professional development focused on up-to-date education legislation and research-proven pedagogy practices. Their formal training imbues school officials with an extensive professional knowledge base that parents lack. This training often establishes a perceived chasm in the teacher-parent relationship.

Upon absorbing the fact that their child is both gifted and has a learning disability, parents must quickly establish a professional knowledge base that will enable them to support their child (see Coleman, Baldwin, & Pereles, this volume). Educators cannot, however, look at parents through a deficit lens; rather, they must be willing to partner with parents to provide the most effective learning environment for children (Besnoy, 2006; Besnoy et al., 2015; Collier, Keefe, & Hirrel, 2015). By establishing strong school-to-home partnerships, educators, parents, and students can pull their collective resources to become more knowledgeable about gifted students with learning disabilities and provide effective interventions that allow these children to maximize their abilities.

Collaborative school-to-home partnerships are nurtured over time and entail a lot of trust building. This chapter describes strategies educators can implement to create strong school-to-home partnerships that result in more informed parents and better services for gifted children with learning disabilities (see Coleman et al., this volume). Furthermore, it will help school officials build collaborative relationships with parents gifted children with learning disabilities.

## DEFINING GIFTED STUDENTS WITH DISABILITIES

While there is no universally accepted definition of giftedness, Sternberg's (1985) theory allows us to think about the needs of children with disabilities who exhibit extraordinary aptitudes or competences in one or more domains. According to the National Association for Gifted Children (2016), domains refer to "any structured area of activity with its own symbol system (e.g., mathematics, music, language) and/or set of sensorimotor skills (e.g., painting, dance, sports)."

Baum (1990) classified gifted students with learning disabilities students into one of three categories: (a) those identified as gifted but whose learning disability is not identified, (b) those who have an identified disability but whose giftedness is unrecognized, and (c) those whose giftedness and disability mask each other. According to Besnoy (2006), "regardless of the category, each twice exceptional student has distinguishing characteristics that must be addressed by teachers, parents, and school administrators" (p. 8).

## DEFINING POSITIVE SCHOOL-TO-HOME COLLABORATIVE RELATIONSHIPS

A child's most important advocate is her/his parent(s). The diverse demographic make-up of today's schools, however, means that there is an unevenness in the amount of time and resources that parents have to collaborate with school officials. While some parents can meet with school officials at a moment's notice to discuss their child's educational needs, others work hourly jobs that require advanced noticed in order to take time off of work to make a school meeting.

Most parents want to be effective advocates for their child; however, many are unsure of official school processes and are unaware of possible services (Matthews, Georgiades, & Smith, 2011). The literature is rich with examples of various models that detail successful strategies for parents to follow as they advocate for their child (Crozier, 1999; Duquette, Orders, Fullerton, & Robertson-Grewal, 2011; Holcomb-McCoy & Bryan, 2010). The general consensus among these researchers is that parents are more successful advocates when they are knowledgeable of school policies and able to articulate their child's needs. The gap between wanting to be an effective advocate and knowing how to be one is often frustrating for parents.

The research is pretty clear that good things happen where there are effective school-to home collaborative relationships (Boss, 2011; Collier et al., 2015). In situations where positive relationships exist, parents feel as though school officials have taken a personal and professional interest in the child. From parents' perspectives, this is powerful because they often feel powerless to maintain their parental responsibly during the time while their child is at school. In addition to positive parental perspectives, school officials also feel empowered because they know that their well-intentioned efforts are welcomed. The synergy created by mutual trust yields effective, individualized, and student-centered programming.

Developing positive school-to-home relationships requires a purposeful attempt by educators to connect with parents and empower them to be part of the process in determining their child's educational outcomes. In order to build collaborative relationships and provide gifted students with learning disabilities with appropriate interventions and programming strategies, all stakeholders need to understand the child's learner profile (i.e., social-emotional and learning characteristics) (Barber & Mueller, 2011; Galbraith, this volume). In addition, stakeholders should be knowledgeable of federal laws regarding students with disabilities, and they should be well versed in state regulations governing gifted education (Yssel, Prater, & Smith, 2010). Finally, everyone involved must collaborate in such a manner that they feel their expert voices are heard, valued, and respected. Arriving at this common ground, where all stakeholders equally share knowledge and respect, can be a lengthy and frustrating process.

The number one characteristic of a positive school-to-home collaborative relationship is consistent communication (Davern, 2004). In fact, there is a direct correlation between teachers' communication home frequency and children's positive academic and social/emotional growth (Davern; Boss, 2011; Collier et al., 2015). Despite the existing body of research documenting the positive outcomes associated with strong school-to-home collaborative relationships, teachers and parents alike know that establishing, and maintaining, a trusting relationship is difficult. Barriers to creating such relationships range from economic constraints and time limitations to ineffective communication outlets and a lack of understanding of school policies and procedures.

The type of commutation is equally as important as the frequency. Communication with parents should be inviting, informative, and inspiring. By adhering to a communication style that exhibits these characters, school officials project a message that parental input is valued and goes a long way to establishing a trusting school-to-home partnership. Responsiveclassroom.org (2011) identified the following effective communication strategies: (a) send letters home to parents at the start of each grading period, (b) schedule parent conferences (face-to-face or video) within the first few weeks of school, and (c) survey parents about the quality of services provided. In each of these communications, parents should be informed of student progress toward meeting stated goals, key deadlines for meeting and filing paper work, and other general school information.

## RESPONSIBLE PARTIES

When describing student success and the correlation to parental involvement, there is saying among educators, "Parents that need to be involved aren't and those that don't need to be involved are." The meaning of this statement is that student success improves when parents attend PTA events and parent-teacher conferences. In fact, Henderson and Mapp (2002) determined there existed a strong relationship between family involvement and student success. At the same time, research also shows that parents need to be invited into the school before they will fully engage in collaborative partnerships with school officials. To help promote positive school-to-home collaborative partnerships, the National Parent Teacher Association created the National Standards for Family-School Partnerships (n.d.), which outlines the following six standards: (a) welcoming all families into the school community, (b) communicating effectively, (c) supporting school success, (d) speaking up for every child, (e) sharing power, and (f) collaborating with community.

There are several programs that meet these standards, but all include a high-level communication that treats all parties are equals. Some examples include but are not limited to (a) parent study rooms, (b) weekly pep rallies where parents are invited to celebrate in student success, (c) community social media groups, and (d) parent celebration days. Schools that take on this type of community approach send the message that all stakeholders are valued and critical to a student's success.

## Administrator's Role

Administrators need to observe how faculty and staff describe and interact with students' families. Is there a school climate that expresses positive perceptions that all parents want their children to succeed academically and socially? Are faculty and staff willing to learn from parents about how best to create an engaging and meaningful learning environment for children? Is there an appreciation for families from diverse backgrounds? Administrators need to model affirmative responses to these questions and establish an expectation that gifted children with learning disabilities have unique needs. The answers to these questions are important because they establish the expectations that parents' perspectives are valued and need to be considered, even if they contradict a child's school persona. Responsiveclassroom.org (2011) offers administrators advice about how they can deliberately address staff's beliefs. Three specific tips include (a) modeling respect for parents in one's own speech and actions, (b) holding conversations on the topic in staff meetings, and (c) reminding staff of parents' positive intentions for their children.

No matter their leadership style, administrators establish a school's priority list and are ultimately responsible for the attention that the school community focuses on various programs. As such, administrators must make parental involvement a top priority. Not only it is important to establish a positive attitude among faculty/staff, administrators must also create an expectation about how parents need to engage with school officials. By communicating with parents multiple times throughout the year administrators can establish a school culture where parents are encouraged to be part of the team.

## Parents' Role

Research shows that most parents attend all of their child's Individualized Education Program (IEP) meetings (Spann, Kohler, & Soenksen, 2003). This finding is not all that surprising, given the fact that federal law requires that school officials afford parents every opportunity to attend such meetings. What is surprising in the same research is that parents felt that they were rely involved in the creation of interventions, goals, or evaluation methods. In addition, parents are also less satisfied with their level of involvement as their child gets older.

To counter this, parents need to specifically ask for a copy of any proposed goals, interventions, or evaluation methods before meeting with school officials. A simple written request to school officials ahead of time will satisfy this aspect. This will enable parents to review the proposals, formulate questions, and offer suggestions. Furthermore, it sets the tone that the parent is fully engaged and supportive of school officials. It is important, however, for parents to communicate with school officials in a professional manner. All communications (written and verbal) should be cordial and free of accusatory language. While schools should be seen as community centers, parents must remember that school officials are the caretakers. As such, they deserve to be communicated with the same level of respect that other professionals hold.

## Teacher's Role

The teacher is the foundation through which positive school-to-home relationships are built. Research shows that parents of gifted students with disabilities initially engage with teachers with the belief that their child's best interests are going to be cared for. Furthermore, most parents are understanding and realize that a teacher's job is tough and an inexact science. Parents know that teachers have to worry about all the children in their classroom, not just one. At the same time, they do not want their child's needs to be ignored or overlooked. They want to feel as though their child's academic and social needs are being addressed in a caring manner and with a professional approach.

As such, teachers need to be transparent with parents about how best to meet a child's needs. Teachers need to listen to parents' concerns for a child's development and be willing to find common ground on how best to create a pedagogically sound learning program. The key is to adopt and implement an open lines of communication system that informs parents of their child's current level of performance and progress to meeting developmental goals.

## Student's Role

Teaching gifted students with learning disabilities to take ownership of their educational outcomes is one hallmark of a successful school-to-home collaborative partnership. One way to promote this is to implement student-led IEP meetings. By becoming an active participant in the IEP meetings, students develop a deep understanding of their needs, are able to articulate their academic and social/emotional strengths and weaknesses, and learn lifelong self-advocacy skills. As a result of these attempts, students become the catalyst for positive school-to-home collaborative partnerships.

Establishing an environment where student-led IEP meetings is commonplace does not happen overnight; rather, it requires that all parties (administrators, parents, teachers, and students) are willing participants. In order to lead their own IEP meeting students need to (a) know their own strengths, weaknesses, and learning preferences; (b) be able to set personal learning goals and transition goals; (c) take actions to achieve goals; (d) evaluate progress toward meeting established goals; and (e) adjust goals and actions to achieve goals accordingly.

## STRATEGIES FOR CREATING STRONG SCHOOL-TO-HOME PARTNERSHIPS

Understanding everyone's role in creating strong school-to-home partnerships is important because these types of relationships cannot develop unless everyone is a contributing participant. There are a few research proven strategies that can be leveraged to help promote stronger relationships. Each of the strategies discussed here adhere to the National Standards for Family-School Partnerships and can be modified to fit any situation.

### School-to-Home Communication Books

One effective method for creating and maintaining open lines of communication is the implementation of school-to-home communication books. A significant characteristic of communications books is that it establishes two-way communication channel. Research shows that typical teachers and parents dialogue usually only happens when concerns about the child's academic or social/emotional development is present. As two-way dialogue matures, trust emerges, an appreciation for contrasting perspective materializes, and a collaborative partnership develops (Deslandes & Rivard, 2013; Lawrence-Lightfoot, 2004; Zarate, 2007). Whether used on a daily or weekly basis, the premise of these communication books is for students, parents, and teachers to establish open lines of communication.

The use of family message journals, one common form of such communication tools, improves school-to-home partnerships by helping to establish common language about learning among all parties. Furthermore, it allows students to begin taking control of their own learning because they are responsible for establishing the content of the communication and articulating their learning preferences (Zarate, 2007). This critical element empowers gifted students with learning disabilities to develop self-advocacy skills and enables them to articulate their own learning needs.

### Crowdsourcing Information

The growth of social networks to disseminate ideas and create communities of like-interests people has made it easier for school officials to create positive school-to-home partnerships. The challenge in using social networks in this manner is to develop a community that encourages and sustains engagement. Two of the biggest obstacles to effective collaboration are time and caseload. As more gifted students are added to special education caseloads, it is important to leverage social media platforms where communities can be built, questions can be asked, and resources shared. One solution to this situation is to Crowdsource information. According to Scott (2015), "*Crowdsourcing* is the practice of obtaining needed ideas or content by soliciting contribution from crowds of people in an online community . . . where each one adds a small portion that combines to create a greater result" (p. 11).

Of course, it is important for parents to be involved in the creation of a school sanctioned social media, or Crowdsourcing group, but school officials should be responsible for creating and monitoring these groups. When creating these groups, ground rules must be established so that productive lines communications are maintained. A "Bill of Rights" should be posted and agreed upon before members are granted access to the group.

- Share feedback and questions.
- Keep comments positive and brief.
- Practice collegial discourse.
- Notify site administrators of inappropriate comments.
- Share useful resources.
- Do not publicly attack other members.
- Do not use profanity.
- Do not share student names or personal information.
- Do not get into online arguments.
- Do not post comments that are off topic.

Adhering to these few basic guidelines will create a safe space where honest dialogue can occur and proactively deescalate many festering concerns.

## STUDENT TALENT SHOWCASE

As stated earlier, there is no single definition that encompasses all of gifted education. However defined, though, it is the responsibility of all stakeholders to develop the talent that young people possess. Gagné (2011) defines talent development as "the progressive transformation of outstanding natural abilities (gifts) into outstanding knowledge and skills (talents) in a specific occupational field" (p. 11). One strategy to help students transform their gifts into talents, while simultaneously fostering strong school-to-home collaborative partnerships, is to host student talent showcase events.

Rather than a talent show where students are required to perform live for an audience, student talent showcases allows organizers to vary the showcasing of student talent. Of course there can be live performance sessions, but students can also develop their products ahead of time and showcase them in a museum-style format. Another advantage of this strategy is the flexibility of when it can be delivered. For example, instead of hosting the event at night or during school hours, an entire day can be devoted to delivering the showcase, thus allowing parents and community members to visit the school around their work schedules.

## CONCLUSION

In moving forward with establishing strong school-to-home collaborative partnerships, the step that needs to be taken first is fostering a school climate that caters to the needs of the child but also establishes a positive relationship with the parents. In order to give students and parents a voice when it comes to collaborative partnerships, school officials must teach them how to have a voice. School officials hold the key to extending an olive branch to parents in the hopes that they will accept it so that educational outcomes can be achieved.

## FAMILY INTERVIEW QUESTIONS

- What makes your family unique?
- Describe three family traditions that are important to you.
- What do you like best about your family?
- How are the teachers at school similar to the people in your neighborhood?
- How are the teachers at your school different from the people in your neighborhood?
- What are your family's favorite meals?
- Who is the cook in your family?
- What is the best thing about your child coming to school? How do you feel about your child's teachers?
- What is the most difficult thing about coming to school?
- Tell me two things your teachers don't know about your child that you think they should know.
- Tell me two things your child's friends don't know about your child that you think they should know.
- Describe what your ideal school day would be like for your child.
- Describe what you want your child's life to be like when he or she grows up.

## COMMUNICATING WITH PARENTS GUIDELINES

The information here is a guide to follow when communicating with parents in any medium (face-to-face, email, phone, social media). The key for school officials is to imagine that they are the parent and think about how they would want someone to communicate with them about their child.

1. Greet the parent with a warm welcome; do not begin with detailed information.
2. Identify two to three things that the child is doing well in school/class; do not begin by detailing problems or concerns.
3. Clearly identify the concern that you have; do not be ambiguous about the child's growth areas.
4. Invite the parent to come to school for a face-to-face meeting, do not end the conversation without the parent knowing that he or she can follow-up at a later date.
5. Ask the parents if they have any questions; do not end the conversation without making sure the parent understands next steps.
6. Create a consistent line of communication that documents successes; do not communicate with the parent only when there is an issue to discuss.

## REFERENCES

Barber, C., & Mueller, C. T. (2011). Social and self-perceptions of adolescents identified as gifted, learning disabled and twice-exceptional. *Roeper Review, 33*(2), 109–120.

Baum, S., Council for Exceptional Children, & ERIC Clearinghouse on Handicapped and Gifted Children. (1990). *Gifted but learning disabled: A puzzling paradox* (ERIC Digest #E479). Washington, DC: US Department of Education.

Besnoy, K. D. (2006). *Successful strategies for twice-exceptional children.* Waco, TX: Prufrock Press.

Besnoy, K. D., Swoszowski, N. C., Newman, J. L., Floyd, A., Jones, P., & Byrne, C. (2015). The advocacy experiences of parents of elementary age, twice exceptional children. *Gifted Child Quarterly, 59*(2), 108–123.

Boss, S. (2011). Home-to-school connections guide: Tips, tech tools, and strategies for improving family-to-school communication. *Edutopia.* Retrieved from http://www.edutopia.org/pdfs/edutopia-home-to-school-guide.pdf

Collier, M., Keefe, E. B., & Hirrel, L. A. (2015). Preparing special education teachers to collaborate with families. *School Community Journal, 25*(1), 117–135.

Crozier, G. (1999). Is it a case of 'We know when we're not wanted'? The parents' perspective on parent-teacher roles and relationships. *Educational Research, 41*(3), 315–328.

Davern, L. (2004). School-to-home notebooks: What parents have to say. *TEACHING Exceptional Children, 36*(5), 22–27.

Deslandes, R., & Rivard, M. C. (2013). A pilot study aiming to promote parents' understanding of learning assessments at the elementary level. *School Community Journal, 23*(2), 9–31.

Duquette, C., Orders, S., Fullerton, S., & Robertson-Grewal, K. (2011). Fighting for their rights: Advocacy experiences of parents of children identified with intellectual giftedness. *Journal for the Education of the Gifted 34*(3), 488–512.

Gagné, F. (2011). Academic talent development and the equity issue in gifted education. *Talent Development & Excellence*, *3*(1), 3–22.

Holcomb-McCoy, C., & Bryan, J. (2010). Advocacy and empowerment in parent consultation: Implication for theory and practice. *Journal of Counseling and Development*, *88*, 259–268.

Lawrence-Lightfoot, S. (2004). Building bridges from school to home. *Instructor*, *114*(1), 24–28.

Matthews, M. S., Georgiades, S. D., & Smith, L. F. (2011). How we formed a parent advocacy group and what we've learned in the process. *Gifted Child Today*, *34*(4), 29–34.

National Association for Gifted Children. (2016, October 2). Definitions of giftedness. Retrieved from https://www.nagc.org/resources-publications/resources/definitions-giftedness

Scott, C. (2015). Designing mathematics instruction utilizing crowdsourcing as a professional development model. *Journal of Higher Education Theory and Practice*, *15*(2), 11–18.

Spann, S.J., Kohler, F.W., & Soenksen, D., (2003). Examining parents' involvement in and perceptions of special education services: An interview with families in a parent support group. *Focus on Autism and Other Developmental Disabilities*, *18*(4), 228–237.

Sternberg, R. J. (1985). *Beyond IQ: A triarchic theory of intelligence.* Cambridge, UK: Cambridge University Press.

Yssel, N., Prater, M., & Smith, D. (2010). How can such a smart kid not get it? Finding the right fit for twice-exceptional students in our schools. *Gifted Child Today*, *33*(1), 54–61.

Zarate, M. E. (2007) *Understanding Latino parental involvement: Perception, expectations, and recommendations.* Los Angeles, CA: Tomas Riviera Policy Institute.

# PART III

# Special Populations

11

# Attention Divergent Hyperactive Giftedness

## *Taking the Deficiency and Disorder out of the Gifted/ADHD Label*

C. MATTHEW FUGATE

During my years as an elementary teacher and gifted coordinator, I had the pleasure of working with children who were at a variety of academic levels of achievement. There is one student in particular who stands out and who I often describe as my *muse*, crediting him with inspiring me to follow my current path in education research. I first had the honor of meeting this student when he entered kindergarten. Our district universally tested for gifted identification at this age, and he quickly stood out as a student with an advanced vocabulary, a keen sense of humor, an inquisitive nature, and a flair for imagination and creativity.

Unfortunately, by the end of his kindergarten year and throughout first grade, it became clear that something else was going on. He quickly fell behind his peers in reading and often found himself in the principal's office due to his inability to control his behavior in the classroom. He was the typical *Alphabet Child* (Baum & Olenchak, 2002) with every letter of the labeling alphabet attached to his name. By the time he walked into my classroom in the second grade, his self-perception had changed to the point that during the second week of classes he walked up to me and stated, "Mr. Fugate, I am stupid. Everyone else in the class can read but me." I was brought to tears hearing this, shocked that a child who I knew to be so gifted could possibly see himself as "stupid." His dyslexia and impulsivity control issues related to his attention deficit hyperactivity disorder (ADHD) had started taking their toll and his love for school was beginning to wane.

Unfortunately, there are many students who feel "stupid" in classrooms all around the country. They may know that they are gifted, but their ADHD and co-occurring conditions can make them feel isolated and alone. Moon and Reis

(2004) have stated that, because giftedness is outside the norm, it is by definition an exceptionality. When a student presents characteristics of giftedness—evidence of potential for high intellectual, creative, or leadership abilities—combined with a learning or behavioral difference, they are said to be *twice* exceptional (Baum & Olenchak, 2002; Foley-Nicpon, 2013; Moon & Reis, 2004). There are an estimated 385,000 twice exceptional students in our schools (Assouline, Colangelo, VanTassel-Baska, & Lupkowski-Shoplik, 2015). However, this number may actually be much greater due to the lack of a systematic identification approach for these students (Foley-Nicpon, Allmon, Sieck, & Stinson, 2011), combined with the tendency for educators to focus on a child's challenges rather than their strengths and then using this as evidence that the child could not possibly be gifted (Assouline, Foley-Nicpon, & Huber, 2006; Schultz, 2012).

According to the *Diagnostic and Statistical Manual of Mental Disorders* (5th ed.; American Psychiatric Association, 2013), ADHD can be diagnosed based upon the level of inattentiveness and/or hyperactivity-impulsivity exhibited in an individual when observed in more than one setting. Indeed, ADHD has been identified as the most commonly diagnosed childhood behavioral disorder (American Academy of Pediatrics, 2011) with a prevalence rate in the United States estimated to be 6.4 million school-aged children (Visser et al., 2016). Although ADHD is most commonly thought of as a behavioral disorder, these children can face a multitude of challenges including, first and foremost, the potential for the presence of co-occurring learning deficiencies in reading and/or mathematics (Zentall, 2006). They are also at risk of being three to seven times more likely to be suspended or expelled and/or provided with special education services (LeFever, Villers, Morrow, & Vaughn, 2002) and are more likely to experience failure in school with significantly higher dropout rates than their non-ADHD peers (Barron, Evans, Baranik, Serpell, & Buvinger, 2006).

## GETTING TO KNOW THE GIFTED/ADHD LEARNER

Students who are gifted with ADHD face unique academic challenges. A normal distribution of IQ scores has been found in children with ADHD (Kaplan, Crawford, Dewey, & Fischer, 2000), suggesting that there is no reason to think that there are any more or less instances of ADHD in the gifted population. However, due to cognitive processing problems often found in these students, it has been found that their composite IQ scores can typically be 5 to 10 points lower than their non-ADHD peers of similar ability (Castellanos, 2000; Hughes, 2011). Because these scores do not reflect the true potential of these students, educators often fail to recognize gifted potential in students with ADHD, particularly in school districts that rely on IQ scores for identification (Hughes, 2011; Moon, 2002; Silverman, 2002). Other common characteristics affecting the academic performance of students who are gifted with ADHD are a lack of organizational skills (Nielsen, 2002), poor working memory (Fugate, Zentall, & Gentry, 2013), the inability to maintain attention (Zentall, Moon, Hall, & Grskovic, 2001), and poor metacognitive skills (Davis, Rimm, & Siegle, 2010).

In addition to academic challenges, these twice exceptional students may also face many social-emotional difficulties. Baum and Owen (1988) have suggested that disruptive behaviors in class may be an outward sign of these students' feelings of inadequacy and low self-esteem related to their achievement in school when compared with their peers. Further, they can display emotional intensity (Olenchak & Reis, 2002), suffer from low self-concept and self-esteem (Foley-Nicpon, Rickles, Assouline, & Richards, 2012), and experience frustration that leads to a general lack of motivation (Baum & Owen, 1988). These characteristics, combined with an inability to control verbal and/or physical impulsivity, often cause difficulties for these students when relating to their same-age peers, leading to feelings of alienation (Johnson & Kendrick, 2005; Moon, Zentall, Grskovic, Hall, & Stormont, 2001) and difficulties making and maintain friendships (Grskovic & Zentall, 2010). Renzulli and Reis (2009) highlighted the following quote that sums up the difficulties experienced by many twice exceptional students.

> I believe I didn't have friends because I was different. . . . I didn't think the way most kids thought. I didn't care about a lot of the things that they did, and I would spend a lot of time alone because I was comfortable alone, and why you would go out to recess walking alone being comfortable by yourself, people start to think you are strange. So that made the cycle worse. (p. 186)

Interestingly, in a recent collective case study of five gifted girls with ADHD, it was found that although they had difficulties relating to most of their same-age peers, the girls in this study all reported maintaining long-term relationships with a small, close-knit group of friends who they felt understood them because they were alike behaviorally. One of the girls reported that when she was with her friends, she could "let myself behave how I want myself to behave; not how my brain wants me to, but how my heart feels" (Fugate, 2014, p. 78).

## CREATIVITY AND THE *ADHG* LEARNER

Although these twice exceptional students may demonstrate varying degrees of difficulty in their academic and social worlds, there is evidence, dating as far back as the late 1980s, to suggest that students who are gifted, or with above average intelligence, with ADHD may have a greater potential for creativity and creative achievement (e.g., Fugate et al., 2013; Kuester & Zentall, 2011; Shaw & Brown, 1999; Zentall, 1988). Specifically, researchers have found that gifted students with ADHD scored higher on tests of creative thinking (Cramond, 1994; Fugate et al., 2013); told more creative stories with novel themes (Zentall, 1988); used more visual imagery and strategies during problem-solving in response to high states of arousal, such as when watching and playing videos and games (Lawrence et al., 2002; Shaw & Brown, 1999); and contributed to higher percentages of correct problem solutions in cooperative groups (Kuester & Zentall, 2011) when compared with their same-age peers. Further, when comparing college students with and without ADHD, White and Shah (2006) found that the students with ADHD outperformed their non-ADHD peers in measures of divergent thinking in the areas of fluency, flexibility, and originality. Additionally, these students were found to be more innovative in their thinking (White & Shah, 2016) and reported higher levels of creative achievement (White & Shah, 2011).

Based upon these findings, Fugate and Gentry (2016) have suggested that these students be viewed as attention *divergent* hyperactive *gifted* (ADHG). This type of paradigm shift alters the focus from the challenges that these students face and instead highlights their potential for creativity, innovation, and motivation.

## PRACTICAL APPROACHES TO ADDRESSING THE NEEDS OF ADHG STUDENTS

It is important that educators pay attention to and cultivate the creativity and innovation inherent in these ADHG students, rather than to let these qualities remain dormant and underdeveloped. In order to accomplish this, it is important that schools implement a systematic approach to the identification of these students combined with in-class supports and strategies that highlight the strengths of these students and leverages those strengths to address their challenges.

### Identification

As previously stated, the 385,000 twice exceptional students estimated by Assouline et al. (2015) could be a conservative number, due to the lack of systematic procedures to identify these students. One reason for this is due to a phenomenon known as the *masking effect* (McCoach, Kehle, Bray, & Siegle, 2001; Pfeiffer, 2013). Children who are gifted and have a learning and/or behavioral disability display characteristics of both conditions with one often hiding the characteristics of the other, the frequent result being that the student presents as "average" with neither his/her strengths nor challenges being adequately addressed (Baum, Cooper, & Neu, 2001; Zentall et al., 2001). This can have serious academic consequences for these students, particularly under the Response to Intervention model, because although they may be working below their potential, their performance may not be below that of their grade-level peers and therefore they are never identified with an intervention need. Baum and Olenchak (2002) found it to be extremely rare for assessments for identification in gifted programs to occur once a diagnosis for ADHD or another disability had been made. It has also been reported that in those instances when students were identified as both gifted and ADHD, the students were apt to have been retained more often; performed poorly on standardized tests; and experienced higher rates of mood and anxiety disorders when compared to their gifted, non-ADHD peers (Antshel, 2008).

To address these concerns, Nielsen (2002) encouraged schools to establish a multidisciplinary task force who would advocate for, and raise awareness of, the needs of twice exceptional students. This task force should include gifted education, special education, and general education teachers, as well as any diagnosticians responsible for the testing and identification of students for special education services. The primary functions of this group would be to establish and oversee a process of identification and the development of a continuum of service options that meets the unique needs of these ADHG students and "[focuses] on developing the talent while compensating for the disability" (Renzulli & Reis, 2009, p. 187). To increase awareness, the task force should seek out professional development opportunities for all stakeholder—teachers, administrators, diagnosticians, paraprofessionals, *and parents*. These opportunities would focus on recognizing the characteristics associated with these students for identification, as well as best practices for differentiation to meet their needs.

Nielsen (2002) recommends that identification begins with a thorough examination of the special education records to identify students who have an IQ score of 120 or higher (Nielsen, 2002). I would argue that records also be carefully examined for students with an IQ of 110 or higher, due to the 5- to 10-point difference that can exist when compared to their similar-ability peers (Castellanos, 2000; Hughes, 2011). Additionally, an examination of the records of identified gifted students should also be conducted for any indications of a special need that might require further evaluation for special education services. During this process of records examination, Nielsen stresses the importance of carefully exploring any discrepancies between the results of abilities tests and measures of academic performance, as well as any extreme score variation on individual abilities subtests. Because students with ADHD often have deficiencies in cognitive processes related to indicators such as coding and digit span, the discrepant subscores and full-scale scores may not accurately reflect the ability of the student. Finally, it is important that multiple data sources be used for identification. Because creative thinking has been found to be a strength in ADHG students (see Cramond, 1994; Fugate et al., 2013, for review), the use of measures that evaluate divergent thinking, such as the Torrance Tests for Creative Thinking (Torrance, 2006), may be important when developing identification plans for these students.

## Classroom Strategies

It is important that teachers incorporate a variety of classroom strategies that recognize that these ADHG students are gifted *first*, addressing and enhancing their strengths, then using those strengths to address the challenges that they face. The challenge for teachers, then, is to create classroom environments in which "creativity is emphasized as a *pathway to* learning as well as an outcome of learning" (Fugate et al., 2013, p. 242). This type of environment encourages students to ask questions and make connections beyond just finding the correct answer. It is an environment in which teachers encourage their students' interests and passions and provides them with timely, positive feedback on work that is challenging with realistic goals and time frames established with and/or by the students (Drapeau, 2014).

Hayes (2016) suggests some specific strategies that can be easily incorporated in the classroom when working with ADHG students. For instance, these students should be allowed to test out of units of study in which they demonstrate mastery. Additionally, when they are working on larger projects or are involved in coursework that is new or more challenging, it is important to break tasks down into smaller, more manageable chunks. The ability to successfully complete these subtasks builds positive self-efficacy that can help them take on larger tasks in the future. Further, offering students choice in how they learn and in the types of products that they produce to demonstrate understanding gives them an opportunity to develop autonomy and take responsibility for their own learning. As previously stated, researchers have found that students with ADHD were able to maintain high states of arousal when involved in games and videos. Therefore, the utilization of technology for high-level research, online classes, and educational games and programs can increase student interest and attention.

Finally, these students have a reverse hierarchy of learning that is focused on "the big picture" as opposed to the discrete skills emphasized in the learning objectives often associated with district and state standards. For example, when reading from a science textbook is the primary source of learning for a student with attention and processing deficiencies related to ADHD, a deficiency is created in science (Hughes, 2011). Rather, these students need to be exposed to authentic learning experiences that emphasize applied content knowledge over the process of acquisition of knowledge. Project-based learning is one example of a learning experience that provides this type of authentic learning and may be especially appropriate for ADHG students. Implications for creative writing and problem-solving within science, social studies, literature, and mathematics can yield a variety of interest-based student products including cartoons, role-playing, blogs, videos, and newspaper articles. Learning can then be deepened and broadened through the revision of these products for different audiences (Fugate et al., 2013).

Hayes (2016) offers several suggestions for teachers to consider when planning for authentic learning experiences. First, when planning their lesson, it is important to keep in mind what teachers would like their ADHG students to be able to demonstrate to show understanding. This requires that teachers identify the specific cognitive skills (e.g., using algebra as a tool to solve everyday problems), affective skills (e.g., working with others/team-building), and metacognitive skills (e.g., how to conduct research) that they want their students to develop. Once this has been accomplished, they should create a list of those areas of mastery that they want them to develop (e.g., cause and effect relationships). To get them started, include on this list specific questions that they could answer, topics they might explore, and/or online resources. Next, determine the amount of time that it will take to complete the project-based learning experience, understanding that ADHG students often need extended time to fully develop their ideas. Providing them with opportunities to "walk away" for a period of time allows for reflection in order to further build upon their ideas when they return to the project.

When teachers are ready to present the student with the project-based learning experience, it is important to clearly explain that the objective is to demonstrate mastery of the content through the process of the project, not through the final product itself. This will allow the student to develop products that demonstrate his or her learning based upon individualized areas of interests. The prospect of choosing their own learning product may be new to the ADHG learner; therefore, Hayes (2016) suggests providing them with examples of possible projects to spark their creativity (e.g., design a living history museum, design and develop a community garden, develop a website). To further promote opportunities for choice and to enhance learning, provide students with occasions to engage with others; "the beauty of teaching through individual projects is that children can work on their own, in a group, with a partner, or engage in a combination of solo and group endeavors" (Hayes, 2016, p. 5). Next, work with students to create a self-checklist that breaks the project into smaller parts with periodic check-in times to obtain teacher support as needed. This will help students learn to self-regulate and stay on-task while building their self-efficacy. Finally, it is important to allow students time to present their work in class. As Hayes points out, this allows them to not only share their own learning but to learn from their peers "in a multi-modality, high-interest way" (p. 5).

## CONCLUSION

For decades, researchers have focused on the importance of creativity in education and the connections between levels of divergent thinking skills related to creativity and students who are diagnosed with ADHD. In order to foster creativity in the classroom, it is important to approach education from a strength-based perspective as opposed to one that is focused on remediating weaknesses. This is particularly beneficial for ADHG students who we must start to see not as having a deficiency or disorder but as motivated individuals with strengths, perseverance, and resilience—innate qualities that make them so very special.

## REFERENCES


American Academy of Pediatrics. (2011). ADHD: Clinical practice guidelines for the diagnosis, evaluation, and treatment of attention-deficit/hyperactivity disorder in children and adolescents. *Pediatrics, 128*(5), 1007–1022

American Psychiatric Association. (2013). *Diagnostic and statistical manual of mental disorders* (5th ed.). Arlington, VA: Author.

Antshel, K. M. (2008). Attention-deficit hyperactivity disorder in the context of a high intellectual quotient/giftedness. *Developmental Disabilities Research Reviews, 14*, 293–299.

Assouline, S. G., Colangelo, N., VanTassel-Baska, J., & Lupkowski-Shoplik, A. (2015). *A nation empowered: Evidence trumps the excuses holding back America's brightest students, Vol. 2.* Iowa City, IA: Connie Belin & Jacqueline N. Blank International Center for Gifted Education and Talent Development.

Assouline, S. G., Foley-Nicpon, M., & Huber, D. H. (2006). The impact of vulnerabilities and strengths on the academic experiences of twice-exceptional students: A message to school counselors. *Professional School Counseling, 10,* 14–24.

Barron, K., Evans, S., Baranik, L., Serpell, Z., & Buvinger, E. (2006). Achievement goals of students with ADHD. *Learning Disability Quarterly, 29,* 137–158.

Baum, S. M., Cooper, C. R., & Neu, T. W. (2001). Dual differentiation: An approach for meeting the curricular needs of gifted students with learning disabilities. *Psychology in the Schools, 38,* 477–490.

Baum, S. M., & Olenchak, F. R. (2002). The alphabet children: GT, AHDH, and more. *Exceptionality, 10,* 77–91.

Baum, S., & Owen, S. (1988). High ability/learning disabled students: How are they different? *Gifted Child Quarterly, 32,* 226–230.

Castellanos, X. (2000, November). *ADHD or gifted: Is it either/or?* Paper presented at the annual meeting of the National Association for Gifted Children, Atlanta, GA.

Cramond, B. (1994). Attention-deficit hyperactivity disorder and creativity: What is the connection? *The Journal of Creative Behavior, 28,* 193–210.

Davis, G. A., Rimm, S. B., & Siegle, D. (2010). *Education of the gifted and talented,* 6th Ed. Boston, MA: Prentice Hall.

Drapeau, P. (2014). *Sparking student creativity: Practical ways to promote innovative thinking and problem solving.* Alexandria, VA: ASCD.

Foley-Nicpon, M., Allmon, A., Sieck, B., & Stinson, R. D. (2011). Empirical investigation of twice-exceptionality: Where have we been? Where are we going? *Gifted Child Quarterly, 55,* 3–17.

Foley-Nicpon, M., Rickels, H., Assouline, S. G., & Richards, A. (2012). Self-esteem and self-concept examination among gifted students with ADHD. *Journal for the Education of the Gifted, 35,* 220–240.

Fugate, C. M. (2014). *Lifting the cloak of invisibility: A collective case study of girls with characteristics of giftedness and ADHD.* (Unpublished doctoral dissertation). Purdue University, West Lafayette, IN.

Fugate, C. M., & Gentry, M. (2016). Understanding adolescent gifted girls with ADHD: Motivated and achieving. *High Ability Studies, 27,* 83–109.

Fugate, C. M., Zentall, S. S., & Gentry, M. (2013). Creativity and working memory in gifted students with and without characteristics of attention deficit hyperactive disorder: Lifting the mask. *Gifted Child Quarterly, 57,* 234–236.

Grskovic, J. A., & Zentall, S. S. (2010). Understanding ADHD in girls: Identification and social characteristics. *International Journal of Special Education, 25,* 170–183.

Hayes, M. (2016, September/October). Teaching 2e children. *2e Newsletter,* 3–6.

Hughes, C. E. (2011). Twice-exceptional children: Twice the challenges, twice the joys. In J. A. Castellano & A. D. Frazer (Eds.), *Special populations in gifted education: Understanding our most able students from diverse backgrounds* (pp. 153–174). Waco, TX: Prufrock Press.

Johnsen, K., & Kendrick, J. (Eds.). (2005). *Science education for gifted students.* Waco, TX: Prufrock Press.

Kaplan, B. J., Crawford, S. G., Dewey, D. M., & Fisher, G. C. (2000). The IQs of children with ADHD are normally distributed. *Journal of Learning Disabilities, 33*, 425–432.

Kuester, D. A., & Zentall, S. S. (2011). Social interaction rules in cooperative learning groups for students at-risk for ADHD. *Journal of Experimental Education, 80*, 69–95.

Lawrence, V., Houghton, S., Tannock, R., Douglas, G., Durkin, K., & Whiting, K. (2002). ADHD outside the laboratory: Boy's executive function performance on tasks in videogame play and on a visit to the zoo. *Journal of Abnormal Child Psychology, 30*, 447–462.

LeFever, G. B., Villers, M. S., Morrow, A. L., & Vaughn, E. S. (2002). Parental perceptions of adverse educational outcomes among children diagnosed and treated for ADHD: A call for improved school/provider collaboration. *Psychology in the Schools, 39*, 63–71.

McCoach, D.B., Kehle, T.J., Bray, M.A., & Siegle, D. (2001). Best practices in the identification of gifted students with learning disabilities. *Psychology in the Schools, 38*(5), 403–411.

Moon, S. (2002). Gifted children with attention deficit/hyperactivity disorder. In M. Neihart, S. Reis, N. Robinson, & S. Moon (Eds.). *The social and emotional development of gifted children: What do we know?* (pp. 193–204). Waco, TX: Prufrock Press.

Moon, S. M. & Reis, S. M. (2004). Acceleration and twice-exceptional students. In N. Colangelo, S. G. Assouline, & M. U. M. Gross (Eds.), *A nation deceived: How schools hold back America's brightest students, Vol. I,* (109–119). Iowa City, IA: The Connie Belin & Jacqueline N. Blank International Center for Gifted Education and Talent Development.

Moon, S., Zentall, S. S., Grskovic, J., Hall, A. M., & Stormont, M. (2001). Social and family characteristics of boys with giftedness and/or attention deficit/hyperactivity disorder. *Journal for the Education of the Gifted, 24*, 207–247.

Nielsen, M. E. (2002). Gifted students with learning disabilities: Recommendations for identification and programming. *Exceptionality, 10*, 93–111.

Olenchak, F. R., & Reis, S. M. (2002). Gifted children with learning disabilities. In M. Neihart, S. M. Reis, N. M. Robinson, & S. M. Moon (Eds.), *The social and emotional development of gifted children: What do we know?* (pp. 177–192). Waco, TX: Prufrock Press.

Pfeiffer, S. I. (2013). *Serving the gifted: Evidence-based clinical and psychoeducational practice.* New York, NY: Routledge.

Renzulli, J. S., & Reis, S. M. (2009). *Light up your child's mind.* New York, NY: Little, Brown.

Schultz, S. M. (2012). Twice exceptional students enrolled in advanced placement classes. *Gifted Child Quarterly, 56*, 119–133.

Shaw, G. A., & Brown, G. (1999). Arousal, time estimation, and time use in attention-disordered children. *Developmental Neuropsychology, 16*, 227–242.

Silverman, L. K. (2002). *Upside-down brilliance: The visual-spatial learner.* Denver, CO: DeLeon.

Torrance, E. P. (2006). *TTCT—Torrance Tests of Creative Thinking.* Bensenville, IL: Scholastic Testing Services.

Visser, S. N., Danielson, M. L., Wolraich, M. L., Fox, M. H., Grosse, S. D., Valle, L. A., . . . Peacock, G. (2016). Vital signs: National and state-specific patterns of attention deficit/hyperactivity disorder treatment among insured children ages 2–5 years—United States, 2008–2014. *Morbidity and Mortality Weekly Report, 65*, 443–450.

White, H. A., & Shah, P. (2006). Uninhibited imaginations: Creativity in adults with attention-deficit/hyperactive disorder. *Personality and Individual Differences*, *40*, 1121–1131.

White, H. A., & Shah, P. (2011). Creative style and achievement in adults with attention-deficit/hyperactive disorder. *Personality and Individual Differences*, *50*, 673–677.

White, H. A., & Shah, P. (2016). Scope of semantic activation and innovative thinking in college students with ADHD. *Creativity Research Journal*, *28*, 275–282.

Zentall, S. S. (1988). Production deficiencies in elicited language but not in the spontaneous verbalizations of hyperactive children. *Journal of Abnormal Child Psychology*, *16*, 657–673.

Zentall, S. S. (2006). *ADHD and education: Foundations, characteristics, methods, and collaboration*. Upper Saddle River, NJ: Pearson Education.

Zentall, S. S., Moon, S., Hall, A. M., & Grskovic, J. (2001). Learning and motivational characteristics of boys with giftedness and/or attention deficit/hyperactivity disorder. *Exceptional Children*, *67*, 499–519.

12

# Appreciating and Promoting Social Creativity in Youth with Asperger's Syndrome

MATTHEW D. LERNER AND REBECCA M. GIRARD ■

## AUTISM SPECTRUM DISORDER

Autism spectrum disorders (ASD) describe a constellation of social, communicative, and learning challenges, which themselves encompass a group of children representing a wide range of abilities. Included within this—indeed, now representing a distinct plurality of children with ASD—are those with average to exceptional measured intellectual capacity, a group sometimes referred to as having Asperger's syndrome (while Asperger's disorder no longer appears in the *Diagnostic and Statistical Manual of Mental Disorders* as of the 2013 fifth edition, Asperger's syndrome is still often used informally, colloquially, and sometimes professionally to delineate this subgroup of the population and so is employed judiciously in this chapter). Youth with Asperger's syndrome are often considered to be twice exceptional in a profound and pervasive sense (Cash, 1999), inasmuch as they often exhibit deep knowledge of specific topics yet sometimes have difficulty applying this knowledge flexibly, especially in social situations.

Such difficulty in processing and flexibly adapting to social information is often described as being related to the social deficits often described as "core" to ASD (Hobson, 2013; Mendelson, Gates, & Lerner, 2016). Indeed, dating almost all the way back to Kanner's (1943) original work defining ASD, rigidity of thought and action—as well as a lack of consequent novel or creative expression—has long been considered a hallmark of ASD, especially in social domains. In this chapter, we discuss this claim, while showing evidence that, in fact, many individuals with ASD show normative or even exceptional creativity (including social creativity), that such abilities can act as a source of social connection for this population, and that they can be fostered in individuals.

## CREATIVITY IN ASD

Due to common cognitive rigidity and "sticky thinking," youth with ASD, including those with Asperger's syndrome, have long been described as lacking imagination or creativity (Wing & Gould, 1979). From early accounts describing a limited repertoire of creative play to educational approaches advocating structured learning (i.e., rote and systematic approaches to teaching skills and knowledge) as optimal for youth with ASD, this claim pervades understanding of ASD. While the controversial notion of the "autistic savant" has long been evident in the field (Donnelly & Altman, 1994), this has generally been viewed through the lens of extreme splinter skills (e.g., the ability to reproduce visual images with great detail via pencil drawing) rather than an extension of creativity as it is usually understood. Indeed, claims of an inability to "generalize" skills arise from this premise: if a person is not capable of creative expression, surely he or she must also extrapolate from one type of situation to another with great difficulty, and vice versa.

Challenges in creative and pretend play are often considered diagnostic hallmarks of ASD (Jarrold, 2003; Kang, Klein, Lillard, & Lerner, 2016). In fact, the *Autism Diagnostic Observation Schedule* (ADOS; Lord, Rutter, DiLavore, & Risi, 1999), which is the "gold standard" diagnostic measure of ASD, itself even includes assessment of creative play as part of its evaluative process, especially in the modules targeting more cognitively able individuals. Across several activities, children who fail to come up with flexible, independent, creative play procedures often score higher (i.e., more ASD symptoms) on certain ADOS items. However, interestingly, the "creativity" items do not load highly on the core ADOS diagnostic algorithm, suggesting that, while difficulties in creative or flexible play are common, they are not sufficient to effectively differentiate those with and without ASD.

This failure of "lack of pretend play" to effectively differentiate those with and without ASD has strong ecological validity—and, indeed, contemporary understanding of ASD undercuts the notion that creativity and imagination are precluded (Roth, 2007). Even a cursory examination of online communities of individuals with Asperger's syndrome reveals a rich and vibrant creative universe (SomethingWitty, 2012). Individuals with Asperger's have written award-winning books (of fiction and nonfiction; Angleberger, 2012; Robison, 2008) and created novel technologies and research discoveries (Dawson, Soulières, Gernsbacher, & Mottron, 2007). Such creative outlets are fast becoming not only venues for expression but also a rallying point for others in the community to express themselves as well.

Recently, for instance, the first all-ASD sketch comedy troupe in the world, unironically called Asperger's Are Us, began experiencing a surge in popularity.

After touring for several years, the eponymous documentary about them received rave reviews at the SXSW film festival and was picked up for production by the Duplass Brothers and Netflix. This documentary reveals the creative process of Asperger's Are Us, which relies heavily on word-play, dark comedy, and blatant silliness. It is their shared sense of the absurd and desire to stretch sketch comedy to new limits that brought them together and solidified their friendship. It is also what endears them to their fast-growing audience—they are doing comedy differently, in novel, interesting ways that are, in part, attributed to their ability to conceive not only comedy but life in general differently (and less constrained by normative social expectation), through the lens of their Asperger's syndrome.

## SOCIAL CREATIVITY

One domain in which creativity has long been particularly implicated in Asperger's syndrome is flexible social responding. Sometimes called *social creativity* (Mouchiroud & Lubart, 2002), this construct represents the ability to come up with novel scenarios to social problems. Its measurement is not dissimilar from other creativity instruments—a child is given a set of scenarios (e.g., coming up with ways to get other children to play with him) and is asked to generate as many responses as possible, trying to think of ideas that others might not have. Their responses are rated by a set of reliable judges and then corrected for generativity (i.e., an average score is generated for each participant by dividing the sum of the creativity scores by the total number of responses, thereby not biasing individuals who simply provide *more* responses). What is interesting about such a measure is that it is conceptually distinct from (and, in some cases, even inversely related to) knowing what the *correct* response to a social scenario is. For instance, when responding to the aforementioned scenario of trying to get other children to play, the response "I would ask them to please play with me," would likely yield a score of 2 or less on a 1 to 7 Likert scale (with 1 being not at all creative and 7 being highly creative). This is, of course, a "correct" and normative social response and certainly one that would typically be taught to children with Asperger's syndrome in traditional social interventions. However, the response "I would add a twist to their game and make it about pirates and astronauts," or "I would pretend to call forth aliens to mind control the kids to play with me" might be rated at a 7 or above. Importantly, this is not necessarily an a priori adaptive response. Indeed, a child who tries this in real life might not achieve social success. Nonetheless, it is unambiguously a more creative response.

Crucially, as measured this way, social creativity is linked to a number of adaptive outcomes, including teacher-reported social competency and popularity (Mouchiroud & Bernoussi, 2008). Indeed, even factors that typically relate to such outcomes (like verbal ability and/or IQ) were not found to do so. This suggests that, rather than being a hindrance or necessitating atypical social behavior that other children would not accept, social creativity may present an avenue, or at least a way of thinking, that permits children to attempt social experiences that might otherwise be difficult or stressful for them; it also suggests that such attempts may indeed be met with success.

## SOCIAL CREATIVITY IN ASD

As described already, contemporary accounts of ASD that preclude creative capacity strain credulity. However, does this extend to social creativity? Again, most accounts of social behavior in ASD highlight a rigid or rote capacity and focus, with difficulties in generalization of skills across settings and adapting to new information. It is plausible, though, that we have traditionally sought to understand social behavior in individuals with ASD (and particularly Asperger's syndrome) through a refracted lens. That is, researchers and clinicians often seek specific, prescriptive, putatively adaptive behaviors (such as saying hello, shaking hands, or asking questions) as indications that a child "has social skills" in this population. Yet, in typically developing children, such a framework would be criticized as overly reductionistic, failing to account for the complexity and novelty of social interaction that most often yields social success (e.g., friendship-making). Indeed, as described in the previous section, it is precisely the ability to come up with novel, creative responses to social situations—and not necessarily the ability to come up with "correct" responses—that appears to predict social success in typically developing youth (Mouchiroud & Bernoussi, 2008). Perhaps social creativity, then, is indeed quite present in youth with Asperger's syndrome, but it is either ignored, missed, or even discouraged at times in favor or more "normative" behaviors. As well, perhaps it can—and in some cases does—serve a similar social connective role for individuals with Asperger's syndrome, providing opportunities to flourish and feel welcome in a world in which they may otherwise feel ill at ease.

Clinically, this is certainly a phenomenon we have observed often in our practices. Rather than being constrained by the range of behaviors and responses prescribed by social norms, individuals with ASD/Asperger's syndrome are able to access a much broader array of creative social responses. While in some cases these may be considered "quirky," they can, in fact, represent a broadened vista of potential social behaviors and means of connection.

Some children, for instance, may quickly develop shared inside jokes arising from the simplest experiences. In one group of children with Asperger's, we observed a child note, "I like chairs" as a *non sequitur* during an otherwise straightforward conversation. This observation was found to be immediately hilarious for its simultaneous literalness and absurdity, both by the children and the adults in the group. It then became a running joke for several weeks, providing a natural icebreaker and tension-reducer in a way that such a statement rarely would among typically developing youth.

Other children may, for instance, elaborate on a snippet of a thought, which then becomes a source of a whole repertoire of interactions. One child with whom we worked, for instance, was very interested in the realization that "some fish bite." However, despite this being a potential perseverative interest, he would often have elaborate discussions on this topic and would engage the adults with whom he was working in genuinely informative, inquisitive back-and-forth conversations on the topic that were engaging, reciprocal, and—indeed—creative. Thus engagement and elaboration around this simple point of interest can broaden the topography of the social landscape. Such interactions may, of course, preclude surface-level, "cocktail party conversations." In the field, this has often been taken to mean that such individuals cannot access social interactions successfully at all. Instead, perhaps it means that social interactions for individuals with ASD are more likely to be bimodal—either minimal (i.e., getting one's needs met), or significantly more profound and connected. This, then, shifts the perspective of the typically developing individual. Rather than expecting the child with ASD to meet you where *you* are socially, instead it is incumbent upon the neurotypical to *earn the right* and ability to engage with the sometimes vastly more complex and creative social world of that child.

We subsequently conducted a study to examine the relationship between social creativity, rote social knowledge, and prosocial behavior among individuals with ASD (Lerner, Lucchetti, & Mikami, 2013). In this study, we recruited 41 adolescents with so-called "high functioning" ASD (a term used loosely here, since there is much appropriate debate about the implications of using the term "high functioning" to delineate verbal ability but not adaptive functioning) or Asperger's syndrome; that is, they all had average to exceptional measured IQ and all met criteria for ASD (including via the ADOS). We then had them complete measures of social creativity (the Social Creativity Task, in which they provide an array of novel solution to social problems and situations); social knowledge (the Children's Assertive Behavior Scale, which is adapted to ask "what is the right thing to do" in given social situations; Michelson & Wood, 1982), current (ADOS) and lifetime (Social Communication Questionnaire; Rutter, Bailey, & Lord, 2005) ASD symptoms, and observed prosocial behavior (they were observed during free play, with these interactions coded using the Social Interaction Observation Scale; Bauminger, 2002).

For the social creativity tasks, all answers were double-coded by blinded, randomly assigned coders, counterbalanced by coder pair. This approach achieved excellent reliability (interclass correlation coefficient (1,2) = .79). We found that the range of creativity of our participants did not differ much from that of typically developing peers. We also found that their social knowledge was, on average, not different from typically developing peers but that they exhibited an especially wide range (i.e., some children knew few if any "correct" answers, while others knew almost all of them perfectly).

In terms of relationships between variables, we first found that social knowledge and social creativity were uncorrelated with each other (see Figure 12.1; $r = .03$, $p = .83$); social knowledge ($r = -.11$, $p = .48$) and social creativity ($r = .08$, $p = .62$) were each individually uncorrelated with IQ. This suggests that, as suspected, knowing correct social responses to social situations and being able to generate novel, creative responses to those solutions represent different constructs; it also suggests that neither is accounted for simply by being highly verbally able.

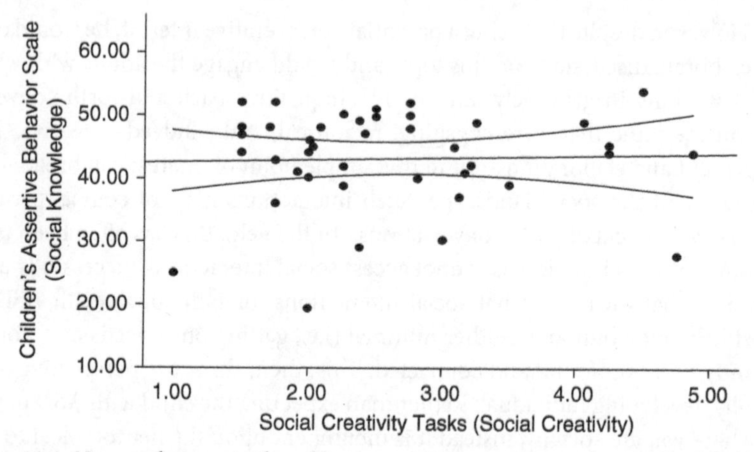


**Figure 12.1** No correlation was found between social creativity and social knowledge in adolescents with ASD.

Both social knoweldge ($r = -.31, p = .03$) and social creativity ($r = -.41, p < .01$) correlated with ADOS scores, such that higher scores in both domains related to fewer current ASD symptoms; the relationship was somewhat stronger for social creativity. However, only social creativity (see Figure 12.2; $r = -.25, p = .06$) but not social knowledge ($r = .02, p = .46$), correlated marginally with lifetime ASD symptoms, suggesting that social creativity may have a broader relationship to social symptoms of ASD.

Finally, when examining the relationship with prosocial behavior during free play, social knowledge exhibited no correlation ($r = -.27, p > .05$); that is, knowing the rules for effective prosocial behavior did not relate to using those rules. However, social creativity exhibited a modest correlation with prosocial behavior ($r = .32, p < .05$), and this correlation maintained even after partialling out the effect of social knowledge ($r_{partial} = .34, p < .05$), suggesting that the ability to generate novel social responses, even if they are themselves not *prima facie* "adaptive," may be especially valuable to support prosocial behavior in youth with ASD.

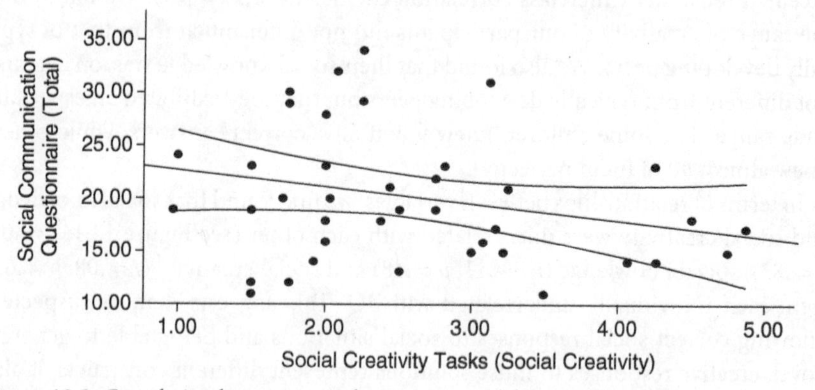


**Figure 12.2** Correlation between social creativity and lifetime ASD symptoms.

Overall, this suggests that the capacity for novel, flexible social responses, rather than knowledge of concrete social rules, may be especially critical for development of real-world social communication skills in ASD.

## PROMOTING SOCIAL CREATIVITY

How, then, might one examine whether there is indeed a direct, predictive relationship between social creativity and social outcomes in youth with Asperger's syndrome? Likewise, how might one promote such creativity? One option might be via group social activities designed to improve social competence in this population—so-called social skills groups. However, despite evidence for modest efficacy of such interventions (Gates, Kang, & Lerner, 2017), most tend to focus on promoting social knowledge rather than creative social response (McMahon, Lerner, & Britton, 2013).

In recent years, though, there has been a surge of new approaches that do focus on expanding social creativity (Gabriel, Angevin, Rosen, & Lerner, 2016). Blythe Corbett and colleagues (2011, 2014), for instance, provides a theater training experience, including peer partners, for youth with ASD to both engage in collaborative, creative activities and generate shared novel social experiences. Shaugnessey (2016) and Trimingham and Shaugnessey (2016), via the Imagining Autism project, create "pods" for children with ASD—immersive environments that are entirely driven by (and are designed to promote) the spontaneous, creative expression of each individual.

In the model we developed, called Socio-dramatic Affective Relational Intervention (SDARI; Lerner & Levine, 2007; Lerner, Mikami, & Levine, 2011), promotion of social creativity is a core aim. That is, rather than aiming to promote rote knowledge of social rules, SDARI employs improvisation and related activities to encourage individuals to generate a wide (often absurd or silly) array of responses to unexpected social scenarios. Thus, the goal of the model is to help participants to "flex" their social creativity "muscle" so that it is more practiced and well-developed when facing the complexities of the social world. For instance, in a game called "change," two children interact in a spontaneous scene. Occasionally, the group leader yells "change" after one child speaks, which indicates that the child must change the last thing they said to something else; the leader may continue to yell "change" multiple times in a row, and the first child must continue to come up with new phrases, while the second child must respond only to the final statement. Such an approach is designed to promote the ability to generate—and respond to—many different social scenarios in rapid succession.

Across a number of studies, the efficacy of this approach has been supported (Lerner, 2013; Lerner & Levine, 2007; Lerner & Mikami, 2012; Lerner et al., 2011; McMahon et al., 2013; Mendelson et al., 2016), with SDARI promoting generalized and (for at least several weeks postintervention) maintained gains in emotion recognition, prosocial behavior, and (reduced) social anxiety according to task-based measures, parent report, self-report, peer report, and (in some studies) even teacher report. In one randomized, controlled study (Lerner & Mikami, 2012), it was found that such an approach produced improved friendship-making and prosocial play at a faster rate than more traditional approaches, while in another (Lerner, 2013) it was found that relatively greater peer interaction took place during and after the SDARI approach after less than 20 minutes of the target activities. A similar model, the Social Competence Intervention Program (Guli, Wilkinson, & Semrud-Clikeman, 2008), has shown improvements in prosocial behavior in naturalistic settings (Guli, Semrud-Clikeman, Lerner, & Britton, 2013). Crucially, the SDARI approach is often reported to be not only effective but *fun,* providing shared joy and connection among the participants. Indeed, the aforementioned Asperger's Are Us troupe originally trained in SDARI, providing a cardinal example of how shared social creativity can sometimes yield lasting social connective tissue.

Overall, this burgeoning area of practice and study suggests that improvisation may provide a distinctive and parsimonious venue to both capitalize on and promote the capacity for social creativity—and corollary benefits—in youth with Asperger's syndrome.

## CASE EXAMPLES

### Tom

Tom, 17 years old, was enrolled in an eight-week after-school "transitions" program designed to help highly able young adults on the autism spectrum learn postgraduation skills related to adult independence. The program curriculum focused on skills such as money management, time management, and job skills training. He was originally referred to the program by his parents, both professionals, who believed that despite Tom's intellect and capabilities, he would be overlooked by employers because of his unconventional interaction style. He was described by people in his life as "blunt," and a person with "no filter." He said aloud things he was thinking without considering the social consequences. He also presented with a "stiff" affect and lack of facial expressions. Over the years, he was frequently reminded by his parents and teachers that he should become more aware of himself and how he is perceived by others socially and work to change these qualities to conform to social norms, fit it better socially, and ultimately have a successful life.

As part of the job skills aspect of the program, Tom was scheduled to complete an informational interview at a local video game store. The owner of the store had agreed to interview Tom, take notes, and give constructive feedback for how Tom could improve his interview skills and employability. During the interview, Tom was relaxed and unbound by the expectation of impressing this person. The interviewer found that, despite Tom not necessarily saying the "right" things or giving conventional answers to his interview questions, he was enjoying his time Tom and appreciated his thorough knowledge and focus throughout the 45-minute interview.

It was not only that his quirks translated differently in a new context or a context that catered to his strengths. It was that he was unencumbered by social norms or other conventions that could otherwise cause self-consciousness or situational anxiety. Most people believe that a job interview is an evaluation of their ability and to not get a job offer can feel like a personal rejection. Tom did not place the same value on being evaluated or having a positive outcome. His answers came from a freer and more genuine place, as he was not constrained by what "normal" interview behavior. As a result, the interviewer was refreshed by his concise honesty, his confident demeanor, and his subtle humor. Tom did not have to do it the *right* way, he did it *his* way, with success.

The same can be said for a variety of social interactions—for a person with ASD, it can require an optimal blend of the right context and the right people to allow for social success that does not include the often stressful constraining of their authentic selves to fit the conventional social mold. Instead of focusing on changing their interaction style to suit current social norms, we could allow individuals with ASD to display a whole new set of ideas and responses, even for something as prescriptive as a job interview. If people can evaluate and appreciate a broader range of interaction styles, they can be highly successful and highly social, quirks and all.

## Marie

Marie is 21-year-old female, who was diagnosed with Asperger's disorder (using the fourth edition of the *Diagnostic and Statistical Manual of Mental Disorders*, the current diagnostic criteria for the time) during her senior year of high school. With academic accommodations, she recently graduated a small, urban art and design college with a bachelor's in fine art. She was not diagnosed until age 16, despite a history of symptoms related to an autism diagnosis in early childhood. Growing up, Marie was often described as "sensitive," "shy," and "odd" and would avoid social situations, preferring instead to draw, color, or do small crafts. Marie's teachers often noticed Marie struggle to initiate interactions with her peers and would often be isolated during unstructured times during the school day. After learning about Asperger's disorder in her high school psychology class, she began to suspect she may be on the autism spectrum.

At age 16, she was diagnosed with depression and Asperger's disorder and started weekly, individual therapy. During her sessions she found direct discussion of her emotional state and perceived social skills deficits was too anxiety-producing and, therefore, ineffective. Instead, her therapist encouraged her to use a form of expression she was comfortable with—Marie chose painting and drawing—to help discuss the events of her week, her feelings, and her goals for therapy. Some may have assumed that, due to her autism, abstracting her emotions this way would be too ambiguous not therapeutic. On the contrary, use of painting and drawing allowed Marie to share her thoughts and feelings in a way she was comfortable with and proud of.

When Marie decided to leave her suburban home to live in the city and pursue an education in fine art, her family and educational team were wary. She initially struggled to acclimate to the various social and academic demands of college but found that an arts-based curriculum allowed her to build on her natural strengths and be in an environment that catered to "outsiders" and creative thinkers of all kinds. She began to thrive as her differences and idiosyncrasies were seen as valuable expressions of her true, creative self. As a result, instead of feeling shy and anxious, she was feeling proud of herself and her work. In her second year of college, she cofounded an autism support and neuro-diversity activism group on campus that she called her "besties group."

When Marie was in an environment where her artistry was encouraged (versus dismissed as a "special interest" or shaped to conform to social norms) and her unusual interaction style accepted and celebrated as part of her artistic lifestyle, she displayed more confidence and willingness to reach out to others to form social connections. In her "besties group" she and her peers often engaged in creative collaborations across mediums such as film, animation, and fashion design and used the arts to promote tolerance for individuals with developmental and intellectual disabilities.

## CONCLUSION

In this chapter, we focused on both the presence and the value of creativity—particularly social creativity—for youth with ASD, in particular those with Asperger's syndrome. We provided clinical and empirical evidence, as well as case examples, supporting the importance of social creativity in this population, and described intervention approaches that specifically capitalize on the promotion of social creativity for youth with ASD. We hope that this can provide guidance to clinicians, educators, and parents in appreciating and fostering this vital capacity in these children and teens.

As mentioned, one item on the ADOS (the "gold standard" measure of ASD) focuses on creativity. Another item, though, provides an opportunity for individuals to identify their hopes and dreams for the future. In many cases, responses on this item may be deemed unrealistic by the clinician—overly novel, broad, or imprecise. We suggest that such responses (and, indeed, some aspects of how individuals with ASD view and navigate their social world) could instead be seen as instances of exceptional creativity and that a most valuable approach to supporting youth with Asperger's may be—rather than teaching these children what might be realistic—creating a venue where they can experience the possibility of their dreams.

## REFERENCES

Angleberger, T. (2012). *The strange case of origami Yoda.* New York, NY: Abrams.

Bauminger, N. (2002). The facilitation of social-emotional understanding and social interaction in high-functioning children with autism: Intervention outcomes. *Journal of Autism and Developmental Disorders, 32*(4), 283–298.

Cash, A. B. (1999). A profile of gifted individuals with autism: The twice-exceptional learner. *Roeper Review, 22*(1), 22–27. doi: 10.1080/02783199909553993

Corbett, B. A., Gunther, J. R., Comins, D., Price, J., Ryan, N., Simon, D., . . . Rios, T. (2011). Brief report: Theatre as therapy for children with autism spectrum disorder. *Journal of Autism and Developmental Disorders, 41*(4), 505–511. doi:10.1007/s10803-010-1064-1

Corbett, B. A, Swain, D. M, Coke, C., Simon, D., Newsom, C., Houchins-Juarez, N., . . . Song, Y. (2014). Improvement in social deficits in autism spectrum disorders using a theatre-based, peer-mediated intervention. *Autism Research, 7*(1), 4–16.

Dawson, M., Soulières, I., Gernsbacher, M. A., & Mottron, L. (2007). The level and nature of autistic intelligence. *Psychological Science, 18*(8), 657–662.

Donnelly, J. A., & Altman, R. (1994). The autistic savant: Recognizing and serving the gifted student with autism. *Roeper Review, 16*(4), 252–256. doi:10.1080/02783199409553591

Gabriel, J., Angevin, E., Rosen, T. E., & Lerner, M. D. (2016). Use of theatrical techniques and elements as interventions for autism spectrum disorders. In G. Sofia (Ed.), *Theater and cognitive neuroscience* (pp. 163–176). London: Bloomsbury Academic.

Gates, J. A., Kang, E., & Lerner, M. D. (2017). Efficacy of group social skills interventions for youth with autism spectrum disorder: A systematic review and meta-analysis. *Clinical Psychology Review, 52,* 164–181.

Guli, L. A., Semrud-Clikeman, M., Lerner, M. D., & Britton, N. (2013). Social Competence Intervention Program (SCIP): A pilot study of a creative drama program for youth with social difficulties. *The Arts in Psychotherapy, 40*(1), 37–44. doi:10.1016/j.aip.2012.09.002

Guli, L. A., Wilkinson, A. D., & Semrud-Clikeman, M. (2008). *SCIP, Social Competence Intervention Program: A drama-based intervention for youth on the autism spectrum.* Champaign, IL: Research Press.

Hobson, R. P. (2013). The coherence of autism. *Autism, 18*(1), 6–16.

Jarrold, C. (2003). A review of research into pretend play in autism. *Autism, 7*(4), 379–390.

Kang, E., Klein, E. F., Lillard, A. S.; & Lerner, M. D. (2016). Predictors and moderators of spontaneous pretend play in children with and without autism spectrum disorder. *Frontiers in Psychology, 7.*

Kanner, L. (1943). *Autistic disturbances of affective contact.* N.p.

Lerner, M. D. (2013). *Knowledge or performance: why youth with autism experience social problems* (Unpublished doctoral disseration). University of Virginia, Charlottesville.

Lerner, M. D., & Levine, K. (2007). The spotlight method: An integrative approach to teaching social pragmatics using dramatic principles. *Journal of Developmental Processes, 2*(2), 91–102.

Lerner, M. D., Lucchetti, A. R., & Mikami, A. Y. (2013). *Social knowledge and social creativity: Contributions to symptomatology in adolescents with ASD.* Paper presented at the annual meeting of the Association for Behavioral and Cogntive Therapies, Nashville, TN, Nov. 21–24.

Lerner, M. D., & Mikami, A. Y. (2012). A preliminary randomized controlled trial of two social skills interventions for youth with high-functioning autism spectrum disorders. *Focus on Autism and Other Developmental Disabilities*, *27*(3), 147–157. doi:10.1177/1088357612450613

Lerner, M. D., Mikami, A. Y., & Levine, K. (2011). Socio-dramatic affective-relational intervention for adolescents with Asperger syndrome and high functioning autism: Pilot study. *Autism*, *15*(1), 21–42. doi:10.1177/1362361309353613

Lord, C., Rutter, M., DiLavore, P., & Risi, S. (1999). *Manual for the Autism Diagnostic Observation Schedule*. Los Angeles, CA: Western Psychological Services.

McMahon, C. M., Lerner, M. D., & Britton, N. (2013). Group-based social skills interventions for adolescents with higher-functioning autism spectrum disorders: A review and looking to the future. *Adolescent Health, Medicine, & Therapeutics*, *4*, 23–38.

Mendelson, J. L., Gates, J. A., & Lerner, M. D. (2016). Friendship in school-age boys with autism spectrum disorders: A meta-analytic summary and developmental, process-based model. *Psychological Bulletin*, *142*(6), 601–622.

Michelson, L., & Wood, R. (1982). Development and psychometric properties of the Children's Assertive Behavior Scale I. *Journal of Behavioral Assessment*, *4*(1).

Mouchiroud, C., & Bernoussi, A. (2008). An empirical study of the construct validity of social creativity. *Learning and Individual Differences*, *18*(4), 372–380.

Mouchiroud, C., & Lubart, T. (2002). Social creativity: A cross-sectional study of 6- to 11-year-old children. *International Journal of Behavioral Development*, *26*(1), 60–69.

Robison, J. E. (2008). *Look me in the eye: My life with Asperger's*. New York, NY: Random House.

Roth, I. (2007). *Autism and the imaginative mind* (Vol. 147). Oxford: Oxford University Press.

Rutter, M., Bailey, A., & Lord, C. (2005). *SCQ: The Social Communication Questionnaire manual*. Los Angeles, CA: Western Psychological Services.

Shaughnessy, N. (2016). Curious incidents: Pretend play, presence, and performance pedagogies in encounters with autism. In *Creativity and community among autism-spectrum youth* (pp. 187–216). New York, NY: Springer.

SomethingWitty. (2012, July 29). Are people with aspergers creative or uncreative in general? Retrieved from http://wrongplanet.net/forums/viewtopic.php?t=201436

Trimingham, M., & Shaughnessy, N. (2016). Material voices: Intermediality and autism. *Research in Drama Education: The Journal of Applied Theatre and Performance*, *21*(3), 293–308.

Wing, L., & Gould, J. (1979). Severe impairments of social interaction and associated abnormalities in children: Epidemiology and classification. *Journal of Autism and Developmental Disorders*, *9*(1), 11–29.

13

# The Spectrum of Twice Exceptional and Autistic Learners and Suggestions for Their Learning Styles

RICHARD O. WILLIAMS AND JEFFREY FREED

This chapter develops the idea that the exceptionalities and learning disabilities found in twice exceptional (2e) learners and learners on the autistic spectrum are similar and overlap to such an extent that it is beneficial to compare the two and learn from what is known of the other population. Often autism and any related autistic labels present a stigma for many readers, parents, and professionals because they are associated, incorrectly, with low IQs along with compromised cognitive abilities, handicaps, and disabling social skills. For some, the idea of the exceptional 2e person being in any way related or similar to autism is barely, if at all, acceptable. This chapter demonstrates that both the recent developments in autistic spectrum disorder (ASD) research and the very close similarities of exceptionalities and learning difficulties have direct relevance to the 2e learner.

For the sake of clarity, it is necessary to understand the terms used in this chapter, including exceptionality, 2e learners, autistic spectrum, autistic spectrum disorders, and autistic spectrum conditions. Exceptionalities, as described here, are some recognizable ability (art, music, numbers, intellect, etc.) that is above average and has the likelihood to persist beyond primary and secondary education. These are abilities that when nurtured and developed in early education can have a strong influence on the student's success as an adult. Twice exceptional (2e) learners as used here refers to a minority of students who have mild or strong exceptionalities as well as learning disabilities. Importantly, this group can be very difficult to identify. Mild exceptional abilities can mask mild learning disabilities resulting in either under- or average performance in school. Autistic spectrum disorder is a medical diagnosis given to individuals who display traits and conditions of autism that are milder and less debilitating than the handicaps and disabilities of true autistic individuals. This group can integrate socially and in the workforce if some accommodations are made for their problems. The term autistic spectrum conditions (ASC) is used to describe traits seen in people who have one or more mild conditions that appear in ASDs and autism but both the number of traits and their intensity are subclinical and not sufficient to merit any ASD or related diagnosis. In the social context, these mild autistic traits would represent a group of learners that might be identified as slightly odd or a bit different from their peers. The reference to learners on the autistic spectrum is limited only to that group who carry very mild (subclinical) autistic traits or ASCs along with learning disabilities. None of the learners referenced in this chapter would carry a diagnosis of ASD or autism.

This chapter illustrates that the learning difficulties of 2e learners encountered early in school, both academically and behaviorally, are remarkably similar to the difficulties encountered by people with mild ASCs and that both lie on a spectrum of increasing abilities and difficulties. The perspective argued is that many of the learning difficulties encountered by 2e students result from unusual and exceptional sensory processing issues. Because sensory issues can be widely found in children with learning disabilities, they may possibly be an identification or diagnostic marker for both 2e learners (especially in the case where exceptionality has not been identified) and children with ASCs. By understanding the sensory issues of both 2e and ASC learners, one may be able to appropriately target sensory intervention goals for teachers and professionals to improve classroom performance.

Recent reports in the human genetics literature suggest positive correlations between autism and measures of mental ability (Bulik-Sullivan et al., 2015; Clark et al., 2016; Crespi, 2016; Hagenaars et al., 2016; Hill et al., 2016). If these observations prove correct they would support the hypothesis that people on the autistic spectrum have the same prevalence of exceptionalities as do 2e learners. By a review of the literature and the authors' professional experience, this chapter demonstrates that many ASC learners are virtually identical to the 2e learner in their learning styles, cognitive styles, and learning challenges. As will be described, these two learning groups learn predominantly by visual and spatial thinking. The chapter concludes with targeted teaching suggestions for the visual-spatial (VS) learner.

The 2e and ASC learners along with their exceptional abilities and their learning difficulties can be characterized on a linear spectrum beginning on one end with near neurotypical learners who display very few exceptionalities and only mild forms of learning difficulties. This includes the ASC group who displays the same mild exceptionalities and learning difficulties in the middle while the opposite end lies Asperger's syndrome (see Figure 13.1). Such mild traits, as identified on the left in Figure 13.1, are frequently overlooked and identified only serendipitously. Further into the spectrum, learning difficulties and exceptionalities of 2e

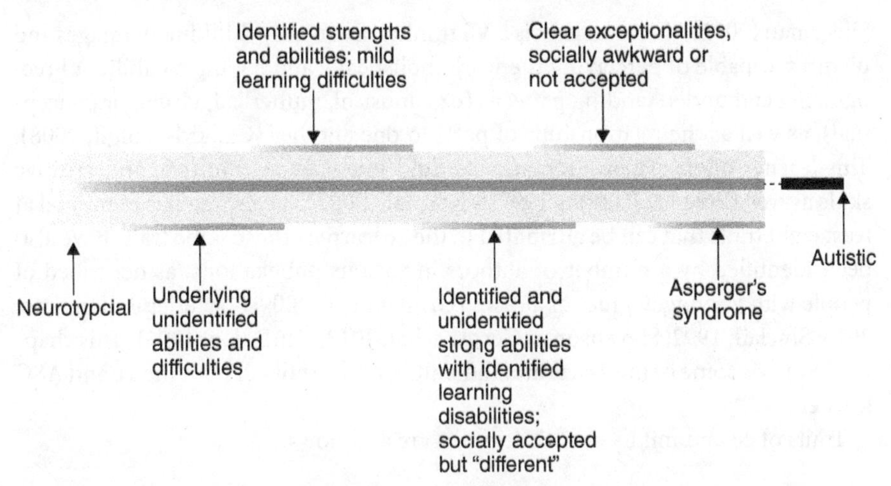


**Figure 13.1** Traits of 2e and ASC learners on a spectrum. The bar above is a gradient of gray on the left progressing to black on the right representing increasing number and intensity of exceptional abilities and learning disabilities. The line describes the overlapping traits of 2e and ASC learners along with the clinical conditions of Asperger's syndrome and autism on the far right. The line is broken on the right, indicating a variable distance between Asperger's syndrome and severe autism. The shorter gradients describe the degrees and relative positions of abilities and difficulties on the continuum. The black gradient can also represent the increasing number of small gene mutations that contribute to both the increasing degree of exceptionalities and learning difficulties.

and ASC learners are recognized only after the appearance and identification of some form of learning disability and occasionally mild but unusual social behavior that present early in schooling. Moving further to the right on the spectrum, giftedness and learning disabilities increase together along with social issues. Asperger's syndrome holds a prominent position on the right end of the autistic spectrum as illustrated. To the right of the Asperger's position, ASCs and autistic traits become more prominent in individuals such that they carry either an ASD or autism diagnosis.

Unless the 2e learners display perfectly normal social behavior, they may frequently have many of the traits of Asperger's syndrome. The gifted talents of Asperger's syndrome students are precisely those 2e traits that frequently make for very exceptional and successful careers when the students are able to accommodate for their deficits and are given the opportunity to recognize and develop their exceptional abilities. The important point to be made here is that gifted abilities and learning difficulties often can be linked and lie on a spectrum.

## TWICE EXCEPTIONAL AND ASC LEARNERS

Twice exceptional learners' and their autistic spectrum cohort's learning style are very similar but are very different from the neurotypical learners. As described by

Silverman (2002), the 2e learner is a VS thinker, frequently thinking in images and pictures, capable of perceiving the world holistically and having an ability of recognizing and understanding patterns (e.g., musical, numerical, visual, or conceptual), as well as the relationships of parts to one another (Callard-Szulgit, 2008). This learner often displays remarkable fluid intelligence, intuitive, and creative skills as well (Freed & Parsons 1997; Silverman, 2002). Silverman has identified at least eight traits that can be attributed to the 2e learner. These same traits have also been identified by a number of authors in various publications, as described of people with varying degrees of autism (Grinter et al., 2009; Schauder & Bennetto, 2016; Sinclair, 1992; Stevenson & Gernsbacher, 2013; VanDalen, 1995). This chapter describes some of the assets and difficulties of the traits in both the 2e and ASC learner.

Traits of 2e and mildly autistic learners are as follows:

- visual rather than auditory
- spatial rather than sequential
- pattern seeking
- sensitive and intense
- holistic rather than detailed
- focused on ideas rather than format
- divergent rather than convergent
- asynchronous (exhibiting large disparities between strengths and weaknesses)

Among the many observations of bright children with learning disabilities (for both 2e learners and ASC learners) is a visual learning style. This is also true for the preponderance of ASC and ASD individuals who are VS learners and thinkers (Grandin, 1996; Stevenson & Gernsbacher, 2013). Silverman (2002) clearly demonstrates that the same is true for the 2e learner.

Visual-spatial learners find it substantially easier to learn and remember in the form of mental images or pictures while their auditory memory is often very poor, thus they require different teaching strategies. Visual-spatial learners also have an excellent ability to visualize in three dimensions. This skill can become a significant asset, especially if nurtured and allowed to develop early in education, in disciplines such as architecture, design, and the visual arts. Another feature of VS learners is their ability to recognize and visualize new associations, relationships, and patterns. The perception of new patterns and associations, sometimes of unrelated parts and their perspectives, plays an important role in the student's capability of intuitive thinking. Intuitive abilities are frequently a central feature of creativity. Pattern recognition and intuitive conceptualization are important components of fluid intelligence or the ability to recognize and reason problems without direct knowledge from previous experience. These are all important attributes of both 2e and ASC learners.

The degree to which the VS learner uses mental images is variable. It can be as simple as learning in the form of simple images, but it can vary to the complex form where all memory is recorded as a catalog of ideas stored with images and pictures (Grandin, 1996; Zeki, 1992). These thinkers sometimes perceive a story like a video in memory. This means that ideas or subjects must undergo a transition from spoken or written words to pictures or mental images to learn or understand a subject or idea. For those who have a superior visual memory, the process of transferring images into words can be both an asset and a liability. Visual learners frequently have exceptionally good memories, and many have photographic memories (Carter, 2010; O'Neill, 1999; Sacks, 1995; Silverman, 2002). Although many can quickly handle the process of converting words into images and images back into words, the conversion process can create time delays. Such delays can appear frequently as a speech difficulty where the learner is incapable of responding in the appropriate short time frame of a normal conversation because the act of word-image conversion takes time. An inability to respond or converse in the normal time frame of conversation can in itself produce learning and social difficulties. *The ability to hold a simple verbal conversation is one of the most important unacknowledged measures of social normality.* The VS learner finds himself wanting to make a contribution to a conversation but when he has his idea fully developed and images converted to words, the conversation has moved beyond the topic and onto other subjects. Interrupting a great conversation and injecting a previous idea is very disruptive to the flow of discourse. Conversation delays can become awkward and socially unusual to the extent that the person can be seen as different from his peers possibly leading to social isolation. It is not unusual to find 2e and ASC learners who avoid conversations with peers, but if they chose to participate, they become silent partners in the conversation. Similarly, many choose simply to withdraw from conversations altogether (Bogdashina, 2016; Callard-Szulgit, 2008).

A strong VS memory can also have an impact on a student's writing performance. Again the decoding of an image does not happen quickly. The act of trying to move from a mental image to writing can be too difficult of a decoding process for many such that writing becomes a very significant difficulty or disability. Visual image decoding in order to write is a multistep process. The individual must learn to decode an image into a word, mentally assemble a sentence with the words, and then write the sentence.

The traditional school classroom has had a heritage and tradition of teaching in a linear, sequential, and auditory format. This style is a direct conflict for the VS learner. Learning using verbal memory presents a serious obstacle for the VS learner yet many teachers find it unusual, or indeed view it as a handicap, if the VS learner fails to learn in the traditional linear sequential format. Special accommodations must therefore be made for VS learners in the traditional classroom.

Strong similarities exist in the cognitive styles of both 2e and ASC learners, and the disparity between strengths and weaknesses are very surprising. One of the hallmarks of these learners is nonuniform and sporadic performance in the classroom along with large variances on IQ tests (see Gilman & Peters, this volume). One very frequently finds a student's report card consists of As and Fs. The performance in each subject can represent the student's interests in the subjects and also possibly the presence or absence of learning difficulties. Such a variance in grades is a prime indicator for both 2e and ASC learners. Achievement on the Wechsler Intelligence Scale for Children (WISC) follows a similar pattern. Large variation in the 10 subtests of the WISC with variations ranging from 1 to 19 is a common finding, which leads to the suggestion that the grouped total score is not representative of the 2e and ASC learner's abilities (Barbeau et al., 2013; Nader, Courchesne, Dawson, & Soulières, 2016; Soulieres, Dawson, Gernsbacher, & Mottron, 2011). There is a strong tendency for service providers to focus on the total score, thereby interpreting a substantially compromised intelligence profile. Therefore, intelligence scores for 2e and ASC learners must be very critically analyzed and interpreted by a professional who has the time and background to understand the student's strengths and weaknesses or supplemented with additional tests. It is important to reiterate that the total WISC score is unreliable and a strongly misleading measurement for this group of students.

The 2e and ASC learners are top to bottom thinkers. They learn holistically and can learn very quickly when a high-level concept is explained first and details and factual data presented afterward. These learners easily remember facts when they understand the reason for doing so. One frequently observes that the introduction of a new concept generates a curiosity that can lead to intensive concentration on the subject that can last for hours at a time. Such strong focusing can produce a library of factual data whereas any approach involving direct or rote memorization is almost certain to fail. Generally, they need to know why they are learning a concept before they learn any details about the subject. These students like to focus on ideas rather than on details or format (Bogdashina, 2016). Approaching new concepts by starting at the bottom with facts, data, or dates and concluding with an overall concept is almost certain to lead to boredom in the 2e and ASC learners. Indeed, boredom is frequently observed and can become a significant issue in a learning environment when concepts are approached in such a way. If new concepts are introduced in a visual format as well as in a top-down fashion, a great deal of information can be acquired very rapidly.

## SENSORY ISSUES AND LEARNING DISABILITIES

Following the trait of VS thinking found in 2e and ASC learners, sensory processing issues are probably the next most common trait influencing learning difficulties in primary education. Sensory abnormalities are found in 70% of the learning-disabled including 2e and ASC students, and they are a central feature in learning and abnormal behavior in autism (Berard, 1993; Bogdashina, 2003). Sensory hypersensitivities and functional integration of sensory input have long been recognized as an ASC (Bogdashina, 2003, 2016). In a recent survey of 925 children, ages 7 to 11 years, parents reported that 16% of their children had multiple tactile or auditory hypersensitivities that bothered their children (Ben-Sasson, Carter, & Briggs-Gowan, 2009).

Hyper- and hyposensory perception can modify normal development and contribute to ancillary cerebral cognition and 2e exceptionalities. The brain adapts and continues to interpret the environment from a different perspective, leading to the child learning in an altered way.

The association of learning disabilities and sensory issues has been recognized for many years (Ayres, 1978; Ben-Sasson et al., 2009; Green, Chandler, Charman, Simonoff, & Baird, 2016; Morrison, 1985). Green et al. reported that atypical sensory behavior was measured in 67% of a group of 10- to 14-year-old children who were in special education classes and without a diagnosis of ASD. The application of sensory integration therapy to improve performance of students with learning disabilities began in the late 1960s (Polatajko, Kaplan, & Wilson, 1992).

Sensory issues can directly cause a learning disability by inhibiting concentration and attention. Such problems in primary students can distract and disrupt the classroom, causing outbursts from significant sensory stress and anxiety; can prevent concentration and create behavioral issues; and, importantly, can mask underlying special skills and abilities. It should be remembered that challenging behaviors in the classroom may result from sensory hypersensitivities; proper accommodations can significantly ameliorate the behavior. This obviously requires that teachers recognize the sensory problems that can cause disruptive behaviors. An incomplete list of the more common types of hypersensitivities observed in and out of the classroom is provided next. It is important to understand that frequently more than one sense can be involved thus amplifying any sensory impact.

- Visual: distraction of flickering fluorescent lights, overly bright lighting, strong contrasts, trees moving, birds flying, color intensities, specific colors, facial expressions or different dressing styles.
- Auditory: turning pages, buzzing of fluorescent lights, scuffling of shoes, whispering, the sound of writing with a pencil, wind blowing outside, doors opening and closing, leaf blowers, tapping of pencils, noise from the next door classroom, vehicles, airplanes, or writing with chalk.
- Smell: food, deodorants, perfume, body odor, residual cleaning agents, soap, hairspray, magic markers, or odor from someone's breath.
- Tactile: sensitivity to texture of certain types of paper, overly sensitive to being touched, feeling different textures like chalk or pencils or uncomfortable clothes.

## A GENETIC SPECTRUM OF ABILITIES AND DISABILITIES

Autism spectrum disorders and autistic traits all originate from the effect of a variable number of genes carried in a large polygenic pool that has been conserved in the human lineage for over 6 million years of evolution. Research estimates there are well over 185 genes and probably many more that constitute the autistic trait polygenic pool (Betancur, 2011; Betancur & Coleman, 2013; Matsunami et al., 2013). As with other polygenic-based diseases, this gene pool is distributed across the genome in the general population (Gaugler et al., 2014; Krumm, O'Roak, Shendure, & Eichler, 2014). A large number of genetic ASC risk factors can be found in people who do not carry a diagnosis of a spectrum disorder and therefore are part of the ASC constituency with mild or hard to identify autistic traits (Chakrabarti et al., 2009; Grinter et al., 2009; Robinson et al., 2016). Each gene each contribute small effects that add to the risk of acquiring autistic traits. Several recent studies on genetic risk factors for acquiring ASD used very large groups to compare people with ASD and the general population. The studies have identified multiple single point mutations in DNA or single nucleotide polymorphisms in the gene pool that account for at least 49% of ASC liability (Bulik-Sullivan et al., 2015; Gaugler et al., 2014; Klei et al., 2012; Krumm et al., 2014; Krumm et al., 2015).

These small effects mediate the risk of autistic traits in both directions: some genes add to the risk of the deleterious effects and some genes reduce the risks of deleterious effects. The acquisition of an autistic trait or a diagnosis of ASD depends upon the number of genes inherited and the degree of risk carried by each gene. For example, the most common gene risk factor (a gene deletion) found in ASD can also be found in a large number of people who have no autistic disorder diagnosis of any kind (Chakrabarti et al., 2009; Grinter et al., 2009). Some genes have a greater impact and therefore mediate greater risk than others. The total risk of acquiring an autistic trait, as in other polygenic systems such as cardiovascular disease, is the total risk contributed by all the genes. If the total is large enough and reaches a threshold, then an autistic trait or an autistic disorder will be likely to appear. The line in Figure 13.1 describes the spectrum of subclinical traits of autistic conditions. As we have depicted in this spectrum, when one moves from the left to the right, the number and effect of polygenic risk genes and the number and strength of autistic traits gradually add together until the trait or traits become significant enough for consideration of a clinical diagnosis. The end of the line to the right constitutes severe autism where many traits and impacts are severely debilitating. The gene burden carried by those with severe autism is unlikely to be passed on to a next generation because of social issues in finding a suitable partner for marriage, therefore eliminated from the gene pool.

For the human lineage to carry such a large pool of genes with the liability to confer deleterious traits, there has to be some corresponding evolutionary or survival benefit that selects for them to be retained in the human gene pool. Many of the genes that carry risks for autism overlap substantially and significantly with genes associated with high intelligence. This observation has been confirmed in several different studies (Bulik-Sullivan et al., 2015; Clark et al., 2016; Hagenaars et al., 2016; Hill et al., 2016). These studies stand in direct opposition with the commonly held beliefs that autism is often associated with intellectual disability. A recent study by Crespi (2016) reviewed the literature and presented a novel paradoxical hypothesis that autism is genetically positively correlated with high intelligence but an imbalanced intelligence, where some of the characteristics of intelligence are increased yet the overall performance on IQ testing is reduced.

The characteristics that are enhanced are in the perceptual domain including fluid intelligence, VS skills, sensory discrimination, and scientific and attentional abilities. This paradox is an extension of earlier studies showing IQ testing can underestimate the true underlying intelligence in people on the autistic spectrum (Barbeau et al., 2013; Dawson, Soulières, Gernsbacher, & Mottron, 2007; Nader et al., 2016).

As an example of how genes that carry a risk for autistic traits can simultaneously contribute improved mental skills at the same time, Crespi (2013) studied two genes known to add to the risk of acquiring autistic traits. PITX-1 and APC are genes that regulate biochemical processes of nerve cells in the brain. These two genes can be found in the general population with point mutations in the DNA that incrementally add to the risk of acquiring autistic traits (Philippi et al., 2007; Zhou et al., 2007). For each gene, an individual inherits one copy (allele) from the maternal side and one allele from the paternal side. Using a test developed by Shepard and Metzler (1971) that measures the VS skill of rotating a mental image in three dimensions, Crespi (2016) quantified the mental rotational skills of people who had one allele of each of these genes with people who had two alleles, one from each parent. The conclusion of this experiment was that when there are two alleles present there was a 10% to 20% quantitative improvement in rotational skills above the scores with only one allele. Point mutations found in each of these genes individually add to the risk of acquiring autistic traits while at the same time measurably improves one's skill on a test of mental rotation.

It is important to note that exceptional and profound mental skills have long been associated with people on the autistic spectrum. Kanner (1971), who originally described autism, noted that 6 individuals from his original 11 cases in 1943 had outstanding musical and memory capabilities. Similarly, of the four cases originally described by Asperger (1944), one had exceptional calculation skills while another had remarkable spelling skills. In a recent study by Howlin, Good, Hutton, and Rutter (2009), approximately 30% of 137 individuals diagnosed with autism had savant skills or exceptional cognitive skills. Treffert and Rebedew (2015) reported that in the Savant Syndrome Registry 75% of the 319 people carried a diagnosis of autism while 25% had other central nervous system disorders. One could conclude from this information that many of the social and behavioral issues found in people with both mild and strong autistic traits mask underlying mental abilities. This becomes particularly relevant to students with learning disabilities. Professionals must scrutinize students who are considered to have learning disabilities for underlying exceptional abilities.

## TEACHING TO VS SKILLS

Teaching to VS learners requires different strategies from that of linear-sequential learners. Here we present several suggestions for teaching and working with 2e and ASC learners. These are successful methodologies that have been adapted from the book *Right-Brained Children in a Left-Brained World* (Freed & Parsons,

1997). (Note that although we use the male pronoun for ease of reading, the same strategies would apply to a female child.)

Twice exceptional learners tend to be perfectionists and are extremely hard on themselves. Coercion will not work, nor will pointing out every mistake. Teachers should modify their expectations. The fear of failure may be overwhelming if the student senses that expectations are too high. The student is highly perceptive and will give up rather than run the risk of trying and letting the teacher down.

Complex topics should be presented in images rather than sequences of facts. It is important to teach to their innate visual ability and "aim" it in presentation of concepts such as math and reading. However, not all visual learners understand they are visual and therefore may need to be made aware of it (Sinclair, 1992). Verbal instructions need to be turned into mental images. To give the child a feel for what it means to visualize, tell him to close his eyes and make a movie in his head of himself completing a sequence of tasks you describe (not to actually do them). Give the instructions slowly to allow him time to turn them into pictures. The directions might go like this: "Get up from the table. Go down to the car. Open and close the driver's side door three times. Come back upstairs. Go into the refrigerator and get out a carton of milk. Pour the milk and don't forget a Coke for me. Bring the drinks back to the table." If the child can "play back his movie" or repeat the instructions back to you, he is visualizing. Note that when instructions are given both auditorily and sequentially, they can be recalled perfectly as long as the student takes the time necessary to turn them into a pictures. This method of visualization can provide significant assistance for the VS learner in planning and remembering a complicated day's agenda.

Another exercise to turn verbal instructions into mental pictures is to give a sequence of numbers, such as "four, seven, three, two," and ask the student to visualize the numbers in his head and give them back to you in reverse order, "two, three, seven, four." Give the numbers slowly and allow the child time to visualize; four digits are quite easy for most VS learners. Once the child masters four digits, move on to five, and so on. Some adolescents can handle numbers up to 20 or more, given in groups of four if visualization skills are well developed.

## SPELLING

Schools teach spelling in black and white usually using white chalk on a blackboard. Zentall and Kruczek (1988) found that color can capture the attention of children labeled with attention deficit disorder and improve their skills in copying written material. When these children see letters on a screen, they are much more likely to pay attention if the letters are in color.

Start the spelling lesson with some white unlined paper and colored pencils, crayons, or markers. Choose a word that is slightly more difficult than what the child is capable of spelling. Write out the word and break it into syllables, using a different color for each syllable. Write in big letters filling the entire page. Hold the paper at least a foot away from the student, and direct him to look at the word until he can visualize it in his mind. Some children prefer to close their eyes or to look at the word and then look away until they can remember what the word looks like. It is important not to rush this step. Ask the child to take as much time as he needs to get a picture, at least 20 seconds. Once the child can visualize the word in his head, turn the paper facedown and instruct him to spell the word aloud. The child will be much more likely to succeed by initially spelling aloud. As learning progresses, select words from books at the appropriate reading level. Have the student look at the word, visualize it, and spell it orally both forward and backward.

## ORAL READING

To teach the VS learner oral reading, find a book he is familiar with that is about one to two years below his current grade level. Ask the child to read aloud as much as he can, using your finger as a visual guide in order to control the pace. Point directly under the words you want the child to read to keep the child's eye focused on one word at a time. This slows down the process, keeping him from jumping ahead or behind and allowing time for visualization to occur. Comprehension is not the main goal. The VS learner visualizes the word on his mental blackboard as well as an image of what the word represents. Check periodically to make sure he is seeing not only the word but also the mental image. If he says he is not getting a picture, gently suggest that he close his eyes and visualize the word and the image in his mind. A VS learner should be able to do this easily because this is an area of strength. He might have a difficult time with words such as "from," "though," and "then" because there is no corresponding visual image.

## SILENT READING

Start by reading to him. Instruct him to take your words and turn them into mental pictures. It might help to ask him to visualize a TV show or a movie running in his head. Tell him that he will use visualization when he reads to himself. He should be getting a picture in his mind. It might not be as detailed as the one he gets when you read to him, but he should be getting a picture nonetheless.

Start with a book that interests the student. Tell him, "We are going to read silently now. Just do it in your head and don't 'mouth' the words." The teacher should preview any difficult words in the passage in order to reduce the pressure of decoding difficult words and to aid the child's visual memory without imprinting the wrong words. Tell the child if he loses the picture at any time while reading to let you know. Then read to him for a short time. Once he gets the picture back, the child can resume reading. Check his progress periodically, asking him to give you details about the picture in his mind.

This process helps the child make the association that reading is about *visualization*. Tell him over and over, "If you are not getting a picture in your mind, you are not reading." The little words such as "the," "from" and "that" become unimportant.

Visual-spatial learners need to slow down to read aloud, but the opposite is true for silent reading. Silent reading is a different skill and should be taught differently. Comprehension is very important. The VS learner's mind moves quickly and visually. These children can speed-read as soon as they can master a few hundred words by sight. Once the child is able to read within one year of grade level, speed-reading techniques should be applied to new material. He should visualize the text to learn it. When studying he should quickly scan the pages first for the big picture. He may need to read the material three or four times to fill in the details, *slowing down for the sections that are most significant*. On the final reading, he can jot down notes to help him remember important dates or names. Or he can use a highlighting pen to help him recall significant passages.

For middle school and high school students who are applying these reading techniques to specific subject areas, the advice is the same:

- Study in short bursts.
- Speed-read the material first, going for general concepts.
- Reread the material several more times, filling in the details.
- Constantly monitor that one is getting a visual image.
- When taking a written test, rapidly scan the test from start to finish, stop when you come to a question you can answer with 100% certainty, continue skipping around, answering the easier questions. This helps achieve some confidence in a test situation, allowing one to relax and focus on the questions rather than fear of failure.

## MATHEMATICS

At the core of learning math is mental math. The teacher writes the exercise and the student answers. This will vary according to the child's math skill level. For example, the teacher writes the number 6, then asks the student to double it, add 2, double that, half it, and half it again to give 7. As the child becomes more adept at math one could write 12, then ask the student to triple it, square root, triple it, add 2, and double it. This technique helps the VS student to learn math patterns, develop auditory sequencing skills, and become proficient at computational math. There is almost no way to do this technique incorrectly. Never do this for more than five minutes, and change operations to make the computation more complex.

Some teachers argue that if you cannot show your steps you will be unable to move on to higher levels of mathematics such as trigonometry and calculus. Math teachers should value the solutions even if they are reached in an alternative way because VS thinkers are intuitive and can find answers without knowing how they did it.

Gifted students may struggle with computation and showing their steps, but if they do not get discouraged, they will find higher math concepts and in sync with their learning style. One should try to instill in them a love of math and a picture of the high-level concept: that math is so much more than being able to memorize times tables or solve an equation in three or four steps. How much loss of potential occurs because children who are potentially brilliant at abstract conceptual math get the message early on that they are poor at this subject?

## ADDITION

Teaching math should begin with addition regardless of the child's grade level. It is the simplest concept to master and a basic building block of math. Later, subtraction is taught as the opposite of addition and multiplication as a shortcut to addition. Write a string of five to six single-digit numbers vertically down a page. Ask the child to add the numbers in his head. If he is reluctant to do it in his head, stress that we are trying something new and what really matters is to try. Perfect accuracy is not important at this time.

## DIVISION

Apply the student's intuitive and visual abilities to solve complex problems. Explain that division need not be intimidating; it is simply the other side of multiplication. To be successful the child will work in reverse—using multiplication tables to reach the solution. If the problem is 67 divided by 9, ask the child to first run through his 9 times tables to find the solution that is closest to but less than 67. In this case it would be $9 \times 7 = 63$. Take the 63 and put it under the 67 and subtract. The answer would be 7 with a remainder of 4.

## CONCLUSION

Twice exceptional and autistic spectrum learners frequently display nearly identical abilities and learning styles; however, the unusual abilities in autistic spectrum learners are more often overlooked. The many traits that constitute exceptional abilities and learning difficulties in twice exceptional and autistic spectrum learners can be conceptualized on a spectrum ranging from mild to intense traits. Two of the more frequently identified traits in both groups, VS thinking and sensory hypersensitivities, must be recognized and understood for teachers to be successful in the classroom. Visual-spatial thinkers require a different teaching approach to match their learning style. This chapter has provided a number of teaching suggestions that have proven successful for these two groups of learners.

## REFERENCES

Asperger. H. (1944). Die "autistischen psychopathen" im kindesalter. *Archiv für Psychiatrie und Nervenkrankheiten*, *117*, 76–136.

Ayres, A. J. (1978). Learning disabilities and the vestibular system. *Journal of Learning Disabilities, 11*(1), 30–41.

Barbeau, E. B., Soulières, I., Dawson, M., Zeffiro, T. A, & Mottron, L. (2013). The level and nature of autistic intelligence III: Inspection time. *Journal of Abnormal Psychology, 122*(11), 295–301.

Ben-Sasson, A., Carter, A. S., & Briggs-Gowan, M. J. (2009). Sensory over-responsivity in elementary school: Prevalence and social-emotional correlates. *Journal of Abnormal Child Psychology, 37*, 705–716.

Berard, G. (1993). *Hearing equals behavior*. New Canaan, CT: Keats.

Betancur, C. (2011). Etiological heterogeneity in autism spectrum disorders: More than 100 genetic and genomic disorders and still counting. *Brain Research, 1380*, 42–77.

Betancur, C., & Coleman, M. (2013). Etiological heterogeneity in autism spectrum disorders: Role of rare variants. In J. Buxbaum (Ed.), *The neuroscience of autism spectrum disorders* (pp. 113–144). Oxford: Academic Press.

Bogdashina, O. (2003). *Sensory perceptual issues in autism and Asperger syndrome*. London: Jessica Kingsley.

Bogdashina, O. (2016). *Sensory perceptual issues in autism and Asperger syndrome* (2nd ed.). London: Jessica Kingsley.

Bulik-Sullivan, B. K., Finucane; H. K., Anttila, V., Gusev, A., Day, F. R., Loh, P. R., . . . Neale, B. M. (2015). An atlas of genetic correlations across human diseases and traits. *Nature Genetics, 47*(11), 1236–1241.

Callard-Szulgit, R. (2008). *Twice-exceptional kids: A guide for assisting students who are both academically gifted and learning disabled*. Lanham, MD: Rowman & Littlefield Education.

Carter, R. (2010). *Mapping the mind*. Berkeley: University of California Press.

Chakrabarti, B., F. Dudbridge, Kent, L., Wheelwright, S., Hill-Cawthorne, G., Allison, C., . . . Baron-Cohen, S. (2009). Genes related to sex steroids, neural growth, and social-emotional behavior are associated with autistic traits, empathy, and Asperger syndrome. *Autism Research, 2*(3), 157–177.

Clark, T.-K., Lupton; M. K., Fernandez-Pujals, A. M., Starr, J., Davies, G. Cox, S., . . . McIntosh, A. M. (2016). Common polygenic risk for autism spectrum disorder (ASD) is associated with cognitive ability in the general population. *Molecular Psychology, 21*(3), 419–425.

Crespi, B. J. (2013, January 18). *Evolutionary biology of autism "risk."* Retrieved from www.uctv.tv/shows/CARTA-Human-Origins-Lessons-from-Autism-Spectrum-Disorders-Bernard-Crespi-Evolutionary-Biology-of-Autism-Risk-24824.

Crespi, B. J. (2016). Autism as a disorder of high intelligence. *Frontiers in Neuroscience, 10*, 300. doi:10.3389/fnins.2016.00300.

Dawson, M., Soulières, I., Gernsbacher, M. A., & Mottron, L. (2007). The level and nature of autistic intelligence. *Psychological Science, 18*(8), 657–662.

Freed, J., & Parsons, L. (1997). *Right-brained children in a left-brained world: Unlocking the potential of your ADD child*. New York: Simon & Schuster Paperbacks.

Gaugler, T., Klei, L., Sanders, S. J., Bodea, C. A., Goldberg, A. P., Lee, A. B., . . . Buxbaum, J. D. (2014). Most genetic risk for autism resides with common variation. *Nature Genetics, 46*(8), 881–885.

Grandin, T. (1996). *Thinking in pictures*. New York, NY: Random House.

Green, D., Chandler, S., Charman, T., Simonoff, E., & Baird, G. (2016). Brief report: DSM-5 sensory behaviors in children with and without an autism spectrum disorder. *Journal of Autism and Developmental Disorders, 46*(11), 3597–3606.

Grinter, E. J., Maybery, M. T., Van Beek, P. L., Pellicano, E., Badcock, J. C., & Badcock, D. R.. (2009). Global visual processing and self-rated autistic-like traits. *Journal of Autism and Developmental Disorders, 39*(9), 1278–1290.

Hagenaars, S. P., Harris, S. E., Davies, G., Hill, W. D., Liewald, D. C. M., Ritchie, S. J., . . . Deary, I. J. (2016). Shared genetic aetiology between cognitive functions and physical and mental health in UK bioback (N = 112,151) and 24 GWAS consortia. *Molecular Psychology*. doi:10.1038/mp.2015.225.

Hill, W. D., Davies, G., CHARGE Cognitive Working Group, Liewald, D. C., McIntosh, A. M., & Deary, I. J. (2016). Age-dependent pleiotropy between general cognitive function and major psychiatric disorders. *Biological Psychiatry, 80*(4), 266–273.

Howlin, P., Good, S., Hutton, J., & Rutter, M. (2009). Savant skills in autism: Psychometric approaches and parental reports. *Philosophical Transactions of the Royal Society B, 364*, 1359–1367.

Kanner, L. (1971) Follow-up study of eleven autistic children originally reported in 1943. *Journal of Autism and Childhood Schizophrenia, 1*(2), 119–145.

Klei, L., Sanders, S. J., Murtha, M. T., Hus, V., Lowe, J. K., Willsey, A. J., . . . Devlin, B. (2012). Common genetic variants, acting additively, are a major source of risk for autism. *Molecular Autism, 3*(1), 9. doi:10.1186/2040-2392-3-9.

Krumm, N., O'Roak, B. J., Shendure, J., & Eichler, E. E. (2014). A de novo convergence of autism genetics and molecular neuroscience. *Trends in Neuroscience, 37*(2), 95–105.

Krumm, N., Turner, T. N., Baker, C., Vives, L., Mohajeri, K., Witherspoon, K., . . . Eichler, E. E. (2015). Excess of rare, inherited truncating mutations in autism. *Nature Genetics, 47*(6), 582–588.

Matsunami, N., Hadley, D., Hensel, C. H., Christensen, G. B., Kim, C., Frackelton. E., . . . Hakonarson, H. (2013). Identification of rare recurrent copy numbers variants in high-risk autism families and their prevalence in a large ASD population. *PLoS ONE, 8*(1), e52239. doi:10.1371/journal.pone.0052239

Morrison, D. C. (1985). Signs of neurobehavioral dysfunction in a sample of learning disabled children: Stability and concurrent validity. *Perceptual and Motor Skills, 61*(3), 863–872.

Nader, A.-M., Courchesne, V., Dawson, M., & Soulières, I. (2016). Does WISC-IV underestimate the intelligence of autistic children? *Journal of Autism and Developmental Disorders, 46*, 1582–1589.

O'Neill, J. L. (1999). *Through the eyes of aliens: A book about autistic people*. London: Jessica Kingsley.

Philippi, A., Tores, F., Carayol, J., Rousseau, F., Letexier, M., Roschmann, E., . . . Hager, J. (2007). Association of autism with polymorphisms in the paired-like homeodomain transcription factor I (PITXI) on chromosome 5q31: A candidate gene analysis. *BMC Medical Genetics, 8*, 74. doi:10.1186/1471-2350-8-74

Polatajko, H. J., Kaplan, B. J., & Wilson, B. N. (1992). Sensory integration treatment for children with learning disabilities: Its status 20 years later. *OTJR: Occupation, Participation and Health 12*(8), 323–341.

Robinson, E. B., St. Pourcain, B., Anttila, V., Kosmicki, J. A., Bulik-Sullivan, B., Grove, J., . . . Hager, J. (2016). Genetic risk for autism spectrum disorders and neuropsychiatric variation in the general population. *Nature Genetics, 48*, 552–555.

Sacks, O. (1995). *An anthropologist on Mars*. London: Picador.

Schauder, K. B., & Bennetto, L. (2016). Toward an interdisciplinary understanding of sensory dysfunction in autism spectrum disorder: An integration of the neural and symptom literatures. *Frontiers in Neuroscience, 10*(51), 268. doi:10.3389/fnins.2016.00268.

Shepard, R. N., & Metzler, J. (1971). Mental rotation of three-dimensional objects. *Science, 171*, 701–703.

Silverman, L. K. (2002). *Upside-down brilliance*. Denver, CO: DeLeon Publishing.

Sinclair, J. (1992). Bridging the gaps: An inside-out view of autism. In E. Schopler & G. Mesibov (Eds.), *High-functioning individuals with autism* (pp. 289–306). New York: Plenum Press.

Soulieres, I., Dawson, M., Gernsbacher, M. A., & Mottron, L. (2011). The level and nature of autistic intelligence II: What about Asperger syndrome? *PLoS ONE, 6*(9), e25372. doi:10.1371/journal.pone.0025372.

Stevenson, J. L., & Gernsbacher, M. A. (2013). Abstract spatial reasoning as an autistic strength. *PLoS ONE, 8*(3), e59329. doi:10.1371/journal.pone.0059329.

Treffert, D. A., & Rebedew, D. L. (2015). The savant syndrome registry: A preliminary report. *Wisconsin Medical Journal, 114*(4), 158–162.

VanDalen, J. G. T. (1995). Autism from within: Looking through the eyes of a mildly afflicted autistic person. *Link, 17*, 11–17.

Zeki, S. (1992). The visual image in mind and brain. *Scientific American, 267*(3), 68–76.

Zentall, S. S., & Kruczek, T. (1988). The attraction of color for active attention-problem children. *Exceptional Children, 54*(4), 357–362.

Zhou, X.-L., Giacobini, M., Anderlid, B.-M., Anckarsäter, H., Omrani, D., Gillberg, C., . . . Linblom, A. (2007). Association of adenomatous polyposis coli (APC) gene polymorphisms with autism spectrum disorder (ASD). *American Journal of Medical Genetics: Part B, Neuropsychiatric Genetics, 144B*(3), 351–354.

14

# Visuo-Spatial Skills in Atypical Readers

## *Myths, Research, and Potential*

MARYAM TREBEAU CROGMAN, JEFFREY W. GILGER, AND FUMIKO HOEFT

## OVERVIEW

Atypical learners including those with developmental dyslexia (also called decoding-based reading disability [RD]) and twice exceptionality (2e), where 2e refers to having an RD co-occurring with giftedness, often exhibit a wide variety of cognitive profiles. Following a medical historical tradition of a symptom-cure perspective, however, these individuals have typically been addressed by focusing more on *disabilities* than on *abilities* and on specifically salient behavioral outcomes such as improvement in reading-related challenges. While data on nonlinguistic skills remain relatively unconsidered in general definitions of RD, we argue that these abilities may be an important part of the RD and 2e-RD picture. To develop such an argument, we start by providing an overview of current definitions of RD (Lyon, Shaywitz, & Shaywitz, 2003) and 2e (Foley-Nicpon, Allmon, Sieck, & Stinson, 2011), and summarize the past 40 years of research on how nonverbal visual-spatial (VS) reasoning is expressed in people with RD. While results generally suggest that RD individuals as a group do not exhibit overall superior VS abilities, there appear to be specific types of VS skills that RD individuals show strengths in, but more rigorous and systematic research is needed. We also note that regardless of the data on VS skills in heterogeneous RD samples, there is a subset of RD individuals who could be classified as 2e-RD and who often demonstrate superiority in the VS domain. The special needs of these 2e-RD individuals needs to be better addressed with an extended focus beyond their reading challenges.

This chapter aims to highlight the need for a different theoretical and applied approach to how nonverbal VS skills in RD populations are considered; it also suggests the need for shifting the methodological approach of researchers when it comes to assessing those skills. The goal is to contribute to a change in the educational and clinical infrastructures that support and enhance nonverbal skills in these populations. Recommendations are made for future research in order to characterize the VS aspects of the RD profile and what, if any, links there are between the neurological underpinnings of 2e-RD and what may be unique VS processing mechanisms in RD and 2e-RD populations. We also make recommendations on how to translate such research into mainstream education and other venues catering to these groups. Researchers, educators, and parents are invited to focus on what may be processing and learning "uniqueness" or cognitive differences in RD and 2e-RDs when it comes to nonverbal VS skills and are invited to seek answers as to how to best support these learners.

## INTRODUCTION

### Reading Disorder

Developmental dyslexia or decoding-based RD is one of a set of specific learning disorders recognized by educational and medical professionals. According to Lyon et al. (2003, p. 2), it is

> A specific learning disability that is neurobiological in origin . . . characterized by difficulties with accurate and/or fluent word recognition and by poor spelling and decoding abilities . . . typically resulting from a deficit in the phonological component of language that is often unexpected in relation to other cognitive abilities and the provision of effective classroom instruction. Secondary consequences may include problems in reading comprehension and reduced reading experience that can impede growth of vocabulary and background knowledge.

Prevalence estimates of RD in the school-age population run around 7% to 10%, with approximately 1.5 boys to every girl where the ratio may be higher as with greater severity (Boyle et al., 2011; Goswami, 2006; Hawke, Olson, Willcut, Wadsworth, & DeFries, 2009; Shaywitz & Shaywitz, 2005; Willcutt & Pennington, 2000).

The consensus of brain imaging studies is that people with RD show an underactivation during phonological reading tasks in parts of the reading circuit (left parietotemporal and occipitotemporal regions). There may also be a developmentally inappropriate over activation of the right and left inferior frontal regions (Cao, Bitan, & Booth, 2008; Hoeft et al., 2007; Richlan, Kronbichler, & Wimmer, 2009, 2011). For example, research has shown that normal reading activation profiles change with age, with a natural shift to reliance on left hemisphere processing, yet in RD samples (especially at younger ages) there remains a relative overactivation of the right hemisphere (Frye, Wu, Liederman, & McGraw Fisher, 2010; Hoeft et al., 2011). Appropriate and intensive remediation can change these atypical neurological patterns and "normalize" the reading circuit with more appropriate activation of brain regions and a more typical pattern of hemispheric reliance (Keller & Just, 2009; Simos et al., 2002).

In general, RD is defined on the basis of a reading problem. In practice, however, we see that individuals with RD often exhibit a wide variety of cognitive profiles. In addition to the reading problem, other symptoms such as delays in oral language and motor development, auditory processing deficits, and secondary academic problems are common, as are certain co-occurring conditions such as attention deficit hyperactivity disorder (Chaix et al., 2007; Greven, Harlaar, Dale, & Plomin, 2011; King, Lombardino, Crandell, & Leonard, 2003; Ramus, 2003; see Fugate, this volume). There are also data indicating that individuals with RD may show nonlinguistic behavioral or sensory deficits, such as those related to visual-orthographic processing, cognitive-temporal sequencing, and functioning of the parvo-magnocellular visual system (Fawcett & Nicolson, 1994; Howard, Howard, Japikse, & Eden, 2006; Schneps, Brockmole, Sonnert, & Pomplun, 2012; Skottun, 2005; Stein, 2001). However, the contribution that these nonlinguistic or sensory deficits may make to the etiology of the reading issue is unclear, and more research is needed (Goswami, 2006, 2015). Thus people with RD constitute a very diverse group, with developmental challenges and etiologies that require multidisciplinary approaches to support and research.

## RD and Giftedness

Further complicating the RD profile is the potential for reading deficits to occur alongside cognitive strengths or talents. The presence of cognitive gifts/talents such as high ability to process verbal (Berninger & Abbott, 2013) or nonverbal information (Gilger, Tavalage, & Olulade, 2013) may mask RD traits, complicate RD diagnoses, or, more positively, help individuals with RD to compensate for their reading weaknesses (Silverman, 2009; van Viersen, Kroesbergen, Slot, & de Bree, 2016). In educational settings, it is common to label children who have a learning or cognitive disability but also learning or cognitive gifts/talents as twice exceptional (2e; Foley-Nicpon, 2013; Kalbfleisch, 2012; Nielsen & Higgings, 2005). Many different disorders can co-occur with a superior ability (e.g., Treffert, 2009), but this chapter focuses on one of the most common forms of 2e, 2e-RD. The superior component of the 2e-RD condition can take many forms, such as measurable verbal IQ or performance IQ, special talents in math or art, extreme memory skill, and other (Kay, 2000; Nielsen, 2002; Nielsen et al., 2005).

Twice exceptionality rates vary greatly across studies, and some of the best estimates have placed the prevalence of 2e in K–12th grade in heterogeneous special education or gifted populations at around 3% to -5% (with some as low as 1% and as high as 36%; Foley-Nicpon et al., 2011; Ruban & Reis, 2005). Given that reading/language-related disabilities are the most common of the specific learning disorders (Cortiella, & Horowitz, 2014), it is not surprising that a majority of these 2e children will have reading impairments as part of their profile. While the reading-related deficits may be the focus of remediation in children with 2e-RD, best practices suggest that a thorough treatment plan should attend to the entire profile of student strengths and weaknesses (Berninger et al., 2013; Jones, 1986; Kalbfleisch, 2012; Kappers, 1991; LaFrance, 1997; Paulesu et al., 2001; Snowling, 2000; Snowling, Bishop, & Stothard, 2000).

## Neural Systems of RD

The disease model of RD has, understandably, dominated the neurobiological studies, and researchers have tended to focus on the left hemisphere language-based systems or the classic reading circuit: left hemisphere inferior frontal, inferior temporo-occipital, and temporo-parietal areas (Linkersdörfer, Lonnemann, Lindberg, Hasselhorn, & Fiebach, 2012; Richlan et al., 2009, 2011; Vandermosten, Hoeft, & Norton, 2016). Research, however, shows that individuals with RD often have broader differences in brain functions and structures not limited to the left hemisphere, with behavioral consequences we do not fully understand (Diehl et al., 2014; Eckert, 2004; Gilger & Hynd, 2008; Hynd, Semrud-Clikeman, Lorys, Novey, & Eliopulos, 1990; Galaburda, LoTurco Ramus, Fitch, & Rosen, 2006; Gilger & Kaplan, 2001; Linkersdörfer et al., 2012; Maisog, Einbinder, Flowers, Turkeltaub, & Eden, 2008; Olulade, Gilger, Talavage, Hynd, & McAteer, 2012; Richlan et al., 2009, 2011). In addition to the reading pathway of the left hemisphere, the brains of people with RD show structural and/or functional differences in the right hemisphere, subcortical and cerebellar regions (Eckert, 2004; Gilger & Kaplan, 2001; Galaburda et al., 2006; Galaburda, 1992; Hynd et al., 1990; Lindell, 2006; Linkersdörfer et al., 2012; Maisog et al., 2008; Pugh et al., 2000; Richlan et al., 2009, 2011; Temple et al., 2003). While the processing of language-related information is not constrained to the left hemisphere, these other regions where RD differences have been found are known to be important for other functions as well, such as processing visuo-spatial information, social, affective, and musical information. Again, we know little about how these other neurological differences in RD individuals manifest in behavior or what factor they may play in response to remediation; nor do we understand how reading remediation might in turn influence the development of these associated skills.

## Considering the Nonverbal Profiles of Individuals with RD

We must keep in mind that despite similarities in behavioral and cognitive characteristics, each individual in the general RD population is different. Thus categorizing individuals, though helpful in many respects, can also become a limitation to the full consideration of skills and challenges encountered by these individuals.

Indeed, science has truly advanced our understanding of the causes and expression of RD. The relatively neglected questions deal with why and how the brains of people with RD may be unique in other ways and how that uniqueness may manifest itself in behavior.

Twice exceptional-RD individuals, as mentioned earlier, likely constitute a subpopulation within the RD group. But some have proposed that 2e-RD is more than a subgroup and that RD individuals *in general* show a tendency to excel in certain VS skills as part of their RD profile, perhaps reflecting a unique neurology present at birth (Eide & Eide, 2011; Galaburda, 1992; Geschwind & Behan, 1982; Geschwind & Galaburda, 1987; von Károlyi, Winner, Gray, & Sherman, 2003). Skills in the nonverbal and VS domain are, in fact, those most often represented in 2e populations, including savants and gifted children with specific learning disorders (Treffert, 2009). Seminal research initiated discussions on how the neurology of RD could be linked to special skills in the nonverbal domain (Galaburda, 1992; Geschwind et al., 1982; Geschwind et al., 1987). Geschwind and colleagues hypothesized that pathological or atypical prenatal development of the left hemisphere, and secondary right hemisphere neurological compensation and development, could lead to both the language-related weaknesses *and* nonverbal strengths simultaneously.

Partly based on these early hypotheses about RD and 2e-RD neurology and partly because of subsequent research and additional anecdotal reports, some authors have suggested that we destigmatize individuals with RD by moving away from a purely deficit perspective and emphasizing their possibly inherent strengths such as VS abilities. For example, some have suggested that people with RD are gifted in nonverbal areas and/or the status of being RD is a gift in itself (e.g., Davis, 2010; Eide, 2013; Kaufman, 2015; West, 1997). Because individuals with RD may be talented in the nonverbal areas, they may therefore excel at careers or avocations related to these special aptitudes (e.g., West, 1997).

Indeed, there are data suggesting that people with RD tend to adopt and perform well in VS-oriented professions or professions involving more mathematical and artistic skills than verbal skills (Cowen, 2004; Eide & Eide, 2011; Logan & Martin, 2012; Steffert, 1998; Taylor & Walter, 2003; West, 1997, 2009; Wolff & Lunberg, 2002). There are also some reports that people with RD do better than non-RD groups on the processing of complex visual forms (e.g., Diehl et al., 2014; Von Karolyi et al., 2003). Our experience with people that have RD is that they often do "think differently" and in creative ways (see Daniels & Freeman, this volume), but the precise ways they do so have yet to be empirically resolved. As we detail in this chapter, research over the past 40 years is inconsistent on this question. Some studies report better performance in RD samples, while many do not. The best conclusion at this time seems to be that there are large individual differences, with some being gifted or talented and others not.

We suggest that it is important to take a more individual differences approach rather than categorizing individuals into RD or 2e-RD groupings and stopping there. The end result may be a better way to consider innovative perspectives, aimed at supporting individuals in all their dimensions, rather than further refinement of labels and limiting boxes (Gilger & Hynd, 2008; Rose, 2016).

## MYTH OR REALITY: ARE PERSONS WITH RD SUPERIOR IN VS THINKING?

Quality data on what may be a dyslexic advantage in nonverbal and creative domains is limited. While only a few studies have provided career assessment data, a number of studies have addressed the aptitude question, which we detail next.

### Careers

While the literature does show an elevated rate of individuals with RD in nonverbal careers (fine arts, astronomy, etc.; Hickman & Brens, 2014; Schneps et al., 2011), these findings are largely anecdotal reports or self-report surveys, and there is a paucity of experimental studies of good design in this area (Taylor et al., 2003; Wolff et al., 2002). In contrast, other reports (Fink, 2002; Finucci, Gottfredson, & Childs, 1985; Gottfredson, Finucci, & Childs, 1984) show that people with RD choose fields that are considered more "verbal" (nursing, business, law). It has been proposed that many RD individuals have strong oral language skills and that some of these "verbal" professions may require certain creative thinking abilities characteristic to people with RD (Fink, 2002; Finucci et al., 1985; Gottfredson et al., 1984). Thus, whether in positions that appear nonverbal or verbal, the argument is that people with RD choose careers based on a set of unique abilities that they possess more often that people without RD. It is possible, however, that career choice is more a matter of preferences or practice based on compensations for reading-related weaknesses or *within-person relative strengths* (and not necessarily that their nonreading skills are in the gifted domain).

For example, Wolff and Lunberg (2002) suggest that career choice is more a function of compensation and practice. They worked with art students and through both interviews and tests concluded that art students were more often likely to report issues with phonological skills than non-art students. They reported that art students tended to choose this field more often when they are RD because of their challenges with reading. In the same vein, Hickman and colleagues (2014) interviewed and observed art teachers with severe dyslexia to find out what coping strategies they had employed in their teaching and to see if those strategies could be used as tools to help students with RD. One conclusion was that these teachers had not only a hyper-awareness about VS information but were also very socially attuned and particularly empathetic to struggling students due to their own experiences.

In other domains such as the sciences, few reports are available, and sometimes they are contradictory (e.g., people with RD are wired for and choose more scientific careers [Schneps et al., 2011] versus they choose careers that are more "people oriented" [Taylor, et al., 2003]). For example, Schneps and colleagues observed astronomy students with RD and professional astrophysicists and discovered that they were better at detecting signals and had unique visual strategies to solve problems. They posited that many struggling individuals with RD may find success in careers that build on the type of strengths they naturally possess; however, the authors suggested that these abilities may not be manifested without proper training and guidance (see also Gilger et al., 2016; Gilger et al., 2013). Thus Schneps and colleagues imply that a special potential ability for these types of skills is inherent to the RD profile, but these abilities need to be trained.

Finally, Taylor and Walter (2003) did a simple comparison between the occupations of adults with and without RD and found that people with RD were more often in "people-oriented" professions such as nursing or business rather than science. They stressed the possibility of a pattern of career choice correlated with having RD. Logan (2009) found similar results with some nuances as to the type of business venture, for example people with RD were more often entrepreneurs than corporate managers, and used strategies such as delegation for tasks that involved verbal demands. In the same vein, Finucci and colleagues (1985) tracked boys with RD into adulthood to assess their career choices and found the majority to be employed in the business area with differences correlated to the degree of their original reading deficits as young children.

The variety of the reports and the lack of consensus on what people with RD choose as careers is a testimony to the confusion that still exists around inherent RD abilities and that representation in careers. An important remaining question is if the career choices made are reactionary to reading weaknesses and compensation over time, reflect the practice of relative strengths, or are due to some innate ability or brain-behavior skill set that is linked to being RD. It is valuable to address this question to adequately support individuals with RD from birth through their adult life.

## Visuo-Spatial Ability

There are many more studies on VS aptitude in people with RD than there are regarding RD careers. Before summarizing this research, we must point out that despite a general belief that RD may exhibit superiority in VS skills, a large body of research has looked at VS *deficits* and VS associations with RD. For example, Facoetti and colleagues (2010) have shown connections between visuo-spatial attention and auditory processing deficits in families at risk for RD, and the work of Valdois and colleagues (2004) and Vidyasagar and Pammer (2003) demonstrates that visuo-spatial attention issues may be a predictor dyslexia. There is also a body of work looking at the role that specific neurological visual system may contribute to the RD profile (e.g., Eden, Stein, & Wood, 1993; Facoetti et al., 2009; Goswami, 2012; Gould & Glencorss, 1990; Howard et al., 2006; Koenig, Kosslyn, & Wolff, 1991; Schneps et al., 2012; Stein, 2001). While phonological decoding problems are considered the hallmark of RD, there are multiple factors that contribute the expression of the disorder, and this research suggests a multi-deficit view of dyslexia, including connections to VS abilities.

Before beginning our review of VS skills it is noteworthy that a significant amount of research has focused on the more basic or primary aspects of visual processing or perceptual skills in RDs, and this work is not part of our review here. These studies have considered such behaviors as peripheral visual abilities, visual memory, motion perception, the analysis of variable spatial frequencies, and functions of the parvo-magnocellular system in RD subjects (see Eden, Stein, & Wood, 1993; Facoetti et al., 2009; Goswami, 2012; Gould & Glencorss, 1990; Howard et al., 2006; Koenig et al., 1991; Schneps et al., 2012; Stein, 2001). While studies of these more basic visual abilities or perceptual processes are important, they do not represent the type of skill most often studied and considered as an RD gift or as an explanation for the overrepresentation of successful RDs in artistic, nonverbal reasoning, or creative fields. These skills do, however, likely influence the more dynamic spatial reasoning or processes we review.

Our aim in the following sections is to review the literature on experiments assessing VS abilities in RD samples. We emphasize dynamic and complex spatial visualization, reasoning, rotation, nonverbal holistic processing, and nonverbal creativity. These abilities have been well researched and linked to the effects of genes, hormones, gender, age, and training (Cohen, Kosslyn, Breiter, & DiGirolamo, 1996; Jung & Haier, 2007; Linn & Peterson, 1985; Moore & Johnson, 2008; Newcombe & Dubas, 1987; Uttal et al., 2013). They are also correlated with nonverbal IQ (and to a lesser extent verbal IQ; Colom, Rebollo, Palacios, Juan-Espinosa, & Kyllonen, 2004). Other studies have also found relationships between VS skills and performance in math, engineering, music, and art, as well as interpersonal communication styles (e.g., Stieff, Dixon, Ryu, Kumi, & Hegarty, 2014; Winner Casey, DaSilva, & Hayes, 1991). The term *visual-spatial* (VS) skill or ability is a broad term that includes a plethora of separate yet related behaviors, and it is assessed in a number of different ways. Lohman (1996) defines VS ability as "the ability to generate, retain, retrieve, and transform well-structured visual images," and he included several subfactors that comprise VS in general: spatial relations, spatial orientation, and spatial visualization, inclusive of tasks requiring encoding, remembering, transforming, and matching and cognitive activities involving closure speed, perceptual speed, visual memory, and kinesthetic left-right orientation. For the purpose of this chapter we use Lohman's definition and include additional VS skills categories such as dynamic versus static VS tasks, navigation in 3D space and the processing of virtual environments, and so on (Newcombe & Shipley, 2015; Uttal et al., 2013). Additionally, we incorporate abilities that involve recognizing pattern frequencies, memory, attention, or creativity as they relate to processing of information in space. Note that these separate VS skills are not uncorrelated, and the list is not necessarily exhaustive.

## Literature Review

We reviewed the literature for the past 37 years, 1978–2015. Like Gilger and colleagues (2016), we reviewed only those studies that included a control (non-RD comparison) group. A total of 43 articles were found to meet our selection criteria. Collapsing the VS measures of these 43 we found 192 (partially overlapping and repeated) tests comparisons between individuals with and without RD (non-RD).[1] Participants tested in these studies ranged from four years old to adulthood and accounted for a wide range of populations, genders, and participant backgrounds. Databases searched included HEBSCO, PsychInfo and PsychArticles, and Google Scholar. The bibliographies of identified articles were crosschecked with database results to help ensure that no significant articles were missed. Key words searched alone or in combination were: dyslexia, reading disorder, RD, spatial, spatial ability, spatial aptitude, VS talent, nonverbal skill, ability or aptitude, VS learning, VS training, VS tasks, spatial, performance, rotation, visualization, VS skills, intervention, training. Accepted publications had to include comparisons of RD to non-RD samples, or at least present adequate data to deduce how subjects with RD performed relative to a population norm. Excluded from this review are books, chapters, conference presentations, single subject case studies and anecdotal reports, and publications with a primary focus other than dynamic and complex VS skills as defined previously (e.g., peripheral abilities, visual attention, etc.).

Table 14.1 provides descriptions of the seven main categories of VS skills we focused on. Brief descriptions of each of the 43 studies are shown in Table 14.2. Finally, summary statistics for each of the seven categories of VS are provided in Table 14.3. Table 14.3 allows the reader to see at a glance the overall average performance of individuals with RD compared to non-RD controls on the 192 VS task comparisons found in the review. It is important to remember that when we speak of RD "superiority" on certain tasks, we do not necessarily mean "gifted" performance but rather superior performance relative to controls. Gifted performance would require levels in the exceptional range, say, 1.5 to 2 standard deviations above the population mean on a standardized test (Stephens & Karnes, 2000). The reader is free to examine the studies in Table 14.2 on his or her own; *however, our conclusion is that rarely did RD groups achieve a high enough level of mean performance to classify as gifted.*

Out of the 192 VS tasks recorded across 43 studies, individuals with RD relative to non-RDs demonstrated superior performance on 30 (16%) comparisons, lower performance on 70 (36%), and equal performance on 92 (48%). These findings clearly show that people with RD do not typically outperform their non-RD counterparts, and, in fact, individuals with RD perform equal to or worse than non-RD

1. Some papers included more than one VS test that was used to make RD/non-RD statistical comparisons. There were 192 useable statistical comparisons for VS skills in these 43 articles.

*Table 14.1.* Visuo-Spatial Skills and Constructs[a]

| Task Category | Task Type | Example | Illustration | Associated Literature Assessed |
|---|---|---|---|---|
| Spatial Visualization | Complex, multistep manipulations of spatially presented information, may involve rotations, dynamic movement, part-to-whole analysis | Paper from board, block design, paper folding | b | Thomson (1982); Kamhi, Catts, Mauer, Apel, & Gentry (1988); Siegel & Ryan (1989); Everatt (1997); Winner et al. (2001); Brosnan et al. (2002); Helland & Asbjørnsen (2003); Duranovic, Dedeic, & Gavrić (2014); Lockiewicz, Bogdanowicz, & Bogdanowicz (2014). |
| Spatial relations or rotations | Perceive an object from different positions, mentally rotate one stimulus to align it with a comparison stimulus, involves rotations and/or reflections | Shephard Metzler cubes | c | Stanley, Kaplan et al. (1975); Pontius (1981); Thomson (1982); Corballis, Macadie, & Beale (1985); Eden, Stein, & Wood (1993); Singh (1993); Karádi, Kovács, Szepesi, Szabó, & Kállai (2001); Winner et al. (2001); Rüsseler, Scholz, Jordan, & Quaiser-Pohl (2005); von Károlyi & Winner (2005); Rusiak et al. (2007); Attree, Turner, & Cowell (2009); Wang & Yang, (2011); Olulade, Gilger, Talavage, Hynd, & McAteer (2012); Diehl et al. (2014); Lockiewicz, Bogdanowicz, & Bogdanowicz (2014). |
| Global-holistic processing, closure speed, flexibility of closure | Rapid identification of incomplete or distorted pictures and figures impossible in normal 3D environments | Impossible figures, Gestalt completion | d | von Karolyi (2001); Winner et al. (2001); Brosnan et al. (2002); von Károlyi et al. (2003); von Károlyi & Winner (2005); Brunswick et al. (2010); Diehl et al. (2014). |
| Drawing | 2D drawing or reproduction of shapes or patterns | Draw a man, free drawing, pattern reproduction | e | Pontius (1981); Everatt (1997); Winner et al. (2001); Eden, Wood, & Stein, (2003); von Karolyi et al. (2005); Alves & Nakano (2014); Duranovic et al. (2014). |

| | | | | |
|---|---|---|---|---|
| Pattern Recognition/ Recall / Target Recognition | Perceptual organization | Matrices, Rey-Osterrieth Complex Figure Task, hidden figures, block design | f, g | Siegel & Ryan (1989); Koenig, Kosslyn, & Wolff (1991); Eden, Stein, & Wood, (1993); Everatt (1997); Fischer & Hartnegg (2000); Nicolson & Fawcett (2000); von Karolyi (2001); Winner et al. (2001); Brosnan et al. (2002); Helland & Asbjørnsen (2003); Howard, Howard, Japikse, & Eden (2006); von Karolyi et al. (2005); Attree et al. (2009); Brunswick et al. (2010); Olulade et al. (2012); Schneps, Brockmole, Sonnert, & Pomplun (2012); Alves & Nakano (2014); Ruffino, Gori, Boccardi, Molteni, & Facoetti (2014); Martinelli & Schembri (2015). |
| Virtual world navigation / 3D navigation / speed of recognition | Navigating 2D–3D space | Maze, navigating virtual environments, | h | Siegel & Ryan (1989); Winner et al. (2001); Nicolson & Fawcett (2000); Sigmundsson (2005); von Karolyi et al. (2005); Attree et al. (2009); Mammarella et al. (2009); Brunswick et al. (2010); Wang & Yang (2011). |
| Other | Right-left orientation, visuo-motor and visuo-constructive performance, perceptual organization | Finger recognition, queen's head direction | i | Benton (1984); Winner et al. (2001); Brunswick et al. (2010); Duranovic et al. (2014). |

NOTE: Some studies appear several times as they tested diverse types of skills. [a]Constructs and table format borrowed from Gilger, Allen, and Castillo (2016). [b]Modified example from the Minnesota Paper From Board Test (Likert & Quasha, 1941). [c]Example from Vandenberg and Kuse (1978) based off of the Shepard-Metzler Cubes Mental Rotation Tasks (1988). [d]Example from Schacter, Cooper, and Delaney (1990). [e]Example from Winner et al. (2001). [f]Test stimulus from Osterrieth (1944) and Rey (1941). [g]Example from Winner et al. (2001). [h]Example from Brunswick et al. (2010). [i]Illustration for one of the tasks in Brunswick et al. (2010).

*Table 14.2.* Studies Featuring RD Performances Compared to Controls[a]

| Authors | Sample and Age Group | Tools & Tasks | Higher Performance | Lower Performance | Equal Performance |
|---|---|---|---|---|---|
| van Bergen et al. (2014) | 212: 100 at risk w/o RD<br>44 RDs, 68 controls<br>(Age 4 and 4 years later) | Block design, patterns (copying patterns), object assembly (jigsaw puzzle), picture completion (adding missing parts), analogies (assembling pieces in small trays by shape, color, size) | | PR (block design)<br>PR (patterns), PR (analogies)<br>SV (object assembly)<br>SV (picture completion) | |
| Kamhi et al. (1988) | 30, 10 RDs (6–8) | Minnesota Paper Form Board, paper folding | | SV (Minnesota Paper), SV (paper folding) | |
| Siegel & Ryan (1989) | 641, 200 RDs (6–14)<br>**Grouped as** 6–8, 9–14:<br>PDG,<br>CDG,<br>RDG | Block design, object assembly, picture completion, picture arrangement, mazes, PIQ | | **PDG:**<br>SV (block design in PIQ) 6–8<br>PR (object assembly) 6–8<br>PR (picture completion) 6–8<br>**CDG:**<br>SV (Block design in PIQ) 6–8 / 9–14<br>PR (object assembly) 6–8<br>PR (picture completion) 6–8<br>PR (picture arrangement) 6-8<br>**RDG:**<br>SV (block design in PIQ) 6–8 / 9–14<br>PR (object assembly) 9–14<br>PR (picture arrangement) 6–8<br>N (mazes) 9–14 | **PDG:**<br>SV (block design in PIQ) 9–14<br>PR (object assembly) 9–14<br>PR (picture completion) 9–14<br>PR (picture arrangement) 9–14<br>N (mazes) 6–8 / 9–14<br>**CDG:**<br>PR (object assembly) 9–14<br>PR (picture completion) 9–14 |

| | | | | |
|---|---|---|---|---|
| | | | | PR (picture arrangement) 9–14<br>N (mazes) 6–8 / 9–14<br>**RDG:**<br>PR (object assembly) 6–8<br>PR (picture completion) 6–8<br>PR (picture arrangement) 9–14<br>N (mazes) 6–8 |
| Ruffino et al. (2014) | 75, 32 RDs (7–14), | Target detection and identification of masked objects | TR (spatial and temporal attention) | |
| Tobia & Marzocchi (2014) | 160, 32 RDs (7–10) | Visual search: cancel a stimulus in an array. Visuo-spatial attention (click a button when detecting a dot on screen) | PR (cancel picture in array, RT) TR (spot dot, RT) | Both eccentricity and visual field PR (cancel picture in array), TR (spot dot) |
| Rüsseler, Scholz, Jordan, & Quaiser-Pohl (2005) | 70, 34 RDs (7–9) | FRT 3D figures, symbols, and pictures mental rotation tasks, EFT | SR (in all three mental rotation tasks and EFT) | |
| Stanley, Kaplan, & Poole (1975) | 66, 33 RDs (8–12) | Visual matching spatial transformation, identify similarities of 3D objects | | SR (visual matching spatial transformation) |

(*continued*)

*Table 14.2.* Continued

| Authors | Sample and Age Group | Tools & Tasks | Higher Performance | Lower Performance | Equal Performance |
|---|---|---|---|---|---|
| Pontius (1981) | 356 children: 104 RDs (8–15) | Bender Gestalt Rotation task, drawing | | SR (mental rotation)<br>DW (drawing a person) | SR (mental rotation) |
| Thomson (1982) | 83 RDs (8–16) | British Ability Scales: Letter-like form rotation, visualization of cubes, block Design (level), block design (power), recall of design | | | SR (letter rotation)<br>SV (blocks level), SV (blocks power)<br>SV (cubes) |
| Benton (1984) | Multiple studies with children and adults | Show right left limbs, finger recognition | | O (right-left orientation)<br>O (finger recognition) | |
| Singh (1993) | 40, 20 RDs (8–11) | Mental rotation | | SR (mental rotation) | |
| Fischer & Hartnegg (2000) | 85 RDs (8–15) | Practice on pattern orientation to detect targets in visual field | | | PR (pattern detection after training) |
| Karádi et al. (2001) | 55, 27 RDs (8–9) | Angled drawing recognition | | SR (mental rotation) | |
| Duranovic, Dedeic, & Gavrić (2015) | 80, 40 RDs (9–11) | Mental rotation, paper folding, Rey-Osterrieth complex figures, electric grid task, drawing memory | SV (paper folding) | PR (Rey-Osterrieth complex figure, recall)<br>DW (drawing memory long term but results nonsignificant) | SR (mental rotation)<br>PR (Rey O. complex figure copy)<br>PR (electric grid)<br>DW (drawing memory short term) |
| Mammarella et al. (2009) | 39, 22 RDs (9–12) | Outdoor spatial description surveys and route description | | N (outdoor spatial description surveys and route description) | |

| | | | | | |
|---|---|---|---|---|---|
| Alves & Nakano (2014) | 26, 13 RDs (9–11) | Raven matrices, figural creativity | | | DW (creative drawing), PR (Raven matrices) |
| Eden, Stein, & Wood (1993) | 17 (10–13) | Complex figures, judgment of lines | | SR (judgment of lines) | PR (complex figures) |
| Eden, Wood, & Stein (2003) | 93, 26 poor readers (10–12) | Clock drawing, handedness (Edinburg test), visuospatial skills (WISC block design test) | | DW (clock drawing) | DW (clock drawing) |
| Wang & Yang (2011) | 120, 60 RDs (10–12) | Columns (cover) a ball (target), must rotate 3D figures to find a ball | SR, N (rotation response time) | | SR, N (rotation accuracy) |
| Corballis, Macadie, & Beale (1985) | 20, 10 RDs (11–13) | Rotation of letters, discriminating Bs from Ds | SR (left hemisphere advantage for unrotated letter recognition in space) | | SR (accuracy) |
| Corballis, Macadie, Crotty, & Beale (1985) | 20, 10RDs (11-13) | Recognizing rotated letters F, G, and R. | | SR (1/accuracy letter recognition, more errors with G; results nonsignificant) (2/speed of recognition (rotated and unrotated) but results nonsignificant) | SR (letter recognition accuracy and speed of F and–R) |

(*continued*)

*Table 14.2.* Continued

| Authors | Sample and Age Group | Tools & Tasks | Higher Performance | Lower Performance | Equal Performance |
|---|---|---|---|---|---|
| Vakil, Lowe, Goldfus (2015) – *Practice study* | 53, 23 RDs (11–13) | ToH puzzle (SV), pattern skill learning task (PR) | PR (pattern skill learning task, RT after practice)<br>SV (time by first move after picture | SV (time per moves) | PR (pattern skill learning task, learning rate)<br>SV (number of moves to find solution, RT) |
| Helland & Asbjørnsen (2003) | 39 RDs (12–13) | Aston Index (visual-sequential memory tasks pictures and symbols), WISC (block design, object assembly) | PR (visual-sequential tasks for the subgroup with math skills | PR (visual-sequential tasks) for the mathematics-impaired subgroup<br>PR (block design), SV (object assembly) | PR (visual-sequential tasks for RD subgroup with language and math impairments) |
| Attree, Turner, & Cowell (2009) | 42, 21 RDs (12–14) | BAS pattern construction and design recall tasks, virtuality "pseudo-real life test" | PR (spatial recognition memory); N (real-world, target recognition) | PR (BAS but results nonsignificant) | SR (global rotation) |
| Martinelli & Schembri (2015) | 36, 16 RDs (12–13) | Hidden shapes, sections, jigsaws, wallpaper and right angles<br>(Smith & Lord, 2002). | PR (Raven matrices -progressive)<br>PR (jigsaw)<br>PR (wallpaper but results nonsignificant)<br>PR (right angles) | PR (hidden figures, sections) | |

| | | | | | |
|---|---|---|---|---|---|
| von Károlyi, Winner, Gray, & Sherman (2003) | 64, 29 RDs (13–18) | S1 and S2: Impossible Figures test | S1 and S2: FC (Impossible Figures, in RT) | S1 and S2: FC (Impossible Figures in accuracy but results nonsignificant) | |
| Nicolson & Fawcett (2000) | S1: 21, 13 RDs, (13–15). S2: 22, 11 RDs, (15–16) | PacMan maze practice | | S1 and S2: PR (automatization "strength" after training) | |
| Diehl et al. (2014) | 53 RDs; 27 did the fMRI (13–22) | fMRI, mental rotation (accuracy and RT), Impossible Figures (accuracy, RT), Navon task (accuracy, RT) | FC (Impossible Figures RT out of scanner) | SR (mental rotation accuracy)<br>FC (Navon RT)<br>FC (Impossible Figures RT and accuracy in scanner) | FC (Impossible Figures accuracy)<br>FC (Navon accuracy)<br>SR (mental rotation RT) |
| von Karolyi (2001) | 40 RDs (15–18) | Computerized global task (Impossible Figures), feature oriented task (Celtic Matching Task) | FC (Impossible Figures for RT not at expense of accuracy) | PR (Celtic Matching Task but results nonsignificant) | FC (Impossible Figures for accuracy) |
| Winner et al. (2001) | S1: 60, 21 RDs (15–24). S2: 37, 15 RDs (grades 9–12). S3: 63, 40 RDs | S1: Vandenberg Test of Mental Rotation, Rey–Osterrieth Figure, hidden figures. S2: all above + Archimedes' screw, pyramid puzzle, drawing, K-Bit matrices. S3: Gestalt Completion Test, spatial orientation, card orientation, boat test, form board test, figural flexibility (storage task), closure speed, reference memory (maze test) | | SR (mental rotation, card rotation (in S3)) SV (Archimedes screw)<br>SV (form board in S3 if untimed)<br>PR (Rey complex figure in S2 but results nonsignificant)<br>PR (K-bit matrices in S2), O (storage test)<br>N (spatial reference memory in maze test) | PR (Rey complex figure)<br>PR (hidden figure)<br>SV (Archimedes screw)<br>SV (form board)<br>SR (mental rotation)<br>O (storage test), FC (Gestalt completion)<br>DW (drawing hands) |

(*continued*)

*Table 14.2.* Continued

| Authors | Sample and Age Group | Tools & Tasks | Higher Performance | Lower Performance | Equal Performance |
|---|---|---|---|---|---|
| Koenig, Kosslyn, & Wolff (1991) | 12 RDs males (16–18) | Memorizing shape or letters patterns in a grid | | PR (letter patterns) | PR (shapes pattern) |
| Everatt (1997) | 36 (18–55) | Spatial reasoning, Ravens matrices, drawing | DW (creative drawing) | SV (spatial reasoning)<br>PR (matrices but results nonsignificant) | |
| Sigmundsson (2005) | 23, 10 RDs (18–23) | Simulator car driving while pushing buttons (condition 1) or a voice-activated microphone (condition 2) immediately when a road sign appears | | N (RT) | |
| Brosnan et al. (2002) | S1: 18, 9 RDs. (Mean age 34); S2: 60, 30 (14) RDs. S3: 30, 15 RDs (18–29) | S1: Group Embedded figure test GEFT (for inhibition), ToH task (planning);<br>S2: Group Embedded figure test GEFT (for inhibition);<br>S3: spatial span, spatial recognition, matching complex figures, pattern recognition | | S1&2: FC (Group Embedded figure test) | S1: SV (ToH ball task)<br>S3: PR (spatial span), PR (spatial recognition), PR (matching complex figures), PR (pattern recognition) |

| | | | | | |
|---|---|---|---|---|---|
| von Károlyi & Winner (2005) | S1: 60, 21 RDs (young adults). S2: 37, 15 RDs (college). S3: 63, 40 RDs. (highschool); S4 & 5: 64, 29 RDs (Middle and Highschool) | S1: Vandenberg mental rotation test, Rey Osterrieth and hidden figures. S2: S1 + K-Bit, drawing task, 3D puzzle, Archimedes' screw; S3: spatial orientation (card rotation, Vandenberg TMR, boat test), mental visualization (Form Board Task), figural flexibility (storage task), closure speed (Gestalt completion test), spatial memory (Morris maze); S4 and 5: Impossible Figures task. | S4 and 5: FC: Impossible Figures | SR: (Vandenberg test of mental rotation (RD females))<br>PR (K-Bit matrices)<br>S3: SR (card rotation)<br>SR (boat test when timed)<br>FC (storage test when timed)<br>N (Morris maze) | PR (Rey-Osterrieth complex figure)<br>PR (hidden figures);<br>SV (Archimedes' screw);<br>DW (drawing ability);<br>S3: SR (boat test when untimed);<br>FC (storage test when untimed)<br>FC (Gestalt completion) |
| Howard, Howard, Japikse, & Eden (2006) | 23, 11 RDs (20) | Alternating serial RT and spatial context learning, computer screens letters and shapes series | PR (pattern recognition in spatial context learning) | PR (pattern recognition in sequence learning) | |
| Barnes, Hinkley, Masters, & Boubert (2007) | 60, 30 RDs (20-30) | Detecting motion in rotated or linear static images on screen, identifying if image presented corresponds to the previous screen picture | | SV (perception of static spatial movement organization) | |

(*continued*)

*Table 14.2.* CONTINUED

| Authors | Sample and Age Group | Tools & Tasks | Higher Performance | Lower Performance | Equal Performance |
|---|---|---|---|---|---|
| Rusiak et al. (2007) | 28, 16 RDs (19, 20) | S1 and S2: Letters oriented differently, press key when stimuli appears | | S1 and S2: SR (letters mental rotation RT) | S2: SR (mental rotation of shapes) |
| Brunswick, Martin, & Marzano (2010) | 41, 20 RDs (college students) | WAIS PIQ (picture completion, block design, object assembly), Rey Osterrieth complex figure, ambiguous figure test, visuospatial knowledge: queen's head direction, Herman virtuality environment, Gollin incomplete figure test | PR (PIQ picture completion)<br>PR (object assembly)<br>FC (ambiguous figure) for RDs men;<br>PR (Rey-Osterrieth complex figures)<br>PR (pattern reproduction)<br>O (recalling image direction)<br>N (navigating)<br>N (recreating virtual environment) | PR (PIQ block design) | |
| Stothers & Klein (2010) | 49 RDs (college-age and adults) | Gestalt closure, block design | | | FC (Gestalt closure), PR (block design) |

| | | | | | |
|---|---|---|---|---|---|
| Olulade et al. (2012) | 21, 9 RDs (18–25) | fMRI 3D rotation task | PR (WASI PIQ)<br>SR (MRI Rotate response time but the result was non significant) | SR (MRI rotate % accuracy, results nonsignificant)<br>SR (MRI non-rotate % accuracy and RT, results nonsignificant) | |
| Schneps, Brockmole, Sonnert, & Pomplun (2012) | 29, 10 RDs (college age) | S1: object search in sets, S2: finding objects in real-world scenes, S3: finding objects in low-pass filtered scenes | S3: TR (object search in low-pass filtered scene) | | S1: TR (object search in set)<br>S2: TR (object search in real-world scene) |
| Lockiewicz, Bogdanowicz, & Bogdanowicz (2014) | 180 high school up to 30, 93 RDs | The APIS-Z Battery visuo-spatial subtests (2, 7), Urban-Jellen Test for Creative Thinking–Drawing Production, Polish adaptation | | | SV (test2 square)<br>SR (test7 cube) |

[a]Detailed by age range, year, tasks used, and level of performance by type of visuo-spatial skill tested.

NOTE: RD = reading disorder. SV = spatial visualization; PDG = phonetics deficit group; CDG = comprehension deficit group; RDG = rate deficit group; PIQ = performance IQ; PR = pattern recognition/recall; N = navigation; TR = target recognition/recall; FRT = Figure Rotation Test; EFT = Embedded Figures Test; SR = spatial relations or rotations; DW = drawing; BAS = British Ability Scales; O = other; WISC = Wechsler Intelligence Scale for Children; ToH = Tower of Hanoi; RT = response time; S1 = Study#1; S2 = Study#2; S3 = Study#3; S4 = Study#4; fMRI: functional magnetic resonance imaging; FC = flexibility of closure; GEFT = Group Embedded Figures Test; K-BIT = Kaufman Brief Intelligence Test; TMR = Test of Mental rotation; MRI = magnetic resonance imaging; WASI = Wechsler Abbreviated Scale of Intelligence; APIS-Z = Test Battery from Matczak, et al. (1995).

*Table 14.3.* Summary of Empirical Research Results on RD Performance versus. Controls on VS Tasks[a]

| **Tasks Types** | **Superior Performance (%)** | **Lower Performance (%)** | **Equal Performance (%)** | **Total Tasks Occurrences Per Skill** |
|---|---|---|---|---|
| *Spatial visualization* | 2 (8.0) | 13 (52.0) | 10 (40.4) | **25** |
| *Spatial relations or rotations* | 3 (10.0) | 14 (46.7) | 13 (43.3) | **30** |
| *Global-holistic processing, closure speed, flexibility of closure* | 5 (31.2) | 5 (31.2) | 7 (43.7) | **16** |
| *Drawing* | 1 (11.1) | 3 (33.3) | 5 (55.5) | **9** |
| *Pattern recognition/recall* | 13 (15.3) | 25 (29.4) | 47 (55.3) | **85** |
| *Target recognition/recall* | 1 (12.5) | 2 (25.0) | 5 (62.5) | **8** |
| *Virtual world navigation/ 3D navigation* | 4 (30.8) | 5 (38.5) | 4 (30.8) | **13** |
| *Other* | 1 (20.0) | 3 (60.0) | 1 (20.0) | **5** |
| **Total Tasks per Performance Level** | **30 (15.6)** | **70 (36.4)** | **92 (47.9)** | **192** |

NOTE: The table classifies by performance levels and types of visuo-spatial skill. Units = number of tasks among the 192 occurrences reported in the reviewed literature and representative percentages over all skills in parentheses).[a]

counterparts 84% of the time. Where individuals with RD did do better, the data suggest that this is most likely to occur on tests of global/holistic processing and virtual world navigation (over 30% of the time better than non-RDs). A similar conclusion was made by Gilger and colleagues (2016).

### Summary

In this review, we have assessed VS abilities from a purely functional point of view, without looking at the connections to deficits and to the development of RD. At this point in time, a majority of the experimental VS data suggest that there is no generalized advantage across individuals with RD when it comes to VS abilities, and there is more often equality or disadvantage in individuals with RD for a variety of subskills related to the VS domain, particularly those that require complex dynamic thinking. This finding may support in part the multiple-deficit theory described earlier and it also reifies that the RD population is not homogenous in terms of skills and potential. We also found an exception to the equal or underperformance results in the domains of global/holistic and virtual world navigation (see also Gilger et al., 2016). This domain is worthy of further attention. Finally, there were a number of gaps in the literature, such as a lack of studies specifically on 2e-RD children, and there was a tendency for certain VS tasks to be commonly studied and others only minimally.

In terms of careers, people with RD were found to be slightly overrepresented in artistic, scientific, as well as "people-oriented" professions (nursing, business). However, these data come largely from self-reports, observations, interviews, and surveys and not always from peer reviewed research. This in itself warrants more concrete nationally driven studies to allow for drawing definitive conclusions. Furthermore, none of the career studies are longitudinal thus preventing conclusions about the etiology of career trajectory (i.e., choice driven by weakness avoidance, practice, or inherent strengths).

## DISCUSSION ON KEY ISSUES

Given the results of our review, it is unclear that there is an ontological or naturally occurring "RD advantage" per se (see Davis, 2010, and West, 1997, for contrary views) across a gamut of VS skills or in career choice for people with RD. Similarly, at this point there is little or no empirical support that individuals with RD are more likely to be especially talented at complex spatial reasoning, although there is some very preliminary data that 2e-RDs may be overrepresented in the 2e population (see the Conclusions section for caveats). There is, for instance, reason to expect a higher frequency of RD co-occurring with giftedness given the high rate of RD compared to other specific learning disorders, and there is also some preliminary data (see Gilger et al., 2008) to suggest that prevalence of 2e-RD individuals may be roughly eight times higher than we would expect if the two exceptionalities co-occurred just by chance.

In spite of our general conclusions based on the data reviewed, we feel there is still more to be learned in this area, and we next highlight next some of the remaining questions that need to be addressed. Specifically, we identify needs in four areas of research and practice: a consideration of learning versus aptitude, age and development questions, the range of behavioral assessments used, and the behavior-process distinction. While we address each of these areas separately, they are interrelated.

## The Phenomenon of Learning

We can distinguish learning measures from measures of discrete aptitude or ability, and there is a need to examine VS abilities in the framework of learning processes rather than single point in time behavioral performance. Aptitude is a measure of performance given the subject's knowledge and capacity at a certain point in time, whereas learning is a measure of response over time given certain experiences. Using reading as an analogue, RD is not just an unusual lower aptitude to read per se as it is a difficulty with *learning* and retaining skills relevant to reading. This learning-ability distinction has been well studied for the linguistic aspects of RD but has not been studied for the VS aspects of the RD condition. Our review suggests that the VS studies available have only assessed aptitude at a single point in time or, at best, a secondary look at the effects of practice as a result of pre- and posttesting (e.g., Fischer & Hartnegg, 2000, Table 14.2; Nicolson & Fawcett, 2000). There is, however, one interesting 3D practice study in our review using a virtual reality task created by Nicolson and Fawcett (2000), which did look at training and learning of VS information over time. The authors concluded that practice helped RD participants to gain a normal level of automatization catching up to their counterparts. However, they still lagged behind controls' skills after a year. Such studies are rare but point to the fact that training, even implicit training, specifically in VS could be an important asset in the support of students with RD. This study, however, dealt with basic automatization of simple VS tracking, and it did not include measures of complex or dynamic VS reasoning. Indeed, prior research has shown clearly that training and experience in more dynamic spatial areas can have significant effects in non-RD samples (Uttal et al., 2013); thus testing how training is responded to by RD samples is called for.

Key research questions on the horizon include (a) do individuals with RD possess a learning difference for VS skills, irrespective of ability? and (b) do they respond differently than normal readers to training or experience in VS areas? This requires short- or long-term longitudinal studies, perhaps with training on such skills over time. Research that includes this reformulation will be important in the future, and combining behavioral learning and brain imaging technologies has the potential to bring additional information about RD brain processing. Teachers can play a fundamental role in collaboration with researchers to address these questions in the future, perhaps by combining curricula and research in programs or tasks that may assess these learning abilities in order to inform the field in more organic environments outside of the research lab.

## Age and Developmental Trajectory

Age is another variable that has not been well considered in the research to date. The vast majority of the work on VS skills in RD samples has been on adults. There is to date no substantial information on VS skill in individuals with RD at ages less than four years and minimal research on preteens. Thus, if no RD/non-RD difference is found, we are unsure that it may not have been found in younger ages and before the person's neurology has been changed by experience, reading interventions, normal maturation (e.g., puberty), or lack of appropriate stimulation/practice. Similarly, if differences are found in older samples, we cannot be certain of their etiology: these could be inherent differences or differences acquired through choice or practice (e.g., Winner et al., 2001).

Age and experiential effects are correlated, and they may be particularly important to consider for several reasons. First, as noted, spatial skills can be affected by experience or practice (Uttal et al., 2013). People subjected to, or with more access to VS practice would, on average, do better than their contrasting cohort. If there is a differential amount of experience across RD and non-RD groups, this may mask (or enhance) VS ability differences. Second, studies have hinted that RD individuals, relative to those without RD, have a prolonged developmental period where they rely more on the right hemisphere for reading (Keller & Just, 2009; Shaywitz & Shaywitz, 2005; Simos et al., 2002). This right hemisphere reliance is thought to help those with RD to compensate for left hemisphere deficits. Gilger and colleagues (2013) suggested that, as people with RD get older, continuing to rely on these right hemisphere areas to solve reading-related problems may cause permanent neurological changes, and the possibility that any inherent right hemisphere advantage, if it exists, for above-average spatial thinking could be lost (see also McBride-Chang et al., 2011). This illustrates further the call to take a developmental perspective when looking at nonverbal skills in 2e-RD and RD children.

Because of the complicating factors of age, and the comparative lack of research on younger age groups, we propose that the neurology and behavior of persons with RD, along with the neurological changes from childhood to adulthood, be given more careful consideration, particularly in the VS learning and ability domains. More specifically, it is important to assess VS skills in the *very young* and later compare this data to that in older children to get at the question of causation, the developmental trajectories of VS abilities, and their relationships with reading.

## Differentiating Cognitive Skills

Some studies have focused on basic visual perceptual skills using tasks (e.g., Table 14.1) tapping into cognitive processes that require *simpler* levels of spatial analysis such as recall or recognition of simple patterns in the visual field, detecting collections of similar objects, and so on (Alves & Nakano, 2014; Duranovic, Dedeic, & Gavrić, 2015; Ruffino, Gori, Boccardi, Molteni, & Facoetti, 2014). Others have looked at tasks requiring higher level thinking, creativity or dynamic nonverbal cognition such as rotating objects in the mind, or identifying rapidly Impossible Figures in space (Diehl et al., 2014; Gilger et al., 2013; Olulade et al., 2012; Winner et al., 2001). Although some of these skills rely on related neurocognitive components, they often represent different behaviors and processing systems and should be considered clearly so as not to encourage the combining of skills into overly generalized conclusions about VS aptitude. Understanding these nuances will help fine-tune our comprehension about individual differences in RDs' VS skills and could provide a window into their unique neurology beyond the nonverbal abilities.

Second, the differentiation must also be at the level of the *type of performance*. For example, some tasks look at accuracy (Franceschini et al., 2013), while others look at speed of response (Diehl et al., 2014; von Károlyi et al., 2003). Individuals with RD have sometimes been found to perform differently than controls for one of these indices while underperforming in the other. Accuracy and speed of response speak both to very different cognitive processing of VS information and can be informative as to where deficits or strengths lie. This adds a level of complexity (Diehl et al., 2014) to the interpretation of VS tasks performance and learning. Including both accuracy and timing will be important in future work. Considering both indexes combined, say through a signal detection methodology (Abdi, 2007), allows us to disentangle strategy and task approach from "true" ability.

Finally, our review and that by Gilger and colleagues (2016) suggests that out of all the VS tests used on RD samples, the speed of solving Impossible Figures may be one measure that shows a somewhat reliable difference in favor of RD participants. This task has been used mostly on computer screens, and could be explored at other levels such as 3D or manipulatives, to gather more precise data on that apparent superior performance and what it means for people with RD. Further, while virtual reality methods are fairly new to the field, they may represent another type of task worthy of further study in RD samples, and some interesting work by a few authors has reported that RD differences may exist with a marked advantage of RD performance (see Attree, Turner, & Cowell, 2009; Wang & Yang, 2011; and others in Table 14.2). These methods may allow us to track more accurately RD VS abilities and learning by facilitating access to real-time behaviors, allowing to track timing, accuracy, and type of tasks that are best responded to. Using such technologies also matches more closely the interactive and cyber world in which individuals with RD live (Shams & Seitz, 2008).

## Observable Behavior versus Underlying Neural Process

Educators and researchers have long known that different strategies can be used to arrive at the same answer. These different strategies are presumably reflected in different neural processes, such as reliance on different cognitive processes and hence brain networks. Studying these processes are important because it gives us information about mechanism and may hint at ways we can support these students. Individuals with or at risk of RD have been widely shown to present very atypical neurocognitive profiles as detailed by Pugh and colleagues (2011) looking at their basic verbal circuitry, their compensatory behaviors, and unique anatomical patterns. They also make the suggestion that exploring talent will be beneficial to better serve this population (Pugh & McCardle, 2011, pp. 43–56).

As reviewed here, there are a number of papers that look at VS behavior in RD samples. But there are very few published studies that examine VS neurology in RD samples. For example, Olulade and colleagues showed that the VS behavioral performance of individuals with RD may be similar to that of controls, even though the neurological processing used to solve VS problems can be quite different (Olulade et al., 2012). Other work also compared the functional neurology of RD and 2e-RD samples while performing a VS task (Gilger, Tavalage, & Olulade, 2013). These were the first brain imaging studies on adults with RD and the only study of 2e-RD adults using complex VS tasks. Subsequent work by Deihl and colleagues (2014) supported the central conclusion that people with RD process VS information in neurologically different ways than those who do not have RD, and they also showed that those with RD were faster (not more accurate) on tests of holistic processing. Additional work by Craggs and colleagues (2006) and Gilger, Bayda, Olulade, Altman, and O'Boyle (2017) also shows that there may be neuroanatomical differences in RD and 2e-RD subjects compared to controls that may underlie the VS brain processing differences observed.

Our review highlights an existing imbalance in the use of modern methodologies to study nonverbal skills in RD samples, with the majority of past research studies (except for the several listed here) focusing on psychometric behavioral performance without a consideration of neurology. While deficits in phonological processing may be the hallmark symptom and one of the major risk factors of reading-related problems in RD, such a focus might be expanded to include VS processing, which may yield important insights.[2] The neurology work this far also reminds us that similar behavior does not mean the same neurological processes are at work.

2. Gilger and colleagues (2006, 2012, 2016, 2017), further proposed that the unique neurological signature observed in individuals with RD and 2e could be a residual sign of the same developmental neurology that leads to dyslexia (e.g., Geschwind, 1985), although it may have been modified with age and compensation for reading weaknesses (Birch & Chase, 2004). This neurological profile may set certain people up not only to deal with spatial information differently but to be better able to learn VS-related skills (e.g. Schneps, et al., 2011, 2012); especially if the necessary learning experiences occur at an early age.

## CONCLUSION: TYING IT TOGETHER FOR PARENTS AND EDUCATORS

While the conclusion of our review points to a lack of VS talents in RD individuals overall, the reader should bear in mind that this is limited to experimental data based on commonly used spatial tests. We again emphasize that there may be other ways of assessment that may better detect RD-non-RD differences. Future research, for example, may consider nonverbal tests that better measure creativity or fluidity of thought than typical measures that have been used in the past. Our own personal experience suggests that many people with RD take a less linear approach to problem-solving and this may in turn lend itself to unique solutions, or the same solution through different paths (see also Daniels & Freeman, this volume). Preliminary neurological research, in fact, supports the idea of dyslexics having different ways of solving problems compared to nondyslexics whether or not the behavioral outcome is the same (Diehl et al., 2014; Gilger et al., 2013; Olulade et al., 2012).

Research has an important role in addressing the needs of special populations. Progress can only be made if on the back-end of programs catering to atypical learners there exists a strong research base that is well translated and its recommendations carefully applied. Catering better to RD and 2e-RD populations, however, will take the efforts of all. Parents, educators, and researchers are the driving force.

Parents can be keen observers of true abilities and potentials, and they are the strongest advocates for more funding and better services. They can also be allied to researchers by facilitating accessibility to their children and their experience. Being a correctly informed parent is therefore critical. Similarly, educators can facilitate our understanding by channeling their observations up to academic research centers, staying abreast on the latest research, and requesting that crucial information be better distilled to their professional circles and educational programs.

Finally, researchers can help by

- extending the current research to cover the gaps we have highlighted
- focusing on a more multifaceted strength/deficits apprehension of the RD verbal and nonverbal skills problem (i.e., multifactorial liability models) and designing studies adapted to this type of models
- advocate for more comprehensive approaches to studying people with RD that focuses on individual differences across the profile of skills as much as we have focused on common deficits thus far

An empirical lack of a VS advantage in RDs does not mean that there exist no strengths or advantages at all. Until additional research is performed utilizing different types of assessments, we cannot recommend a specific type of program that could cater to more targeted strengths of RD and 2e-RD groups. Studies are also unavailable that address how people with RD *learn* VS information, as opposed to the plethora of data on how they are learning verbal material. Yet, having a knowledge base of how learning takes place is the very foundation of teaching and supporting intellectual development and nonverbal abilities. We also found that we know very little about the developmental trajectory of VS skills in RD populations from birth to adulthood. There are too few studies investigating these skills at young ages, as the majority of studies have focused on adults and adolescents. It is thus difficult to tell parents or teachers, for example, how to support these potential skills at home or at school, although some common activities can be suggested (e.g., building games, drawing, playing with blocks, etc.).

Our review also briefly highlighted that the methodological approach to studying VS cognitive processes in RD could be modified. We have technologies readily available allowing us to observe cognitive processing in real time such as functional magnetic resonance imaging and others, yet we mainly focus on a limited number of VS skills (e.g., spatial rotation) using paper and pencil, or basic computer tasks. Additionally, such important factors as speed and accuracy of execution and complexity of the skills (static/dynamic) have often been lumped together. These aspects need to be broken down, and they need to be explored within the context of a wider variety of progressive methodologies and nuances and with a wider age range.

We hope in this chapter to have established a clearer picture of the need to understand better what specifically constitutes nonverbal strengths in individuals with RD beyond their difficulty to learn how to read and spell. Twice exceptional individuals with RD are a subgroup presenting with specific needs and a unique profile that further emphasizes the need to look beyond deficits. In the case of 2e-RD, future research will dictate whether 2e-RD and RD by itself represent groups with specific abilities when it comes to learning and processing VS information and if these abilities should be supported better in early childhood educational curricula. Additional data may help change views and considerations pertaining to treating and educating these special groups, shifting the ideology that the RD brain has to be "normalized" to the view that it should also be strengthened in areas of relative strengths (Keller & Just, 2009; Simos et al., 2002). Such findings have the potential to influence many aspects surrounding the development of RDs and 2e-RDs.

Knowing the basis of nonverbal abilities can be the subject of remediation recommendations, and this can translate into special education, tutoring, tailored class activities, games at home, and so forth. Having a better understanding will also bolster parental support in that they may understand better how to direct their child's activities and attention; it will also indicate where to focus efforts in their advocacy with schools, districts, and healthcare providers. We invite researchers and practitioners to consider how to integrate these findings and suggestions into their work, as well as to maintain a feedback loop in order to assess in real time the progress of the newest findings as applied to the development and support of RDs and 2e-RDs.

## REFERENCES

Abdi, H. (2007). Signal detection theory (SDT). In N. Salkind (Ed.), *Encyclopedia of measurement and statistics* (pp. 1–9). Thousand Oaks, CA: SAGE.

Alves, R. J. R., & Nakano, T. C. (2014). Creativity and intelligence in children with and without developmental dyslexia. *Paidéia, 24*(59), 361–369.

Attree, E. A., Turner, M. J., & Cowell, N. (2009). A virtual reality test identifies the visuospatial strengths of adolescents with dyslexia. *CyberPsychology & Behavior, 12*(2), 163–168.

Barnes, J., Hinkley, L., Masters, S., & Boubert, L. (2007). Visual memory transformations in dyslexia. *Perceptual and Motor Skills, 104*(3), 881–891.

Benton, A. L. (1984). Dyslexia and spatial thinking. *Annals of Dyslexia, 34*(1), 69–85.

Berninger, V. W., & Abbott, R. D. (2013). Differences between children with dyslexia who are and are not gifted in verbal reasoning. *Gifted Child Quarterly, 57*(4), 223–233.

Boyle, C. A., Boulet, S., Schieve, L. A., Cohen, R. A., Blumberg, S. J., Yeargin-Allsopp, M., . . . Kogan, M. D. (2011). Trends in the prevalence of developmental disabilities in US children, 1997–2008. *Pediatrics, 127*(6), 1034–1042.

Brosnan, M., Demetre, J., Hamill, S., Robson, K., Shepherd, H., & Cody, G. (2002). Executive functioning in adults and children with developmental dyslexia. *Neuropsychologia, 40*(12), 2144–2155.

Brunswick, N., Martin, G. N., & Marzano, L. (2010). Visuospatial superiority in developmental dyslexia: Myth or reality?. *Learning and Individual Differences, 20*(5), 421–426.

Cao, F., Bitan, T., & Booth, J. R. (2008). Effective brain connectivity in children with reading difficulties during phonological processing. *Brain and Language, 107*(2), 91–101.

Chaix, Y., Albaret, J. M., Brassard, C., Cheuret, E., De Castelnau, P., Benesteau, J., . . . Démonet, J. F. (2007). Motor impairment in dyslexia: The influence of attention disorders. *European Journal of Paediatric Neurology, 11*(6), 368–374.

Colom, R., Rebollo, I., Palacios, A., Juan-Espinosa, M., & Kyllonen, P.C. (2004). Working memory is (almost) perfectly predicted by g. *Intelligence, 32*, 277–296.

Corballis, M.C., Macadie, L., & Beale, I. L. (1985). Mental rotation and visual laterality in normal and reading disabled children. *Cortex, 21*(2), 225–236.

Corballis, M. C., Macadie, L., Crotty, A., & Beale, I. L. (1985). The naming of disoriented letters by normal and reading-disabled children. *Journal of Child Psychology and Psychiatry, 26*(6), 929–938.

Cortiella, C., & Horowitz, S. H. (2014). *The state of learning disabilities: Facts, trends and emerging issues.* New York: National Center for Learning Disabilities.

Cowen, C. D. (2004). *Dyslexia and visuospatial processing strengths: New research sheds light.* IDA Perspectives. Retrieved from https://dyslexiaida.org/dyslexia-and-visuospatial-processing/

Craggs, J. G., Sanchez, J., Kibby, M. Y., Gilger, J. W., & Hynd, G. W. (2006). Brain morphology and neuropsychological profiles in a family displaying dyslexia and superior nonverbal intelligence. *Cortex, 42*(8), 1107–1118.

Davis, R. D. (2010). *The gift of dyslexia: Why some of the smartest people can't read . . . and how they can learn.* New York, NY: Penguin Group.

Diehl, J. J., Frost, S. J., Sherman, G., Mencl, W. E., Kurian, A., Molfese, P., . . . Rueckl, J. G. (2014). Neural correlates of language and non-language visuospatial processing in adolescents with reading disability. *NeuroImage, 101*, 653–666.

Duranovic, M., Dedeic, M., & Gavrić, M. (2015). Dyslexia and visual-spatial talents. *Current Psychology, 34*(2), 207–222.

Eckert, M. (2004). Neuroanatomical markers for dyslexia: A review of dyslexia structural imaging studies. *The Neuroscientist, 10*(4), 362–371.

Eden, G. F., Stein, J. F., & Wood, F. B. (1993). Visuospatial ability and language processing in reading disabled and normal children. Facets of dyslexia and its remediation. *Studies in Visual Information Processing, 3*, 321–335. http://dx.doi.org/10.1016/B978-0-444-89949-1.50028-6

Eden, G. F., Wood, F. B., & Stein, J. F. (2003). Clock drawing in developmental dyslexia. *Journal of Learning Disabilities, 36*(3), 216–228.

Eide, F. (2013). Proceedings from the Conference on Dyslexia and Talent. Retrieved from http://www.dyslexicadvantage.org/conference-on-dyslexia-and-talent/

Eide, B. L., & Eide, F. F. (2011). *The dyslexic advantage: Unlocking the hidden potential of the dyslexic brain.* New York, NY: Hudson Street Press.

Everatt, J. (1997). The abilities and disabilities associated with adult developmental dyslexia. *Journal of Research in Reading, 20*(1), 13–21.

Facoetti, A., Corradi, N., Ruffino, M., Gori, S., & Zorzi, M. (2010). Visual spatial attention and speech segmentation are both impaired in preschoolers at familial risk for developmental dyslexia. *Dyslexia, 16*(3), 226–239.

Fawcett, A. J., & Nicolson, R. I. (1994). Naming speed in children with dyslexia. *Journal of Learning Disabilities, 27*(10), 641–646.

Finucci, J. M., Gottfredson, L. S., & Childs, B. (1985). A follow-up study of dyslexic boys. *Annals of Dyslexia, 35*(1), 117–136.

Fink, R. P. (2002). Successful careers: The secrets of adults with dyslexia. *Career Planning and Adult Development Journal, 18*(1), 118–135.

Fischer, B., & Hartnegg, K. (2000). Effects of visual training on saccade control in dyslexia. *Perception, 29*(5), 531–542.

Foley-Nicpon, M. (2013). *Gifted Child Quarterly*'s special issue on twice-exceptionality: Progress on the path of empirical understanding. *Gifted Child Quarterly, 57*(4), 207–208.

Foley-Nicpon, M., Allmon, A., Sieck, B., & Stinson, R. D. (2011). Empirical investigation of twice-exceptionality: Where have we been and where are we going? *Gifted Child Quarterly, 55*(1), 3–17.

Franceschini, S., Gori, S., Ruffino, M., Viola, S., Molteni, M., & Facoetti, A. (2013). Action video games make dyslexic children read better. *Current Biology, 23*(6), 462–466.

Frye, R. E., Wu, M. H., Liederman, J., & McGraw Fisher, J. (2010). Greater pre-stimulus effective connectivity from the left inferior frontal area to other areas is associated with better phonological decoding in dyslexic readers. *Frontiers in Systems Neuroscience, 4*, 156.

Galaburda, A. M. (1992). Neurology of developmental dyslexia. *Current Opinion in Neurology and Neurosurgery, 5*, 71–76.

Galaburda, A., LoTurco Ramus, F., Fitch, H. R., & Rosen, G. R. (2006). From genes to behavior in developmental dyslexia. *Nature Neuroscience, 9*, 1213–1217.

Geschwind, N., & Behan, P. (1982). Left handedness: Association with immune disease, left handedness, and developmental learning disorder. *Proceedings of the National Academy of Science, 79*, 5097–5100.

Geschwind, N., & Galaburda, A. M. (1987). *Cerebral lateralization: Biological mechanisms, associations and pathology.* Cambridge, MA: MIT Press.

Greven, C. U., Harlaar, N., Dale, P. S., & Plomin, R. (2011). Genetic overlap between ADHD symptoms and reading is largely driven by inattentiveness rather than hyperactivity-impulsivity. *Journal of the Canadian Academy of Child & Adolescent Psychiatry*, *20*(1), 6–14.

Gilger, J. W., Allen, K., & Castillo, A. (2016). Reading disability and enhanced dynamic spatial reasoning: A review of the literature. *Brain and Cognition*, *105*, 55–65.

Gilger, J. W., & Hynd, G. W. (2008). Neurodevelopmental variation as a framework for thinking about the twice exceptional. *Roeper Review*, *30*(4), 214–228.

Gilger, J. W., & Kaplan, B. (2001). The neuropsychology of dyslexia: The concept of atypical brain development. *Developmental Neuropsychology*, *20*(2), 469–486.

Gilger, J. W., & Olulade, O. A. (2013). What happened to the "superior abilities" in adults with dyslexia and high IQs? A behavioral and neurological illustration. *Roeper Review*, *35*(4), 241–253.

Gilger, J. W., Olulade, O. A., Altman, M. N., & O'Boyle, M. (2017). Preliminary report on neuroanatomical differences among reading disabled, nonverbally gifted, and gifted-reading disabled college students. *Developmental Neuropsychology*, *42*(1), 25–38.

Gilger, J. W., Talavage, T. M., & Olulade, O. A. (2013). An fMRI study of nonverbally gifted reading disabled adults: Has deficit compensation effected gifted potential? *Frontiers in Human Neuroscience*, *7*. https://doi.org/10.3389/fnhum.2013.00507

Goswami, U. (2006). Neuroscience and education: From research to practice? *Nature Reviews Neuroscience*, *7*(5), 406–413.

Goswami, U. (2015). Sensory theories of developmental dyslexia: three challenges for research. *Nature Reviews. Neuroscience*, *16*(1), 43.

Gottfredson, L. S., Finucci, J. M., & Childs, B. (1984). Explaining the adult careers of dyslexic boys: Variations in critical skills for high-level jobs. *Journal of Vocational Behavior*, *24*(3), 355–373.

Gould, J. H., & Glencross, D. J. (1990). Do children with a specific reading disability have a general serial-ordering deficit?. *Neuropsychologia*, *28*(3), 271–278.

Hawke, J. L., Olson, R. K., Willcut, E. G., Wadsworth, S. J., & DeFries, J. C. (2009). Gender ratios for reading difficulties. *Dyslexia*, *15*(3), 239–242.

Helland, T., & Asbjørnsen, A. (2003) Visual-sequential and visuo-spatial skills in dyslexia: Variations according to language comprehension and mathematics skills. *Child Neuropsychology*, *9*(3), 208–220.

Hickman, R., & Brens, M. (2014). Art, pedagogy and dyslexia. *International Journal of Art & Design Education*, *33*(3), 335–344.

Hoeft, F., McCandliss, B. D., Black, J. M., Gantman, A., Zakerani, N., Hulme, C., . . . Gabrieli, J. D. (2011). Neural systems predicting long-term outcome in dyslexia. *Proceedings of the National Academy of Sciences*, *108*(1), 361–366.

Hoeft, F., Meyler, A., Hernandez, A., Juel, C., Taylor-Hill, H., Martindale, J. L., . . . Deutsch, G. K. (2007). Functional and morphometric brain dissociation between dyslexia and reading ability. *Proceedings of the National Academy of Sciences*, *104*(10), 4234–4239.

Howard, J. H., Howard, D. V., Japikse, K. C., & Eden, G. F. (2006). Individuals with dyslexia are impaired on implicit higher-order sequence learning, but not on implicit spatial context learning. *Neuropsychologia*, *44*, 1131–1144.

Hynd, G. W., Semrud-Clikeman, M., Lorys, A. R., Novey, E. S., & Eliopulos, D. (1990). Brain morphology in developmental dyslexia and attention deficit disorder/hyperactivity. *Archives of Neurology*, *47*(8), 919–926.

Jones, B. H. (1986). The gifted dyslexic. *Annals of Dyslexia, 36*(1), 301–317.

Jung, R. E., & Haier, R. J. (2007). The Parieto-Frontal Integration Theory (P-FIT) of intelligence: Converging neuroimaging evidence. *Behavioral and Brain Sciences, 30*(2), 135–154.

Kamhi, A. G., Catts, H. W., Mauer, D., Apel, K., & Gentry, B. F. (1988). Phonological and spatial processing abilities in language-and reading-impaired children. *Journal of Speech and Hearing Disorders, 53*(3), 316–327.

Kalbfleisch, M. L. (2012). Twice-exceptional students. In C. M. Callahan & H. L. Hertberg-Davis (Eds.), *Fundamentals of gifted education: Considering multiple perspectives* (pp. 358–368). London: Routledge.

Kappers, E. J. (1991). Neuropsychological treatment of highly gifted dyslexic children. *European Journal of High Ability, 1*(1), 64–71.

Karádi, K., Kovács, B., Szepesi, T., Szabó, I., & Kállai, J. (2001). Egocentric mental rotation in Hungarian dyslexic children. *Dyslexia, 7*(1), 3–11.

Kaufman, S. (2015). *Ungifted: Intelligence redefined.* New York, NY: Basic Books.

Kay, K. (2000). *Uniquely Gifted: Identifying and Meeting the Needs of Twice-Exceptional Students. An Avocus Advocacy in Education Title.* Gilsum, NH: Avocus Publishing.

Keller, T. A., & Just, M. A. (2009). Altering cortical connectivity: Remediation-induced changes in the white matter of poor readers. *Neuron, 64*(5), 624–631.

King, W. M., Lombardino, L. J., Crandell, C. C., & Leonard, C. M. (2003). Comorbid auditory processing disorder in developmental dyslexia. *Ear and Hearing, 24*(5), 448–456.

Koenig, O., Kosslyn, S., & Wolff, P. (1991). Mental imagery and dyslexia: A deficit in processing multipart visual objects? *Brain and Language, 41*, 381–394.

LaFrance, E. D. B. (1997). The gifted/dyslexic child: Characterizing and addressing strengths and weaknesses. *Annals of Dyslexia, 47*(1), 163–182.

Likert, R., & Quasha, W. (1941). *Revised Minnesota Paper Form Board (Series AA).* New York, NY: Psychological Corporation.

Lindell, A. K. (2006). In your right mind: Right hemisphere contributions to language processing and production. *Neuropsychology Review, 16*(3), 131–148.

Linkersdörfer, J., Lonnemann, J., Lindberg, S., Hasselhorn, M., & Fiebach, C. J. (2012). Grey matter alterations co-localize with functional abnormalities in developmental dyslexia: An ALE meta- analysis. *PLoS ONE, 7*(8), e43122.

Linn, M. C., & Peterson, A. C. (1985). Emergence and characterization of sex differences in spatial ability: A meta-analysis, *Child Development, 56*(6), 1479–1498.

Lockiewicz, M., Bogdanowicz, K. M., & Bogdanowicz, M. (2014). Psychological resources of adults with developmental dyslexia. *Journal of Learning Disabilities, 47*(6), 543–555. doi:10.1177/0022219413478663

Logan, J. (2009). Dyslexic entrepreneurs: The incidence; their coping strategies and their business skills. *Dyslexia, 15*(4), 328–346.

Logan, J., & Martin, N. (2012). Unusual talent: A study of successful leadership and delegation in entrepreneurs who have dyslexia. *Inclusive Practice, 4*, 57–76.

Lohman, D. F. (1996). Spatial ability and g. *Human abilities: Their nature and measurement, 97*, 116.

Lyon, G. R., Shaywitz, S., & Shaywitz, B. (2003). Defining dyslexia, comorbidity, teachers' knowledge of language and reading. *Annals of Dyslexia, 53*, 1–14.

Maisog, J. M., Einbinder, E. R., Flowers, D. L., Turkeltaub, P. E., & Eden, G. F. (2008). A meta-analysis of functional neuroimaging studies of dyslexia. *Annals of the New York Academy of Sciences, 1145*(1), 237–259.

Mammarella, I. C., Meneghetti, C., Pazzaglia, F., Gitti, F., Gomez, C., & Cornoldi, C. (2009). Brain and cognition representation of survey and route spatial descriptions in children with nonverbal (visuospatial) learning disabilities. *Brain and Cognition, 71*(2), 173–179. doi:10.1016/j.bandc.2009.05.003

Martinelli, V., & Schembri, J. (2015). Dyslexia and visuospatial ability in maltese male adolescents. *Journal of Educational and Social Research, 5*(3), 111.

McBride-Chang, C., Zhou, Y., Cho, J. R., Aram, D., Levin, I., & Tolchinsky, L. (2011). Visual spatial skill: A consequence of learning to read?. *Journal of Experimental Child Psychology, 109*(2), 256–262.

Moore, D. S., & Johnson, S. P. (2008). Mental rotation in human infants: A sex difference. *Psychological Science, 19*(11), 1063–1066.

Newcombe, N., & Dubas, J. S. (1987). Individual differences in cognitive ability: Are they related to timing of puberty? In R.M. Lerner, T.T. Foch (Eds.), *Biological–psychosocial interactions in early adolescence* (pp. 249–302). Hillsdale, NJ: Lawrence Erlbaum Associates.

Newcombe, N. S., & Shipley, T. F. (2015). Thinking about spatial thinking: New typology, new assessments. In J. S. Gero (Ed.), *Studying visual and spatial reasoning for design creativity* (pp. 179–192). Amsterdam, The Netherlands: Springer.

Nicolson, R. I., & Fawcett, A. J. (2000). Long-term learning in dyslexic children. *European Journal of Cognitive Psychology, 12*(3), 357–393.

Nicpon, M. F., Allmon, A., Sieck, B., & Stinson, R. D. (2011). Empirical investigation of twice- exceptionality: Where have we been and where are we going? *Gifted Child Quarterly, 55*(1), 3–17.

Nielsen, M. E. (2002). Gifted students with learning disabilities: Recommendations for identification and programming. *Exceptionality, 10*(2), 93–111.

Nielsen, M. E., & Higgins, L. D. (2005). The eye of the storm: Services and programs for twice- exceptional learners. *Teaching Exceptional Children, 38*(1), 8.

Olulade, O. A., Gilger, J. W., Talavage, T. M., Hynd, G. W., & McAteer, C. I. (2012). Beyond phonological processing deficits in adult individuals with dyslexia: Atypical fMRI activation patterns for spatial problem solving. *Developmental Neuropsychology, 37*(7), 617–635.

Osterrieth, P. A. (1944). Filetest de copie d'une figure complex: Contribution a l'etude de la perception et de la memoire [The test of copying a complex figure: A contribution to the study of perception and memory]. *Archives de Psychologie, 30*, 286–356.

Paulesu, E., Démonet, J. F., Fazio, F., McCrory, E., Chanoine, V., Brunswick, N., . . . Frith, U. (2001). Dyslexia: Cultural diversity and biological unity. *Science, 291*(5511), 2165–2167.

Pontius, A. A. (1981). Geometric figure-rotation task and face representation in dyslexia: role of spatial relations and orientation. *Perceptual and motor skills, 53*(2), 607–614.

Pugh, K., & McCardle, P. (Eds.). (2011). *How children learn to read: Current issues and new directions in the integration of cognition, neurobiology and genetics of reading and dyslexia research and practice*. London: Taylor & Francis.

Pugh, K. R., Mencl, W. E., Shaywitz, B. A., Shaywitz, S. E., Fulbright, R. K., Constable, R. T., . . . Liberman, A. M. (2000). The angular gyrus in developmental dyslexia: Task-specific differences in functional connectivity within posterior cortex. *Psychological Science, 11*(1), 51–56.

Ramus, F. (2003). Developmental dyslexia: Specific phonological deficit or general sensorimotor dysfunction? *Current Opinion in Neurobiology, 13*(2), 212–218.

Rey, A. (1941). L'examen psychologique dans les cas d'encephalopathie traumatique. (Les problemes). *Archives de Psychologie, 28*, 215–285.

Richlan, F., Kronbichler, M., & Wimmer, H. (2009). Functional abnormalities in the dyslexic brain: A quantitative meta-analysis of neuroimaging studies. *Human Brain Mapping, 30*(10), 3299–3308.

Richlan, F., Kronbichler, M., & Wimmer, H. (2011). Meta-analyzing brain dysfunctions in dyslexic children and adults. *NeuroImage, 56*(3), 1735–1742.

Rose, T. (2016). *The end of average: How to succeed in a world that values sameness.* London: Penguin.

Ruban, L. M., & Reis, S. M. (2005). Identification and assessment of gifted students with learning disabilities. *Theory into Practice, 44*(2), 115–124.

Ruffino, M., Gori, S., Boccardi, D., Molteni, M., & Facoetti, A. (2014). Spatial and temporal attention in developmental dyslexia. *Frontiers in Human Neuroscience, 8*, 331. http://doi.org/10.3389/fnhum.2014.00331

Rusiak, P., Lachmann, T., Jaskowski, P., & van Leeuwen, C. (2007). Mental rotation of letters and shapes in developmental dyslexia. *Perception, 36*(4), 617–631.

Rüsseler, J., Scholz, J., Jordan, K., & Quaiser-Pohl, C. (2005). Mental rotation of letters, pictures, and three-dimensional objects in German dyslexic children. *Child Neuropsychology, 11*(6), 497–512.

Schacter, D. L., Cooper, L. A., & Delaney, S. M. (1990). Implicit memory for unfamiliar objects depends on access to structural descriptions. *Journal of Experimental Psychology: General, 119*(1), 5.

Schneps, M. H., Brockmole, J. R., Rose, L. T., Pomplun, M., Sonnert, G., & Greenhill, L. J. (2011). Dyslexia linked to visual strengths useful in astronomy. *Bulletin of the American Astronomical Society, 1*, 21508.

Schneps, M. H., Brockmole, J. R., Sonnert, G., & Pomplun, M. (2012). History of reading struggles linked to enhanced learning in low spatial frequency scenes. *PLoS ONE, 7*(4), e35724.

Shams, L., & Seitz, A. R. (2008). Benefits of multisensory learning. *Trends in Cognitive Sciences, 12*(11), 411–417.

Shaywitz, S. E., & Shaywitz, B. A. (2005). Dyslexia. *Biological Psychiatry, 57*(11), 1301–1309.

Shepard, S., & Metzler, D. (1988). Mental rotation: Effects of dimensionality of objects and type of task. *Journal of Experimental Psychology: Human Perception and Performance, 14*(1), 3.

Siegel, L. S., & Ryan, E. B. (1989). Subtypes of developmental dyslexia: The influence of definitional variables. *Reading and Writing, 1*(3), 257–287.

Sigmundsson, H. (2005). Do visual processing deficits cause problem on response time task for dyslexics? *Brain and Cognition, 58*(2), 213–216.

Silverman, L. K. (2009). The two-edged sword of compensation: How the gifted cope with learning disabilities. *Gifted Education International, 25*(2), 115–130.

Simos, P. G., Fletcher, J. M., Bergman, E., Breier, J. I., Foorman, B. R., Castillo, E. M., . . . Papanicolaou, A. C. (2002). Dyslexia-specific brain activation profile becomes normal following successful remedial training. *Neurology, 58*, 1203–1213.

Singh, R. R. (1993). Spatial and linguistic abilities in dyslexic children. *Journal of Personality and Clinical Studies, 9*, 55–58.

Skottun, B. C. (2005). Magnocellular reading and dyslexia. *Vision Research, 45*(1), 133–134.

Snowling, M. J. (2000). *Dyslexia.* New York, NY: Blackwell.

Snowling, M., Bishop, D. V. M., & Stothard, S. E. (2000). Is preschool language impairment a risk factor for dyslexia in adolescence?. *Journal of Child Psychology and Psychiatry, 41*(5), 587–600.

Stanley, G., Kaplan, I., & Poole, C. (1975). Cognitive and nonverbal perceptual processing in dyslexics. *Journal of General Psychology, 93*, 67–92.

Steffert, B. (1998). Sign minds and design minds. In S. M. Dingli (Ed.), *Creative thinking: Towards broader horizons* (pp. 28–46). Msida: Malta University Press.

Stieff, M., Dixon, B. L., Ryu, M., Kumi, B. C., & Hegarty, M. (2014). Strategy training eliminates sex differences in spatial problem solving in a STEM domain. *Journal of Educational Psychology, 106*(2), 390–402.

Stein, J. (2001). The magnocellular theory of developmental dyslexia. *Dyslexia, 7*(1), 12–36.

Stephens, K. R., & Karnes, F. A. (2000). State definitions for the gifted and talented revisited. *Exceptional Children, 66*(2), 219–238.

Stothers, M., & Klein, P. D. (2010). Perceptual organization, phonological awareness, and reading comprehension in adults with and without learning disabilities. *Annals of Dyslexia, 60*(2), 209–237.

Taylor, K. E., & Walter, J. (2003). Occupation choices of adults with and without symptoms of dyslexia. *Dyslexia, 9*(3), 177–185. doi:10.1002/dys.239

Temple, E., Deutsch, G. K., Poldrack, R. A., Miller, S. L., Tallal, P., Merzenich, M. M., & Gabrieli, J. D. (2003). Neural deficits in children with dyslexia ameliorated by behavioral remediation: Evidence from functional MRI. *Proceedings of the National Academy of Sciences, 100*(5), 2860–2865.

Thomson, M. E. (1982). The assessment of children with specific reading difficulties (dyslexia) using the British Ability Scales. *British Journal of Psychology, 73*, 461–478.

Tobia, V., & Marzocchi, G. M. (2014). Cognitive profiles of Italian children with developmental dyslexia. *Reading Research Quarterly, 49*(4), 437–452.

Treffert, D. A. (2009). The savant syndrome: An extraordinary condition. A synopsis: Past, present, future. *Philosophical Transactions of the Royal Society of London B: Biological Sciences, 364*(1522), 1351–1357.

Uttal, D. H., Meadow, N. G., Tipton, E., Hand, L. L., Alden, A. R., Warren, C., & Newcombe, N. (2013). The malleability of spatial skills: A meta-analysis of training studies. *Psychological Bulletin, 139*(2), 352–402.

Vakil, E., Lowe, M., & Goldfus, C. (2015). Performance of children with developmental dyslexia on two skill learning tasks—serial reaction time and Tower of Hanoi puzzle: A test of the specific procedural learning difficulties theory. *Journal of Learning Disabilities, 48*(5), 471–481.

Valdois, S., Bosse, M. L., & Tainturier, M. J. (2004). The cognitive deficits responsible for developmental dyslexia: Review of evidence for a selective visual attentional disorder. *Dyslexia, 10*(4), 339–363.

van Bergen, E., de Jong, P. F., Maassen, B., Krikhaar, E., Plakas, A., & van der Leij, A. (2014). IQ of four-year-olds who go on to develop dyslexia. *Journal of Learning Disabilities, 47*(5), 475–484.

van Bergen, E., van der Leij, A., & de Jong, P. F. (2014). The intergenerational multiple deficit model and the case of dyslexia. *Frontiers in Human Neuroscience, 8*, 346.

Vandenberg, S. G., & Kuse, A. R. (1978). Mental rotations, a group test of three-dimensional spatial visualization. *Perceptual and Motor Skills, 47*(2), 599–604. doi:10.2466/pms.1978.47.2.599

Vandermosten, M., Hoeft, F., & Norton, E. S. (2016). Integrating MRI brain imaging studies of pre-reading children with current theories of developmental dyslexia: A review and quantitative meta-analysis. *Current Opinion in Behavioral Sciences, 10*, 155–161.

van Viersen, S., Kroesbergen, E. H., Slot, E. M., & de Bree, E. H. (2016). High reading skills mask dyslexia in gifted children. *Journal of Learning Disabilities, 49*(2), 189–199.)

Vidyasagar, T. R., & Pammer, K. (2010). Dyslexia: A deficit in visuo-spatial attention, not in phonological processing. *Trends in Cognitive Sciences, 14*(2), 57–63.

von Károlyi, C. (2001). Visual-spatial strength in dyslexia: Rapid discrimination of Impossible Figures. *Journal of Learning Disabilities, 34*(4), 380–391.

von Károlyi, C., & Winner, E. (2005). Investigations of visual-spatial abilities in dyslexia. In F. Columbus (Ed.), *Focus on dyslexia research* (pp. 1–25). Hauppauge, NY: Nova Science.

von Károlyi, C., Winner, E., Gray, W., & Sherman, G.F. (2003). Dyslexia linked to talent: Global visual-spatial ability. *Brain and Language, 85*(3), 427–431.

Wang, L. C., & Yang, H. M. (2011). The comparison of the visuo-spatial abilities of dyslexic and normal students in Taiwan and Hong Kong. *Research in Developmental Disabilities, 32*(3), 1052–1057.

West, T. G. (1997). *In the mind's eye: Visual thinkers, gifted people with dyslexia and other learning difficulties, computer images, and the ironies of creativity.* Amherst, NY: Prometheus.

West, T. G. (2009). *In the mind's eye: Creative visual thinkers, gifted individuals with dyslexia, and the rise of visual technologies* (2nd ed.). New York, NY: Prometheus Books.

Winner, E., Casey, M., DaSilva, D., & Hayes, R. (1991). Spatial abilities and reading deficits in visual art students. *Empirical Studies of the Arts, 9*, 1, 51–63.

Winner, E., von Karolyi, C., Malinsky, D., French, L., Seliger, C., Ross, E., & Weber, C. (2001). Dyslexia and visual-spatial talents: Compensation vs deficit model. *Brain and Language, 76*(2), 81–110.

Willcutt, E. G., & Pennington, B. F. (2000). Comorbidity of reading disability and attention-deficit/hyperactivity disorder differences by gender and subtype. *Journal of Learning Disabilities, 33*(2), 179–191.

Wolff, U., & Lundberg, I. (2002). The prevalence of dyslexia among art students. *Dyslexia, 8*(1), 34–42.

15

# Gifted Dyslexics

## *MIND-Strengths, Visual Thinking, and Creativity*

**SUSAN DANIELS AND MICHELLE FREEMAN**

Research in neuroscience and learning disabilities establishes a connection between certain cognitive challenges and certain cognitive strengths for students with dyslexia (Cowan, 2014; Crogman, Gilger, & Hoeft, this volume; Eide, 2015; Eide & Eide, 2011; Martinelli & Schembri, 2014; Silverman, 2002; Tafti, Hameedy, & Baghal, 2009; von Karolyi, Winner, Gray, & Sherman, 2003; West, 2009; Wolf & Lundberg, 2002). Eide and Eide (2011) identified four patterns of strengths in their dyslexic clients that they call MIND-Strengths. These include (a) M-Strength: Material Reasoning, (b) I-Strength: Interconnected Reasoning, (c) N-Strength: Narrative Reasoning, (d) D-Strength: Dynamic Reasoning. Further, dyslexic students have been found to exhibit characteristics of creativity and a preference for original thinking (Tafti, Hameedy, & Baghal, 2009; West, 2009).

Thomas West's (2009) findings suggest that left-hemisphere deficiencies, such as dyslexia, are fundamentally linked to right-hemisphere strengths. Right-hemisphere strengths include visual thinking, spatial ability, pattern recognition, problem-solving, heightened intuition, and creativity. In his thorough discussion of learning disabilities, West cites neurological research that demonstrates a clear association between visual talents and verbal difficulties.

Extending these findings, we provide four student vignettes that are representative of the gifted dyslexic students we see in our clinical practice. For the purposes of this chapter, we define gifted dyslexic students as having a score at or above 130 on an intelligence test who have also been diagnosed with dyslexia. Beyond the IQ, we gather information in the clinical setting through an initial parent interview and an assessment protocol that includes achievement data, screening for dyslexia, a creativity checklist, parent and teacher checklists of strengths, personality assessments, and executive functioning measures. These four students have been reported to have creative strengths by teachers and parents.

In these case vignettes, we identify and describe the unique patterns of MIND-Strengths, visual strengths, and creative strengths of each student. Each case is accompanied by a table that lists strengths, challenges, recommended strategies, interventions, and common professions. The recommended teaching and learning strategies build upon the MIND-Strengths, visual strengths, and creative strengths of each of the four cases.

## DYSLEXIA—A LEARNING DIFFERENCE NOT DEFICIT

Dyslexia is a specific learning disability that is characterized by difficulties in word recognition, reading, writing, and spelling. This has recently been termed "stealth dyslexia" (or dyslexia, stealth subtype) in bright individuals, as they tend to *compensate* by their advanced thinking, *get the gist* of what they read, and *appear* to be sufficient readers when they actually have some form of difficulty with the core aspects of reading and writing (Eide, 2011). Common traits that coincide with dyslexia include difficulties with visual and auditory attention, processing, executive functioning, verbal fluency, math fluency, trouble solving word problems, and such.

Difficulty with fine detail processing specific to the phonological and/or visual processing system contributes to the reading and language challenges many individuals with dyslexia experience. Many students with dyslexia have trouble processing word sounds. While some students have a shortened echoic memory for word sounds, others are more challenged in distinguishing the sounds of similar phonemes (e.g., *ba* and *ga, duh* and *buh*). The aforementioned examples involve basic skills needed to support higher language functions required to learn and use words to proficiently read and write. Those with visual processing challenges struggle to use their eyes to visually track and process what they see. Some students report that letters move, wobble, and blur. When letters seem to overlap, it is difficult for the child to distinguish which is which. Others may not be as aware of the visual processing issues but have a tendency to skip over words and even entire lines while reading. They might tend toward scanning rather than reading line by line and word for word. While it may appear that the student comprehends what is being read, oftentimes a person with stealth dyslexia may compensate for processing challenges by using context and verbal reasoning to make sense of what the passage says. However, as demands increase, and as reading material becomes less familiar, it becomes much more difficult to compensate for visual processing challenges. Learning new material becomes more challenging. The student may misread the word "do" as "don't" or may skip over essential information required to learn material.

In our clinical work, we often hear students say that they have to reread sentences repeatedly to comprehend written passages. When this happens, students find themselves losing focus, feeling tired, or feeling overwhelmed by the reading material. Often, "reading for school" takes an incredibly long time, and even when investing the time and energy, students still struggle to retain the information.

A number of phonological and visual processing challenges come into play when students with dyslexia report the need to reread sentences repeatedly to comprehend written passages. The student may come across an unfamiliar word with many more syllables than what can be held in phonological memory. By the time the later sounds or syllables in a longer word are formed, the earlier syllables may slip out of memory, impacting reading fluency. Less developed visual tracking require the student to use more energy to read the sentences and can cause fatigue, poor reading accuracy, and visual memory overload. As such, reading becomes a demanding task for those with phonological and visual processing challenges.

The different processing style associated with dyslexia may be attributable to differences in brain structure (see Crogman, Gilger, & Hoeft, this volume). As an example, problems with phonological processing are related to structural variations in the brain's left hemisphere. Some of the functions performed in the neurotypical individual's left hemisphere are processed in the right hemisphere of dyslexic individuals. Dyslexic students tend to place greater demand on their right hemisphere for reading than do their counterparts. Thomas West (2009) suggested that the right-hemisphere preference for processing certain types of information and strengths exhibited by some dyslexics are directly related to their co-occurring visual and spatial talents.

As such, dyslexia has more recently been viewed as predisposing individuals to a number of concomitant strengths. These include

- Three-dimensional spatial reasoning and mechanical ability
- The ability to perceive relationships (analogies, paradoxes, differences, etc.).
- A strong memory for personal experiences and understanding of abstract information related to specific examples.
- The ability to perceive and take advantage of subtle patterns in complex and shifting systems or data sets.

## DIFFERENT WIRING: RIGHT-HEMISPHERE STRENGTHS, VISUAL THINKING, AND CREATIVITY

Several years ago (Sperry, 1982), the idea of right-brained thinking and left-brain thinking was presented as a dichotomous model. The left-brain/right-brain discussion oftentimes was presented as though individuals had a significant preference of left-brain (organized and analytical) or right-brain (holistic and synthetic) thinking.

More recently, West (2009), author of *In the Mind's Eye: Creative Visual Thinkers, Gifted Dyslexics, and the Rise of Visual Technologies*, discusses the functions of the right and left hemispheres at length.

> The view of the two hemispheres now commonly accepted is that certain skills and abilities are specialized in one hemisphere while other skills and

abilities are specialized in the other. *However, there is often complex interaction between the two hemispheres on any given task.* Abilities, such as logic, language, orderliness, sequential time, and arithmetic are seen to be largely specialized in the left hemisphere whereas the processing of visual images, spatial relationships, face and pattern recognition, gesture, and proportion are seen to be specialized in the right hemisphere." (p. 26; emphasis added)

Generally, the left hemisphere thinks in words and numbers, and the right hemisphere thinks in pictures and images in three-dimensional space. The right hemisphere processes large-scale, big-picture features, and the left hemisphere processes fine details. Yet, in contrast, research utilizing functional magnetic resonance imaging to identify the brain regions activated when individuals with dyslexia and individuals without dyslexia read indicates that the dyslexic brain consistently utilizes more right-hemisphere structures than left-hemisphere structures while reading (Eide & Eide, 2011).

This pattern of processing presents challenges in reading for individuals with dyslexia, yet right-hemisphere strengths also confer certain advantages. In this vein, West (2009) provides a list of positive traits that are associated with learning difficulties, creativity, and visual thinking. These traits include

- High talents in spatial, mechanical, and related right-hemisphere skills, with early sophistication in these skills.
- Love of construction toys, models, and craftwork.
- Love of and great skill at drawing, although may have difficulty with handwriting.
- An especially good ability to visualize and manipulate images in the mind.

## MIND-STRENGTHS AND DYSLEXIA

For dyslexic brains, excellent function typically means traits like the ability to see the gist or essence of things . . . multidimensionality of perspective; the ability to see new, unusual, or distant connections; inferential reasoning . . . the ability to recombine things in novel ways and a general inventiveness; [along with] greater mindfulness and intentionality during tasks that others take for granted. (Eide & Eide, 2011, p. 42)

Brock and Fernette Eide—researchers, neurologists, and clinicians who specialize in dyslexia—have developed a model that illustrates four patterns of strengths found in many individuals with dyslexia. The Eides' conception of MIND-Strengths developed through clinical observation of and work with hundreds of dyslexic individuals and families. They discovered that dyslexic individuals did not just share one pattern of cognition but two. The first is the set of challenges that we typically associate with dyslexia: challenges with reading, writing, spelling, and other related academic skills. The second pattern they identified was a common set of strengths.

The Eides conducted a literature search to substantiate their clinical observations. They investigated three types or "levels" of research literature, including (a) research on brain structure, (b) research on brain cognition, or functional processing, and (c) research on areas in which individuals with dyslexia found success in learning or career pursuits (Jung-Beeman, 2005; Turkeltaub, Gareau, Flowers, Zeffro, & Eden, 2003).

In their book, *The Dyslexic Advantage* (Eide & Eide, 2011), four patterns of dyslexia-related strengths were described:

- M-Strengths that represent Material Reasoning—reasoning about the position, form, and movement of objects in 3D space.
- I-Strengths that represent Interconnected Reasoning—reasoning related to the ability to identify, understand, and interpret the meaning of connections and relationships, such as analogies, metaphors, systems, and patterns.
- N-Strengths that represent Narrative Reasoning—reasoning that uses fragments of memory from past experience, such as: cases, examples, and simulations rather than abstract reasoning.
- D-Strengths that represent Dynamic Reasoning—reasoning that applies the ability to accurately make predictions by using patterns derived through conceptions of the future or the unwitnessed past.

In the following sections, we provide one case example for each of the four patterns of strengths: Material-strengths, Interconnected-strengths, Narrative-strengths, and Dynamic-strengths. A description of each child's unique confluence of strengths and challenges is presented. The description is accompanied by a table that lists these strengths and challenges along with strategies for optimizing strengths and supporting areas of challenge.

## MATERIAL REASONING STRENGTHS AND CHALLENGES: NOAH

Noah is extremely bright, creative, and has strong reasoning skills. At the young age of seven, he is known to create extraordinary structures, come up with solutions to hypothetical questions using science and imagery, and has a love for aesthetics. He can describe how structures, cars, and other mechanical objects can be improved in great detail. Often, Noah provides vivid descriptions of inventions and structures he has created in his mind, and, by the next day, Noah has used ordinary items to build what he has imagined. Noah enjoys coming up with unique solutions to problems. His parents reported that Noah has successfully demonstrated alternative ways to solve complex mathematical problems.

Noah has strong reasoning abilities and is highly gifted, yet he was described to have a number of challenges in the classroom that contribute to his below grade level performance. Noah does not show his work in science lab and math. Even though he can come up with solutions to problems, Noah often does not follow instructions or needs a significant amount of time to complete his work. He often misreads information written on the board, will make simple calculation errors, and, even when he has a wealth of information about a topic, will spend numerous hours struggling to "find the words" to describe what he knows when having to write a few sentences about it (see Table 15.1).

## INTERCONNECTED REASONING STRENGTHS AND CHALLENGES: EMMA

> My brain is like a teapot with magical jelly beans inside. It looks like an ordinary teapot, but when you tilt the teapot, you end up with a cup of jelly beans instead of a cup of tea. You lick the outside of the jelly bean, and it doesn't taste like anything at all. You bite in to it, and it bursts with flavor! My teapot is full of magical ideas that others don't quite understand.

Emma is an exceptionally gifted nine-year-old girl. She is highly creative and has a strong imagination but has difficulties staying focused and takes a long time to "get to the point."

Emma's teacher reported that she has difficulties responding to simple questions, misunderstands instructions, and has difficulties with reading comprehension. Emma has a wealth of knowledge and writes elaborate answers to open-ended test questions but does not do well on multiple-choice exams. It takes Emma a very long time to complete homework assignments. She complains of not having enough time to complete school assignments or tests, even when given access to extended time. Emma makes fine detail processing errors like mistaking a word for a similar-sounding word. On the flip side, Emma will come up with a new idea based on a word that sounds similar to one she hears, but this is not always "useful" when in school. Emma is easily distracted, but, on the other hand, her distractibility brings strength. One idea can lead to another idea, bursting with creativity and meaning. "It is a jelly bean that bursts with magical flavor! You never know what you'll get!" (See Table 15.2.)

## NARRATIVE REASONING STRENGTHS AND CHALLENGES: LOGAN

> An aroma means a fragrance, like the aroma of chocolate chip cookies baking in the kitchen. Doesn't that sound delicious? Now all I can think about is the aroma of baked goods. I want to write a story about a scene from when I was five. I used to watch my grandmother bake cookies in her kitchen and

*Table 15.1.* Noah: Material Reasoning Strengths and Challenges

| Material Reasoning Strengths: Visual Thinking and Creativity | Material Reasoning Challenges | Challenges Observed | Strategies or Interventions to Consider | Common Professions Associated with Strengths in Material Reasoning |
|---|---|---|---|---|
| • Strong ability to create multidimensional, vivid images in his mind<br>• Creating and building using physical objects and materials<br>• Generates unique and new ways to problem-solve | Visual processing of 2D images | • Difficulties distinguishing letter and number orientation<br>• Impacts speed and accuracy when processing and learning material<br>• Difficulties using the proposed strategy taught in the classroom due to dyslexic processing | • Visual processing evaluation<br>• Vision therapy<br>• Additional time to complete assignments and take tests<br>• Consideration of unique problem-solving strategies when being graded<br>• Use of creative projects to demonstrate knowledge | • Architect<br>• Designer<br>• Engineer<br>• Inventor<br>• Mechanic<br>• Film maker<br>• Medicine<br>• Illustrator |
| | Language output | • Challenges with formulating, organizing, and using words to describe ideas<br>• Bright, verbally advanced students struggling to express their advanced, complex, and often creative, multidimensional ideas<br>• Struggles with academic material in the classroom | • Projects instead of written assignments<br>• Encourage use of a visual aid to organize ideas<br>• Provide concrete examples of what is expected<br>• Dictation<br>• Facilitate strengths in creating and building through extracurricular activities | |

*Table 15.2.* Emma: Interconnected Reasoning Strengths and Challenges

| Interconnected Reasoning Strengths: Visual Thinking and Creativity | Interconnected Reasoning Challenges | Challenges Observed | Strategies or Interventions to Consider | Common Professions Associated with Strengths in Interconnected Reasoning |
|---|---|---|---|---|
| • Strong ability to create a connection between ideas and concepts using words<br>• Creating and building new ideas based on concepts<br>• Generates unique and new ways to problem solve by way of identifying "distant and unusual connections" (Eide, 2011)<br>• Takes multiple perspectives and different types of information to get the overall gist and "identify its central essence" (Eide, 2011). | Performance is impacted negatively when in a situation where "speed, accuracy, reliability, and precision are more valued than creativity, novel, or insight" (Eide, 2011). | • Difficulties comprehending literal information (i.e., reading material)<br>• Impacts the rate and ability to answer a question with a direct answer (i.e., seems to get off topic)<br>• Difficulties with multiple-choice exams | • Need to tie information to previous learning<br>• Provide examples so the student knows what is expected<br>• Additional time to complete assignments and take tests<br>• Consideration of unique problem-solving strategies when being graded<br>• Allow time for brainstorming and concept building | • Philosopher<br>• Lawyer<br>• Entrepreneur<br>• Scientist<br>• Chef<br>• Trainer |
| | Organization<br><br>Strong need for understanding background information and context | • Might think of multiple places and ways to file information (i.e., papers) impacting organization.<br>• Without having the general understanding and background, it is harder to learn and remember information | | |

> imagined her opening a bakery offering rows and rows of unique-baked goods. Customers would have the option of chocolate chip cookies, coconut cake, macaroons, and other warm goodies filled with ice cream! The aroma of my grandmother's bakery could be detected miles and miles away.

Logan is a very bright, gifted, seven-year-old boy. His parents describe Logan as highly creative and as having a strong imagination. Logan loves to tell stories and enjoys writing his stories, but, rather than using words when writing, he prefers to illustrate what he imagines in his mind. Logan does not like to read but enjoys being read to. He relates information back to past experiences and speaks in narrative form. Logan has a gift for vividly describing stories he remembers from the past. While Logan possesses exceptional story-telling abilities, he refuses to complete writing assignments. (See Table 15.3.)

## DYNAMIC REASONING STRENGTHS AND CHALLENGES: ZOE

Zoe is a profoundly gifted 13-year-old girl who has a knack for taking patterns, bits of information, and experiences to construct a vision for how something came to be, to make strikingly accurate predictions, and to create new possibilities based on the patterns.

> One moment, I am listening to my teacher, and don't realize when my mind is drifting off. All of a sudden I envision this elaborate idea of what will be. How did I come up with it? At first, I have no idea. Then, in my mind, I get these scenes that flash in to my mind. It starts with the picture of the final product, and instead of visualizing the evolution from start to finish, it is the complete opposite. I get a time lapse that I can vividly see playing out in my mind that starts off with the final product and ends with what you would consider the beginning. The pieces come together in my mind. I realize how something has come to be, and then I just know what is going to happen. I can build on a concept and come up with a solution for a problem that others may have not found a solution for. Interestingly, when I am asked to come up with a solution, I can't in that moment. When I have to sit down and write a hypothesis based on facts, I can't seem to get myself to come up with something. If I try to force myself, it just doesn't work. I have to be relaxed, and then, I experience the "aha moment."

While Zoe can accurately predict outcomes and use information to solve problems, she struggles to get through tests, "freezes" when she is called upon in class, and can take many hours and many nights to complete her science homework. Stress makes things harder for Zoe. Yet, when relaxed and in the "right mood," Zoe comes up with exceptional solutions to scientific problems. If Zoe is having a "good day," the information comes to her at an amazing rate, "like a lightning bolt hit her with the solution." (See Table 15.4.)

*Table 15.3.* Logan: Narrative Reasoning Strengths and Challenges

| Narrative Reasoning Strengths: Visual Thinking and Creativity | Narrative Reasoning Challenges | Challenges Observed | Strategies or Interventions to Consider | Common Professions Associated with Strengths in Narrative Reasoning |
|---|---|---|---|---|
| • Strong ability to use memory and apply it toward understanding present situation, understanding concepts, and predicting scenarios | Similar to Interconnected Reasoning, performance is impacted negatively when in a situation where "speed, accuracy, reliability, and precision are more valued than creativity, novel, or insight" (Eide, 2011). | • Remembering facts, rote, and abstract information is much harder<br>• Impacts the rate and ability to answer a question with a direct answer (i.e., take longer and have a harder time "getting to the point" as they describe answers)<br>• Difficulties with multiple choice exams | • Need to tie information to previous learning or put within context<br>• Use narrative-style of teaching new information<br>• Allow for sharing knowledge through story form, creatively, through acting, etc. | • Creative writer<br>• Historian<br>• Screen writer<br>• Counseling<br>• Psychologist<br>• Ministry<br>• Game designer<br>• Attorney<br>• Marketing and advertising |

*Table 15.4.* Zoe: Dynamic Reasoning Strengths and Challenges

| Dynamic Reasoning Strengths: Visual Thinking and Creativity | Dynamic Reasoning Challenges | Challenges Observed | Strategies or Interventions to Consider | Common Professions Associated with Strengths in Dynamic Reasoning |
|---|---|---|---|---|
| • Individuals with dynamic reasoning strengths can identify patterns that allows one to recreate past events without having experienced it, foresee potential situations, and come up with plausible hypotheses<br>• Strong use of instinct to gather insight on situation<br>• Ability to find connection and patterns that are unique and unusual<br>• Uses insight to problem-solve | • Ability to work efficiently and quickly greatly impacted<br>• Being overly focused can "inhibit creative connections" | • Appears to be daydreaming or unfocused, but the "magic" happens when the mind is relaxed enough to allow for exploration, creativity, and imagination | • Need to allow space for relaxation, creativity, and imagination<br>• Positive mood and well-being is correlated with strong insight<br>• Use of creative writing to demonstrate knowledge<br>• Use of graphics and illustrations to teach material<br>• Encourage visualization and imagination when teaching new material<br>• Use of analogies to put new material into context<br>• Encourage use of narratives to demonstrate knowledge | • Entrepreneur<br>• Scientist<br>• Inventor<br>• Writer<br>• Finance<br>• Business consultant |

## CONCLUSION

In this chapter, we have illustrated that dyslexia is not just a reading impairment. Dyslexia is also a different pattern of brain organization and information processing. As such, dyslexia brings with it patterns of strengths and certain challenges.

The children we work with—who are gifted and who have dyslexia—often have strengths in big-picture, holistic processing while they may also have difficulties with processing details. Research and clinical practice have provided evidence that individuals with dyslexia may show strengths in material reasoning, interconnected reasoning, narrative reasoning, and dynamic reasoning (Eide & Eide, 2011). As we have outlined in the presentation of these four case examples, teachers, parents, and other caregivers can positively nurture the gifted, dyslexic child by focusing on developing the MIND-Strengths, visual strengths, and creative strengths associated with giftedness and dyslexia while also providing support for related challenges.

## REFERENCES

Cowan, C. D. (2014). Dyslexia and visuospatial processing strengths: New research sheds light. International Dyslexia Association. Retrieved from https://dyslexiaida.org/

Eide, F. E. (2015). Defining dyslexia: Difference not deficit. Dyslexic Advantage. Retrieved from http://www.dyslexicadvantage.org/?s=defining+dyslexiA/

Eide, B. L., & Eide, F. E. (2011). *The dyslexic advantage: Unlocking the hidden potential of the dyslexic brain.* New York, NY: Plume.

Jung-Beeman, M. (2005). Bilateral brain processes for comprehending natural language. *TRENDS in Cognitive Sciences, 9*, 512–518.

Martinelli, V., & Schembri, J. (2014). Dyslexia, spatial awareness, and creativity in adolescent boys. *Psychology of Education Review, 38*(2), 39–47.

Silverman, L. K. (2002). *Upside down brilliance: The visual-spatial learner.* Denver, CO: DeLeon Publishing.

Sperry, R. W. (1982). *Science and moral priority: Merging mind, brain and human values.* Vol. 4. New York, NY: Columbia University Press.

Tafti, M. A., Hameedy, M. A., & Baghal, N. M. (2009). Dyslexia, a deficit or a difference: Comparing the creativity and memory skills of dyslexic and nondyslexic students in Iran. *Social Behavior and Personality, 37*(8), 1009–1016.

Turkeltaub, P., Gareau, L., Flowers, L., Zeffro, T. A., & Eden, G. (2003). Development of neural mechanisms for reading. *Nature Neuroscience, 6*, 767–773.

von Karolyi, C., Winner, E., Gray, W., & Sherman, G. (2003). Dyslexia linked to talent: Global visual-spatial ability. *Brain and Language, 85*(3), 427–432.

West, T. G. (2009). *In the mind's eye: Creative visual thinkers, gifted dyslexics, and the rise of visual technologies.* Amherst, NY: Prometheus Books.

Wolf, U., & Lundberg, I. (2002) The prevalence of dyslexia among art students. *Dyslexia, 8*(1), 34–42.

16

# Being 3e, A New Look at Culturally Diverse Gifted Learners with Exceptional Conditions

*An Examination of the Issues and Solutions for Educators and Families*

JOY LAWSON DAVIS AND SHAWN ANTHONY ROBINSON ■

## INTRODUCTION

The underrepresentation of culturally diverse gifted students is a pervasive and egregious problem across the nation. Although Black and Latino students combined make up 42% of the student populations in school that have gifted and advanced learner programs nationwide, they comprise only 28% of the students identified and enrolled in those programs (US Department of Education, 2016). This underrepresentation persists due to many factors: the lack of teacher referrals of students of color for gifted services, biased identification protocols, inadequate teacher training in cultural competency, limited parent and family engagement in gifted education, and bias deeply rooted in the American educational system of injustices that have worked for majority-population students and against cultural minority population groups (specifically Black and Latino students) for generations (Davis, 2010; Ford, 2013; Stambaugh & Ford, 2015; Symanski & Shaff, 2013). Even more troubling is the continuing underachievement of high-ability students who are participants in gifted programs nationwide (Plucker & Peters, 2016). This continuing waste of talent in America's schools should be cause for concern for all educators, community and civic leaders, and families.

According to the National Association for Gifted Children (2014), gifted education program services are classes and programs characterized by providing enrichment, advanced instruction, and independent study in specialized areas; access to these courses and programs provide challenge, enhance student interest, and improve their preparation for rigorous coursework in postsecondary training and allow students opportunities to work with their intellectual peers. Enabling equitable access to these services is a major challenge for school districts—in particular, ensuring that these specialized programs are available to high-ability Black and Latino students. Even more difficult is ensuring that Black students with other exceptional learning needs (i.e., learning disabled [LD], dyslexic, behavior disordered) are provided available and appropriate services for their intellectual and academic strengths while having their perceived or identified disabilities mediated (Mayes & Moore, 2016). The 3e label signifies three exceptional conditions: being culturally diverse (members of a socially oppressed group); being gifted or having high potential, and simultaneously being LD or having another disabling condition (such as dyslexia). This chapter explicates the concerns and issues relevant to this uniquely challenged group of students and offers strategies that teachers and parents can utilize to enrich children's educational experiences and improve their chances for life success.

## BRIEF REVIEW OF THE LITERATURE

Scholars DeCuir-Gunby (2009) and Ferguson and Nusbaum (2012) both asserted the importance of examining student development (i.e., African Americans) through understanding who they are and how their identities are constructed. In support of their positions, both Lovett and Sparks (2011) and Wang and Neihart (2015) noted that focusing on student's exceptionalities will develop how they see themselves and increases their overall self-concept.

Earlier, in a dated but relevant study, Peterson (1997) asserted that African Americans students are written off and given little attention in the literature on exceptionalities, and that little is known about this population regarding their identities, particularly around the intersection of LD (i.e., dyslexia) and giftedness (Annamma, Connor, & Ferri, 2013; Blanchett, 2010; Gillborn, 2015; Robinson, 2016a). For purposes of this chapter, it is critical to provide a working definition of the terms "learning disabled" and "giftedness." First, according to the Learning Disabilities Association of America (2016),

> Learning disabilities are neurologically based processing problems. These processing problems can interfere with learning basic skills such as reading, writing and/or math. They can also interfere with higher level skills such as organization, time planning, abstract reasoning, long or short term memory and attention. It is important to realize that learning disabilities can affect an individual's life beyond academics and can impact relationships with family, friends and in the workplace.

Further, LD is an umbrella term that describes a variety of specific learning categories (e.g., dyslexia). For example, Lyon, Shaywitz, and Shaywitz (2003) capture the essence of dyslexia as a

> Specific learning disability that is neurobiological in origin. It is characterized by difficulties with accurate and/or fluent word recognition and by poor spelling and decoding abilities. These difficulties typically result from a deficit in the phonological component of language that is often unexpected in relation to other cognitive abilities and the provision of effective classroom instruction. Secondary consequences may include problems in reading comprehension and reduced reading experiences that can impede growth of vocabulary and background knowledge. (p. 2)

As part of the Jacob Javits Gifted and Talented Students program of the Elementary and Secondary Education Act—the federal government defines gifted and talented students as

> Students, children, or youth who give evidence of high achievement capability in areas such as intellectual, creative, artistic, or leadership capacity, or in specific academic fields, and who need services and activities not ordinarily provided by the school in order to fully develop those capabilities.

The literature on giftedness has clearly noted that gifted children of color are underrepresented and underserved in programs nationwide (Davis & Moore, 2016). Thus, when considering the intersection of these terms, gifted Black students have been historically neglected from proper diagnostic assessments and are victimized by teacher biases and lack of appropriate identification protocols intervention (Hoyles & Hoyles, 2010; Mayes & Moore, 2016; Naglieri & Ford, 2011; Petersen, 2006).

Ford, Lisbon, and Little-Harrison (2016) discussed how using assessments to address student achievement is not only at the center of educational debate but also a sensitive topic marked by controversy when African American students are concerned. Scholars generally recommend employing a preventive and anti-deficit approach and encourage more teachers to be culturally competent, as well as understand, affirm, and be responsive to African American students' culture and identities, disrupt their negative experiences, and ensure academic success by nurturing their exceptionalities (Ladson-Billings, 2014; Mayes & Moore, 2016). Robinson (2015) discusses a new model of exceptionality articulating three identities of students who may be identified or perceived as exceptional or disabled who also are also members of the African American or Latino community, two traditionally oppressed groups; these students are regularly affected by negative reactions by educators and the general community to their cultural group (Robinson, 2016b).

Ensuring the academic success of students of color by nurturing their exceptionalities provides a platform for students to not only feel like their voices are being heard within the context of the classroom but also like they are active contributors and demonstrators of their own knowledge (Connor, 2006; Ferri, 2006). The two cases described here are those of Black male students who were served in their respective school districts' special education program when they were students in K-12 programming. Later in their school careers, each demonstrated high ability as is typical of students served in advanced learner programs.

## TWO STUDENT VIGNETTES: AFRICAN AMERICAN 3E MALES

The stories that follow are those of two Black males who originate from two very distinct environments. The first is Ronnie, who grew up in a small rural school district in the South. Lawrence, on the other hand, is a Nigerian immigrant who grew up in a large urban school district in the North. Both young men are now practicing professionals.

### Ronnie's Story

1. What specific strategies do you recall your parents using to engage with school personnel?
   I grew up in a very small community, and my father was a very popular minister. He was also a member of the PTA and very active, especially while my older sister was in school. My teachers would often see him at Food Lion or elsewhere and speak to him. They didn't have any problems calling home and talking to my parents. My parents attended IEP meetings—my dad told me that I didn't attend any of them.
2. Do you recall any specific teacher and what he or she did to encourage you?
   I only found a few favorable comments on my report cards, and a majority of them came from my resource teacher Mrs. Tobey. Mrs. Tobey was my special education teacher in sixth and seventh grade. Her comment read "The student is trying very hard. Encourage your child to write down study and written homework assignments in a small tablet." It was the only comment that alluded to how hard I was working. The other comments read "The student is not working up to potential" and "The student does not seem to have a serious attitude about school." It made me think: what was different about her class? Then I remembered the way she made me feel. Her classroom was the only place in school where it felt like nothing was wrong with me. Even though it was a special education class I never felt "slow" or stigmatized. In her classroom I felt like my life mattered; I felt like she was truly invested in me. She helped me improve my handwriting and organizational skills.

3. What barriers did you face as a diagnosed LD student? Academic or personal?
   The biggest barrier was a lack of access to college prep classes. I was placed on a lower academic track with low performing, misbehaved students. I had to fight each year to at least get one class with the "White people." I wasn't allowed to take a foreign language until the 11th grade, which meant I had to take two years in college. When my 11th grade Algebra II teacher found out I had a D in Geometry and Algebra I, she wanted the guidance counselor to place me back in Algebra I. This was the first year of state standardized testing and she didn't think I would pass. I didn't like her attitude and we clashed throughout the whole year. I clashed with a lot of my teachers. I went to the principal one year and told him that one of my teachers was racist. Not only did I get placed back in her class, but the principal told her what I said. I was often targeted in classes where a majority of the students were White. My Black friends and I would be split up and placed on opposite ends of the classroom. I felt like I didn't fit in anywhere.
4. Do you have any specific recommendations you can provide for teachers and administrators who may read your story?
   I would recommend they give students with disabilities the power to self-determine and the support to help them succeed. I wanted to be in the "smart" classes, but there were no supports in place. I feel like my teachers' expectations dictated my academic performance and behavior. Earn your students' trust by treating them like human beings who you feel are capable of doing amazing things. Speak to their purpose and their strengths. Don't be afraid to challenge them—they may just surprise you.

Today, Ronnie is a very successful social worker, entrepreneur, and author. He received a master's of social work from Virginia Commonwealth University in 2014. He graduated with a 3.5 GPA. Ronnie was raised in Tappahannock, Virginia, and attended Essex County Public Schools (ECPS). While attending ECPS, he spent seven years in special education after being diagnosed with a specific LD. The stigmatization of special education created a lack of interest in school. Nevertheless, he graduated from Essex High School in 2001 but with a 1.81 GPA. He was ranked 73 in a class of 95 students. With limited options regarding four-year colleges, he decided to enroll in J. Sargeant Reynolds Community College in Richmond, Virginia. The following year, he transferred to Old Dominion University, where he received a bachelor of science degree in human services in 2006. Sidney minored in business management and had a 3.09 GPA.

Ronnie's early academic challenges ignited a passion within him to pursue social justice and to work with youth. He has spent over eight years in the mental health and academic counseling fields and currently works as an outpatient therapist at the Middle Peninsula-Northern Neck Community Services Board. Ronnie is an active member of the Richmond Association of Black Social Workers. He founded Creative Medicine: Healing Through Words, an expressive writing program for offenders. He facilitated the program at the Northern Neck Regional Jail in Warsaw, Virginia, for six months before expanding the program into an limited liability corporation. The company's mission is to improve participants' social, emotional, and physical health through therapeutic writing and dialogue. He is also the author of a popular children's book titled *Nelson Beats the Odds*, the story tells about Ronnie's experiences as a student diagnosed as LD whose teachers had low expectations of him in elementary school.

## Lawrence's Story

Lawrence shares his story of being in school settings where the expectations for him were very low, but later in life his schooling took a complete turnaround because of his mother's advocacy.

> It has taken me well over three days to put to written word my story of how I was almost drowned as a little Black boy in the deep end of a pool called Special Education, only to kick and splash my way to the shallow end of the same pool labeled Gifted and Talented Education. I know what you might be thinking right now: "what an odd analogy to describe one's experience through their formative education."
>
> My family moved to the United States of America from Saudi Arabia, where my father had completed his undergraduate education. The move to America was for similar reasons to many other immigrant families; we were filled with the hope of a better life than that available in our native country of Nigeria. It goes without saying that my parents and their children struggled to adjust to this, at the time, peculiar and foreign land.

Even more peculiar and foreign to me was the American school, classroom, and teachers. We ended up in South Central Los Angeles and I attended elementary school. I was terrified of the foreign world in which I found myself. The teachers yelled and the students did not listen. To make things worse I was the new boy, with a funny accent and African. I was bullied by classmates almost from day one. I quickly shrunk into myself feeling culturally inept and constantly intimidated by other children and at times unknowingly by teachers who deemed me intellectually impaired. I remember school becoming a place that evoked a level of anxiety that eventually led to a stammer that only increased the ridicule that I received from the other kids. This eventually led to my emotional explosion into physical fights. I went from being a kind and somewhat shy little boy to a boy that preempted verbal and physical assaults by dishing the first strike.

> Eventually, the change in my behavior labeled me a difficult child to deal with. I could see the way I was treated by the adults around me taking a turn for the worst. At the time, all my teachers were White and as an eight-year-old I just

didn't feel as though they cared. Whenever I was made fun of or mocked in class they simply did nothing, other than telling me to "ignore them." When I fought back I was repeatedly told that I needed to learn to control my temper. Soon my parents were invited to the school for a meeting to discuss my behavior. I remember being present with my parents and my eight-year-old mind zoning out as my third-grade teacher told my parents that though I could be "a sweet child, but you just never know when and what would set him off." My mother recently revealed to me that after we had gotten home from that meeting she wept.

Soon after that meeting, I met a few times with a White man at the school (now I recognize as having been the school psychologist). Before I knew it I was no longer a full-time member of my third-grade classroom. I spent several periods a week in different classrooms, with speech therapists, and in counseling sessions. Interestingly enough, it was my classmates who made it clear to me that I was now labeled as "special ed." The mockery continued and I shrank deeper into myself. Plagued with constant anxiety, I simply stopped speaking. I hated school.

In 1985, due to financial hardship, we moved back to Nigeria. My father stayed here to support us. Once more I was in a peculiar and foreign land, having not been in Nigeria since the age of two. I continued with the fourth grade in Nigeria, a country without a formalized special education program. So, the "services" I received in Los Angeles were pretty much over and done with. Interestingly, the expectations from my new teachers were extremely high, mainly because I was coming from America. The thought was that all that comes from America must be superior. I quickly proved all my teachers wrong, as I failed all my subjects and was ranked 40th out of 42 students in the class. My mother, being unwilling to shed another tear, resolved that she would do whatever it took to provide me with the best tutoring and academic enrichment she could afford.

I went to school from 8:00 AM until 2:30 PM. I would get home, have a snack, and expect to have one of my subject-specific tutors arrive by 4:00 PM for a two-hour session. This occurred Monday through Friday, including 9:00 AM until noon on Saturdays. I remember at first being so intimidated by both of my tutors. The two were imposing Nigerian men. Mr. Mike also happened to be my math and science teacher at school, and Mr. Igwe was my English and history teacher. They gave me no slack; if anything, they expected me to rise above my classmates in every subject. With a lot of work and newfound determination, I did just that. I completed the fourth grade ranked fourth out of 42 students.

My mother didn't stop there. She purchased me books instead of toys. She rewarded for time spent reading or in study, and by the end of the summer of 1986, before the start of the fifth grade I had read Chinua Achibe's *Things Fall Apart, No Longer At Ease, and The Arrow of God;* George Orwell's *Animal Farm,* William Golding's *Lord Of The Flies*; and my favorite Charles Dickens'

*Oliver Twist, David Copperfield, A Christmas Carol,* and *Great Expectations.* Can you imagine that? I was the same boy that a little over a year before hated school, and I became madly in love with it. Learning became my joy.

I would return to Los Angeles with my family in November of 1988. I was 12 years old enrolled in junior high school in Inglewood, California, a primarily Black suburb of South Central Los Angeles. First off, I was placed a grade level behind, in the sixth grade, because I was transferring from a school in Africa. It was assumed that I would be academically deficient. However, due to my father's unwillingness to have me repeat the sixth grade, the school's officials reluctantly agreed to have me in the seventh grade on a trial basis. Things would take a turn for the best, when on my first day in seventh-grade mathematics class, I solved a couple of double- and triple-digit division problems in my head as the rest of the class penciled away in long division. The teacher was impressed with me, then had me work out various problems in the seventh-grade mathematics textbook until she moved me on to eighth-grade mathematics. The next thing I knew, at the end of the class period, she took me by the hand and dragged me to another classroom to meet the science teacher. From there I was sitting in the main office, listening to both women's muffled voices behind the principal's closed door. By the end of the day, not only was I advanced to the eighth grade, but I was also placed in the GATE program (Gifted and Talented Education). In just about five years I had gone from being labeled learning disabled to being recognized as gifted and talented.

The question is often asked how do Black boys without disabilities end up in special education? Toldson (2011) speaks to the differences among all students and how behavior patterns are often different than expectations of the typical school environment. This was my circumstance. Rather than my teachers helping me deal with the huge cultural shift of moving from Saudi Arabia to America, or even addressing the bullying that I was facing on a daily basis, instead I was made to be the villain. In Nigeria, I found teachers that had high expectations, expecting nothing less than my best. This expectation also covered all children in their care.

Anyone in the position of caring for the intellectual and emotional life of any child should learn from my story. The misdiagnosis of Black boys is far too common. As an educator, I fight for justice in the education of all students, especially those who find themselves more likely to be victimized by an unfair educational system. I sometimes wonder what those teachers at my elementary school would say of me now, the Black boy that they expected so little of.

Today, Lawrence is a high school principal in New York City for high-ability students interested in math and science. In 2011, he graduated from Teacher's College Columbia University. His career continues to develop as he works with young people, their families, and his community.

## DEVELOPING CULTURALLY RELEVANT SOLUTIONS AND HIGH EXPECTATIONS FOR ALL

While these are only two stories, the experiences of both students from totally different environments (one southern rural and other northern urban) are like those of thousands of Black male students (in particular) with high ability who have gone through the special education system in our nation. In consideration of the unique, and often misunderstood, academic needs of Black students who possess both high ability and who may also have exceptional learning needs, it is most prudent to look first at recommendations for teaching students who are most like themselves. For this, it is imperative that all teachers receive training in culturally responsive pedagogy (Ford, 2013). Perhaps even more important, that classroom teachers of students from culturally diverse communities should engage in training to help them understand the impact of high expectations for their students. Using culture as a mediator or framework for designing and delivering instruction can help teachers meet student interests and align instruction with academic goals simultaneously. Using culture brings the student into the learning process with familiarity and increases interest and the likelihood of attention, and it improves racial identity and self-esteem (Delpit & Dowdy, 2008).

In addition to "cultural mediation," providing opportunities for students to build self-regulation are highly recommended with high-potential students who may have experienced low expectations from teachers whose approach to working with them was deficit-based rather than strength-based (Ford et al., 2016). When self-regulation strategies are taught, high-potential students take control of their own learning and achievement (Cash, 2016). Finally, emphasis on rigor ensures that these unique students are utilizing their innate potential for critical thinking, creativity, and challenge. Providing early and sustained access to intellectually rigorous classroom and enrichment programs increases student interest and preparation for rigorous coursework at the secondary and postsecondary levels.

Families of 3e students can be their best advocates when they are active, well-informed collaborators with educators. Working with families to strengthen their advocacy skills and create stronger relationships between families and schools is highly recommended (Davis, 2010; Wood & Davis, 2016). The following are recommendations for families working in collaboration with schools:

- Ensure that teachers of are those who set high expectations and believe in the potential and strengths of one's children.
- Ask school administrators to convene meetings with three key clientele/educational leaders in gifted education, diversity/inclusion specialists, and special education coordinators with families in attendance.
- Allow parents to serve as "cultural agents" and provide information about family and community norms and traditions that impact student achievement and the way that families engage with students in other environments outside of schools.

- Invite community leaders and faith leaders to serve as mentors, role models, and providers of other supports needed by 3e students.
- Develop a cadre of family leaders who can be trained in the specific language and strategies of special education and gifted education to train other families. This tiered approach is valuable for both the community and the school.

In summary, to further understand the lived experiences of African American students who are 3e, we highly recommend that additional research and special programs be supported (Robinson, 2016b; Stambaugh & Ford, 2015). Examining this specific student body may offer enhanced solutions that lead to decreasing and preventing the significant academic disparities within the system (Wright, 2013). There is no greater social justice issue in America. Developing a body of literature specifically addressing the exceptionalities is the first step to preventing academic failure and underachievement among African American and other minority students (McDonald, Keys, & Balcazar, 2007; Robinson, 2013).

It is crucial that educators and families fully understand the social and intellectual challenges faced by these students in the classroom, in the community, and among their peers. The two stories in this chapter are just the tip of the iceberg, yet they are very compelling and cause us to pause and understand how the relationships between students, families, and educators can create positive or negative outcomes over time. The loss for individuals, communities, and society is immeasurable when any student is devalued, overlooked, and denied access to enriching educational opportunities.

## REFERENCES

Annamma, S., Connor, D. J., & Ferri, B. A. (2013). Disability critical race studies: Theorizing at the intersections of race and disability. *Race Ethnicity and Education, 16*, 1–31.

Blanchett, J. W. (2010). Telling like it is: The role of race, class, & culture in the perpetuation of learning disability as a privileged category for the white middle class. *Disability Studies Quarterly, 30*(2), 6.

Cash, R. (2016). *Self-regulation in the classroom: Helping students learn how to learn.* Minneapolis, MN: Free Spirit Press.

Connor, D. (2006). Michael's story: "I get into so much trouble just by walking": Narrative knowing and life at the intersections of learning disability, race, and class. *Equity & Excellence in Education, 39*, 154–165.

Davis, J. L. (2010). *Bright, talented & Black: A guide for families of African American gifted learners.* Scottsdale, AZ: Great Potential Press.

Davis, J. L., & Moore, J. L. III (2016). (Eds.). *Gifted children of color around the world: Diverse needs, exemplary practices, and directions for the future* (Advances in Race and Ethnicity in Education 3). London: Emerald Group.

DeCuir-Gunby, J. (2009). A review of the racial identity development of African American adolescents: The role of education. *Review of Educational Research, 79*, 103–124.

Delpit, L., & Dowdy, J. K. (2008). *The skin that we speak: Thoughts on language and culture in the classroom*. New York, NY: New Press.

Ferguson, P. M., & Nusbaum, E. (2012). Disability studies: What is it and what difference does it makes? *Research & Practice for Persons with Severe Disabilities, 37*, 70–80.

Ferri, B.A. (2006). Voices in the struggle: In response to "Reigning in special education." *Disability Studies Quarterly. 26*(2), 10–14.

Ford, D. Y. (2013). *Recruiting and retaining culturally different students in gifted education*. Waco, TX: Prufrock Press.

Ford, D. Y., Lisbon, A. J., & Little-Harrison, N. (2016). #Black intellect matters: Inequitable practices yield inequitable results. *Wisconsin English Journal, 58*, 81–101.

Gillborn, D. (2015). Intersectionality, critical race theory, and the primacy of racism: *Race, Class, Gender, and Disability in Education. Qualitative Inquiry, 21*, 277–287.

Hoyles, A., & Hoyles, M. (2010). Race and dyslexia. *Race Ethnicity and Education, 13*, 209–223.

Ladson-Billings, G. (2014). Culturally relevant pedagogy 2.0: Aka the remix. *Harvard Educational Review, 84*, 74–84.

Learning Disabilities Association of America. (2016). Types of learning disabilities. Retrieved from https://ldaamerica.org/types-of-learning-disabilities/

Lovett, B. J., & Sparks, R. L. (2011). The identification and performance of gifted students with learning disability diagnoses: A quantitative synthesis. *Journal of Learning Disabilities, 46*, 304–316.

Lyon, R. G., Shaywitz, S. E., & Shaywitz, B. A. (2003). Defining dyslexia, comorbidity, teachers' knowledge of language and reading. *Annals of Dyslexia, 53*, 1–14.

Mayes, R. D., & Moore, J. L. III. (2016). The intersection of race, disability, and giftedness: Understanding the education needs of twice-exceptional, African American students. *Gifted Child Today, 39*, 98–104.

McDonald, K., Keys, E., & Balcazar, C. (2007). Disability, race/ethnicity and gender: Themes of cultural oppression, acts of individual resistance. *American Journal of Community Psychology, 39*, 145–161.

Naglieri, J. A., & Ford, D. Y. (2011). Addressing underrepresentation of gifted minority children using the Naglieri Nonverbal Ability Test (NNAT). In T. C. Grantham, D. Y. Ford, M. S. Henfield, M. Trotman-Scott, D. A. Harmon, S. Porcher, & C. Price (Eds.), *Gifted & advanced Black students in school* (pp. 243–253). Waco, TX: Prufrock Press.

National Association for Gifted Children. (2015). Gifted education in the U.S. Retrieved from https://www.nagc.org/resources-publications/resources/gifted-education-us

Petersen, A. (2006). An African-American woman with disabilities: the intersection of gender, race and disability. *Disability & Society, 21*(7), 721–734.

Peterson, J. S. (1997). Bright, troubled, and resilient, and not in a gifted program. *Journal of Secondary Gifted Education, 8*, 121–136.

Plucker, J. S., & Peters, S. J. (2016). *Excellence gaps in education: Expanding opportunities for talented students*. Cambridge, MA: Harvard Education Press.

Robinson, S. A. (2013). Educating Black males with dyslexia. *Interdisciplinary Journal of Teaching and Learning, 3*, 159–174.

Robinson, S. A. (2016a). Introduction: Supporting twice exceptional African American students: Implications for classroom teaching. *Wisconsin English Journal, 58*, 76–80.

Robinson, S. A. (2016b). Triple Identity Theory: A theoretical framework for understanding gifted Black males with dyslexia. *Urban Education Research and Policy Annuals, 4*, 147–158.

Stambaugh, T., & Ford, D. Y. (2015). Microaggressions, multiculturalism, and gifted individuals who are Black, Hispanic, or low income. *Journal of Counseling & Development, 93*, 192–201.

Symanski, T., & Shaff, T. (2013). Teacher perspectives regarding gifted diverse students. *Gifted Children, 6*. Retrieved from http://docs/lib.urdue.edu/giftedchildren/vol6/iss1/1

Toldson, I. A (2011). How Black boys with disabilities end up in honors classes while others without disabilities end up in special education. *The Journal of Negro Education, 80*, 439–443.

United States Department of Education (1993). National Excellence: A Case for Developing America's Talent. Office of Educational Research and Improvement, Washington, D.C.

US Department of Education. (1994). Jacob Javits Gifted and Talented Students program biennial report. Retrieved from https://www2.ed.gov/pubs/Biennial/618.html

US Department of Education. (2016). Persistent disparities found through comprehensive civil rights survey. Retrieved from http://www.ed.gov/news/press-releases/

Wang, C. W., & Neihart, M. (2015). Academic self-concept and academic self-efficacy: Self-beliefs enable academic achievement of twice-exceptional students. *Roeper Review, 37*, 63–73.

Wood, E. L., & Davis, J. L. (2016). Family engagement and advocacy for culturally diverse 2E learners. *Wisconsin English Journal, 58*, 189–192.

Wright, C. (2013). Understanding Black academic attainment: Policy and discourse, educational aspirations and resistance. *Education Inquiry, 4*(1), 87–102.

17

# Where the Rubber Meets the Road

## *Supporting the Educational Success of Twice Exceptional African American Students*

RENAE D. MAYES, ERIK M. HINES, AND JAMES L. MOORE III ■

## INTRODUCTION

As the US population continues to change, K-12 schools are also growing rapidly and becoming much more culturally diverse than ever before. These shifts in the student population also indicate a potential shift in representation in both special education and gifted education programs as well. Currently, African American students account for 17% of the student population but are underrepresented in gifted education at only 8.8% of the students enrolled in gifted and talented programs and overrepresented in special education at 19.1% of students being served under the Individuals with Disabilities Education Act (IDEA; Mayes & Moore, 2016b; Office of Civil Rights Data, 2012). As such, African American students have a greater propensity to fall into what is known as the "excellence gap," which are achievement gaps that persist in advanced proficiency levels (Hardesty, McWilliams, & Plucker, 2014; Plucker & Peters, 2016). These gaps are perpetuated by the underrepresentation of African American students in gifted education and are caused by a host of factors, including limited resources in schools that serve predominately low-income students of color, greater attention and focus on minimum proficiency standards gaps, and limited parent awareness and advocacy for resources for gifted education (Hardesty et al., 2014; Plucker & Peters, 2016). What still remains unknown is the proportion of African American students being served in both special education and gifted education.

Students who are both gifted and have a disability, also known as twice exceptional students, have been receiving greater attention from both educators and researchers, each eager to understand and find the best ways to support this population. However, much of the scholarly literature focuses on the intersection of giftedness and disability alone, rarely integrating other aspects of identity that can have a significant influence on educational experiences. As such, this chapter expands on the twice exceptionality literature by integrating racial identity through the discussion of African American twice exceptional students.

## TWICE EXCEPTIONAL STUDENTS

Twice exceptional students are identified as being gifted and talented while having a disability (Mayes, Harris, & Hines, 2016; Trail, 2011). Specifically, the National Gifted Association for Gifted Children (NAGC; 2009), stated, "in the field of gifted education, the more commonly used term for a gifted student with a concurring disability is 'twice exceptional learner'" (p. 1). Between 2 and 7 percent of the K-12 student population is estimated to be twice exceptional (Trail, 2011). Moreover, NAGC (2009) believes the number of twice exceptional students in the United States is 360,000 (see also National Education Association, 2006). Mayes et al. (2016) noted this estimation is conservative as students may not be properly identified for this designation.

Researchers (Bianco, 2005; Rinn & Nelson, 2009) suggest that twice exceptional students are more likely to be known for their disability as it can overshadow their giftedness. More research is needed into understanding twice exceptional students and how to properly identify students to ensure they receive the support needed to be academically successful. However, it is also likely that students "are underidentified due to the phenomena of masking, where one exceptionality is masked due to the presence of the other exceptionality" (Mayes et al., 2016, p. 55).

Table 17.1 lists several characteristics of twice exceptional students.

This list is not exhaustive, and other characteristics of twice exceptional students may include a specific learning disability, autism, or attention deficit hyperactivity disorder. The largest percentage of students labeled as twice exceptional are in the specific learning disability category (NAGC, 2010). IDEA recognized an additional 10 categories: heath impairment, speech/language impairment, emotional disturbance, hearing impairment, visual impairment, orthopedic impairment, intellectual disability, multiple disabilities, deaf/blindness, and traumatic brain injury (Montgomery County Public Schools, 2014; US Department of Education, 2007).

## RACE, GIFTEDNESS, AND DISABILITY

Much of the literature on gifted students with learning disabilities is helpful, but it also lacks attention to the cultural context of diverse students. As such, more

*Table 17.1.* Characteristics of Twice Exceptional Students

| | | |
|---|---|---|
| Great expressive language skills | Hypersensitive | Strong mathematical skills |
| Great reasoning (verbal/ nonverbal) | Perfectionism | Difficulty with retrieving words |
| Class clown behaviors | Highly critical or self | Excellent language skills |
| Creative | Large and expansive vocabulary | Verbally elaborate with unlimited description and detail |
| Struggle to synthesize and organize ideas | Difficulty with number sense or visual spatial skills | Exhibit disruptive behaviors like crying frequently |

NOTE: Adapted from *A Guidebook for Supporting the Achievement of Gifted Students with Disabilities* (Montgomery County Schools, 2014).

research is needed that highlights the unique strengths and needs of students at the intersection of their multiple identities (race, gender, ability status, etc.). Literature regarding twice exceptional African American students is growing. Current literature suggests that African American students are more likely than White students to be identified as having a disability and less likely to be identified as being gifted (Mayes & Moore, 2016b). Further, once an African American student is identified as having a disability, the chances that they will be recognized for their giftedness dwindles. While masking may make gifted African American students with disabilities harder to identify, there are also challenges with the identification process for giftedness, which often relies on teacher referral and assessments that can be culturally biased (Ford, 2013).

Should African American students with disabilities be identified as gifted, they must navigate many potholes in the education process in order to be successful. First, it may be that they are identified as gifted but do not receive gifted education services. For example, in their study, Mayes and Moore (2016a) found that the majority of twice exceptional African American students in a large urban school district were identified as artistically gifted in the areas of dance, vocal and instrumental music, and visual arts. However, these students did not receive gifted services as gifted education only occurred in academic subjects (i.e., math, science, English). Further, these students often lacked opportunities to be involved in elective courses that would allow them to grow their gifts as their electives became time spent in pull-out special education services.

Once gifted African American students with disabilities are receiving gifted services, they may still be faced with socioemotional and academic challenges. A twice exceptional African American student may be one of only a few students of color in the gifted education program (Mayes & Moore, 2016b). Further, there most likely will be few students with disabilities in gifted education and certainly there will not be very many, if any, twice exceptional African American students in the program. Because of their uniqueness, these students may struggle to find both peers and educators who share in and understand their experiences and perspectives (Ford, 2013; Ford, Trotman Scott, Moore, & Amos, 2013). Also, their special needs as outlined in their Individualized Education Program (IEP) may be overlooked or seen as a reason they should not be receiving gifted education services. As such, twice exceptional African American students may be left to battle negative messages and low expectations about both their disability and their cultural identity from the school environment and society as a whole (Mayes & Moore, 2016a, 2016b; Stambaugh & Ford, 2015). Messages, if left unchallenged, can negatively shape self-concept and self-esteem and lead to underachievement and eventual school dropout.

Not surprisingly, when gifted African American students have these negative experiences, they are less likely to reach out for support. They will often "grin and bear it" rather than challenge the negative environment or individuals sending negative messages (Mayes & Moore, 2016a). That is why educators must take a proactive and preventative approach in creating a supportive environment where all students, including twice exceptional African American students, can be successful. Educators must also step in and advocate for students when current policies and practices lead to inequities and disparities in student outcomes, including those involving student access, attainment, and achievement.

## THE CASE OF MARCUS

Marcus is a 12-year-old Black seventh-grade student in a predominately African American and Latinx, urban middle school. Marcus is the youngest of four children, all of whom have attended the same schools. Marcus comes from a household where both parents and grandparents are caregivers. Additionally, members of his extended family are a part of the same community.

When Marcus was in fourth grade, he was identified as having a learning disability. While Marcus is a bright and capable student, his writing and reading skills lagged behind many of his peers. Like many students with disabilities, Marcus struggles with feeling confident in his abilities, but through the support of his general education and special education teachers, he has been able to earn As and Bs in all of his courses. Soon, his mathematics teacher saw that, despite his learning disability, Marcus had incredible potential in mathematics. His mathematics teacher noticed a quiet confidence that Marcus had in learning and finding creative ways to approach problem-solving that in many ways was more advanced than his peers. As such, the mathematics teacher recommended that Marcus be assessed for gifted education.

Once it was declared that Marcus should be in gifted education, the school counselor and gifted education teacher called a meeting with Marcus's family. They shared that Marcus would be provided with gifted education services in the area of mathematics while continuing his other courses in the general education classroom. Although apprehensive, Marcus's family believed this could be an important learning opportunity.

Once in gifted education, Marcus's teachers and family noticed a change in him. He was no longer engaged in and excited about learning. His confidence that had grown so much prior to being in the gifted program had faded to apathy. Across all of his courses, his As and Bs quickly became Cs and Ds. When his school counselor shared her concern, Marcus explained that he did not feel welcomed into the class and that gifted classes were for "White kids." Ideally, Marcus would like to go back to the way things were before gifted education. While Marcus's family was initially excited about the academic rigor of gifted education, they are now concerned that his love of learning is being sacrificed.

## STRATEGIES TO SUPPORT MARCUS

Next we discuss specific strategies regarding the case of Marcus. Strategies are provided using the American School Counseling Association (2012) domains, which include academic, personal/social, and career development. This framework provides a holistic understanding of student development and functioning in schools as well as points of prevention and intervention for educational stakeholders including teachers, school counselors, administrators, and families.

### Academic Domain

The academic domain refers to strategies and activities to support and maximize a student's ability to reach their learning potential. As stated in the case, Marcus has a learning disability and giftedness in mathematics. It seems that, in general education, Marcus was receiving appropriate support from teachers as outlined in his IEP, which enabled him to be academically successful. However, the addition of gifted services in mathematics drastically changed Marcus's academic performance. As a teacher of gifted education, it would be important to not only understand Marcus's giftedness but also the manifestation of his special needs. How was the IEP shared with the gifted education teacher? What accommodations outlined in his IEP need to also be incorporated into this particular course? Should the IEP team including his family meet to discuss what additional accommodations may be necessary in this gifted mathematics course?

Although in this case the IEP has already been drafted and implemented in the general education classes, the shift into the gifted mathematics course would call for some additional attention to Marcus's needs as the learning environment is different. For example, despite being in a math course, the typical way students engage learning is through reading. As this is an area where Marcus needs extra support, this cannot be overlooked.

Marcus may also be adjusting to the different expectations there may be in the gifted mathematics classroom. If these expectations are not communicated clearly and he is not provided sufficient support, Marcus can easily disengage from the learning environment. Instead, as students transition into gifted education, it would be important to provide students information on the structure, expectations, and support systems in place for the course. For example, is it typical for students to struggle in the beginning as they adjust to the rigor of this course? How is the course set up (primarily lecture and independent work or group modules, etc.)? What kind of support (e.g., tutoring, study groups, office hours) are provided to students in this course? How can families support learning at home?

Finally, Marcus's disengagement may also be linked to his lack of representation in the curriculum and the classroom. For example, representation of diversity in curriculum as well as staff indicate what and who is valued as a part of a hidden curriculum. The lack of cultural connection with peers and perhaps that of learning material can push students like Marcus to the margins and lead to academic disengagement and underachievement. As such, educators and school counselors must be intentional with curriculum materials and resources to represent the diversity of the student body.

## Personal/Social Domain

The personal/social domain refers to strategies and activities that meet personal and social needs while students progress through school and into adulthood. Despite the move to gifted education in math being an academic shift, it is also a shift with Marcus's peer group. With particular attention to urban schools, it is likely that Marcus moved from a general education classroom with peers of similar cultural backgrounds to one that has very few culturally similar peers. Further, it is likely that he is one of very few students with special needs in the gifted classroom. Although not explicit, the message became clear to Marcus that he is indeed an outsider and does not belong in this space.

Marcus's reaction points to a larger systemic issue with how students are identified and placed in gifted education. For example, in an urban school where the population is predominately students of color, Marcus found that gifted education did not look like people with his cultural identity. Both teachers and educators should be concerned about the disparity of representation in gifted programs to ensure that identification procedures are culturally responsive, allowing for a diverse study body to have access to gifted education.

Additionally, Marcus's reaction to gifted education indicates that specific support is needed to help him reconcile his own identities. Being considered gifted is a new situation for Marcus; how does he make sense of that with his learning disability? How does that interact with his cultural identities? Current literature suggests that while Black students in special education or gifted education may struggle initially, success is often a result of positive identity development, meaning that students have been able to make sense of their exceptionalities as well as their cultural identities in ways that counter the negative stereotypes that they face. Teachers and school counselors can foster their development directly through mentorship where students can openly discuss their unique learning experiences as gifted African American students with disabilities while directly challenging myths and stereotypes that exist about their identities. School counselors, in particular, may create a growth-centered counseling group around exploring diverse identities to build connections among students (see Mayes et al., 2016).

Communication between the school and Marcus's family regarding the intervention activities, particularly around building positive identity, is also important. As middle school is a primary age where students begin to understand themselves in relation to others, these questions or ideas of who Marcus believes himself to be are still forming, and his family will play a big role in that process. As such, school counselors and teachers should consider working directly with Marcus's family to provide more insight on twice exceptionality while learning more from the family about their particular culture. This collaborative process can guide work being done at school with Marcus but also provides opportunities for Marcus's family to continue to be a strong support both inside and outside of school. Given that Marcus's family is well regarded in the community, there may be connections or opportunities to connect Marcus with others with similar identities and talents in the community who can serve as formal and informal role models and mentors.

## Career Domain

The career domain refers to strategies and activities that allow students to acquire skills, attitudes, and knowledge need for successful transition from school to the world of work and from job to job across their lifespan. In particular, school counselors can use the National Office of School Counselor Advocacy (NOSCA) Eight Components of College and Career Readiness (NOSCA, 2010). The eight components are college aspirations, academic planning for college and career readiness, enrichment and extracurricular engagement, college and career exploration and selection process, college and career assessments, college affordability planning, college and career admission processes, and transition from high school to college enrollment process (NOSCA, 2010). Specifically, the school counselor can work with Marcus in understanding how gifted class can help with the rigor of college as well as match these courses to potential careers. The school counselor can talk to Marcus about careers involving mathematics since he tends to do well in this area. They can also read up on famous African American and Latino individuals who used math in their careers to show Marcus that there are individuals like himself who are successful. Further, the school counselors can work to understand why students of color are underrepresented in gifted education and to figure out why Marcus feels isolated and uncomfortable being the only person of color. The school counselor can advocate for cultural shift and a change in practices to increase representation of students of color.

Additionally, the school counselor can connect career development to Marcus's IEP to ensure that his accommodations are taken into consideration when discussing career and college readiness. It is important for the school counselor to work with other education stakeholders to ensure Marcus receives the assistance he needs to successfully prepare for postsecondary opportunities as well as for any career of his choice. Career ideas can be infused throughout the curriculum so that Marcus can understand how life after high school is impacted by his current circumstance as a twice exceptional student.

## CONCLUSION

As educators and school counselors consider working with twice exceptional children and adolescents, students' multiple identities must be considered. As the Marcus's case illustrates, disability and giftedness are important, but identity matters as well. Each of these identities shape students and their experiences in school. Educators and school counselors can take a proactive systemic approach to supporting twice exceptional African American students by examining curriculum as well as the school environment to see how culturally diverse students are represented, welcomed, and included. This means understanding how policy and perhaps bias leads to disproportional representation in gifted education and working to resolve it through fair identification practices and procedures. Further, taking a holistic view of twice exceptional African American students is necessary to understand what is needed to be academically and personally healthy and successful as well as to help students think beyond the present moment to understand that life after K-12 school can involve careers that fit their interests.

## REFERENCES

American School Counselor Association. (2012). *The ASCA national model: A framework for school counseling programs.* Alexandria, VA: Author.

Bianco, M. (2005). The effects of disability labels on special education and general education teachers' referrals for gifted programs. *Learning Disability Quarterly, 28,* 285–293.

Ford, D. Y. (2013). *Recruiting and retaining culturally different students in gifted education.* Waco, TX: Prufrock Press.

Ford, D. Y., Trotman Scott, M., Moore, J. L. III, & Amos, S. O. (2013). Gifted education and culturally different students: Examining prejudice and discrimination via microaggressions. *Gifted Child Today, 36,* 205–208.

Hardesty, J., McWilliams, J., & Plucker, J. A. (2014). Excellence gaps: What they are, why they are bad, and how smart contexts can address them . . . or make them worse. *High Ability Studies, 25*(1), 71–80. doi:10.1080/13598139.2014.907646

Mayes, R. D., Harris, P. C., & Hines, E. M. (2016). Meeting the academic and socioemotional needs of twice exceptional African American students through group counseling. In J. L. Davis & J. L. Moore, III (Eds.), *Gifted children of color around the world* (pp. 53–69). Charlotte, NC: Information Age.

Mayes, R. D., & Moore, J. L. III. (2016a). Adversity and pitfalls of twice exceptional urban learners. *Journal of Advanced Academics, 27*(3), 167–189.

Mayes, R. D., & Moore, J. L. III. (2016b). The intersection of race, disability, and giftedness: Understanding the education needs of twice-exceptional, African American students. *Gifted Child Today, 39*(2), 98–104.

Montgomery County Public Schools. (2014). *Twice exceptional students: A staff guidebook for supporting the achievement of gifted students with disabilities.* Retrieved from http://www.montgomeryschoolsmd.org/uploadedFiles/curriculum/enriched/programs/gtld/0470.15_TwiceExceptionalStudents_Handbook_Web.pdf

National Association for Gifted Children. (2009). Twice exceptionality. Position paper. Washington, DC: Author.

National Association for Gifted Children. (2010). *Twice-exceptionality* [White paper]. Retrieved October 1, 2016, from https://www.nagc.org/sites/default/files/Position%20Statement/twice%20exceptional.pdf

National Education Association. (2006). *The twice-exceptional dilemma.* Washington, DC: Author.

National Office of School Counselor Advocacy. (2010). *The eight components of college and career readiness.* Retrieved from https://secure-media.collegeboard.org/digitalServices/pdf/nosca/11b_4416_8_Components_WEB_111107.pdf

Plucker, J. A., & Peters, S. J. (2016). *Excellence gaps in education: Expanding opportunities for talented students.* Cambridge, MA: Harvard Education Press.

Rinn, A. N., & Nelson, J. M. (2009). Preservice teachers' perceptions of behaviors characteristic of ADHD and giftedness. *Roeper Review, 31*(1), 18–26.

Stambaugh, T., & Ford, D. Y. (2015). Microaggressions, multiculturalism, and gifted individuals who are Black, Hispanic, or low income. *Journal of Counseling and Development, 93*(2), 192–201.

Trail, B. A. (2011). *Twice-exceptional gifted children: Understanding, teaching, and counseling gifted students.* Waco, TX: Prufrock Press.

US Department of Education. (2007). Elementary and Secondary Education Act, Public Law, 107–110.

# PART IV

# Models

18

# Bridges Academy

## *A Strengths-Based Model for 2e*

CARL A. SABATINO AND CHRISTOPHER R. WIEBE

Students come to Bridges defined by their challenges and labels. They leave defined by their abilities and accomplishments.

—Carl A. Sabatino, *Head of School, Bridges Academy*

## INTRODUCTION

Bridges Academy is a dynamic educational ecostructure comprised of growth-minded faculty members, policies, beliefs, attitudes, and practices. This chapter provides a brief overview of our school, expounding upon these factors and discussing the strength-based and talent-focused principles that guide our decision-making and inform our community, program, and pedagogy. Given the complexity of the subject, we approach the topic with broad strokes, with a few examples, in an effort to provide useful information to parents and educators about applying our principles, frameworks, and perspectives in all schools working with twice exceptional (2e) students. These students are highly gifted but have learning differences or other factors that can thwart success in traditional settings. While there is no single formula that defines the Bridges model, there is an unmistakable dynamic system, which involves the interplay of stakeholders, school culture, roles, and beliefs.

## OUR SCHOOL

Bridges Academy's history is one of self-determination, self-discovery, and entrepreneurialism. Founded in 1994, the school initially hosted a small group of struggling students in an in-home tutorial setting. Though these students demonstrated high intelligence and cognitive ability, they suffered from severe anxiety, aggravating teachers and peers, failing their classes, and, in some cases, dropping out of school entirely. Over time the tutorial center came to understand its population as 2e. In 1999, Bridges joined the independent school ecosystem and was accredited by California Association of Independent Schools and Western Association of Schools and Colleges, giving it the flexibility it needed to design curricular and instructional approaches with the 2e student in mind. Bridges has grown its elementary, middle, and high school programs with a faculty whose practices reflect two decades of research and experience working with 2e students. Bridges Academy has committed itself to being a college preparatory school and remains true to the mission of educating complex 2e students. We provide a student-centered model to optimize the 2e student's unique cognitive, academic, and psychological development, implementing an effective strength-based program that identifies students' abilities and uses that information to personalize their educational experience.

## OUR STUDENTS

Just as there is no single formula that characterizes the Bridges model, there is no single profile of a 2e student. In general, students come to Bridges with a diagnosis of attention-deficit disorder, attention deficit hyperactivity disorder, mild to moderate autism spectrum disorder, dyslexia, and/or anxiety, often having sensory-integration or self-regulation issues. Cognitively, their results on the Wechsler Intelligence Scale for Children (WISC) generally are above 125 ("superior" or "very superior") on the verbal and/or perceptual reasoning sections. We have observed that our students' scores for working memory and processing speed vary greatly and often are much lower than verbal and perceptual reasoning scores, which depresses their full-scale scores (also see Gilman & Peters, this volume). Scores on the Woodcock-Johnson Tests of Cognitive Abilities typically are average to above average but show wide variations across disciplines. Some students have a manifest gift in an academic or artistic area and may submit a portfolio. During the admissions process, anecdotal remarks from parents typically recount early reading and speaking or a demonstration of unique talents and gifts sometimes coupled with accounts of frustration, cognitive overload, meltdowns, and/or an estrangement from school, teachers, and peers. Students also submit recommendation letters from current teachers that, more often than not, show strong aptitudes in certain subjects and struggles in others. Similarly, comments on behaviors diverge from teacher to teacher, providing a somewhat heterogeneous account of a student's temperament and level of maturity.

It is important to note that while diagnoses, test results, and portfolios provide an initial view of a student, these factors comprise only a partial perspective of a student's profile. Once a student is admitted, additional—and often more useful—information is gathered through direct observation and experience with the students and ongoing communication among and between teachers, advisors, parents, and other professionals. This totality of diagnostic and experiential knowledge informs our instructional and programmatic approaches over time. At Bridges we do not develop our program in response to diagnostic criteria. We develop programming and use strategies in response to the child in front of us.

## OUR FOUNDATIONS AND BELIEFS

Our experience with the Bridges twice exceptional population over the past 20 years has provided us with many insights into the educational needs of the "whole" 2e child. While research on practice in 2e classrooms may be limited, a significant body of research exists in the fields of psychology, neurology, and pedagogy that provide equally important information to guide classroom practices. In particular, the positive education movement is shining a brighter light on these important issues, drawing on positive psychology's emphasis of individual strengths and personal motivation to promote learning. Chief among our insights is that cognitive and psychological needs of 2e students often are significantly different from the needs of students commonly understood as more neurotypical, necessitating specific programmatic decisions. Twice exceptional students thrive academically, socially, and emotionally when they are valued for what they can do. Their learning differences and challenges in one or more areas do not preclude their gifts and talents in other contexts. We have found that 2e students succeed when they become aware of their strengths and challenges, self-advocate, and become the principal architects of their learning. To support their development, they also need intellectual and social peers to stimulate learning and create friendships. They benefit from faculty and staff members who are highly intelligent and patient, who respect student abilities, and who perceive them as talented young people with great potential. Finally, 2e students need parents who understand and accept that their children are unique and capable of forging their own future and identities.

Strength-based and talent-focused frameworks augment the foundational beliefs for our program. We have found these frameworks to be highly effective in meeting both the academic and social goals of 2e students. Additionally, formal research in gifted and twice exceptional education informs our curriculum, instruction, and campus culture (Baum, 1988; Baum, Renzulli, & Hebert, 1995; Renzulli Enrichment Triad Model, 1976). We have learned that strength-based education invariably involves getting to know students well personally, developing comprehensive student profiles, and creating an educational culture that values time spent on strength and talent development. It is a culture that prides itself on providing opportunities, resources, and encouragement for students to wonder, explore, and produce. Lopez and Luis (2009) synopsized these points as five principles that define a strengths-based education: (a) measurement of student (and educator) characteristics must include strengths assessment, which supplements the typical focus on academic achievement and behavioral data; (b) educators personalize the learning experience by practicing individualization whereby they think about and act upon the strengths of each student; (c) networking with personal supporters of strengths development affirms the best in people and provides praise and recognition for strengths-based successes; (d) deliberate application of strengths within and outside of the classroom fosters development and integration of new behaviors associated with positive outcomes; and (e) intentional development of strengths requires that educators and students actively seek out novel experiences and previously unexplored venues for focused practice of their strengths through strategic course selection, use of campus resources, involvement in extracurricular activities, internships, mentoring relationships, or other targeted growth opportunities.

In general, Bridges defines "strength-based" as "curricular and instructional approaches that are differentiated to align with students' cognitive styles, learning preferences, and profiles of intelligences" (Baum, Schader, & Hébert, 2014, p. 214). Given the diversity of our students' profiles, we tend to talk about strengths in the broadest sense, drawing from frameworks as disparate as the WISC, Gardner's theory of multiple intelligences, the Baum-Nicols personality indicator, and discipline-specific strengths, as well as strengths that manifest in other contexts such as leadership, social situations, and/or other "soft skills." Baum et al. also provided definitions of "talent-focused" and "talent development" that add a level of clarity and specificity that is highly useful to classroom teachers. "Talent-focused" involves ongoing identification and recognition of a student's advanced abilities as well as budding interests, along with explicit options for exploring and expressing those abilities and interests within and outside the curriculum. "Talent-focused" is used as an overarching term that includes "talent development," which specifically refers to encouragement and support of identified talents and abilities that are nurtured in their own right rather than as an entry point for remediation or a reward or motivator for achievement.

Honing our thinking about our foundational beliefs and value is Baum et al.'s (2014) longitudinal case study that found five factors to be critical in the education environment of 2e students: (a) a *psychologically safe environment* is essential. Twice exceptional students often feel estranged, alienated, and ostracized in mainstream settings. Ensuring students' psychological safety means validating the uniqueness of their profiles and empathizing with the difficulties inherent in being twice exceptional. (b) A *tolerance for asynchrony* calls for a faculty mindset and school culture that not only accepts the ways in which neurological complexity manifests in academic and behavioral settings but also understands how to interpret students' words and actions. (c) *Time* needed for growth and timelines for each student is unique to the individual. This is somewhat of a self-evident, critical factor that can go unacknowledged in a program that does not embrace all implications of twice exceptional education. Baum et. al. noted that when growth can take place "without rushing or demanding that students perform at grade level, the students were able to come to terms with extreme anxieties and developmental asynchronies" (p. 320). (d) *Positive relationships* with the faculty are essential. Students come to know the faculty as advocates, confidants, and even colleagues. The dynamic more closely resembles a family than a program or institution. (e) *Consistent use of a strengths-based, talent-focused practice* both reinforces and reprises the several factors expressed previously. Our teachers tap students' strengths as passageways for learning and employ creative methods both to grow a student's talent and develop core academic skills.

These insights regarding the social-emotional and academic needs and approaches borne of extensive classroom experience and research in the fields of gifted education and psychology combine to form the theoretical and practical foundation of our dynamic program. Moreover, they provide touchstones for our decision-making, representing ideas and attitudes that inform our people, our practices, and our policies.

## THE MULTIPLE PERSPECTIVES MODEL

We make choices all the time that can dramatically impact our students and their school experiences. Sometimes those educational decisions center on whether to accelerate or compact curriculum, whether to emphasize social-emotional growth over academic goals, whether to assign less or different better-aligned course and homework, or whether to refer a student for therapeutic support. To answer these and many other questions, the faculty and staff developed a multiple perspectives decision-making model (MPM) (Figure 18.1) that synthesizes important elements critical to understanding 2e students and formulating appropriate strategies to promote growth.

We have refined the model over the years and continue to review it to assure that the variables are relevant and useful to parents, teachers, support personnel, and students. The MPM encourages collaboration among all professionals working with the students and their families to support a cohesive, consistent approach where different perspectives are considered and aligned. The model highlights the dynamic interplay between and among six critical variables: (a) gifts and talents, (b) interests, (c) family context, (d) asynchrony, (e) social and emotional profile, and (f) learning differences. When questions arise, the model reminds us to ask critical questions such as: Are we fully considering student's gifts and talents? learning differences? social-emotional profile? Do we fully understand the impact of the family context? Answers to these questions provide guidelines for conversations about strategies for promoting student growth. To maximize the effectiveness of the model, the relationship between the student-specific topics and each critical variable must be understood both independently and in connection to the whole.

The model enables us to look more deeply into important questions related to academic and social-emotional issues that may not have obvious answers. For

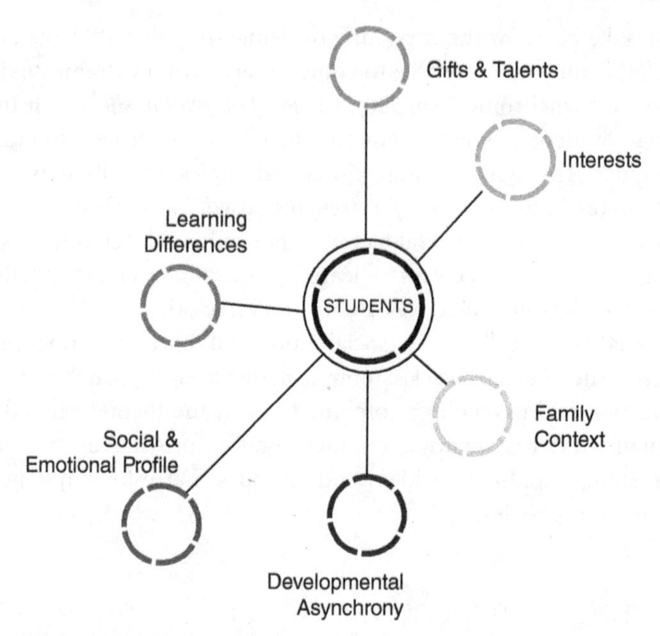


**Figure 18.1** Multiple Perspectives Model.

example, the response to a student at the onset of a diagnosed depression might typically be medication or talk therapy, both of which may seem perfectly appropriate strategies in context of the student's *social and emotional profile*. But a shift of perspective may suggest another interpretation and strategy. One of our former students, Frank, had always presented as highly anxious in previous schools—so much so that increasing production demands in multiple Advanced Placement (AP) courses became unbearable. He became depressed, dropped out of the AP courses, was sent to a therapist, and was put on medication. While these responses seemed in keeping with his then social-emotional profile, it did little to promote his academic development, self-efficacy, or positive identity. Neither his academic performance nor his depression were much improved when the presenting issues were understood *only* as social-emotional and psychological in nature. When Frank enrolled at Bridges, we considered the possibility that his difficulty with homework was due to processing speed, low intellectual demand of homework, and perfectionism. There was a misalignment between rigorous academic goals and the strategies he required to achieve them. His mathematical and scientific knowledge was extraordinary. He was able to write with great depth, complexity, and sensitivity but took a long time to produce. He could apply all knowledge and understanding in many different directions. He was a highly creative problem-solver in any subject area. Focusing on his areas of strength, we fine-tuned his academic program to provide acceleration in some courses—preparation for AP tests in calculus, biology, and chemistry—while making interest-based accommodations to alleviate the anxiety that had hampered progress in language arts courses, mostly related to the writing process. Over the course of his first year, Frank's chronic school avoidance gave way to engagement in his classes and pride in his work. When he graduated from our program he was bound for a top-tier engineering college. This example is not meant to argue that Frank's doctors were ineffective, nor that our program is solely responsible for his turnaround, only that Frank's pathway to improvement came from multiple variables and that it took the thoughtful coordination of multiple perspectives to move him forward. Frank's story is but one example.

Posing and answering important questions within the context of our MPM drives changes in curriculum, shifts in our understanding, and transformations of ourselves that can help improve student performance and mental health and maintain a high level of challenging and creative rigor so many students crave. Time for exploration of these variables in relation to each child's individual situation is critical to understanding the evolving profile of each student and deciding on the most beneficial strategies to promote growth. Parents, teachers, administrators, and outside supports must collaborate as we create and apply the reasoning behind our programming, curriculum design, and differentiation choices. All of our efforts are directed toward bringing these six spheres into productive alignment in the classroom and the socioeducational environment.

## OUR FACULTY

Faculty members must share a sense of purpose, driven by a cause and common goals. While this sense of purpose can evolve over time, faculty must bring life experiences and sensibilities that enable them to engage each day with the possibilities of student growth and their own growth as people and educators. It is important to keep in mind that schools are social environments as well as academic institutions. The best learning takes place when students have positive relations with teachers, administrators, administrative assistants, gardeners, security people, and anyone else part of the educational ecostructure. Students must exist in a space where they come together around creative problem-solving, discussing and debating ideas, sharing experiences, interests, and passions, and creating an atmosphere of excitement and forward thinking about the wonderful opportunities and challenges the future holds.

In a learning community where some students excel in all areas of human thought and activity while many others have specific niches where they shine, the known and potential gifts, interests, and talents of our students must find their counterparts in the faculty and in mentoring relationships. Teachers need to know their subject. They need to be excited about their subject, and about sharing it, and they need to model lifelong learning. We have found that our students often are interested in our teachers' own projects and pursuits outside the classroom, which, in our case, includes an abundance of activities that both bestow educative potential and model a constructive learning trajectory. Our drama teacher, for instance, runs a small theater and is often employed to handle technical theater for professional productions. One of our math teachers is a published writer who also produces films. Our science teachers are either still engaged in professional research or have done professional research in the past. Before joining our faculty, our humanities teacher was a professional journalist who was published in *Rolling Stone*. Teachers with professional experience outside of a school context, related and unrelated to the subject they teach, often appeal to students who have trouble connecting what they do in school and what they may choose as a career. Students look to them as mentors and deeply value their input and perspectives, often progressing beyond a perspective that artificially separates school learning and lifelong learning.

A framework of *strategic flexibility* is perhaps the best way to describe our approach to learning and instruction, endowing students with core academic skills and 21st-century competencies such as critical thinking, communication, and collaboration, while personalizing the learning experience to leverage strengths and accommodate differences. Our faculty's decision-making process is constantly in flux, attending not only to the uniqueness of our students' profiles but also to the nature of their struggle or aptitude on any given day. In order to accomplish these things within the twice exceptional population, our faculty must have a depth of experience and expertise that goes beyond conventional teacher training and certification. As the previous examples demonstrate, our faculty members often come to us from rich, successful careers before moving into teaching. For them, teaching is not so much job as it is a vocation that they evolved into over the course of their lives. Most, if not all, of our teachers are deeply committed to their own personal growth and engage in entrepreneurial activities outside of their teaching careers. They are not only subject-specific teachers but working artists, actors, writers, musicians, martial artists, equestrians, computer programmers, political organizers, research scientists, and environmental advocates. Some teachers are involved with nonprofit and affinity-based organizations. They live their lives taking initiative, setting goals that are personally meaningful, persevering through challenges and setbacks, and accomplishing creative and entrepreneurial objectives—and the students notice. Our students are learning in an environment where their teachers are also visibly active learners, providing a model of what it means to truly be a lifelong learner. It is not uncommon for a student who is gifted in a certain area to take on a quasi-apprenticeship related to the teachers' own projects. We also look for similar opportunities with parents and friends of the community.

In addition to an interest in their field, faculty also must take a profound and genuine interest in the interests of others. They must engage students in conversations about their gifts, interests, and talents, valuing and affirming each student's own vision. Teachers must be teachers, role models, mentors, facilitators, and coaches, and each of these roles suggests the possibility of a different relationship with children in the educational setting. Our teachers are most fulfilled when they share their knowledge with students. They encourage students to learn what they know but also must find satisfaction in being a proverbial "guide on the side," stepping back and demonstrating an appreciation for what their students want to experience and learn. While teachers have their learned preferences and/or skills as teachers, mentors, and facilitators, they must also learn to switch roles in a varied and dynamic environment. As such, our faculty's approaches, attitudes, and temperaments are critical. Just as companies look to hire people who share beliefs in the vision and mission of the company, Bridges seeks out faculty members who share our worldview and are positive thinkers who identify what is good in people and what talents they have. We make personnel decisions with a mind toward maintaining a critical mass of people with an orientation toward flexibility, creative thinking, professional experience inside and outside of their own field, and an entrepreneurial perspective. Among the chief considerations guiding our faculty's thinking is that what is best for the child should always be held above adherence to an external policy.

The model detailed here is perhaps best captured in the Bridges motto—"Imagine, Persevere, Achieve," which is more than just a tagline on our website and promotional materials. The phrase, which was crafted by our students, frames both the trajectory we envision for our students and the ideal mindset of our faculty members. It is an attitude that enables faculty members to intuit a student's potential, often before there is an empirical way to identify it. Years ago, a middle school student who was struggling with writing was astounded when her humanities teacher, a former professional journalist, told her she was a writer. A profoundly gifted visual artist, she would sometimes melt down at the assignment of even the most straightforward written reflection. Though the teacher had not seen evidence of her strengths or giftedness in writing, he had identified in her questions and verbal contributions to discussions not only a fascination with language but the inexhaustible desire to speak and hear others speak with specificity and lucidity—in short, a writer's disposition. After work with this teacher and subsequent writing teachers, by her senior year she learned to attend to her written compositions with the same seriousness and confidence that she applied to her visual works. Our faculty, in the spirit of this middle school teacher, often imagines a world based on what he had observed, creating an environment where this student could grapple with challenges and persevere, and setting her prudently on the path to achievement. Had he and the rest of the faculty not done this, this talent for writing may not have manifested at all.

Our faculty's temperament is one of patience and optimism as they invest in the process, no matter how long and winding it may seem. All goals are valuable goals, as long as they are based on students' developmental needs and set them up for success. Both teachers and students must be comfortable with setbacks, casting so-called failures as lessons to be acknowledged and moved beyond. Most importantly, whereas our students may have encountered teachers in other environments who either did not understand them or sought to stifle their creativity and eccentricities, our teachers, some twice exceptional themselves, celebrate our students' differences, having deep compassion for the challenges they face and an awareness of their extraordinary potential. Ultimately teachers must work in an environment where they feel empowered to design and implement creative and customized instructional strategies, learning from experiences, successes, and mistakes without fear of failure. The culture of our school gives teachers implicit permission to enlist students as partners in their own learning, which requires a curriculum that is organic, experiential, and in flux. This framework shares much in common with Dweck's (2006) growth mindset, in which belief in one's own improvement and development drive learning and personal progress. Our program therefore is designed to maximize encouragement, opportunity, and resources for teachers and students to explore the world of thought and action in a variety of ways.

## OUR PROGRAM

The Bridges program may resemble many other independent schools in basic structure, in the focus on core required subjects, electives, after-school activities, and in skill-building in critical thinking, communication, and collaboration. However, the diverse learning profiles of our students require a higher level of differentiation in scheduling, program, and curriculum than typically found in most schools. We seek to develop self-efficacy and successful intelligence through engagement in personally relevant, meaningful work. The program is designed to be lived and enjoyed in the moment with an eye to higher education and a world of opportunities for future careers, cultivating students' strengths and talents to build proficiency and expertise. The common programmatic thread uniting our elementary (Phoenix), middle school, and high school programs is the coexistence of high cognitive rigor, intellectual-creative explorations, and substantial student support. At the most basic level, our program is comprised of three types of courses: core, elective, and talent focused. These three course types all involve student input and are all dual-differentiated to the extent possible to accommodate both strengths and challenges. The fundamental differences among course types might best be described by answering the question, "Who is the primary curriculum designer?"

## CORE

The differentiated core program courses are built within a liberal arts curriculum, which is required by the school and governing-accrediting bodies. This broad liberal arts exposure is essential to a high-quality education. Deep exposure to the riches of human cultures and civilization is becoming more challenging, as the sum of knowledge increases exponentially over time and as students and the economy focus toward more narrow areas of skills and talents in the workforce. In a content-rich world, it is important to provide students with the broadest possible liberal arts experience while fostering their ability to explore, understand, analyze, and apply new information throughout their lives. Teachers inevitably must leave out some cherished literature, topics, and historical periods in designing curriculum to fit a finite time frame. However, the frameworks of big ideas, essential questions, and enduring understandings make it possible to explore the riches of human experience in meaningful ways, providing a strong fund of multidisciplinary, interdisciplinary, and transdisciplinary knowledge necessary for a fullest appreciation of historical figures, movements, events, and ideas of many kinds.

## ELECTIVES AND ENRICHMENT

Opportunities for exciting exploration outside the core arise in electives, enrichment clusters, and after-school specialty programs like robotics, music, and drama, as well as during intersessions when students take a break from their regular classes for in-depth work in a chosen area. Elective and enrichment-course curricula are created by teachers based on expressed interests and profiles of students and their own expertise. Students choose electives and then are given opportunities to take the coursework in various directions. Gentry and Reis (2007) have shown the value of enrichment activities to promote authentic learning based on students' interests and real-world inquiry. Enrichment clusters are opportunities for students to "increase their knowledge base and expand their creative and critical thinking skills, cooperative group work skills, and task commitment by applying their time and energy to self-selected problems or areas of study" (p. 40). Embracing this philosophy, our electives, enrichment clusters, and student-driven learning program invite students to self-select and pursue a course of study under the guidance of experts in the field and learning coaches. In the high school, students can choose from electives such as art, drama, film, debate, creative writing, computer programming, and many others. These courses are not regarded as "extra" or "add-on" courses but as vital learning experiences that complement the high school program as a whole. Electives and enrichment clusters provide a setting in which students' interests drive content mastery, skill-building, and creative production. Sometimes an elective is an area of talent as well as interest and can guide college and career decisions. Students who demonstrate particular talent in an area can pursue a customized talent development plan with a faculty mentor. Having the opportunity to explore numerous topics and define oneself by one's strengths is a core Bridges value.

In addition to this emphasis, inspiring creativity is important. We encourage our students to take on projects and tasks that require outside the box, imaginative thinking and provide opportunities for self-expression. Creativity is a process and not an end. We want students to experiment with a variety of processes, see what they can develop, and create artifacts that have a tangible impact, even if that significance is personal in nature. We hope to instill attitudes and habits that drive students to ask questions about how to improve something, take something apart, or invent something new. We work to maintain an environment where necessary space, materials, and encouragement enable our students to take chances, make mistakes, and relish in their successes. Many of our students, whether naturally convergent or divergent thinkers, need simply to have permission to explore, an environment that supports them, and a teacher who knows when to get out of the way.

In the middle school, interest- and strength-based courses are offered through our enrichment cluster program. These semester classes meet twice per week and are created through faculty and student collaboration. Students are given the opportunity to apply acquired communication and creative skills in an environment where they contribute to the curriculum and manage the pace of the course. Course titles include the Science of Video Games, Science Fiction Film and Writing, Cooking and Baking, and Filmmaking. The Phoenix and middle school programs also undertake a group intersession project, during which the whole division splits into groupings to complete a common project. For example, based on students' profiles and discussions among teachers, our Grade 5- to 6-age students chose to organize themselves into field-based groups, such as architects, historians, scientists, and artists. The designer built the pyramid, the artists decorated it with artifacts, the scientists embalmed everything they could get their hands on, and the historian wrote the messages on interior walls.

Enrichment in the high school also includes a schoolwide symposia program, through which seminars, documentaries, guest speakers, artists, musicians, and TedxKids presentations take place regularly, both on and off campus. They cover relevant contemporary themes, life-skill development and careers, and topics related to students' interest and research. These symposia aim to expose students to new interest areas, further knowledge of a particular domain, build interdisciplinary awareness, model what scholars and career professionals think about and do, and inspire intellectual curiosity. In addition, students in the Badges program (discussed later) can use the symposium forum to give talks about their in-progress project work or summative presentations.

## TALENT DEVELOPMENT

Both core courses and electives can and do contribute to talent development, but our talent-focused courses tend to be student-generated and student-driven and situated primarily in the high school. The Grades 4 through 8 enrichment clusters, electives, and division projects help instill wonder, joy, and engagement. They help prepare students for the in-depth exposure they need to pursue intensive study in high school. In talent-development courses, faculty tend to operate more as mentors and facilitators of learning rather than "teachers." Institutionally, there are no hard lines between curricular, cocurricular, and extracurricular. Although core courses may be required, that does not make them necessarily more important. Robotics in the life of a budding engineer, for instance, occupies a more important and significant place in the overall, long-term learning path for that particular student versus a core course. Therefore, these highly focused courses emerge primarily for students with emergent or manifest talents: young engineers have an opportunity to participate in robotics, animators create films, entrepreneurs create business plans and small businesses, musician form bands and perform at public venues—and the list goes on.

The most nuanced and compelling talent-development opportunities occur in the Bridges Academy Student Driven Learning Program, or Badges. The Badges program represents a major shift away from traditional instruction toward our most progressive ideals. The structure of our master schedule, which engages 10th-, 11th-, and 12th-graders in two core subjects at a time, affords regular time in the afternoon for students to pursue highly personalized learning. Twice exceptional students often have strong interests and passions that make them well-suited for advanced work. The Badge program invites students to dive deeply into a chosen subject area, developing a substantial fund of knowledge and valuable real-world skills that could provide pathways to continued work in higher education and future careers. Under close guidance from faculty coaches and mentors, students design their own courses of study, maturing into self-driven learners as they absorb complex and expansive information, identify and solve problems, and poise themselves to make original contributions to their fields of interest. The scope of all Badges work must involve explicit interdisciplinary awareness, resulting in a thorough, expert-level coverage of the topic and/or area of exploration. Students who demonstrate disciplinary expertise through concentrated work in a field-related cluster of badges (and additional work required by the professional mentors) may earn formal certification as a "young expert" as graduating seniors.

The Badges/Young Expert program is one of Bridges Academy's ongoing projects to dismantle the artificial walls between so-called core academics and enrichment. Already many of our students take their Badges work with them beyond the school day, which offers exciting implications about the potential for a fluidity among in-school and outside-of-school learning experiences. Fully realized, our Badges program aims to develop core skills and competencies within the context of students' personalized work. Given the constraints of the college admission process, we will need to represent this phenomenon more traditionally for external communication, but it is clear that we are on the cusp bringing of secondary school education closer to the reality of the outside world, where learning does not occur within discipline-specific silos but as a part of a broader ecosphere of learning.

## APPROACHES

While it is the rigor, sophistication, and far-reaching conceptual scope of our academic program that keeps students intellectually engaged, differentiation and dual differentiation are vital tools to facilitate students' participation in learning activities and their ability to produce meaningful and independent work. This approach in our curriculum and instruction owes a great deal to scholars such as Washburne (1953), Tomlinson (2001), and Reis, Neu, and McGuire (1995), among many others. It is employing dual differentiation as a strategy that enables us to account for our students' developmental asynchrony (Baum, Cooper, &

Neu, 2001). While traditional grade-level norms can be helpful for designing and implementing curricula, they often fail in providing useful strategies for the students who operate considerably above or below the norm. As mentioned, Bridges students are typically asynchronous in their development, meaning that in one social, academic, intellectual, or creative area they may be developing ahead of their age peers, and in other areas they are developing more slowly, at their own natural rate. Therefore, students need an approach to curricula that simultaneously takes into account students' advanced cognitive abilities, learning challenges, and motivators. In order to inform this approach, student profile information is gathered by standard evaluations, observation, one-on-one interaction, and the "getting to know you" suite of instruments (Schader & Baum, 2016). This information is critical for planning curriculum and differentiated learning activities.

For instance, a social science teacher may leverage a student's visual-spatial strengths as demonstrated in the Picture Concepts subtest of the WISC to trace historical trends for an medieval history class via storyboards rather than presentations or essays. Personality and social-emotional strengths provide equally as fruitful passageways to using strengths in the curriculum. Or, in the context of Gardner's multiple intelligences, a mathematics teacher may tap the musical strengths of a student who is otherwise struggling with the numeric intervals, using musical theory as a framework for exploring arithmetic concepts. A Japanese teacher working with a student who struggles with foreign language but excels in art may eschew traditional quizzes and exams in favor of an approach that invites the student craft an original textbook, pages overflowing with creative representations of grammar and vocabulary. In this way and others, addressing areas of weakness or poor performance does not preclude supporting gifts and talents. Additionally, it often the case that after students has worked in a challenging area in a preferred symbol system, like art for the Japanese language student, they often transfer this experience, becoming more accomplished in the traditional skills of a discipline. Differentiation strategies like this target content, process, and product, shaping how the student goes about making connections between key concepts as well as how the final assignment will be constructed and assessed.

## STRUCTURES

Schedules and routines impact community development and the rhythms of the school day and are important to the life of a vibrant and effective school. Therefore, our schedules vary from division to division—and within each division—to support students' abilities to make transitions and manage independent work on in-class assignments and projects. Throughout the day we provide a balanced distribution of "preferred" and "nonpreferred" activities and tasks, varying the overall number of courses and course-related work according to students' executive-function abilities, after-school activities, and function or dysfunction of their family life.

In the high school program, we implement the liberal arts core through a modified block schedule, influenced by a Copernican framework. Students take two to three subjects per rotation in humanities, math, science, foreign language, and physical education. Focusing on two or three classes at a time enables students to delve deeply into the content and skills of the discipline and develop the habits and routines of a successful student. Each discipline has a four-year scope and sequence that covers required high school content and skills and emphasizes the interdisciplinary nature of all knowledge, a theme also present in the middle school. The Copernican framework also opens up opportunities for integrated and interdisciplinary learning, as well as the student-driven learning program discussed later.

In addition to their clinical diagnoses, academic levels, personalities, and temperaments, learning styles play a large part in positive and effective group dynamics. Both Phoenix (Grades 4–6) and middle school (Grades 7–8) utilize mixed-age groupings to deemphasize fixed grade-level arrangements, instead organizing students in primary academic cohorts. These groupings are fluid and can change in advisory, physical education, drama, art, and technology. Some students do need "breaks" from each other during the day, and flexible cohorts can provide this. In Phoenix, opportunities exist for students to be in self-contained classrooms, two-transition classrooms, or a rotating schedule where they transition from teacher to teacher throughout the day. Some courses are rotated to occur in the schedule at different times of the day in order to adjust for variation in students' arousal and ability to engage. Decisions about these placements are formed according to profile information, observation, and interactions with students, with adjustments made for enrichment opportunities.

## A SUPPORTIVE COMMUNITY

We often are asked who is responsible for the development of social skills and understandings and the ongoing advisement of academic and social support. When we answer that question with "Everyone," it can cause some confusion. Many are familiar with social-emotional support structures within silos among specialists, each contributing only in their own specific way with no organized synthesis of efforts. But it takes a coordinated community in context, often with the support of outside specialists, to teach, model, advise, and support our students' development. Implementing continual, low-keyed, nonjudgmental guidance over time best supports our students' social-emotional development. While we are not a therapeutic environment, we have specialists—a clinical psychologist, three counselors, and an educational therapist—on our faculty. They work collectively with parents, teachers, and faculty to create our "wrap-around" educational programs and services. All teachers are expected to have the skills to provide the appropriate academic or social support and advisement commensurate with the issue at hand, and all members of the community are expected to anticipate and respond to students' needs.

When students enroll at Bridges, they meet with our educational therapist to create an educational plan that anchors ongoing conversation about students' needs and growth and enables the team—comprised of faculty and administrators, parents, educational therapists, psychologists, and other professionals—to develop, implement, assess, and augment strategies as necessary. Information and observations gleaned day to day by the classroom teacher also provide a critical, if not the foremost, element of student support. Our small class sizes provide a setting for close work among teachers and students. Standard response-to-interventions sometimes do not meet the unique challenges that 2e students pose. Our experiences have shown that a faculty-led team firing on all cylinders recognizes issues and obstacles to growth; develops customized, creative, and sophisticated strategies in response; and can adapt its strategies as circumstances inevitably change and the outcomes of strategies suggest the need for others.

A particularly important member of a student's support team is the advisor, who serves as a case manager to help students keep on top of their academic work while developing the habits and routines of a successful student. In the high school, the advisor, with whom students meet three or four times per week in groups of six, helps promote growth in prioritizing, organizing, and planning daily assignments and more involved summative products such as projects or papers. In addition, the advisor can be a guide to help students self-advocate, navigate complex social interactions, or pursue increased opportunities to cultivate strengths, interests, or gifts. Our advisory programs offer a rich curricula in addition to opportunities for support. Topics such as teamwork, community building, hygiene, nutrition, and public speaking are infused into the curriculum, and there also is focus on development of social and emotional intelligence and executive functioning. Students and advisors develop rich, collaborative relationships that support the students and families throughout their experiences in the Bridges program.

## POLICY

The only thing I'm dogmatic about is flexibility.

—Carl A. Sabatino

At Bridges, flexible policies must guide our practice to ensure that our students have the best possible learning experience appropriate to their age, grade, and developmental stage, particularly as they complete their high school requirements and prepare for opportunities in the future. As such, administrators serve both as leaders and support, modeling strategies and responses that advance the school's vision while supporting teacher independence and being responsive to the uniqueness of each student's dynamic emerging profile and trajectory. There is a balance between top-down directives, requirements, and initiatives and a teacher's need to be autonomous and take initiative in their classroom in the face of ever-changing reality. Overall, policy must reflect a willingness to think in terms of responses that are conducive to the best and authentic development for our students. For instance, some schools have an academic disciplinary action policy to suspend students from drama or sports when grades fall below a certain threshold—which, theoretically, uses negative consequences to motivate students to prioritize their core subjects. Bridges would not *necessarily* exclude a student from an "extracurricular" as a result of a low grade in a core class, especially if the extracurricular is in the area of an emergent or manifest gift or talent, where social, psychological, and/or creative development goals are being well met. There are indeed many other methods for improving on weaker performance areas.

Like all schools, there are academic scopes, sequences, and requirements at all levels to successfully move through the system and earn college requirements. But Bridges teachers need flexible ways of helping students achieve them. With encouragement from the administration, teachers can determine time frames for students' projects and homework that are flexible when needed, and assessment—both formative and summative—that is differentiated to allow for the best opportunity to demonstrate students' learning and readiness for future work. This can require flexibility about understandings of what it means to be educated and what sorts of experiences comprise a meaningful education for the individual. What is best for the individual student can never be superseded by administrative convenience, general school policy, or immoveable guidelines for student performance.

This expectation of flexibility and creative problem solving also carries over into behavior/disciplinary decisions. With 2e students, whose diagnoses are complex, consequences for nonacceptable behaviors must be understood as natural and authentic in order to affect changing of the behaviors. Responses are tailored to the situation and the child and always involve both consequences and counseling. While some students will respond well to parent involvement and reflection, others require meeting with their therapist, in-school suspension, or the loss of a privilege, such as computer time, over the weekend. However, we have found that many behaviors are environmentally induced as opposed to exclusively resulting from the perceived shortcomings of the individual student. When analysis of behaviors takes into consideration data available in all variables in the multiple perspectives model, better decisions are made and we see more engagement and fewer behavioral issues. Students can begin to see themselves as partners in understanding and improving behaviors that they themselves want to change. A newer student called in to talk about a behavioral issue will often express disbelief that he is not "in trouble" but rather invited to a conversation to share his feelings about a pattern or course of events. Certainly there is a place for consequences and concrete responses, but not without first appraising the students' perception and understanding of an event or interaction in order to come to a shared conclusion about went wrong and how to avoid such situations in the future. As discussed, this holistic approach also undergirds our academic policies, where decisions about classes and coursework balance the strengths and needs of our students with the realities of external requirements.

Our program is mindful of our role in preparing students for the college years, equating that trajectory beyond the traditional four-year experience to the ages of 18 to 25, when considerable brain development occurs. Consequently, policies surrounding the college counseling process aim to find the "best fit," which may mean going to a top-tier four-year college upon graduation, a small private school, or a community college or pursuing employment or a gap year. A holistic, long-term perspective combined with flexible policies enable us to promote students strengths and develop their talents, which resides at the core of our school's mission. This is a different mindset that holds what is good for the student as paramount above bureaucracy and external pressures. We see ourselves as neo-progressive pragmatists, filling the proverbial teacher toolbox with multiple—and sometimes conflicting—educational philosophies, policies, and practices. By doing so we are in a position to apply the best thinking and strategies at the right time to the individual student at hand.

## CONCLUSION

In his book, *Neurotribes: The Legacy of Autism and the Future of Neurodiversity*, Steve Silberman (2015) writes about the challenges of persons who are on the autism spectrum or are neurodivergent in other ways. He observes that "at home with other members of their tribe, in an environment designed for their comfort, they [do not] feel disabled; they just felt different from their neighbors" (p. 430). Such a sentiment poignantly encapsulates our students' assimilation as they begin to identify with their tribe, becoming comfortable with themselves and forming friendships like they have never had before. The culture of our tribe is at once earnest about its identity and light-heartedly aware of its stature as outside the norm. One of our students once remarked that "You know you are at Bridges when a student walks through the hall with riding boots, a cane, and a top hat and no one bats an eye." Humorous though it may be, this comment is a reflection of our students' tribal identity that is nonjudgmental, reassuring, and sympathetic and provides fertile territory for growth and self-expression. It is fitting that we should end this chapter with a reference to our community and to belonging. The challenges our students face in schools and in the culture at large are daunting. It is not easy getting up in the morning motivated to enter an environment that is full of uncertainty and challenge; not sure if you really are as smart as people tell you; not sure if you will or can be successful; and concerned about grades, friendships, and future. But, when respect replaces shame, hope replaces fear, and acceptance replaces rejection, children can tackle most anything.

## AFTERWORD: IN THEIR OWN WORDS

> Sometimes it is the people no one imagines anything of who do the things no one can imagine.
>
> —Joan Clarke, *Mathematician*

Student speakers at graduations often speak fondly of Bridges' familial inclusiveness and the vitality of its culture, based on shared perspectives, experience, and the valuing of strengths and talents—in short, the ideals discussed throughout this chapter. The following are two excerpts from students in their own words, reflecting on their time in our program.

## Will Marcil, Class of 2015

When I came to Bridges in 2012, I was in a, shall we say, interesting part of my life. Certain events had occurred that had left me doubting whether or not my eccentricity was a good thing, or if it was a good idea to repress my thoughts and ideas in order to properly integrate into the society of man. However, that all changed when, though the exact details are lost to history, I observed an event that piqued my interest as being odd. As I cannot remember exactly what it was, let us say that it was someone doing an impression of a dead goldfish. I turned to my classmates and asked, "Am I the only one who finds this weird?" to which I got the response that pretty much summed up all my time here: "It's Bridges."

My story, while the (forgotten) specifics are all my own, the overarching theme in it is not. I am certain that all of us before you have had one moment or another when we had doubts that our own particular eccentricities were beneficial in any way . . . most were brought forth and accepted thanks to one part or another of the Bridges establishment. Be it a passion for art, or a passion for numbers, a passion for theater, or a passion just to leave well enough alone, Bridges Academy has not only allowed our eccentricities to be exposed but actively challenged us to use those eccentricities, those sparks of madness to help us to find our ways into our own. To quote the great Robin Williams, "You only have one spark of madness, and you must not lose it." Bridges not only helps you hold onto that spark of madness but helps you turn it into a passionate fire that drives you to prove that the line between madness and greatness is not as thick as we would think it to be. So here is a salute to the madness that Bridges Academy has set loose, not only in me, and those who are before you, but to all who pass through those doors, all who think that their own loose screws are detriments. May you keep proving them wrong long into the future, and never, ever, lose part of you that can only really be explained by "It's Bridges." That is explanation enough for what impact you have on all of us.

## Matthew Rosen, Class of 2016

I must share just how amazing this journey has been. When I first came to Bridges, I was a shy 12-year-old with hardly a friend to call my own. I got upset at the slightest provocation, skulked off to be by myself whenever I could, and was afraid of the minutest changes in routine. While I wouldn't go as far as to say I'm the opposite now to what I was then, I still can say without a doubt that I am a far *better* person, and much of that change can only be attributed to the wonderful work the people here at Bridges Academy have done for me and with me. While I always had a passion for literature, history, and the sciences, with acting joining them not that much later, many people are surprised to hear—as a few of you will probably be—that for a long time, I *hated* writing, to the point that the very word "essay" would send me into rage and panic. Eventually, though, the shift came, and it wouldn't have been possible without the trust my teachers showed me, always seeking to ignite the passion that they must have seen in me, always pushing me to never give up. Their commitment paid off in a most spectacular manner, and now I'm setting off to pursue the fruit of dreams from the seed they planted.

It's not just the faculty and staff at Bridges to whom I owe my thanks. I owe a deep gratitude to the entire community. I don't think I could call a single person dispensable or their role superfluous. Within the community, the part my fellow students played is just as important as that of the parents, staff, and faculty of the community. And not just the students by my side right now (although to ignore them would be a great disservice too): also the students who have walked this stage in years prior, and those whose time has not yet come, and I know will certainly rise to the occasion. All of them have been at my side, in weather fair and foul, whether allies or rivals, either friends or temporary enemies. Whether I worked in perfect sync or in total opposition to them, they all played a part in my story, as have I in theirs.

## REFERENCES


Baum, S. (1988). An enrichment program for gifted learning disabled students. *Gifted Child Quarterly, 32*(1), 226–230.

Baum, S. M., Renzulli, J. S., & Hébert, T. P. (1995). Reversing underachievement: Creative productivity as a systematic intervention. *Gifted Child Quarterly, 39*(4), 224–235.

Baum, S. M., Cooper, C. R., & Neu, T. W. (2001). Dual differentiation: An approach for meeting the curricular needs of gifted students with learning disabilities. *Psychology in the Schools, 38*(5), 477–490.

Baum, S., Schader, R., & Hébert, T. (2014). Through a different lens: Reflecting on a strengths-based, talent focused approach for twice-exceptional learners. *Gifted Child Quarterly, 58*(4), 311–327.

Dweck, C. (2006). *Mindset: The new psychology of success*. New York, NY: Random House.

Lopez, S. J., & Louis, M. C. (2009). The principles of strengths-based education. *Journal of College and Character, 10*(4).

Reis, S. M., Neu, T. W., & McGuire, J. (1995). *Talent in two places: Case studies of high-ability students with learning disabilities who have achieved* (Research Monograph No. 95114). Storrs: The University of Connecticut.

Renzulli, J. S. (1976). The enrichment triad model: A guide for developing defensible programs for the gifted and talented. *Gifted Child Quarterly, 20*(3), 303–306.

Renzulli, J. S., Gentry, M., & Reis, S. M. (2007). Enrichment clusters for developing creativity and high-end learning. *Gifted and Talented International, 22*(1), 39–46.

Silberman, S. (2015). *Neurotribes: The legacy of autism and the future of neurodiversity.* New York, NY: Penguin.

Tomlinson, Carol A. (2001). *How to differentiate instruction in mixed-ability classrooms.* Alexandria, VA: Association for Supervision and Curriculum Development.

Washburne, C. W. (1953). Adjusting the Program to the Child. *Educational leadership*, *11*(3), 139–140.

19

# Integration and Dynamic Adaptation in the Formation of a Novel 2e School Model

KIMBERLY BUSI AND KRISTIN BERMAN ■

With the recent explosion in the awareness of the unique niche of students now labeled "twice exceptional" (2e) early research on gifted and twice exceptional educational practices and clinical supports have hit the spotlight, as if for the first time. June Maker first acknowledged the concept in the mid-1970s (Maker, 1977) dubbing it "gifted and handicapped" evolving to twice exceptional within a decade thereafter. Even though some research has been done since, it is not clear to what extent evidenced-based practices are maintained during the implementation process across and within settings and to what extent this variability affects educational and health outcomes for twice exceptional children.

The Quad Preparatory School in New York City is a novel 2e educational model that uses a purposeful system of integration and dynamic adaptation of evidence-based practices (EBPs) from many disciplines. Our meaning of integration lies in the seamless synthesis of practices that provide both educational excellence and appropriate psychosocial support through the implementation of EBPs. These EBPs are in a state of constant "dynamic adaptation" as the individual child adjusts to a personalized system, becomes more trusting, is open to learning, begins to manifest his or her gifts, and internalizes coping mechanisms for his or her challenges. This is an ongoing process for each child, which requires systematic and continual collaboration on the part of the professionals from a variety of disciplines.

This chapter discusses the rationale behind the choices of the specific, novel components of The Quad Preparatory School model, then outlines The Quad Preparatory School's structure for integration and dynamic adaption of EBPs where continuous feedback allows for simultaneous implementation and the creation of new practices in a truly integrated fashion.

Twice exceptional students are, in a word, complicated. They have been defined as fitting into one of three categories: the disability is recognized but the gift is hidden; the gift is recognized, but the disability is hidden; or the gift and disability negate each other (Baum & Owen, 2004; Reis, Baum, & Burke, 2014). However, we see an even more intricate complexity of traits including not only comorbidity but multimorbidity of diagnoses (i.e., attention deficit hyperactivity disorder, obsessive-compulsive disorder, and oppositional defiant disorder) as well as secondary traits such as anxiety and depression. We offer three scenarios (of composite children) who can fit the typical definition but who demonstrate the complications of a multitude of factors that, in reality, confound the formula.

1. By age five, D was having severe emotional dysregulation with tantrums triggered by everyday situations. Her perceptions of reality were colored by a hypersensitivity to the environment in terms of sounds, light, temperature, and movement around her; these physical discomforts overwhelmed her. Her verbal ability was extraordinary, as was her memory, yet she showed great difficulty in comprehending concepts in reading and especially in mathematics. Due to her behavior, she was not able to function in a regular kindergarten class so was taken to a private school for special education. Due to her sophisticated language ability, adults would converse with her as if she were an adult about issues that she found frightening. For example, she would notice homelessness and ask questions that were addressed in too many details for her emotional maturity, causing nightmares and high anxiety. The tantrums continued, making social interaction and learning impossible. When D was able to attend school, she made up elaborate and detailed fantasy stories incorporating factual information she had absorbed. This fantasy world became a respite, and teachers began to worry that she was confusing reality and fantasy, so she was forbidden to use fantasy in any form of reading or writing. She became obstinate and defiant as her deficits became more and more the focus of her school day. Her anxiety grew. She was "counseled out" of the private special education setting for behavioral disorder.
2. Although F had some developmental delays, including late expressive language, motor planning delays, sensory sensitivities, and social anxieties, he was always able to thrive in non-special education settings and entered kindergarten in a rigorous, highly structured school for the gifted. During his first three years there, he thrived. His issues did not disappear but were not a detriment in the environment: he made friends in a class of 20, had a best friend, and academically soared under a very structured and traditional educational setting with clear, high expectations that fit his concrete, sequential learning style. After much success, his well-being began to unravel at the end of third

grade when his best friends moved away, and at the same time the social demands began to intensify at school. He became more aware that he was perceived as "gifted" yet began to find concentration and motivation more difficult. His self-esteem began to plummet and his anxiety began to mount as he became his own worst critic. He began to feel different from his peers and more socially isolated. Although well-meaning and eager to keep him, the school was not able to support his social cognitive needs. His emotional regulation began to worsen, and, with a neuropsychological evaluation, a hidden learning disability was discovered. The decision was made to move him into a supportive (i.e., special education) setting, which promised to simultaneously meet his advanced cognitive abilities. However, now only the previously hidden disability could be addressed, exacerbating his diminishing sense of security in his strengths.

3. L appeared to have a normal early childhood, reaching all developmental milestones within normal ranges. As he grew, he had a fascination with words and built an impressive vocabulary, asking questions about the meanings of words and then using those words. Abstract ideas and emotional sensitivity appeared at a young age and was acknowledged as part of his charming personality. At kindergarten, routine school testing showed unremarkable scores other than in vocabulary development that ranked at the 98th percentile. This discrepancy was not of note or concern in a kindergarten-aged child. L began to lag in reading skills, and by first grade he needed remedial support that lasted several years even when reading improved and special services were no longer needed. Writing continued to be difficult but was attributed to the slow development of a boy. L was a strong participant in oral discussions and seemed to comprehend ideas very quickly, but the gap between his excellent class participation and mediocre written work widened. Eventually his high levels of energy, loud voice, and impulsivity in actions led to problems with his teachers. He was put on medication without a diagnosis, which did not help, and continued his schooling as an average student with moderate "behavior" problems. He did become a stellar musician but was frustrated at the lack of acknowledgment of his intellectual abilities. Depression hit in high school. Continually average test scores prevented L's eligibility for any reading and writing services and from him being placed in any advanced or gifted classes to serve his advanced intellect.

In just these three children, one sees a myriad of gifts, challenges, and learning issues that reflect the wide heterogeneity of the 2e population. We also see the emotional toll that lack of appropriate environments can engender (Craske & Barlow, 2006; Greene, 2014; Kendall & Hedtke, 2006; Pincus, Ehrenreich, & Mattis, 2008). The children who are enrolled in The Quad Preparatory School come from a wide variety of prior school settings—public schools (general education, Integrated

Co-Teaching classes, and gifted and talented programs), independent schools, home schooling, and special education schools. Other than meeting the definition of 2e, the only thing The Quad Prep students have in common upon entering our school is that their prior educational settings—no matter the type, no matter the level of challenge, no matter the level of giftedness or disability—failed them.

This happened despite a solid base of research and EBPs in twice exceptionality specifically and more broadly in gifted education, special education, child and adolescent psychiatry, psychology, developmental pediatrics, speech and language pathology, child neurology, and occupational therapy. This also happened across school settings—even those with a plethora of available resources. In other words, despite knowledge, access, effort, and resources, children were getting worse (National Education Association, 2006). A simple combination of practices and/or curriculum is not enough to serve the complex needs of these children. Rather, a synthesis of approaches from all of these disciplines must be melded into a model that provides a structure that delivers the benefits in a responsively flexible manner to suit the wide variability of individual traits and the simultaneous rapid/lagging trajectory of their developmental journey. The National Association for Gifted Children first recognized 2e children in 1998 when they articulated a foundation of what a program for these children would need:

> A comprehensive program will include: provisions for the identification and the development of talent; a learning environment that values diversity and individual talents in all domains; educational support that develops compensatory strategies including the appropriate use of technology; and school-based counseling to enhance students' ability to cope with their mix of talents and disabilities. Without appropriate identification and services, the gifts of these students may never be developed. (Position Paper, *Students with concomitant gifts and learning disabilities,* National Association for Gifted Children, 1998)

## DEFINING THE QUAD PREPARATORY MODEL

In the investigation that led to the establishment of The Quad Preparatory School, we identified several key areas that contributed to the troublesome outcomes we were witnessing. First, given the wide heterogeneity of extreme gifts and challenges in any age-matched cohort, successful dual differentiation of curriculum and instruction in a classroom-based model is difficult to achieve, no matter how large or small the group. Second, forced large group instruction as the predominant delivery method seemed to exacerbate difficulties rather than build on strengths. Moreover, evidence-based clinical and educational practices were not fully integrated or adapted in systematic ways to allow for effective results with the children in real time and space. The primary way that The Quad Preparatory model counters these problems is by implementing a one-on-one manner of teaching the 2e student, not as a means of remediation but as the most efficient and effective way to meet the student where they are, identify gaps and address them, compact the curriculum to bypass already mastered material, minimize distractions, address individual interests and pursue them, and address social and emotional issues as they arise in real time. Each teacher can also exercise the dynamic adaptation necessary to address the multifaceted and rapid changes that can take place in the child in the right setting.

Table 19.1 shows the constructs that became key to developing The Quad Preparatory School Model, and the sources based on EBPs that we drew from.

*Table 19.1.* Implementation of TQPS Model

| **Constructs Key to TQPS Model** | **EBPs Implemented and Adapted** |
|---|---|
| Foundational skills of self-regulation, executive functioning, independence, coordination | Zones of Regulation (Kuypers, 2011)<br>Tools of the Mind (Leong & Bodrova, 2007)<br>Montessori methods and materials (Montessori, 2010) |
| Strength- and interest-based instruction, talent development, authentic projects | Project-based learning (Blumenfeld et al., 1991; Stanley, 2011; Strobel & van Barneveld, 2009; Thomas, 2000)<br>Enrichment clusters (Renzulli, Gentry, & Reis, 2005)<br>Schoolwide Enrichment Model (Renzulli & Reis, 2005) |
| Addressing strengths and weaknesses | Dual differentiation (Baum, Cooper, & Neu, 2001; Pereles, Omdal, & Baldwin, 2009)<br>Alternate entry points, multiple methods of assessment (Baum, Slatin, & Viens, 2005) |
| Social, emotional, and psychological support | Cognitive behavioral therapies (Albano & DiBartolo 2007; Craske & Barlow, 2006; Kendall & Hedtke 2006; Pincus, Ehrenreich, & Mattis, 2008; Piacentini & Roblek, 2007)<br>Mentalization and mindfulness-based approaches (Allen & Fonagy, 2006)<br>Positive behavioral interventions (Bradshaw, Pas, Goldweber, Rosenberg, & Leaf, 2012)<br>Resiliency building (Duckworth, 2016)<br>Growth mindset versus fixed mindset (Dweck, 2007)<br>Teacher Child Intervention Therapy (Fernandez, Adelstein, Miller, & Gudiño, 2009)<br>Positive psychology (Gaus, 2011; Seligman & Csikszentimihalyi, 2000; Seligman, Steen, Park, & Peterson, 2005)<br>Social thinking (Hendrix, Palmer, Tarshis, & Winner, 2016; Winner, 2002)<br>Cognitive behavioral therapy (Piacentini, Langley, & Roblek, 2007) |

*Table 19.1.* CONTINUED

| Constructs Key to TQPS Model | EBPs Implemented and Adapted |
|---|---|
| Mind-body connection | Sensory integration therapy and occupational therapy (Ben-Sasson, Carter, & Briggs-Gowan, 2010; Miller & Collins, 2013) |
| | Sensory stimulation in autism (Miller & Collins, 2013) |
| | Sensory overresponsivity (Ben-Sasson, Carter, & Briggs-Gowan, 2010). |
| Creativity | Nurturing creative talent (Crammond, 2006) |
| | Synectics, developing strategies for creative thinking (Davis, 2004) |
| | Passion and imagination (Kaufman & Gregoire, 2016) |
| Collaboration and problem-solving | Collaborative and proactive solutions (Dedousis-Wallace et al., 2016; Greene, 2005, 2016; Greene et al., 2004; Greene & Ablon, 2005; Pollastri, Epstein, Heath, & Ablon, 2013; Ollendick, Greene, & Austin, 2015) |
| Curricular and instructional design and enrichment | Enrichment strategies (Baum, 2004) |
| | Origins curriculum (Berman, 2015) |
| | Integrated curriculum (Callahan, Moon, Oh, Azano, & Hailey, 2015) |
| | Project-based learning (Helm & Katz, 2011; Seligman, Steen, Park, & Peterson, 2005) |
| | Schoolwide Enrichment Model (Renzulli & Reis, 2014) |
| | Parallel Curriculum Model (Tomlinson et al., 2009) |
| Personalized educational plan (for creating a plan and monitoring progress in strengths and weaknesses) | Mentorships/apprenticeships (Berger, 1990) |
| | Finding, addressing, and monitoring strengths and weaknesses (Pereles, Omdal, & Baldwin, 2009) |
| | Curriculum compacting (Reis, Burns, & Renzulli, 1992) |

NOTE: TQPS = The Quad Prepatory School; EBP = evidence-based practices.

However, just following these practices alone is not enough. As we adapted each of these practices, we found that each is "dynamic" in that different components can be implemented at different times and in different settings for individual children. The key is to develop the model and train a staff that can identify the needs and the concordant practices to address those needs at the right time (Kazdin, 2008; Malti, Noam, Beelmann, & Sommer, 2016).

Once the key constructs were defined, the first thing that The Quad Preparatory School created was a multidisciplinary team, responsible for implementation, integration, and dynamic adaptation of the practices that are key to the model. The following cornerstones of our model were developed and implemented.

## The People

Unique to 2e students is the need for deep expertise and experience in EBPs from both educators and clinicians. School leadership was redefined as co-leadership so that there was equal expertise and experience in gifted and twice exceptional educational practices and clinical practice. Thus Quad Prep leaders are highly skilled and experienced in disseminating practice in their respective fields.

1. Quad Prep co-leaders must be exceptionally effective educators of other professionals within the school, bringing expertise and experience in training and in the professional development of educational and clinical staff. Time is protected for leadership teams to meet weekly with both teachers and outside providers and to use ongoing feedback and new information about students to create new "ad hoc" adaptations in real time.
2. Outside expert coaches and a "train the trainer" model is used to support the use of coaches to facilitate the dynamic adaption process (Bradshaw et al., 2012). The needs of twice exceptional children run an extremely wide gamut, and no in-house leadership would be able to attain expert status in all areas. Thus a priority of the school is to cultivate and develop a network of outside experts and align resources and time for systematically including their input and coaching in their respective areas of expertise. This includes a very active and multidisciplinary professional advisory board that meets thrice yearly as well as partnerships with professional organizations and institutes of higher education (e.g., Association for the Education of Gifted Underachieving Students, Cooper Union College, New York University). The result is a growing base of in-house experts trained in EBPs.
3. Staff support and professional development are augmented by Friday team meetings between clinical and educational staff (with a noon dismissal) to discuss issues regarding individual students and possible approaches that can be used during the next week to help with the social and emotional issues with each child. Psychologists check in and monitor the progress of various strategies during the week, and the progress is revisited to assess success and make adaptations where necessary. We also hold half- and whole-day professional development sessions throughout the year focusing on implementation, staff-directed needs, instructional strategies, and culture/collaboration. Implementation is constantly being evaluated and flexibly refined.
4. Our commitment to collaboration and clear communication informs relationships between The Quad Preparatory School, parents, and

clinical service providers engaged by families. The director, head of school, teachers, and clinical staff review weekly progress and hold scheduled monthly phone conferences with parents and outside providers for each child that cover both academics and social emotional development.

## Structure of the School

Our school is organized into preps or cohorts, (currently nine preps) of 8 to 10 students ranging from grades K to 12. The preps are multi-aged typically with children in a two-year chronological age span grouped by developmental level, academic readiness, and social cognitive levels. The preps progress developmentally focuses in the youngest grades on the development of skills necessary to function at school in a successful way. Academic depth and breadth progress quickly as young students develop.

In the Lower School, which encompasses what would traditionally be elementary school (K–5), each prep has two academic teachers, an associate teacher (education background), a psychosocial teacher (psychology background), a special education teacher, and several psychology interns.

### Prep 1, Foundations level

Our Foundations class (K–1) uses a Montessori method combining manipulative materials in a structure that encourages children to choose their own work within a structured environment that is designed to meet developmental needs (Montessori, 2010). The primary foundational skills being developed are concentration, coordination, independence, and self-efficacy. Adaptations to a pure Montessori practice must be made, as many of our younger children come to us with profound asynchronous development. Basic skills that lead to self-regulation and executive functioning must be addressed before academics with four-, five-, and six-year-olds who have taught themselves to read yet do not have the world experience or psychic grounding to process what they hear from the adult world and only partially comprehend. Negative behavior at this stage diminishes quickly when a sense of order and independence is internalized. The Montessori practices help young children to do this. This class is led by Montessori trained teachers, a special education teacher, and a psychosocial teacher. When combined with the early childhood multidisciplinary curriculum *Tools of the Mind* (Leong & Bodrova, 2007), which is specifically designed to strengthen nascent executive functioning skills of self-regulation, the environment is prepared to nurture independence and develop skills to move on to higher academic levels.

### Preps 2, 3, 4, and 5 Transition levels

These preps are comprised of second, third, and fourth-grade-aged children. This group is called transitions as the principles emphasized in Prep 1 continue with the goal of developing further self-regulation and executive functioning, leading to a more independent student in a departmentalized Upper School. Academics include skills in all areas emphasizing exercises that increase fine motor control and promote success in writing. As many 2e children have difficulties with writing, cursive writing is introduced as a more easily managed form of writing (Meyers, 2014). Teachers and occupational therapists work together to decide which students would benefit from this instruction, and they work together to complement the process. This is often the stage at which children begin to show difficulties in a traditional setting, as seen with the case study children described earlier. Instruction is therefore delivered in a one-on-one format with small groups when ready. The academic content must also be presented with multimodal approaches, for example with alternate entry points from dramatization to building to art (Baum, Slatin, & Viens, 2005). When children struggle with the mechanical aspects of writing and are trying to compose at the same time, the task becomes overwhelming. Creating content first through another medium helps children to express what they want to say, to then elaborate and organize thoughts rather than trying to compose, organize, and physically put words on paper all at the same time causing frustration and shut down.

### Prep 6, Signature level

This group consists of children typically in grades 4, 5, and/or 6. Children are placed and moved from one prep to another based on their social, emotional, and intellectual development reflecting the personalized and flexible approach to the rate of growth in each child. Here children have reached our signature level by showing readiness to navigate a more independent schedule yet continuing with their two academic teachers in one-on-one lessons covering subjects in an integrated manner with one teacher specializing in humanities and the other in STEM. Content expands to higher academic and interest levels, yet gaps in skills and understanding can still be addressed relatively quickly by using the curriculum compacting concept (Reis, Burns, & Renzulli, 1992) of systematically pretesting to determine where a student's skills lie on a continuum, addressing the misunderstandings or gaps with enough explanation and practice to master it and then moving on to new material. If a student has a special interest, teachers can engage in dialogue and make connections or help create and mentor projects that might happen in the real world. Students are encouraged to make connections between disciplines and taught how to reflect on their own place in the world and their personal identity (Tomlinson et al., 2009).

### Preps 7, 8, and 9, Upper School

These preps are departmentalized to go deeper into content, but work in collaboration. Preps 7 and 8 are comprised of students in Grades 6 to 7 and 7 to 8, respectively. High-level science and mathematics are taught, with many opportunities for depth in history, literature, and writing that employ the interests of the student. In many cases, once students have gained a sense of self-efficacy, they can achieve understanding of content several years above their chronological age, resulting in some students beginning high school credit courses in $8^{th}$ grade. Art and music are required of every student in all grades along with electives such as engineering, coding, debate, drama, creative writing, film, student government, and foreign language offered to students in the Upper School (Grades 5–12). The Upper School has teachers in each core domain (sciences, mathematics, English language arts, history, and foreign languages), with Advanced Placement courses offered to those who are ready. Teachers from both education and psychology backgrounds collaborate for psychosocial integration in seminar sessions (3–5 students in core academic subjects) and for supervision during work periods (in which students continue work from their academic sessions) as well as offer mini enrichment courses.

## Social Cognition and Engagement through Strength Based Teaching

The foundation of social cognition education and practice at The Quad Prep is based on the Social Thinking framework (Winner, 2002), which includes vocabulary that establishes a common language to discuss social functioning, curriculum lessons, and strategies that break down social concepts into concrete, teachable formats. Social Thinking reveals the hidden rules of social communication and explicitly teaches fundamental social concepts, such as perspective-taking, to help children and adults navigate the nuanced world of social interaction.

Social skills are not developed in isolation. An important class for all students throughout their time with us is called Core, which begins with explicit social thinking strategies at the younger grades through role-play, modeling, stories, and film, but as children develop, they take on projects in interest areas that begin to integrate content areas and ultimately result in authentic products for authentic audiences (Renzulli, Gentry, & Reis, 2003). Interest groups evolve and children work toward a goal in small groups such as creating a cookbook through testing recipes and related scientific concepts, building prototypes of inventions, and participating in social service projects that will reach beyond school walls. The concepts of authentic products for authentic audiences inherent in enrichment clusters (Renzulli et al., 2003) provide a much greater buy-in for students than "simulated" projects, as some of them have called school projects. Our adaptation of both the Social Thinking curriculum and enrichment clusters comes in the integration of both allowing the authentic projects to grow organically from the interests of the children and to provide real life contexts for social skills.

Social and emotional development is completely interwoven with academic and executive functioning at The Quad Preparatory School. Using collaborative problem-solving (Greene, 2014), cognitive behavioral strategies, social cognition, and motivational techniques, teachers and clinicians alike are trained and experienced in integrating social and emotional learning concepts, strategies, and language into all aspects of our students' day. We have found that through the integration of the psychosocial attention, children become available for learning, and then when interests are tapped, negative behaviors diminish, they can use their strengths to compensate for learning difficulties, and success breeds success. The positive spiral allows us to truly educate at their potential in all areas—academic, social and emotional.

## The Curriculum

### Content

The Quad Preparatory School provides students with an academic program that acknowledges individual learning styles and accommodates for the asynchronous development that is characteristic of our students. The curriculum is founded in the understanding that as young minds are building skills, they need challenging material and a foundation in higher order thinking as developmentally appropriate. These skills empower and prepare students to tackle increasingly complex problems and issues as their basic skills develop.

The curriculum framework integrated throughout the school called Origins (Berman, 2015) gives students an overall understanding of the "big picture" of the universe in both time and space. It captures the imagination as our children ask the big questions, "Where did I come from?" or "How did everything get to be made?" which is a seeking to understand the systems, patterns, and relationships that form the networks of all disciplines and knowledge. Children want to make order of their environment and beyond, thus timelines and geographic knowledge give students a foundation to make connections and to have a greater understanding of how all came to be.

Origins focuses on the story of the birth of the universe, elements, solar systems, and planets, and ultimately on Earth. A series of key experiments introduces concepts of physical science such as gravity and centrifugal force, then chemistry as students learn how the elements were formed, and finally life science when life emerged billions of years after Earth came to exist. Classification of plants and animals correlates with simple organisms to the most complex as life developed. We look at the development of humans from the perspective of their basic needs, physical and spiritual, creating a framework from which to study any culture. Science and history are initially one in the same as the events of chronology, formation of galaxies, solar systems, geography, and then early life, classification, and ultimately the appearance and needs of humans are presented in stories, then in later grades studied at a deeper level. In mathematics we look at how and why counting began, and in literacy we explore early alphabets and the origins of writing. A sense of the relationship of each person in and to the world takes on a different perspective in this context, and children come to understand how all humans are connected across time and space and how their individual cultures express their common life experiences in different ways. Personal identity also takes on a new perspective. These topics are not typically taught until much later in a more traditional curriculum, if at all, and then in very isolated segments, but for cognitively advanced children, there is a fascination with such big-picture ideas. Through this engagement, reading and writing become important tools to fulfill boundless curiosity.

Such a curriculum that addresses both the affective development in the question "Who am I?" and that creates a big picture of the universe, planet, and civilization provides a sound foundation for all other study in literature, science, arts, mathematics, philosophy, history, and languages. Units of study present related stories of questions that arise from a sense of wonder of the individual child and the place he or she has in the world. As the child grows, he or she also begins to question "Why am I here?" thus interfacing a sense of identity with purpose. Nurturing this natural need for reflection lays the foundation for the habits of mind necessary for creative productivity presented in the curriculum of the higher grades as well as nurtures a sense of purpose and self-efficacy.

At the upper school level, a curricular model from gifted education, the Parallel Curriculum Model (Tomlinson et al., 2009) offers an opportunity for higher levels of intellectual demand by first presenting core information, then making connections in a cross-disciplinary exploration, with the opportunity to further delve into the real-world practice revealing relevance of the material. The model then comes back to the reflective practice of identity in asking "What can I do to make a difference?" These practices support the integration of key concepts and language of Social Thinking (Winner, 2002) into all aspects of the curriculum as well. This ensures that a robust synergy between affective and intellectual development is maintained throughout the school day.

### Instruction

Teachers at The Quad Prep employ a variety of evidenced-based strategies. Academic instruction is given one-on-one for a third of the day with academic group seminars, supervised work periods, group project periods, electives, counseling, and occupational therapy completing the day. Our students' needs can best be met in this format by either accelerating, modifying, pursuing special interests, or pacing for specific needs to fill in learning gaps while raising the achievement bar. The one-on-one ratio insures that students are taught through their strength areas and that they can move as quickly as they are able. If remediation is necessary for skill building, extra sessions can be held with a special education teacher. The one-on-one periods allow us to go beyond individualization of instruction to truly personalize learning.

### Environment

The Quad Preparatory School's learning environment provides a consistent, calm, and nonjudgmental space in which each child can flourish. We acknowledge the courage that each student displays through the process of learning to renew trust and tackle areas of challenge, and we support each success and near-success with encouragement to build resilience and grit. In addition to our integrated academic, social, and emotional skills curricula, the related services of speech and language therapy, occupational therapy, and counseling (by doctoral-level clinical psychologists) are provided by full-time professionals who are an integral part of our school.

### Parent and Community Partnerships

Utilizing the talents of the adults in our community, be it parents or grandparents, neighboring businesses and professionals, or other friends of the school, gives children an opportunity to learn how "school subjects" have relevance and meaning. Musicians, artists, bankers, architects, and nutritionists are only a sampling of the professionals who have much to offer to our children. Interests are triggered when a visitor presents his or her profession to the students. The skills and methodologies of different disciplines can also become part of the curriculum and lead to mentorships, apprenticeships, and major projects. These experiences can lead to a lifetime of interest and often a career (Renzulli & Reis, 2014).

In addition, Quad Prep has implemented a purposeful system of communication between our psychosocial staff, teachers, parents, and outside providers. With regular monthly conference calls, all parties can share their perspectives of the progress of the child, just as the psychologists do with the academic staff once a week. Time is protected, and parents and any outside providers are given a schedule for conference calls in September for the remainder of the academic year, allowing all the constituents the opportunity to fine-tune goals for the next month.

### Autonomy of Students

Developing a sense of autonomy is the ultimate goal for all of our students, which allows any adult to live a full and satisfying life. Autonomy can only be reached if one has developed the skills of executive functioning, emotional regulation, sensory integration, anxiety management, competency, and resilience. Moreover, by using the Collaborative and Proactive Solutions (Dedousis-Wallace et al., 2016) method for student-led solutions to troubleshooting, conflict resolution, and student buy-in for skill building, students are willing and able to grow ever more independent over time. Autonomy and self-actualization enable 2e students to realize their goals beyond high school such as college, a profession, entrepreneurial endeavors, or whatever else they choose.

## HOW DO WE MEASURE SUCCESS?

The Quad Preparatory School has been collecting data on various relevant outcomes since inception and is continually in the process of analyzing and using the data in germane ways. One construct put in place is our use of psychology interns to track both individual student goals and adoption of strategies we are teaching to reach the identified goals. Thus if the student is able to consistently use a particular strategy but not reach the associated goals, we know in real time that we need to adapt specific teaching strategies. We have developed a research committee that collaborates with outside academic departments of psychology and education to both track outcomes for our use and to contribute to the growing evidence base for twice exceptional children.

Because effective practice requires time and implicit nurturing to develop, staff retention becomes an extremely important priority. For both the clinical and educational staff, we hold regular supervision meetings to both gain information on how to support staff and to give feedback from informal observations. Two times a year, teachers are formally observed and evaluated in the spirit of supporting growth and improving professional practice. We also require that a teacher work a year as an associate teacher in a classroom with an experienced teacher before becoming a head academic teacher. Staff retention metrics are key indicators of progress for us—100% of staff returned from 2015–2016 to 2016–2017.

Finally, The Quad Preparatory School has been collecting and informally recording successes in the form of individual case studies and feedback from outside providers and parents. To date, we have witnessed observable changes of increased confidence and productivity in our students who were previously failing. We have not had the need to "counsel out" any students because we were unable to meet their needs. We have received near universal positive feedback from parents and outside professionals that students are growing both academically and in social and emotional realms simultaneously. For example, a student had a repeat neuropsychological evaluation done after attending The Quad for two years. He exhibited significant improvement in academic indicators and reduction in symptoms of task avoidance and anxiety. Until we have completed more formal and prospective outcome studies over longer time periods, we are grateful that these early exemplars show us that the model is successful. Parent satisfaction also offers a testament to positive direction:

> Quad is a rarity for a school—it actually practices what it preaches!
>
> My child had a hugely successful year his first year at Quad. He advanced emotionally, socially and academically. He went from a kid who hated school and did everything he could to get sent home, to a kid who loved school and was sad for it to end and can't wait for it to start again. The staff is skilled, sensitive and warm and my child formed friendships with them equal to those he formed with the other children. The parents at Quad are as devoted to the school as they are to their own children and are available and supportive! (parent correspondence, 2016)

## WHERE ARE OUR THREE STUDENTS NOW?

Although our students described at the beginning of this chapter are composite profiles, they resemble true-to-life students. D, whose behavior and deficits overshadowed her strengths, was ultimately diagnosed with autism spectrum disorder at age nine. By this time, in the proper setting, her negative behavior had all but disappeared. Even though she was still highly sensitive to physical environmental factors, she had learned how to use mindfulness to manage her hypersensitivities. She continued to struggle with mathematics but progressed, although slowly. Her strong language ability and vivid imagination manifested in beautifully written poetry and stories. At 12 she won a major award from a youth literary magazine and gained the confidence she needed to continue studying writing with the goal of making it a career.

F, whose gifts were so evident at the elementary level but began to diminish as he reached adolescence, was ultimately diagnosed with a learning disability that he had been able to compensate for until the work he was encountering became more complex. This began to manifest in social maladjustment. His anxiety level, due to what he interpreted as his inability to achieve, began to rise until interference was so severe that he began to have debilitating panic attacks and developed symptoms of obsessive-compulsive disorder. With a change to a school that understood the 2e child, counseling, appropriate attention to his learning disability, and a project-based curriculum focusing on his area of interest in political anthropology, he was slowly able to work through the anxiety, take more risks, and found ways to tap into his potential once again.

L was the "hidden" 2e child as he was not eligible for any special services for his learning disability or for his gifts as his test scores showed that he was "average." His music became his passion, which carried him through bouts of depression stemming from a deep sense of frustration, sense of being misunderstood, and isolation. He was able to attend a college that did not require the SAT, as he had never been able to perform on tests to a level commensurate with his potential, even though an early neuropsychological evaluation had shown a 129 IQ. In college, he found for the first time a sense of intellectual challenge, which engaged and empowered him. Although he still struggled with the mechanics of writing, he was stimulated to work hard and seek help when necessary, and he found better than "average" success. He was able to succeed but on his own with many silent struggles. Who knows what he could have achieved had he had support and encouragement from the educational system? This is the profile of the 2e child that we still need to learn how to identify and support in the future.

All of these children represent the kinds of students we see at The Quad Preparatory School, and we have found that many of the best practices that we use not only benefit our students but would work with all children. There is still so much to learn about each of these children and how to unlock their potential. We have a large key ring and need to find the right key for each door. If we cannot find the right key in what we have, we forge a new one until we find success.

## REFERENCES

Albano, A. M., & DiBartolo, P. M. (2007). *Cognitive-behavioral therapy for social phobia in adolescents stand up, speak out*. Oxford: Oxford University Press.

Allen, J. G., & Fonagy, P. (2006). *The handbook of mentalization-based treatment*. West Sussex, UK: Wiley.

Baum, S. M. (2004). An enrichment program for gifted learning-disabled students. In S. Baum, (Ed.), *Twice exceptional and special populations of gifted students* (pp. 1–12). Thousand Oaks, CA: Corwin Press.

Baum, S. M., Cooper, C. R., & Neu, T. W. (2001). Dual differentiation: An approach for meeting the curricular needs of gifted students with learning disabilities. (Education Faculty Publications, Paper 82). Retrieved fromhttp://digitalcommons.sacredheart.edu/ced_fac/82

Baum, S. M., & Owen, S. V. (2004). *To be gifted and learning disabled: Strategies for helping bright students with LD, ADHD and more* (2nd ed.). Waco, TX: Prufrock Press.

Baum, S. M., Slatin, B., & Viens, J. (2005). *Multiple intelligences in the elementary classroom: A teacher's toolkit*. New York, NY: Teachers College Press.

Ben-Sasson, A., Carter, A. S., & Briggs-Gowan, M. J. (2010). The development of sensory over-responsivity from infancy to elementary school. *Journal of Abnormal Child Psychology, 38*, 1193–1202.

Berger, S. L. (1990). *Mentor relationships and gifted learners* (Eric Digest #E486). Retrieved from ERIC Clearinghouse on Disabilities and Gifted Education. https://www.ericdigests.org/pre-9216/mentor.htm

Berman, K. B. (2015). *Origins: A curriculum framework for grades 3-8 for creating interdisciplinary context*. Unpublished document created for Mount Vernon Public Schools Academy of Talent, Leadership, and Scholars Program.

Blumenfeld, P. C., Soloway, E., Marx, R. W., Krajcik, J. S., Guzdial, M., & Palincsar, A. (1991). Motivating project-based learning: Sustaining the doing, supporting the learning. *Educational Psychologist, 26*(3–4), 369–398.

Bradshaw, C. P., Pas, E. T., Goldweber, A., Rosenberg, M. S., & Leaf, P. J. (2012). Integrating school-wide positive behavioral interventions and supports with tier 2 coaching to student support teams: The PBISplus model. *Advances in School Mental Health Promotion* 5(3), 20.

Callahan, C. M., Moon, T. R., Oh, S., Azano, A. P., & Hailey, E. P. (2015). What works in gifted education: Documenting the effects of an integrated curricular/instructional model for gifted students. *American Educational Research Journal, 52*(1), 137–167.

Crammond, B. (2006). Creative talent: Recognizing and nurturing it. Duke University Talent Identification Program. Retrieved from http://www.davidsongifted.org/Search-Database/entry/A10816

Craske, M. G., & Barlow, D. H. (2006). *Mastery of your anxiety and panic*. Oxford: Oxford University Press.

Davis, G. A. (2004). *Creativity is forever* (5th ed.). Dubuque, IA: Kendall Hunt.

Dedousis-Wallace, A., Murrihy, R. C., Ollendick, T. H., Greene, R. W., McAloon, J., Gill, S., . . . Drysdale, S. (June, 2016). *Moderators and mediators of parent management training and collaborative & proactive solutions in the treatment of oppositional defiant disorder in children and adolescents*. Paper presented at Eighth World Congress of Behavioural and Cognitive Therapies, Melbourne, Australia.

Duckworth, A. (2016). *Grit: The power of passion and perseverance*. New York, NY: HarperCollins.

Dweck, C. S. (2007). *Growth mindset: The new psychology of success*. New York, NY: Ballantine Books.

Fernandez, M. A., Adelstein, J. S., Miller, S. P., & Gudiño, O. G. (2009). Effectiveness of teacher-child interaction training (TCIT) in a preschool setting. *Behavior Modification, 33*(6), 855–884.

Gaus, V. L. (2011). *Living well on the spectrum: How to use your strengths to meet the challenges of Asperger syndrome/high-functioning autism.* New York, NY: Guilford Press.

Greene, R. W. (June 2016). *Collaborative & proactive solutions: Applications in schools and juvenile detention settings.* Paper presented at the Eighth World Congress of Behavioural and Cognitive Therapies, Melbourne, Australia.

Greene, R. W., & Ablon, J. S. (2005). *Treating explosive kids: The collaborative problem-solving approach.* New York: Guilford Press.

Greene, R. W. (2014). *Lost at school: Why our kids with behavioral challenges are falling through the cracks and how we can help them.* New York, NY: Scribner.

Greene, R. W., Ablon, J. S., Monuteaux, M., Goring, J., Henin, A., Raezer, L., . . . Rabbitt, S. (2004). Effectiveness of collaborative problem solving in affectively dysregulated youth with oppositional defiant disorder: Initial findings. *Journal of Consulting and Clinical Psychology, 72*, 1157–1164.

Helm, J. H., & Katz, L. G. (2011). *Young investigators: The project approach in the early years* (2nd ed.). New York, NY: Teachers College Press.

Hendrix, R. E., Palmer, K. Z., Tarshis, N., & Winner, M. G. (2016). *We thinkers!* San Jose, CA: Social Thinking.

Kaufman, S. B., & Gregoire, C. (2016). *Wired to create.* New York: TarcherPerigee.

Kazdin, A. E. (2008). Evidence-based treatment and practice: New opportunities to bridge clinical research and practice, enhance the knowledge base, and improve patient care. *American Psychologist, 63*, 146–159.

Kendall, P. C., & Hedtke, K. A. (2006). *Cognitive-behavioral therapy for anxious children: Therapist manual* (3rd ed.). Ardmore, PA: Workbook Publishing.

Kuypers, L. (2011). *The zones of regulation: A curriculum designed to foster self- regulation and emotional control.* San Jose, CA: Think Social Publishing.

Leong, D. J., & Bodrova, E. (2007). *Tools of the mind: The Vygotskian approach to early childhood education* (2nd ed.). Upper Saddle River, NJ: Pearson Education, Merrill/Prentice Hall.

Maker, J. (1977). *Providing programs for the gifted handicapped.* Reston, VA: Council for Exceptional Children.

Malti, T., Noam, G. G., Beelmann, A., & Sommer, S. (2016). Toward dynamic adaptation of psychological interventions for child and adolescent development and mental health. *Journal of Clinical Child and Adolescent Psychology, 45*, 827–836.

Meyers, S. L. (2014). Research highlights benefits of teaching cursive handwriting. Retrieved from http://www.wpr.org/research-highlights-benefits-teaching-cursive-handwriting.

Miller, L. J., & Collins, B. (2013, September–October). Sensory success in the classroom. *Autism Asperger's Digest*, 42–43.

Montessori, M. (2010). *The advanced Montessori method: The Montessori elementary material.* Rockford, IL: Snowball Publishing.

National Association for Gifted Children. (1998). *Students with concomitant gifts and learning disabilities.* Washington DC: Author.

National Education Association. (2006). The twice-exceptional dilemma. Retrieved from https://www.nea.org/assets/docs/twiceexceptional.pdf.

Ollendick, T.A., Greene, R. W., & Austin, K.E. (2015). Parent Management Training and Collaborative & Proactive Solutions: A Randomized Control Trial for Oppositional Youth. *Journal of Clinical Child & Adolescent Psychology*, *0*(0), 1–14.

Pereles, D. A., Omdal, S., & Baldwin, L. (2009), Response to intervention and twice-exceptional learners: A promising fit. *Gifted Child Today*, *32*(3), 40–51.

Piacentini, J., Langley, A., & Roblek, T (2007). *Cognitive-behavioral treatment of childhood OCD.* Oxford: Oxford University Press.

Pincus, D. B., Ehrenreich, J. T., & Mattis, S. G. (2008). *Mastery of anxiety and panic for adolescents riding the wave: Therapist guide.* Oxford: Oxford University Press.

Pollastri, A., Epstein, L., Heath, G., & Ablon, J., (2013). The collaborative problem solving approach: Outcomes across settings. *Harvard Review of Psychiatry*, *21*, 188–195.

Reis, S. M., Baum, S. M., & Burke, E. (2014). An operational definition of twice-exceptional learners: Implications and applications. *Gifted Child Quarterly*, *58*(3), 217–230.

Reis, S. M., Burns, D. E., & Renzulli, J. S. (1992). *Curriculum compacting: The complete guide to modifying the regular curriculum for high ability students.* Mansfield Center, CT: Creative Learning Press.

Renzulli, J. S., & Reis, S. M. (2014). *Schoolwide enrichment model* (3rd ed.). Waco, TX: Prufrock Press.

Renzulli, J. S., Gentry, M., & Reis, S. M. (2003). *Enrichment clusters: A practical plan for real-world, student-driven learning.* Mansfield Center, CT: Creative Learning Press.

Seligman, E. P., Steen, T. A., Park, N., & Peterson, C. (2005). Positive psychology progress empirical validation of interventions. *American Psychologist*, *60*(5), 410–421.

Seligman, M. E., & Csikszentmihalyi, M. (2000). Positive psychology: An introduction. *American Psychologist*, *55*(1), 5–14.

Stanley, T. (2011). *Project-based learning for gifted students: A handbook for the 21st-century classroom.* Waco, TX: Prufrock Press.

Strobel, J., & van Barneveld, A. (2009). When is PBL more effective? A meta-analysis of meta-analyses comparing PBL to conventional classrooms. *Interdisciplinary Journal of Problem Based Learning*, *3*(1).

Thomas, J. W. (2000). A review of research on project-based learning. The Autodesk Foundation, San Rafael, CA. Retrieved from http://www.bie.org/index.php/site/RE/pbl_research/29.

Tomlinson, C. A., Kaplan, S. N., Renzulli, J. S., Purcell, J. H., Leppien, J. H., Burns, D. E.,. . . Imbeau, M. B. (2009). *The parallel curriculum: A design to develop learner potential and challenge advanced learners* (2nd ed.). Thousand Oaks, CA: Corwin Press.

Winner, M. G. (2002). *Thinking about you thinking about me: Philosophy and strategies to further develop perspective taking and communication abilities for persons with autism, hyperlexia, ADHD, PDD-NOS, NVLD.* San Jose, CA: Michelle Garcia Winner.

Dillon, [illegible], Greene, [illegible], Armstrong, [illegible] (2014). [illegible] management: Training and collaborative & Proactive Solutions [illegible]. A Randomized Controlled Trial for [illegible] *[illegible] Journal of Clinical Child & Adolescent Psychology*, [illegible]
[illegible], D. [illegible], Cunningham, [illegible] (2011). Response to intervention [illegible] [illegible] implementation: A [illegible]. *School Psychology Quarterly*, [illegible]
[illegible] (2012). *[illegible]*. [illegible] University Press.
[illegible] (2008). *[illegible]*. Oxford University Press.
[illegible], Hall, [illegible] (2012). [illegible] *Journal of Positive Behavior Interventions*, [illegible]
[illegible] (2014). An [illegible] *School Psychology Quarterly*, [illegible]

[illegible], S. M., Burns, D., & [illegible] (2013). [illegible]. Minneapolis, [illegible]. [illegible] Learning Sites.
Reynolds, [illegible] (2014). [illegible] (3rd ed.). [illegible] Guilford Press.
[illegible], [illegible] (2014). [illegible] in Focus [illegible] Collaborative & Proactive Solutions [illegible] Lives in the Balance.
Seligman, M. E. P., [illegible] (2009). Positive education: Positive psychology and classroom interventions. *Oxford Review of Education*, 35(3), 293–311.
Seligman, M. E. P., & Csikszentmihalyi, M. (2000). Positive psychology: An introduction. *American Psychologist*, 55(1), 5–14.
Stanley, [illegible] (2011). [illegible] *Handbook of [illegible]* (3rd ed.). [illegible] Press.
[illegible] (2009). [illegible] more effective? A meta-analytic [illegible] classroom [illegible] *Journal of Problem-Based Learning*, 3(1).
Thomas, J. W. (2000). A review of research on project-based learning. The Autodesk Foundation. Retrieved from [illegible]
[illegible] (2009). *[illegible]* (2nd ed.). Thousand Oaks, CA: Corwin Press.
Winner, M. G. (2007). [illegible] San Jose, CA: Michelle Garcia Winner.

# INDEX